W9-BWO-087

TAKING SIDES

Clashing Views on

Moral Issues

TWELFTH EDITION

Selected, Edited, and with Introductions by

Stephen Satris
Clemson University

McGraw Hill Higher Education

Boston Burr Ridge, IL Dubuque, IA New York San Francisco St. Louis
Bangkok Bogotá Caracas Kuala Lumpur Lisbon London Madrid Mexico City
Milan Montreal New Delhi Santiago Seoul Singapore Sydney Taipei Toronto

The McGraw·Hill Companies

Mc Graw Hill **Higher Education**

TAKING SIDES: CLASHING VIEWS ON MORAL ISSUES, TWELFTH EDITION

Published by McGraw-Hill, a business unit of The McGraw-Hill Companies, Inc., 1221 Avenue of the Americas, New York, NY 10020. Copyright © 2010 by The McGraw-Hill Companies, Inc. All rights reserved. Previous edition(s) 2008, 2006, 2004. No part of this publication may be reproduced or distributed in any form or by any means, or stored in a database or retrieval system, without the prior written consent of The McGraw-Hill Companies, Inc., including, but not limited to, in any network or other electronic storage or transmission, or broadcast for distance learning.

Some ancillaries, including electronic and print components, may not be available to customers outside the United States.

Taking Sides® is a registered trademark of the McGraw-Hill Companies, Inc.
Taking Sides is published by the **Contemporary Learning Series** group within the McGraw-Hill Higher Education division.

2 3 4 5 6 7 8 9 0 DOC/DOC 0

MHID: 0-07-354562-7
ISBN: 978-0-07-354562-2
ISSN: 1094-7604

Managing Editor: *Larry Loeppke*
Senior Managing Editor: *Faye Schilling*
Senior Developmental Editor: *Jade Benedict*
Editorial Coordinator: *Mary Foust*
Production Service Assistant: *Rita Hingtgen*
Permissions Coordinator: *Shirley Lanners*
Senior Marketing Manager: *Julie Keck*
Marketing Communications Specialist: *Mary Klein*
Marketing Coordinator: *Alice Link*
Senior Project Manager: *Jane Mohr*
Design Specialist: *Tara McDermott*
Cover Graphics: *Rick D. Noel*

Compositor: Macmillan Publishing Solutions
Cover Image: © BrandX Pictures/PunchStock/RF

Library of Congress Cataloging-in-Publication Data

Main entry under title:
Taking sides: clashing views on moral issues/selected, edited, and with introductions by Stephen Satris.—12th ed.

Includes bibliographical references and index.
1. Ethics. 2. Social Ethics. I. Satris, Stephen, *comp.*

170´.22

www.mhhe.com

Clashing Views on

Moral Issues

TWELFTH EDITION

Stephen Satris
Clemson University

Advisory Board

Julius Bailey
University of Redlands

Zaphon Wilson
Armstrong Atlantic State University

Andreas Kiryakakis
Normandale Community College

Bambi Robinson
Southeast Missouri State University

Preface

This text contains 32 essays, arranged in pro and con pairs, that address 16 controversial issues in morality and moral philosophy. Each of the issues is expressed in terms of a single question in order to draw the lines of debate more clearly.

Some of the questions that are included here have been in the mainstream of moral philosophy for hundreds (or even thousands) of years and are central to the discipline. I have not shied away from abstract questions about relativism and the relationship between morality and religion. Other questions relate to specific topics of contemporary concern, such as human cloning, abortion, affirmative action, and drug legalization.

The authors of the selections included here take a strong stand on a given issue and provide their own best defenses of a pro or con position. The selections were chosen for their usefulness in defending a position and for their accessibility to students. The authors are philosophers, scientists, and social critics from a wide variety of backgrounds. Each presents us with a determinant answer on an issue—even if we ultimately cannot accept the answer as our own.

Each issue is accompanied by an *introduction,* which sets the stage for the debate, and each issue concludes with a *postscript* that summarizes the debate, considers other views on the issue, and suggests additional readings. The introductions and postscripts do not preempt what is the reader's own task: to achieve a critical and informed view of the issue at stake. I have also provided relevant Internet site addresses (URLs) on the Internet References page that accompanies each part opener. And at the back of the book is a list of all the *contributors to this volume,* which provides information on the philosophers and social commentators whose views are debated here.

Taking Sides: Clashing Views on Moral Issues is a tool to encourage critical thought on important moral issues. Readers should not feel confined to the views expressed in the selections. Some readers may see important points on both sides of an issue and may construct for themselves a new and creative approach, which may incorporate the best of both sides or provide an entirely new vantage point for understanding.

Changes to this edition Several new articles have been added to this edition which have aided in the currency and refinement of the issue questions. These would include "Is It Right to Prohibit Same-Sex Marriage?" (Issue 5); "Should Human Cloning Be Banned?" (Issue 6); "Should Congress Allow the Buying and Selling of Human Organs?" (Issue 8); "Should Drugs Be Legalized?" (Issue 9); "Is Torture Ever Justified?" (Issue 14); "Does Mortality Require Vegetarianism?" (Issue 16). One Issue was rephrased and given a new article "Should Licensing for Handguns Be More Restrictive?" (Issue 12).

A word to the instructor An *Instructor's Resource Guide with Test Questions* (multiple-choice and essay) is available through the publisher for the instructor using *Taking Sides* in the classroom. A general guidebook, *Using Taking Sides in the Classroom,* which discusses methods and techniques for using the pro-con approach in any classroom setting, is also available. An online version of *Using Taking Sides in the Classroom* and a correspondence service for *Taking Sides* adopters can be found at http://www.mhcls.com/usingts.

Taking Sides: Clashing Views on Moral Issues is only one title in the *Taking Sides* series. If you are interested in seeing the table of contents for any of the other titles, please visit the Taking Sides Web site at http://www.mhcls.com/takingsides/.

Acknowledgments Finally, a unique debt of thanks is owed to those who tolerated my strange hours and the time spent away from them as this book was being prepared and revised: Kim, Angela, and Michelle.

Stephen Satris
Clemson University

To the memory of my mother and father

Contents In Brief

UNIT 1 Fundamental Issues in Morality 1

Issue 1. Is Moral Relativism Correct? 2
Issue 2. Does Morality Need Religion? 24

UNIT 2 Gender, Sex, and Reproduction 49

Issue 3. Is Abortion Immoral? 50
Issue 4. Must Sex Involve Commitment? 70
Issue 5. Is It Right to Prohibit Same-Sex Marriage? 86
Issue 6. Should Human Cloning Be Banned? 110

UNIT 3 Law and Society 127

Issue 7. Is Cloning Pets Ethically Justified? 128
Issue 8. Should Congress Allow the Buying and Selling of Human Organs? 146
Issue 9. Should Drugs Be Legalized? 159
Issue 10. Is Gambling Immoral? 183
Issue 11. Is Affirmative Action Fair? 207
Issue 12. Should Licensing for Handguns Be More Restrictive? 233
Issue 13. Should the Death Penalty Be Abolished? 261
Issue 14. Is Torture Ever Justified? 290
Issue 15. Is Physician-Assisted Suicide Wrong? 314

UNIT 4 Human Beings and Other Species 333

Issue 16. Does Morality Require Vegetarianism? 334

Contents

Preface v

Correlation Guide xiv

Introduction xvii

UNIT 1 FUNDAMENTAL ISSUES IN MORALITY 1

Issue 1. Is Moral Relativism Correct? 2

YES: Gilbert Harman, from "Moral Relativism," in Gilbert Harman and Judith Jarvis Thomson, eds., *Moral Relativism and Moral Objectivity* (Blackwell, 1996) *4*

NO: Louis P. Pojman, from "The Case Against Moral Relativism," in Louis P. Pojman and Lewis Vaughn, eds., *The Moral Life: An Introductory Reader in Ethics and Literature* (Oxford University Press, 2007) *13*

Philosopher Gilbert Harman argues that relativism is true for morality—much as Einstein proved it was true for motion. Just as motion always presupposes some framework in which it occurs (and something can be in motion relative to one person but not to another), morality too always presupposes some framework. Louis Pojman carefully distinguishes what he calls the diversity thesis—that moral rules differ from society to society—from ethical relativism. The diversity thesis is a straightforward description of what are acknowledged differences in the moral beliefs and practices of various human groups. But he argues that moral relativism does not follow from this diversity.

Issue 2. Does Morality Need Religion? 24

YES: C. Stephen Layman, from *The Shape of the Good: Christian Reflections on the Foundations of Ethics* (University of Notre Dame Press, 1991) *26*

NO: John Arthur, from "Religion, Morality, and Conscience," in John Arthur, ed., *Morality and Moral Controversies,* 4th ed. (Prentice Hall, 1996) *35*

Philosopher C. Stephen Layman argues that morality makes the most sense from a theistic perspective and that a purely secular perspective is insufficient. The secular perspective, Layman asserts, does not adequately deal with secret violations, and it does not allow for the possibility of fulfillment of people's deepest needs in an afterlife. Philosopher John Arthur counters that morality is logically independent of religion, although there are historical connections. Religion, he believes, is not necessary for moral guidance or moral answers; morality is social.

UNIT 2 GENDER, SEX, AND REPRODUCTION 49

Issue 3. Is Abortion Immoral? 50

YES: Don Marquis, from "Why Abortion Is Immoral," *Journal of Philosophy* (April 1989) *52*

NO: Jane English, from "Abortion and the Concept of a Person," *Canadian Journal of Philosophy* (October 1975) *60*

Professor of philosophy Don Marquis argues that abortion is generally wrong for the same reason that killing an innocent adult human being is generally wrong: it deprives the individual of a future that he or she would otherwise have. Philosopher Jane English (1947–1978) asserts that there is no well-defined line dividing persons from nonpersons. She maintains that both the conservative and the liberal positions are too extreme and that some abortions are morally justifiable and some are not.

Issue 4. Must Sex Involve Commitment? 70

YES: Vincent C. Punzo, from *Reflective Naturalism* (Macmillan, 1969) *72*

NO: Alan H. Goldman, from "Plain Sex," *Philosophy and Public Affairs* (Spring 1977) *78*

Philosopher Vincent C. Punzo maintains that the special intimacy of sex requires a serious commitment that is for the most part not required in other human activities. Philosopher Alan H. Goldman argues for a view of sex that is completely separate from any cultural or moral ideology that might be attached to it.

Issue 5. Is It Right to Prohibit Same-Sex Marriage? 86

YES: Jeff Jordan, from "Is It Wrong to Discriminate on the Basis of Homosexuality?" *Journal of Social Philosophy,* vol. 26, no. 1 (Spring, 1995) *88*

NO: David Boonin, from "Same-Sex Marriage and the Argument from Public Disagreement," *Journal of Social Philosophy,* vol. 30, no. 2 (Summer 1999) *99*

Philosopher Jeff Jordan defends the claim that there are situations in which it is morally permissible to discriminate against homosexuals, i.e., to treat homosexuals unfavorably. There is a public dilemma (or a clash of views) concerning the moral status of homosexuality and, unless something of overriding importance—such as human rights—is at stake, the government should refrain from favoring one side by publicly recognizing same-sex marriage. Philosopher David Boonin argues directly against Jordan that his argument is unsuccessful. He uses Jordan's argument to address some of the questions that seem to lie, unanswered, in the background of this issue: In particular, is it correct that homosexuality is immoral? Do people have a right to marry only certain other people? Is opposition to same-sex marriage comparable to opposition to interracial marriage?

Issue 6. Should Human Cloning Be Banned? 110

YES: Michael J. Sandel, from "The Ethical Implications of Human Cloning," *Perspectives in Biology and Medicine* (Spring 2005) *112*

NO: John A. Robertson, from "Human Cloning and the Challenge of Regulation," *The New England Journal of Medicine* (July 9, 1998) *118*

Political philosopher Michael. J. Sandel argues that much of the talk about cloning revolves around a few limited concepts (e.g., rights, autonomy, and the supposed unnaturalness of asexual reproduction) that are inadequate and fail to express what is really wrong with cloning. We need, Instead, to address fundamental questions about our stance toward nature. Law professor John A. Robertson maintains that there should not be a complete ban on human cloning but that regulatory policy should be focused on ensuring that it is performed in a responsible manner.

UNIT 3 LAW AND SOCIETY 127

Issue 7. Is Cloning Pets Ethically Justified? 128

YES: **Autumn Fiester,** from "Creating Fido's Twin," *Hastings Center Report* (July/August 2005) *130*

NO: **Hilary Bok,** from "Cloning Companion Animals Is Wrong," *Journal of Applied Animal Welfare Science* (vol. 5, no. 3, 2002) *140*

Autumn Fiester argues in support of cloning animals (in particular, people's pets). She emphasizes the point that pet owners really care about their pets. One result of this is that they spend large amounts of money on veterinary care for their pets. Cloning their pets could serve as a useful extension of this idea—and also serve as a positive demonstration to society in general that individual pets have intrinsic value and cannot simply be replaced by new pets. Hilary Bok argues that cloning pets is immoral first of all because it causes great harm to animals. The animal that results from the cloning, for example, is much more likely to have physical defects than the animal from which it was cloned. Moreover, the process of cloning itself necessarily involves harm to other animals (e.g., the animal that will carry the new pet to term). Finally, the end result simply does not provide pet owners with what they were looking for.

Issue 8. Should Congress Allow the Buying and Selling of Human Organs? 146

YES: **Lewis Burrows,** from "Selling Organs for Transplantation," *The Mount Sinai Journal of Medicine* (September, 2004) *148*

NO: **James F. Childress,** from "Should Congress Allow the Buying and Selling of Human Organs? No," *Insight on the News* (May 7, 2001) *153*

Lewis Burrows, M.D., begins with the observation that the need for organs far outstrips the supply: each year, hundreds of patients die while waiting for transplants. Burrows argues that payment to the donor (or, payment to the donor's family, in cases in which the donor is deceased) would increase the supply of organs, regulations could restrain possible abuses, and a payment-for-organs system could meet relevant medical ethical principles. James F. Childress, professor of ethics and professor of medical education, argues that a free market would cause the loss of important altruistic motivations and would turn organs into commodities; moreover, such an untried market might make fewer—not more—organs available.

Issue 9. Should Drugs Be Legalized? 159

YES: **Meaghan Cussen and Walter Block,** from "Legalize Drugs Now! An Analysis of the Benefits of Legalized Drugs," *American Journal of Economics and Sociology* (July 2000) *161*

NO: **Drug Enforcement Administration,** from "Speaking Out Against Drug Legalization," http://www.DEA.gov (May 2003) *170*

Meaghan Cussen (a student in economics) and Walter Block (her economics professor) argue that the legalization of drugs would provide many sorts of benefits (e.g., crime would fall, the quality of life in inner cities would rise, and taxpayers would no longer have to pay for an unwinnable "war on drugs"). Moreover, the legalization of drugs would promote the American the value of liberty. The Drug Enforcement Administration presents the case that drugs are illegal for good reason—they are harmful. If the legalization proponents were heeded, we as a society would be much worse off. We should be concentrating harder on fighting drug use and drug trafficking, where there is significant progress.

Issue 10. Is Gambling Immoral? 183

YES: Lisa Newton, from "Gambling: A Preliminary Inquiry," *Business Ethics Quarterly* (vol. 3, no. 4, 1993) *185*

NO: Peter Collins, from "Is Gambling Immoral? A Virtue Ethics Approach," in Mark Timmons, ed., *Disputed Moral Issues* (Oxford University Press, 2007) *194*

Lisa Newton, a philosopher at Fairfield University, argues that gambling is immoral on the grounds that it violates stewardship (and not on the grounds that it violates anyone's rights or that it leads to negative results). Most of the paper examines the concept of stewardship and how it relates to gambling. Stewardship, which is an old concept that is known to us primarily through religious tradition, can also be given a modern secular form. Peter Collins, a British philosopher, argues that gambling is not immoral. He addresses gambling from both traditional utilitarian (or consequentialist) and Kantian perspectives—and finds the critiques from these perspectives lacking. He then specifically considers the more recent criticism that is based on the idea of stewardship—this too he finds lacking. Collins concludes with the idea of true happiness, and expresses the judgment that although gambling is not necessarily a part of a truly happy life, it is morally trivial.

Issue 11. Is Affirmative Action Fair? 207

YES: Albert G. Mosley, from "Affirmative Action: Pro," in Albert G. Mosley and Nicholas Capaldi, eds., *Affirmative Action: Social Justice or Unfair Preference?* (Rowman and Littlefield, 1996) *209*

NO: Louis P. Pojman, from "The Case Against Affirmative Action," *International Journal of Applied Philosophy* (Spring 1998) *221*

Professor of philosophy Albert G. Mosley argues that affirmative action is a continuation of the history of black progress since the *Brown v. Board of Education* desegregation decision of 1954 and the Civil Rights Act of 1964. He defends affirmative action as a "benign use of race." Professor of philosophy Louis P. Pojman contends that affirmative action violates the moral principle that maintains that each person is to be treated as an individual, not as representative of a group. He stresses that individual merit needs to be appreciated and that respect should be given to each person on an individual basis.

Issue 12. Should Licensing for Handguns Be More Restrictive? 233

YES: Jon S. Vernick, James G. Hodge, Jr., and Daniel W. Webster, from "The Ethics of Restrictive Licensing for Handguns: Comparing the United States and Canadian Approaches to

Handgun Regulation," *Journal of Law, Medicine & Ethics* (Winter 2007) *235*

NO: **Daniel D. Polsby,** from "The False Promise of Gun Control," *The Atlantic Monthly* (March 1994) *250*

Gun control and health policy professionals Vernick, Hodge, and Webster argue that there are trade-offs and competing values at stake in gun control debates. In particular, a comparison between public health policy and gun control in Canada and the United States shows the benefits of placing the value of public health above that of the right to own guns. Professor of law Daniel D. Polsby asserts that gun control legislation is misguided. He maintains that if there were a ban on handguns, criminals would still arm themselves, but law-abiding citizens would not, resulting in more crime and more innocent victims.

Issue 13. Should the Death Penalty Be Abolished? 261

YES: **Michael Welch,** from *Punishment in America: Social Control and the Ironies of Imprisonment* (Sage, 1999) *263*

NO: **Ernest van den Haag,** from "The Death Penalty Once More," *U.C. Davis Law Review* (Summer 1985) *277*

Criminologist Michael Welch argues that the death penalty encourages murder and is applied in a biased and mistake-laden way to growing groups of people. Much of the recent popular support of capital punishment is due to ignorance of the facts. Professor of law Ernest van den Haag argues that the death penalty is entirely in line with the U.S. Constitution and that although studies of its deterrent effect are inconclusive, the death penalty is morally justified and should not be abolished.

Issue 14. Is Torture Ever Justified? 290

YES: **Mirko Bagaric and Julie Clarke,** from "Not Enough Official Torture in the World?" *University of San Francisco Law Review* (Spring 2005) *292*

NO: **Christopher W. Tindale,** from "Tragic Choices: Reaffirming Absolutes in the Torture Debate," *International Journal of Applied Philosophy* (vol. 19, no. 2, 2005) *301*

Bagaric and Clarke remind us, first of all, that torture, although prohibited by international law, is nevertheless widely practiced. A rational examination of torture, and a consideration of hypothetical (but realistic) cases shows that torture is justifiable in order to prevent great harm. Torture should be regulated and carefully practiced as an information-gathering technique in extreme cases. Christopher Tindale argues that torture is absolutely wrong; it is not just wrong under ordinary circumstances, but even when the stakes are high. Hypothetical cases of imminent danger unless we torture a terrorist are always unrealistic to some extent, since, in the real world, we can never be sure of the facts. And once we become torturers, there is no going back. We have undergone a moral loss, and there is no assurance of gain.

Issue 15. Is Physician-Assisted Suicide Wrong? 314

YES: **Richard Doerflinger,** from "Assisted Suicide: Pro-Choice or Anti-Life?" *Hastings Center Report* (January/February 1989) *316*

NO: David T. Watts and Timothy Howell, from "Assisted Suicide Is Not Voluntary Active Euthanasia," *Journal of the American Geriatrics Society* (October 1992) *323*

Admitting that religiously based grounds for the wrongness of killing an innocent person are not convincing to many people, Doerflinger argues on mainly secular grounds having to do with inconsistencies in the arguments of supporters of physician-assisted suicide. He examines the idea of autonomy, and the tendency for something like physician-assisted suicide to spread once it becomes initially accepted in a limited way. Watts and Howell first claim that it is very important to distinguish between *assisted suicide* and *voluntary active euthanasia.* Basically, the first of these is suicide or killing oneself; the second involves being killing by someone else (e.g., a physician). Watts and Howell argue that most of the opposition to physician-assisted suicide turns out to be really opposition to voluntary active euthanasia; furthermore, they argue that physician-assisted suicide would not have the dire consequence that its opponents predict.

UNIT 4 HUMAN BEINGS AND OTHER SPECIES 333

Issue 16. Does Morality Require Vegetarianism? 334

YES: Michael Allen Fox, from "Why We Should Be Vegetarians," *International Journal of Applied Philosophy* (vol. 20, no. 2, 2006) *336*

NO: Holmes Rolston III, from *Environmental Ethics: Duties to and Values in the Natural World* (Temple University Press, 1988) *348*

Michael Allen Fox believes that the common practice of eating meat is something that we need to apply critical thinking to. He argues that if we care about pain, suffering, and death, and if we are to live up to the demands of justice, then we should take responsibility for our diets and become vegetarians. Environmental thinker Holmes Rolston III maintains that meat eating by humans is a natural part of the ecosystem. He states that it is important that animals do not suffer needlessly, but it would be a mistake to think that animals, like humans, are members of a culture. Rolston concludes that people too readily project human nature on animal nature.

Contributors 355

Correlation Guide

The *Taking Sides* series presents current issues in a debate-style format designed to stimulate student interest and develop critical thinking skills. Each issue is thoughtfully framed with an issue summary, an issue introduction, and a postscript. The pro and con essays—selected for their liveliness and substance—represent the arguments of leading scholars and commentators in their fields.

Taking Sides: Clashing Views on Moral Issues, 12/e is an easy-to-use reader that presents issues on important topics such as *genetic engineering, gambling,* and *same-sex marriage.* For more information on *Taking Sides* and other *McGraw-Hill Contemporary Learning Series* titles, visit www.mhcls.com.

This convenient guide matches the issues in **Taking Sides: Moral Issues, 12/e** with the corresponding chapters in one of our best-selling McGraw-Hill Philosophy textbooks by Rachels/Rachels.

Taking Sides: Moral Issues, 12/e	The Elements of Moral Philosophy, 6/e, Rachels/Rachels
Issue 1: Is Moral Relativism Correct?	**Chapter 2:** The Challenge of Cultural Relativism
Issue 2: Does Morality Need Religion?	**Chapter 4:** Does Morality Depend on Religion?
Issue 3: Is Abortion Immoral?	**Chapter 4:** Does Morality Depend on Religion?
Issue 4: Must Sex Involve Commitment?	**Chapter 8:** The Debate over Utilitarianism
Issue 5: Is It Right to Prohibit Same-Sex Marriage?	**Chapter 6:** The Idea of a Social Contract
Issue 6: Should Human Cloning Be Banned?	**Chapter 10:** Kant and Respect for Persons
Issue 7: Is Cloning Pets Ethically Justified?	**Chapter 7:** The Utilitarian Approach **Chapter 8:** The Debate over Utilitarianism
Issue 8: Should Congress Allow the Buying and Selling of Human Organs?	**Chapter 7:** The Utilitarian Approach **Chapter 8:** The Debate over Utilitarianism
Issue 9: Should Drugs Be Legalized?	**Chapter 5:** Ethical Egoism
Issue 10: Is Gambling Immoral?	**Chapter 5:** Ethical Egoism **Chapter 6:** The Idea of a Social Contract
Issue 11: Is Affirmative Action Fair?	**Chapter 8:** The Debate over Utilitarianism
Issue 12: Should Licensing for Handguns Be More Restrictive?	**Chapter 6:** The Idea of a Social Contract
Issue 13: Should the Death Penalty Be Abolished?	**Chapter 9:** Are There Absolute Moral Rules? **Chapter 10:** Kant and Respect for Persons

Taking Sides: Moral Issues, 12/e	The Elements of Moral Philosophy, 6/e, Rachels/Rachels
Issue 14: Is Torture Ever Justified?	**Chapter 9:** Are There Absolute Moral Rules? **Chapter 10:** Kant and Respect for Persons
Issue 15: Is Physician-Assisted Suicide Wrong?	**Chapter 7:** The Utilitarian Approach **Chapter 8:** The Debate over Utilitarianism **Chapter 9:** Are There Absolute Moral Rules? **Chapter 10:** Kant and Respect for Persons
Issue 16: Does Morality Require Vegetarianism?	**Chapter 12:** The Ethics of Virtue

Introduction

Thinking About Moral Issues

Stephen Satris

Getting Started

If you were asked in your biology class to give the number of bones in the average human foot, you could consult your textbook, you could go to the library and have the librarian track down the answer, you could search the Internet, or you could ask your friend who always gets A's in biology. Most likely you have not previously had any reason to consider this question, but you do know for certain that it has one right answer, which you will be expected to provide for the final exam.

What do you do, however, when faced with a moral question like one of the ones raised in this text? Whereas it is a relatively straightforward matter to find out how many bones there are in the human foot, in addressing moral issues, understanding cannot be acquired as easily. Someone cannot report back to you on the right answer. You will have to discuss the ideas raised by these moral questions and determine the answers for yourself. And you will have to arrive at an answer through reason and careful thought; you cannot just rely on your *feelings* to answer these questions. Keep in mind, too, that these are questions you will be facing your entire life—understanding will not end with the final exam.

In approaching the issues in this book, you should maintain an open mind toward both sides of the question. Otherwise, it will be more difficult for you to see, appreciate, and, most importantly, *learn* from the opposing position. Therefore, you should first ask yourself what your own assumptions are about an issue and become aware of any preconceived notions you may have. And then, after such reflection, you should assume the posture of an impartial judge. If you have a strong prior attachment to one side, do not let it prevent you from giving a sympathetic ear to the opposing side.

Once the arguments have been laid out and you have given them careful consideration, do not remain suspended in the middle. Now is the time for informed judgment.

A natural dramatic sequence is played out for each of the 16 issues discussed in *Taking Sides: Clashing Views on Moral Issues*. A question is posed, and you must open yourself to hear each author's arguments, reasons, and examples, which are meant to persuade you to take the author's viewpoint. But then comes the second part of the drama. Having heard and considered both sides of an issue, what will *you* say? What understanding of the issue can *you* achieve?

You can choose aspects of the "yes" answer and aspects of the "no" answer and weave them together to construct a coherent whole. You can accept one answer and build some qualifications or limitations into it. Or you might be stimulated to think of a completely new angle on the issue.

Be aware of three dangers. The first is a premature judgment or fixed opinion that rules out a fair hearing of the opposing side. The second danger is in many ways like the first, but is somewhat more insidious. It is an unconscious assumption (or set of assumptions) that makes it impossible to hear the other side correctly. (The best antidote for this is to be able to give a fair and accurate account of the issue as it appears to someone on the opposing side.) Finally, the third danger is to lack a judgment after having considered the issue. In this case, two contrary positions simply cannot both be right, and it is up to the reader to make an effort to distinguish what is acceptable from what is unacceptable in the arguments and positions that have been defended.

Fundamental Issues in Morality

The 16 issues in this book are divided into four units, or parts. The first part deals with fundamental questions about morality as a whole. In this context, it might be said that "morality is a religious matter" or perhaps, that "it's all relative." The issues in the first part do not directly confront specific moral problems; they question the nature of morality itself.

Already in Unit 1, we see something that is a recurring feature of moral thought and of this book: Moral issues are interrelated. Suppose, for example, that you answer the question "Is Moral Relativism Correct?" (Issue 1) in the affirmative and also answer the question "Does Morality Need Religion?" (Issue 2) in the affirmative. How can these two answers fit together? A positive answer to the second question is generally thought to involve a source for morality that is supernatural, beyond the customs and traditions of any one particular social group. But an affirmative answer to the first question suggests that morality is grounded in what is cultural and *not* supernatural. (It may be possible to maintain affirmative answers to both of these questions, but a person who does so owes us an explanation as to how these two ideas fit together.) Many other issues that at first sight might seem distinct have connections among one another.

Another point, and one that applies not only to the issues in Unit 1 but to controversial issues in general, is this: In evaluating any position, you should do so on the merits (or lack of merit) of the specific case that is made. Do not accept or reject a position on the basis of what the position (supposedly) tells you about the author, and do not criticize or defend a position by reducing it to simplistic slogans. The loss of articulation and sophistication that occurs when a complex position is reduced to a simple slogan is significant and real. For example, a "no" answer to the question "Does Morality Need Religion?" might be superficially labeled as "antireligion," and a "yes" answer might seem as "proreligion." Yet Saint Thomas Aquinas, who has always been regarded as the foremost theologian of the Christian tradition, would respond with a "no" to that question. Moral questions are complex, and the reduction of answers to simple reactions or superficial slogans will not be helpful. The questions and issues that are raised here require careful analysis, examination, and argumentation.

Gender, Sex, and Reproduction

Unit 2 includes several questions that have to do with ways of looking at society, especially sex roles, sexual relationships, and reproduction. In many ways, the issues in this section are basic to an understanding of our own place in society, our relation to others, and what we expect of men and women.

Specific issues considered in Unit 2 are "Is Abortion Immoral?," "Must Sex Involve Commitment?," "Is It Right To Prohibit Same-Sex Marriage?," and "Should Human Cloning Be Banned?"

The question "Is Abortion Immoral?" (Issue 3) is not at all new, and threatens immediately to polarize people into pro-life and pro-choice camps. But it is best to leave such labels and superficial slogans behind. Whenever an issue seems to demand answers very quickly, as this one might, it is better to go slowly and to first consider the arguments, examples, and rationale of each position before making up your mind. Both of the writers on this topic, for example, stay away from religious arguments—which could very quickly polarize people.

The question "Must Sex Involve Commitment?" (Issue 4) has traditionally been answered in the positive—the conservative answer certainly tends to be positive. But after the social changes that have liberalized society's sexual attitudes, does the traditional answer still stand? What, exactly, has changed in people's attitudes? Have people come to see premarital sex as morally permissible (where it was once thought to be immoral)? Or do people still see it as immoral, but they are no longer shocked by its widespread occurrence in real life, films, etc.? The word *must* in "Must sex involve commitment?" is moral. The view that sex must involve commitment is not intended to be one that reflects how things actually are. In fact, those who answer this question positively would probably think that how things actually are is not at all how they should be.

The question "Is It Right to Prohibit Same-Sex Marriage?" (Issue 5) arises in a social context of changing practices and values. Certainly, same-sex relationships are more widely tolerated now than in the past. Some people may think that this shows a moral decline and would naturally be against same-sex marriage. But even some people who think of this increased tolerance as a good thing are hesitant to accept same-sex marriage. Marriage is something for a man and a woman, they might say. Traditionally, this may have indeed been so. But the question now arises whether any changes should be made to this idea. Is marriage for heterosexual unions only? And if same-sex marriage is allowed, what would be the social repercussions?

The question "Should Human Cloning Be Banned?" (Issue 6) has arisen because technology may some day (soon) exist that could clone human beings. Some people think that science would be going too far here and that cloning people would be akin to "playing God." They also feel that not everything that technology makes possible should actually be done. Others see no problem with proceeding with experimentation toward human cloning. Is cloning just a case of using science to manipulate natural facts and achieve some desired results, or are the results here not to be desired?

Law and Society

Unit 3 focuses on questions that involve our social nature. We ask what particular arrangements will (or will not) be tolerated in society. We also ask what laws we should have (or not have).

This section considers the questions: "Is Cloning Pets Ethically Justified?," "Should Congress Allow the Buying and Selling of Human Organs?," "Should Drugs Be Legalized?," "Is Gambling Immoral?," "Is Affirmative Action Fair?," "Should Licensing for Handguns Be More Restrictive?," "Should the Death Penalty Be Abolished?," and "Is Torture Ever Justified?"

The first question, "Is Cloning Pets Ethically Justified?" (Issue 7), raises many of the same questions that arise in the case of cloning human beings. People may have unrealistic expectations of cloning in both cases. And in both cases the cloned individual may be held to those expectations. On the other hand, it may be felt that human beings are in a class by themselves and should not be cloned—while we can do virtually anything in the case of animals. Yet, here again, objectors to cloning stress the failures of the technique and the problems that it always seems to bring with it. If our pets really are at our mercy (unlike human beings), perhaps it is not right to treat them in ways that seem to be problematic.

The second question, "Should Congress Allow the Buying and Selling of Human Organs?" (Issue 8), is one that might initially sound quite gruesome. But the fact is that there are many more people needing organs than there are organs available for transplant. Part of the problem with the shortage of organs is that there is no financial incentive for donors to provide kidneys. Doctors and hospitals are compensated for their roles in the organ transplant process, but the donor—by law—cannot be compensated. There cannot be payment for organs. Yet there is a demand for organs on the part of those in need. Would a market in which there was buying and selling help? Is this even something we should think about? Why not, if it can help?

Asking "Should Drugs Be Legalized" (Issue 9) raises a number of points that require consideration. Here we ask about the future and what kind of society is worth aiming for. Should we strive for a society in which certain substances are available on the open market to consumers who choose them, or should we aim to eliminate certain substances and legally punish drug dealers and users? This is one of several issues in which we are drawn to two incompatible values; in this case, the values are complete liberty and social order. It seems impossible to have both.

The question "Is Gambling Immoral?" (Issue 10) is puzzling for at least one reason. Gambling has traditionally been counted as a vice, and many people today think it is wrong, but if gambling is immoral, it is surprisingly difficult to articulate just what is wrong with it. Even a traditional view of gambling as wrong usually allows that such activities as church bingo, etc., are not wrong. State lotteries are also another strange case. We might feel the positive pull toward lotteries as a useful means of raising state revenue (without increasing taxes), and at the same time have an uneasy feeling about the fact that the state has always forbidden "games of chance"—but now lets itself run one of the games it forbids to all others. Gambling is definitely a strange area, and one that needs some clear thinking!

The question "Is Affirmative Action Fair?" (Issue 11) confronts a policy that is intended to address problems arising from the history and the current state of race relations in the United States. Most arguments in favor of affirmative action can be seen as either backward-looking or forward-looking. Arguments that regard affirmative action as a form of compensation or as a response to previous injustices are backward-looking because they focus on prior events. Arguments that regard affirmative action as a means of achieving integration or diversity or as a means of providing minority role models are forward-looking because they point to the future. Critics of programs of affirmative action, however, have charged that such programs lead to (or themselves amount to) "reverse discrimination" and unfairly focus on "group rights," whereas the only actual rights are rights of individuals.

The question "Should Licensing for Handguns Be More Restrictive?" (Issue 12) is raised largely in response to the very high number of murders that are committed with handguns in the United States. According to an affirmative answer to this question, the crime problem could be seriously addressed; rifles would still be allowed for hunting and other legal purposes; and a somewhat more restrictive approach could be taken to the sale, transport, and use of handguns. But some people who give a negative answer to this question see the strong arm of the government coming into play and fear that individual rights would be violated. Others argue that restictions on handguns would not stop criminals from committing crimes with these guns; in fact, they argue, it may to some extent encourage them.

Many subsidiary questions enter into the issue of "Should the Death Penalty Be Abolished?" (Issue 13). Does the death penalty deter crime? Does it, in fact, encourage crime? Is it the only way to give some criminals what they deserve? Does it fall unfairly on minorities and the poor? How much should we be concerned about errors? And, finally, even if we had the answers to all these questions, could we use those answers to address the overarching question of whether or not the death penalty should be abolished?

The question "Is Torture Ever Justified?" (Issue 14) was, until 9/11, mainly a hypothetical question. Now, it is asked by government interrogators—who have suspects and want answers, and by concerned citizens as well, who might feel that torture makes us no better than the terrorists. The problem is that arguments on both sides seem fairly strong. To use torture against terrorists who have killed some innocent Americans and may want to kill us too does not seem very far from self-defense. On the other hand, if we engage in torture, then we seem to be the very devils we are said by the terrorists to be. But aren't American supposed to be the "good guys"? With torture, we seem to be stooping to the same level as the terrorists.

The question "Is Physician-Assisted Suicide Wrong?" (Issue 15) is another question about life or death, but this time the person who would die would not be regarded as a criminal. Such a person, who may have a terminal illness and perhaps be in great pain, requests the physician's assistance in killing himself or herself. (Why would such assistance even be needed? Some people may be so bad off as not to be able to do it themselves; still others may be better off—but might end up botching things and making the situation worse. Hence, the physician is asked to lend expertise and assistance.) The question is whether this request should be fulfilled. If so, the end comes quickly. If not, the end will come, but not so quickly. But is helping to bring the situation to a quick end something that physicians should do?

Human Beings and Other Species

Unit 4 has only one question: "Does Morality Require Vegetarianism?" (Issue 16). This is a question that probably would not have been taken seriously in earlier times. However, today there are people and organizations that promote vegetarianism on moral grounds. The simplest idea here is that animals are beings that can be harmed, and they generally do suffer when they are raised and killed for meat. Most people can live without eating meat, so meat-eating seems to be a practice that we have in our power to change. Of course, many people *like* meat-eating and are very reluctant to change. From their point of view, animals are part of nature, human beings are part of nature, and meat-eating—where one species eats another—is also part of nature. But the meat-eating question remains and forces itself upon people, who pride themselves on their ability to be self-aware and have knowledge—knowledge that in this case includes awareness of the fact that they share the planet with other species.

Internet References . . .

The Internet Encyclopedia of Philosophy

This is a very useful reference tool for the serious philosophy student. It contains an excellent collection of readings from classic philosophy texts and original contributions by professional philosophers around the Internet.

http://www.utm.edu/research/iep/

Ethics Updates

Ethics Updates is an online resource edited by Lawrence M. Hinman, a well-respected ethicist at the University of San Diego. The site includes definitions of basic ideas, online articles, audio files, video files, discussion boards, and sophisticated search engines. There is a wide variety of subject matter, running from ethical theory to applied ethics, and the site offers frequent opportunities for user input.

http://ethics.sandiego.edu

Internet Philosophical Resources on Moral Relativism

This *Ethics Updates* site contains discussion questions and Internet resources devoted to moral, cultural, and ethical relativism.

http://ethics.sandiego.edu/theories/Relativism/index.asp

UNIT 1

Fundamental Issues in Morality

Even before confronting particular moral issues, we find that there are several conflicting assertions that have been made about morality considered as a whole. Some people state that there is no such thing as objective moral knowledge and that morality can provide no answers. Among them, relativists contend that all moral talk is simply the expression of subjective feelings or cultural norms, and these vary from case to case. Others maintain that morality does not have a source in purely human experience and interaction. Religion, they say, is the ground of morality. These and other ideas are discussed in this section.

- Is Moral Relativism Correct?
- Does Morality Need Religion?

ISSUE 1

Is Moral Relativism Correct?

YES: Gilbert Harman, from "Moral Relativism," in Gilbert Harman and Judith Jarvis Thomson, eds., *Moral Relativism and Moral Objectivity* (Blackwell, 1996)

NO: Louis P. Pojman, from "The Case Against Moral Relativism," in Louis P. Pojman and Lewis Vaughn, eds., *The Moral Life: An Introductory Reader in Ethics and Literature* (Oxford University Press, 2007)

ISSUE SUMMARY

YES: Philosopher Gilbert Harman argues that relativism is true for morality—much as Einstein proved it was true for motion. Just as motion always presupposes some framework in which it occurs (and something can be in motion relative to one person but not to another), morality too always presupposes some framework.

NO: Louis Pojman carefully distinguishes what he calls the diversity thesis—that moral rules differ from society to society—from ethical relativism. The diversity thesis is a straightforward description of what are acknowledged differences in the moral beliefs and practices of various human groups. But he argues that moral relativism does not follow from this diversity.

Many people are drawn to the idea that moral relativism is correct, but most people who have thought and written about this issue think that it is not. As a result, the supporters of moral relativism are in the minority. Among those, however, who think moral relativism is correct, Gilbert Harman's work—excerpted here—stands out.

Harman draws attention to what is probably one of the most common sources of the idea of moral relativism, namely, the fact that there is vast diversity among the moral views of different people at different times and places; furthermore, he emphasizes there is even a diversity of moral views among people in the very same society.

Diversity of views by itself proves nothing, and Harman acknowledges this. Consider the fact that among people of different times and places, there is also a diversity of views about many other things (e.g., about the origin of the earth, whether thunder is caused by Zeus, and so on). But no one would say that there is no truth of the matter, or that such matters are relative.

Of course, one might argue that *beliefs* are relative, at least in the following sense. If you time-traveled back to ancient Greece and asked people whether it was Zeus who caused thunder, you'd receive a large number of affirmative answers, whereas asking the same question of almost anyone today would most probably yield negative answers. So the *beliefs* might be in some sense relative. Both Harman and Pojman would agree that their own disagreement is not over what the beliefs of people would be but what the situation actually is.

As for the belief that Zeus causes thunder, we can probably chalk that one up to the lack of scientific sophistication of the ancient Greeks. But it is also worthwhile considering a more modern question—such as the origin and nature of black holes. There may be competing theories about black holes, and (unlike the case of thunder) the matter might not be settled at all. But no one would say that the nature of thunder or black holes is *relative*. There's a definite truth there to find out. In the case of thunder, we may know the truth; in the case of black holes, we may not. So here is a case in which we ourselves may lack the knowledge. But that doesn't mean that the matter is relative.

From Pojman's point of view, he could easily grant that the views of the people of different times and places are different. Nevertheless, he might say, what different people (e.g., the ancient Greeks and modern-day scientists) say or believe about something may have little or nothing to do with the truth of the matter. Perhaps one of these groups is correct. Perhaps neither is correct. But in any case, the truth of the matter does not depend on what they might say or believe.

Likewise, an opponent of relativism, such as Pojman himself, will insist that the same holds true for moral belief and for physical belief. In any case, the moral objectivist (or non-relativist) will certainly hold that moral judgments are not dependent on cultural acceptance for their validity. So, it's possible for some people to promote a certain moral position, and for that moral position to be correct, while the majority of the population rejects the position. Pojman would admit that in some cases it's *hard* to see the validity, or lack of validity, behind a moral point of view. (Perhaps many controversial ideas—like those in this book—are *hard* in this sense.) Of course, in some cases it's quite easy to see whether or not we have moral validity. (For example, consider an obvious wrong like rape. No one defends rape, it's not controversial, and there is no issue about it in this book.)

In the following essays, Gilbert Harman first defends relativism, invoking, in fact, Einstein's relativistic theory about physical phenomena. Louis Pojman, a supporter of moral objectivism, then argues that moral relativism is not correct.

YES

Gilbert Harman

Moral Relativism

Introduction

Motion is a relative matter. Motion is always relative to a choice of spatio-temporal framework. Something that is moving in relation to one spatio-temporal framework can be at rest in relation to another. And no spatio-temporal framework can be singled out as the one and only framework that captures the truth about whether something is in motion.

According to Einstein's Theory of Relativity even an object's mass is relative to a choice of spatio-temporal framework. An object can have one mass in relation to one such framework and a different mass in relation to another. Again, there is no privileged spatio-temporal framework that determines the real mass of an object.

I am going to argue for a similar claim about moral right and wrong. That is, . . . I am going to defend *moral relativism.* I am going to argue that moral right and wrong (good and bad, justice and injustice, virtue and vice, etc.) are always relative to a choice of moral framework. What is morally right in relation to one moral framework can be morally wrong in relation to a different moral framework. And no moral framework is objectively privileged as the one true morality.

Einstein's relativistic conception of mass involves the following claim about the truth conditions of judgments of mass.

(1) For the purposes of assigning truth conditions, a judgment of the form, *the mass of X is M* has to be understood as elliptical for a judgment of the form, *in relation to spatio-temporal framework F the mass of X is M.*

The word *elliptical* might be misleading here. Einstein's Theory of Relativity does not involve a claim about meaning or about what people intend to be claiming when they make judgments about an object's mass. The point is, rather, that the only truth there is in this area is relative truth.

Before Einstein, judgments about mass were not intended as relative judgments. But it would be mean-spirited to invoke an "error theory" and conclude that these pre-Einsteinian judgments were all false![1] Better to suppose that such a judgment was true to the extent that an object had the relevant

From *Moral Relativism and Moral Objectivity* (Blackwell 1996), pp. 3–6, 8–15, 17–19 (excerpts).
Copyright © 1996 by Gilbert Harman and Judith Jarvis Thompson, eds. Reprinted by permission of Blackwell Publishing, Ltd.

mass in relation to a spatio-temporal framework that was conspicuous to the person making the judgment, for example, a framework in which that person was at rest.

Similarly, the moral relativism I will argue for is not a claim what people *mean* by their moral judgments. Moral relativism does not claim that people intend their moral judgments to be "elliptical" in the suggested way; just as relativism about mass does not claim that people intend their judgments about mass to make implicit reference to a spatio-temporal framework.

To a first approximation, moral relativism makes the following claim about moral judgments.

> (2) For the purposes of assigning truth conditions, a judgment of the form, *it would be morally wrong of P to D,* has to be understood as elliptical for a judgment of the form, *in relation to moral framework M, it would be morally wrong of P to D.* Similarly for other moral judgments.[2]

As before, it is important not to put too much stress on the word *elliptical.* The moral relativism I will argue for is no more a claim about what people mean by their moral judgments than relativism about mass is a claim about what people mean when they make judgments about mass. Moral relativism does not claim that people intend their moral judgments to be "elliptical" in the suggested way; just as relativism about mass does not claim that people intend their judgments about mass to make implicit reference to a spatio-temporal framework. . . .

(2) is only part of a definition of moral relativism because it is important to distinguish moral relativism both from moral absolutism on the one side and from moral nihilism on the other side. Moral absolutism holds that there is a single true morality. Moral relativism claims instead:

> (3) There is no single true morality. There are many different moral frameworks, none of which is more correct than the others.

Moral nihilism agrees with (3) and takes that conclusion to be a reason to reject morality altogether including any sort of relative morality.

Moral nihilism can be compared to religious nihilism. Religious nihilism would be a natural response to the conclusion that there is no single true religion but only many different religious outlooks, none of which is more correct than the others. Such a conclusion would seem to provide a reason to reject religion and religious judgments altogether, rather than a reason to accept "religious relativism." It might then be possible to assign objective truth conditions to religious judgments in relation to one or another religious framework, but it is hard to see how such relative religious judgments could play a serious role in religious practices. Moral nihilism argues that the same is true of morality: given (3), there is no point to engaging in morality and moral judgment.

Moral relativism rejects moral nihilism and asserts instead

(4) Morality should not be abanboned.

Furthermore, moral relativism insists. . . .

(5) Relative moral judgments can continue to play a serious role in moral thinking. . . .

Explaining Moral Diversity

In this and the following section I argue that the following claim is a reasonable inference from the most plausible explanation of moral diversity.

> There is no single true morality. There are many different moral frameworks, none of which is more correct than the others.

I begin by mentioning data to be explained: the nature and extent of moral diversity.

Members of different cultures often have very different beliefs about right and wrong and often act quite differently on their beliefs. To take a seemingly trivial example, different cultures have different rules of politeness and etiquette: burping after eating is polite in one culture, impolite in another. Less trivially, some people are cannibals, others find cannibalism abhorrent.

The institution of marriage takes different forms in different societies. In some, a man is permitted to have several wives, in others bigamy is forbidden. More generally, the moral status of women varies greatly from one society to another in many different ways.

Some societies allow slavery, some have caste systems, which they take to be morally satisfactory, others reject both slavery and caste systems as grossly unjust.

It is unlikely that any nontrivial moral principles are universally accepted in all societies. The anthropologist George Silberbauer (1993, p. 15) is able to say only that "there are values which can be seen as common to nearly all societies," a remark limited by the phrases "can be seen as" and "nearly all." He further limits this claim by adding, "there are sometimes strong contrasts in the ways in which [these values] are expressed in precepts, principles and evaluations of behaviour."

Some say that there is a universally recognized central core of morality consisting of prohibitions against killing and harming others, against stealing, and against lying to others. Walzer (1987, p. 24) offers a more limited list of universal prohibitions: "murder, deception, betrayal and gross cruelty." It makes sense for Walzer to leave theft off the list, since some societies do not recognize private property, so they would have no rules against stealing.

(Without property, there can be no such thing as stealing. It is trivial to say that all societies that recognize private property have rules against stealing, because having such rules is a necessary condition of recognizing private property!)

It may be that *murder* is always considered wrong, if murder is defined as "wrongful killing." But few societies accept *general* moral prohibitions on killing or harming other people. There are societies in which a "master" is thought to have an absolute right to treat his slaves in any way he chooses, including arbitrarily beating and killing them. Similarly, there may be no limitations on what a husband can do to his wife, or a father to his young children. Infanticide is considered acceptable in some societies. When moral prohibitions on harming and killing and lying exist, they are sometimes supposed to apply only with respect to the local group and not with respect to outsiders. A person who is able successfully to cheat outsiders may be treated as an admirable person. Similarly for someone who is able to harm and kill outsiders.

Any universally accepted principle in this area must verge on triviality, saying, for example, that one must not kill or harm members of a certain group, namely the group of people one must not kill or harm![3]

Thomson (1990) appears to disagree. She states certain principles and says of them, "it is not at all clear how their negations could be accommodated into what would be recognizable as a moral code" (Thomson, 1990, p. 20). The principles she mentions are, "Other things being equal, one ought not act rudely," "Other things being equal, one ought to do what one promised," "Other things being equal, one ought not cause others pain," and "One ought not torture babies to death for fun."

On the contrary, it is clear that many moral codes have accommodated the negations of all these general principles by accepting instead principles restricted to insiders. And, if the phrase "other things being equal" is supposed to include a restriction to insiders, then triviality looms in the manner I have already mentioned.

Now, mere moral diversity is not a disproof of moral absolutism. Where there are differences in custom, there are often differences in circumstance. Indeed, differences in custom are themselves differences in circumstance that can affect what is right or wrong without entailing moral relativism. You do not need to be a moral relativist to recognize that in England it is wrong to drive on the right, whereas in France it is not wrong to drive on the right.

Even where circumstances are relevantly the same, mere differences in moral opinion no more refute moral absolutism than scientific differences in opinion about the cause of canal-like features on the surface of Mars establish that there is no truth to that matter.

But, even though the rejection of moral absolutism is not an immediate logical consequence of the existence of moral diversity, it is a reasonable inference from the most *plausible explanation* of the range of moral diversity that actually exists (Wong, 1984).

One of the most important things to explain about moral diversity is that it occurs not just between societies but also within societies and in a way that leads to seemingly intractable moral disagreements. In the contemporary

United States, deep moral differences often seem to rest on differences in basic values rather than on differences in circumstance or information. Moral vegetarians, who believe that it is wrong to raise animals for food, exist in the same community as nonvegetarians, even in the same family. A disagreement between moral vegetarians and nonvegetarians can survive full discussion and full information and certainly appears to rest on a difference in the significance assigned to animals as compared with humans. Is there a nonrelative truth concerning the moral importance of animals? How might that "truth" be discovered?

In a similar way, disagreements about the moral acceptability of abortion or euthanasia survive extensive discussion and awareness of all relevant information about abortion. Such disagreements appear to depend on basic disagreements concerning the intrinsic value or "sanctity" of human life as compared with the value of the things that life makes possible, such as pleasurable experience and fulfilling activity (Dworkin, 1993).

There are similarly intractable disagreements about the relative value of artifacts of culture as compared with human life. Some people think that it is worse when terrorists bomb famous old museums than when they bomb crowded city streets; others feel that the loss of human life is worse than the loss of architecture and art. Again, there are disagreements about how much help one person should be prepared to give to others. Is it morally wrong to purchase a new record player instead of trying to help people who cannot afford food? Singer (1972) says yes; others say no. There are intractable disputes about whether it is morally worse to kill someone than it is to let that person die (Rachels, 1975) and about the relative importance of liberty versus equality in assessing the justice of social arrangements (Rawls, 1971; Nozick, 1972). . . .

It is hard to see how to account for all moral disagreements in terms of differences in situation or beliefs about nonmoral facts. Many moral disagreements seem to rest instead on basic differences in moral outlook.

Explaining Basic Differences

Suppose that many moral disagreements do indeed rest on basic differences in moral outlook rather than on differences in situation or beliefs about nonmoral facts. What explanation might there be for that?

An "absolutist" explanation might be that some people are simply not well placed to discover the right answers to moral questions.[4] The point to this response is not just that different people have different evidence but that what one makes of evidence depends on one's antecedent beliefs, so that starting out with some beliefs can help one reach the truth, whereas starting out with other beliefs can prevent one from reaching the truth. Rational change in belief tends to be conservative. It is rational to make the least change in one's view that is necessary in order to obtain greater coherence in what one believes (Goodman, 1965; Rawls, 1971; Harman, 1986). Different people with different starting points will rationally respond in different ways to the same evidence. There is no guarantee that people who start sufficiently far apart in belief will tend to converge in view as the evidence comes in. Someone whose initial view is relatively close to the truth may be led by the evidence to come closer to the truth. Someone who starts further away from the truth may be led even further away by the same evidence. Such a person is simply not well placed to discover the truth.

Here then is one absolutist's explanation of why moral disagreements that rest on basic differences in moral outlook cannot be rationally resolved, supposing that is in fact the case.

Moral relativists instead see an analogy with other kinds of relativity.

Consider the ancient question whether the earth moves or the sun moves. Here the relativistic answer is correct. Motion is a relative matter. Something can be in motion relative to one system of spatio-temporal coordinates and not in motion relative to another system. The particular motion an object exhibits will differ from one system to another. There is no such thing as absolute motion, apart from one or another system of coordinates.

A relativistic answer is also plausible in the moral case. Moral right and wrong are relative matters. A given act can be right with respect to one system of moral coordinates and wrong with respect to another system of moral coordinates. And nothing is absolutely right or wrong, apart from any system of moral coordinates.

By "a moral system of coordinates" I mean a set of values (standards, principles, etc.), perhaps on the model of the laws of one or another state. Whether something is wrong in relation to a given system of coordinates is to [be] determined by the system together with the facts of the case in something like the way in which whether something is illegal in a given jurisdiction is determined by the laws of that jurisdiction together with the facts of the case.

Why does it seem (to some people) that there are objective nonrelative facts about moral right and wrong? Well, why does it seem to some people that there [are] objective nonrelative facts about motion or mass? In the case of motion or mass, one particular system of coordinates is so salient that it seems to have a special status. Facts about motion or mass in relation to the salient system of coordinates are treated as nonrelational facts.

In a similar way, the system of moral coordinates that is determined by a person's own values can be so salient that it can seem to that person to have a special status. Facts about what is right or wrong in relation to that system of coordinates can be misidentified as objective nonrelational facts.

To be sure, the system of moral coordinates that is determined by a given person's values cannot in general be *identified* with all and only exactly those very values. Otherwise a person could never be mistaken about moral issues (in relation to the relevant system of coordinates) except by being mistaken about his or her own values!

For the same reason, a legal system cannot be simply identified with existing legislation, the record of prior court decisions, and the principles currently accepted by judges. Otherwise legislation could not be unconstitutional and judges could not be mistaken in the legal principles they accept or the decisions they reach. . . .

Evaluative Relativity: "Good For"

We might compare the relativity of moral wrongness with the way in which something that is good for one person may not be good for another person. If Tom has bet on a horse that runs well in the rain and Sue has bet on a horse that does not run well in the rain, then rain is good for Tom and bad for Sue. This is an uncontroversial example of evaluative relativity. The rain is good in relation to Tom's goals and bad in relation to Sue's.

Similarly, abortion can be immoral with respect to (the moral coordinates determined by) Tom's values and not immoral with respect to Sue's. Moral relativists sometimes express this by saying that abortion is immoral "for Tom" and not immoral "for Sue." Of course, what is meant here is not that abortion is bad for Tom but not bad for Sue in the sense of harmful to one but not the other, not is it just to say that Tom may think abortion immoral and Sue may think it moral. The rain might be good for Tom even if he doesn't realize it and abortion might be immoral for Tom whether or not he realizes that it is.

Notice, by the way, that a speaker does not always have to make explicit for whom a given situation is good. In particular, if Max has bet on the same horse as Alice and he is speaking to Alice, out of the hearing of Sue, he can say simply. "This rain is bad," meaning that it is bad for him and Alice.

Similarly, a moral relativist talking to another moral relativist can suppress reference to a particular set of values if the judgment is supposed to hold in relation both to the (moral coordinates determined by the) values accepted by the speaker and to the (moral coordinates determined by the) values accepted by the hearer. If Sue and Arthur both have values with the same implications for abortion, and Tom isn't listening, Sue might say simply, "Abortion is not morally wrong", meaning that it is not wrong in relation to her and Arthur's values. It is not wrong for either of them. . . .

Relativity Theory

Something that is good for some people is bad for others, indifferent to yet others. Moral relativism says that the same is true of moral values and moral norms. According to moral relativism whether something is morally good, right, or just is always relative to a set of moral coordinates, a set of values or moral standards, a certain moral point of view. . . .

[Moral] relativism makes the following claim about moral judgments:

> For the purpose of assigning truth conditions, a judgment of the form, it would be morally wrong of P to D, has to be understood as elliptical for a judgment of the form, in relation to moral framework M, it would be morally wrong of P to D. Similarly for other moral judgments.

Recall that moral relativism is not by itself a claim about meaning. It does not say that speakers always *intend* their moral judgments to be relational in this respect. It is clear that many speakers do not. Moral relativism is a thesis about how things are and a thesis about how things aren't! Moral relativism claims that there is no such thing as objectively absolute good, absolute right, or absolute justice; there is only what is good, right, or just in relation to this or that moral framework. What someone takes to be absolute rightness is only rightness in relation to (a system of moral coordinates determined by) that person's values.

Earlier, I compared moral relativism with Einstein's theory of relativity in physics, which says that physical magnitudes, like mass, length, or temporal duration, are relative to a frame of reference, so that two events that are simultaneous with respect to one frame of reference can fail to be simultaneous with respect to another. In saying this, Einstein's theory does not make a claim about speakers' intentions. It does not claim that speakers intend to be making relational judgments when they speak of mass or simultaneity. The claim is, rather, that there is no such thing as absolute simultaneity or absolute mass. There is only simultaneity or mass with respect to one or another frame of reference. What someone might take to be absolute magnitudes are really relative magnitudes: magnitudes that are relative to that person's frame of reference.

Imagine a difference of opinion about whether event *E* precedes event *F*. According to Einstein's theory of relativity, there may be no uniform answer to this question: perhaps, in relation to one framework *E* precedes *F*, while in relation to a different framework *E* does not precede *F*.

Similarly, consider a moral disagreement about whether we are right to raise animals for food. Moral relativism holds that there is no uniform answer to this question: in relation to (the system of moral coordinates determined by) one person's values it is permissible to raise animals for food and in relation to (the system of moral coordinates determined by) a different person's values it is not permissible to raise animals for food. To repeat: what someone takes to be absolute rightness is only rightness in relation to (a system of moral coordinates determined by) that person's values.

Moral relativism does not claim that moral differences by themselves entail moral relativism, any more than Einstein claimed that differences in opinion about simultaneity by themselves entailed relativistic physics. We have to consider what differences there are or could be and why this might be so. How are we to explain the sorts of moral differences that actually occur? Can we seriously suppose that there is an answer to the question about the justice of our treatment of animals that is independent of one or another moral framework? What is the best explanation of differences in this and other areas of seeming intractability?

I emphasize again that moral relativism does not identify what is right in relation to a given moral framework with whatever is taken to be right by those who accept that framework. That would be like saying Einstein's theory of relativity treats two events as simultaneous with respect to a given coordinate system if people at rest with respect to the coordinate system believe the events are simultaneous.

Notes

1. Mackie, 1977, chapter one, advocates an error theory of this sort about ordinary moral judgments.
2. So, for example, a judgment of the form, *P ought morally to D,* has to be understood as elliptical for a judgment of the form, *in relation to moral framework M, P ought morally to D.*

3. There will be universal truths about moralities just as there are universal truths about spatio-temporal frameworks. Perhaps all spatio-temporal frameworks must admit of motion and rest. And perhaps all moralities have some rules against killing, harm, and deception. The existence of universal features of spatio-temporal frameworks is compatible with and is even required by Einstein's Theory of Relativity and the existence of universal features of morality is compatible with moral relativism.
4. I am indebted to Nicholas Sturgeon for this suggestion.

Bibliography

Dworkin, R. (1993). *Life's Dominion,* New York: Knopf.

Goodman, N. (1965). *Fact, Fiction, and Forecast.* Cambridge, Mass.: Harvard University Press.

Harman, G. (1986). *Change in View: Principles of Reasoning,* Cambridge, Massachusetts: Bradford Books/MIT Press.

Mackie, J. (1977). *Ethics: Inventing Right and Wrong,* London: Penguin Books.

Nozick, R. (1972). *Anarchy, State, and Utopia,* New York: Basic Books.

Rachels, J. (1975). "Active and passive euthanasia," *New England Journal of Medicine* 292.

Rawls, J. (1971). *A Theory of Justice,* Cambridge, Mass.: Harvard University Press.

Silberbauer, G. (1993). "Ethics in small-scale societies," *A Companion to Ethics,* ed. Peter Singer, Oxford: Blackwell.

Singer, P. (1972). "Famine, affluence, and morality," *Philosophy and Public Affairs* 1.

Thomson, J. (1990). *The Realm of Rights,* Cambridge, Mass.: Harvard University Press.

Walzer, M. (1987). *Interpretation and Social Criticism.* Cambridge, Massachusetts: Harvard University Press.

Wong, D. B. (1984). *Moral Relativity,* Berkeley, California: University of California Press.

Louis P. Pojman

The Case Against Moral Relativism

"Who's to Judge What's Right or Wrong?"

> Like many people, I have always been instinctively a moral relativist. As far back as I can remember . . . it has always seemed to be obvious that the dictates of morality arise from some sort of convention or understanding among people, that different people arrive at different understandings, and that there are no basic moral demands that apply to everyone. This seemed so obvious to me I assumed it was everyone's instinctive view, or at least everyone who gave the matter any thought in this day and age.
>
> —Gilbert Harman[1]

> Ethical relativism is the doctrine that the moral rightness and wrongness of actions vary from society to society and that there are not absolute universal moral standards on all men at all times. Accordingly, it holds that whether or not it is right for an individual to act in a certain way depends on or is relative to the society to which he belongs.
>
> —John Ladd[2]

Gilbert Harman's intuitions about the self-evidence of ethical relativism contrast strikingly with Plato's or Kant's equal certainty about the truth of objectivism, the doctrine that universally valid or true ethical principles exist. . . . "Two things fill the soul with ever new and increasing wonder and reverence the oftener and more fervently reflection ponders on it: the starry heavens above and the moral law within," wrote Kant. On the basis of polls taken in my ethics and introduction to philosophy classes in recent years, Harman's views may signal a shift in contemporary society's moral understanding. The polls show a two-to-one ratio in favor of moral relativism over moral absolutism, with fewer than five percent of the respondents recognizing that a third position between these two polar opposites might exist. Of course, I'm not suggesting that all of these students had a clear understanding of what relativism entails, for many who said they were relativists also contended in the same polls that abortion except to save the mother's life is always wrong, that capital punishment is always wrong, or that suicide is never morally permissible. . . .

From *THE MORAL LIFE: An Introductory Reader in Ethics and Literature,* by Louis P. Pojman and Lewis Vaughn, eds., 2007, 166–180, 190 (excerpts). Copyright © 2007 by Oxford University Press. Reprinted by permission.

1. An Analysis of Relativism

Let us examine the theses contained in John Ladd's succinct statement on ethical (conventional) relativism that appears at the beginning of this essay. If we analyze it, we derive the following argument:

1. Moral rightness and wrongness of actions vary from society to society, so there are no universal moral standards held by all societies.
2. Whether or not it is right for individuals to act in a certain way depends on (or is relative to) the society to which they belong.
3. Therefore, there are no absolute or objective moral standards that apply to all people everywhere.

1. The first thesis, which may be called the *diversity thesis,* is simply a description that acknowledges the fact that moral rules differ from society to society. The Spartans of ancient Greece and the Dobu of New Guinea believe that stealing is morally right, but we believe it is wrong. The Roman father had the power of life and death . . . over his children, whereas we condemn parents for abusing their children. A tribe in East Africa once threw deformed infants to the hippopotamuses, and in ancient Greece and Rome infants were regularly exposed, while we abhor infanticide. Ruth Benedict describes a tribe in Melanesia that views cooperation and kindness as vices, whereas we see them as virtues. While in ancient Greece, Rome, China and Korea parricide was condemned as "the most execrable of crimes," among Northern Indians aged persons, persons who were no longer capable of walking, were left alone to starve. Among the California Gallinomero, when fathers became feeble, a burden to their sons, "the poor old wretch is not infrequently thrown down on his back and securely held while a stick is placed across his throat, and two of them seat themselves on the ends of it until he ceases to breathe."[3] Sexual practices vary over time and place. Some cultures permit homosexual behavior, while others condemn it. Some cultures practice polygamy, while others view it as immoral. Some cultures condone while others condemn premarital sex. Some cultures accept cannibalism, while the very idea revolts us. Some West African tribes perform clitoridectomies on girls, whereas we deplore such practices. Cultural relativism is well documented, and "custom is the king o'er all." There may or may not be moral principles that are held in common by every society, but if there are any, they seem to be few at best. Certainly it would be very difficult to derive any single "true" morality by observing various societies' moral standards.

2. The second thesis, the *dependency thesis,* asserts that individual acts are right or wrong depending on the nature of the society from which they emanate. Morality does not occur in a vacuum, and what is considered morally right or wrong must be seen in a context that depends on the goals, wants, beliefs, history, and environment of the society in question. As William G. Sumner says,

> We learn the morals as unconsciously as we learn to walk and hear and breathe, and [we] never know any reason why the [morals] are what they are. The justification of them is that when we wake to consciousness of life we find them facts which already hold us in the bonds of tradition, custom, and habit.[4]

Trying to see things from an independent, noncultural point of view would be like taking out our eyes in order to examine their contours and qualities. There is no "innocent eye." We are simply culturally determined beings.

We could, of course, distinguish between a weak and a strong thesis of dependency, for the nonrelativist can accept a certain degree of relativity in the way moral principles are *applied* in various cultures, depending on beliefs, history, and environment. For example, Jewish men express reverence for God by covering their heads when entering places of worship, whereas Christian men uncover their heads when entering places of worship. Westerners shake hands upon greeting each other, whereas Hindus place their hands together and point them toward the person to be greeted. Both sides adhere to principles of reverence and respect but apply them differently. But the ethical relativist must maintain a stronger thesis, one that insists that the moral principles themselves are products of the cultures and may vary from society to society." The ethical relativist contends that even beyond environmental factors and differences in beliefs, a fundamental disagreement exists among societies. . . .

In a sense we all live in radically different worlds. But the relativist wants to go further and maintain that there is something conventional about *any* morality, so that every morality really depends on a level of social acceptance. Not only do various societies adhere to different moral systems, but the very same society could (and often does) change its moral views over place and time. For example, the majority of people in the southern United States now view slavery as immoral, whereas one hundred and forty years ago they did not. Our society's views on divorce, sexuality, abortion, and assisted suicide have changed somewhat as well—and they are still changing.

3. The conclusion that there are no absolute or objective moral standards binding on all people follows from the first two propositions. Combining cultural relativism (*the diversity thesis*) with *the dependency thesis* yields ethical relativism in its classic form. If there are different moral principles from culture to culture and if all morality is rooted in culture, then it follows that there are no universal moral principles that are valid (or true) for all cultures and peoples at all times.

2. Subjectivism

Some people think that this conclusion is still too tame, and they maintain that morality is dependent not on the society but rather on the individual. As my students sometimes maintain, "Morality is in the eye of the beholder." They treat morality like taste or aesthetic judgments—person relative. This form of moral subjectivism has the sorry consequence that it makes morality a very useless concept, for, on its premises, little or no interpersonal criticism or judgment is logically possible. Suppose that you are repulsed by observing John torturing a child. You cannot condemn him if one of his principles is "torture little children for the fun of it." The only basis for judging him wrong might be that he was a hypocrite who condemned others for torturing. But suppose that another of his principles is that hypocrisy is morally permissible (for him); thus we cannot condemn him for condemning others for doing what he does.

On the basis of subjectivism Adolf Hitler and the serial murderer Ted Bundy could be considered as moral as Gandhi, so long as each lived by his own standards, whatever those might be. . . .

Notions of good and bad, or right and wrong, cease to have interpersonal evaluative meaning. We might be revulsed by the views of Ted Bundy, but that is just a matter of taste. A student might not like it when her teacher gives her an F on a test paper, while he gives another student an A for a similar paper, but there is no way to criticize him for injustice, because justice is not one of his chosen principles.

Absurd consequences follow from subjectivism. If it is correct, then morality reduces to aesthetic tastes about which there can be neither argument nor interpersonal judgment. Although many students say they espouse subjectivism, there is evidence that it conflicts with other of their moral views. They typically condemn Hitler as an evil man for his genocidal policies. A contradiction seems to exist between subjectivism and the very concept of morality, which it is supposed to characterize, for morality has to do with *proper* resolution of interpersonal conflict and the amelioration of the human predicament. . . . Whatever else it does, morality has a minimal aim of preventing a Hobbesian state of nature . . . , wherein life is "solitary, poor, nasty, brutish, and short. But if so, subjectivism is no help at all, for it rests neither on social agreement of principle (as the conventionalist maintains) nor on an objectively independent set of norms that bind all people for the common good. If there were only one person on earth, there would be no occasion for morality, because there wouldn't be any interpersonal conflicts to resolve or others whose suffering he or she would have a duty to ameliorate. Subjectivism implicitly assumes something of this solipsism, an atomism in which isolated individuals make up separate universes.

Subjectivism treats individuals like billiard balls on a societal pool table where they meet only in radical collisions, each aimed at his or her own goal and striving to do in the others before they themselves are done in. This atomistic view of personality is belied by the facts that we develop in families and mutually dependent communities in which we share a common language, common institutions, and similar rituals and habits, and that we often feel one another's joys and sorrows. As the poet John Donne wrote, "No man is an island, entire of itself; every man is a piece of the continent."

Radical individualistic ethical relativism is incoherent. If so, it follows that the only plausible view of ethical relativism must be one that grounds morality in the group or culture. This form is called *conventionalism.*

3. Conventionalism

Conventional ethical relativism, the view that there are no objective moral principles but that all valid moral principles are justified (or are made true) by virtue of their cultural acceptance, recognizes the social nature of morality. That is precisely its power and virtue. It does not seem subject to the same absurd consequences which plague subjectivism. Recognizing the importance of our social environment in generating customs and beliefs, many people suppose that ethical relativism is the correct metaethical theory. Furthermore, they are drawn to it for its liberal philosophical stance. It seems to be an enlightened response to the sin of ethnocentricity, and it seems to entail or strongly imply an attitude of tolerance toward other cultures. Anthropologist Ruth Benedict says, that in recognizing ethical relativity, "We shall arrive at a more realistic social faith, accepting as grounds of hope and as new bases for tolerance the coexisting and equally valid patterns of life which mankind has created for itself from the raw materials of existence."[5] The most famous of those holding this position is the anthropologist Melville Herskovits, who argues even more explicitly than Benedict that ethical relativism entails intercultural tolerance.

1. If morality is relative to its culture, then there is no independent basis for criticizing the morality of any other culture but one's own.
2. If there is no independent way of criticizing any other culture, we ought to be tolerant of the moralities of other cultures.
3. Morality is relative to its culture. Therefore,
4. We ought to be tolerant of the moralities of other cultures.[6]

Tolerance is certainly a virtue, but is this a good argument for it? I think not. If morality simply is relative to each culture, then if the culture in question does not have a principle of tolerance, its members have no obligation to be tolerant. Herskovits seems to be treating the *principle of tolerance* as the one exception to his relativism. He seems to be treating it as an absolute moral principle. But from a relativistic point of view there is no more reason to be tolerant than to be intolerant and neither stance is objectively morally better than the other.

Not only do relativists fail to offer a basis for criticizing those who are intolerant, but they cannot rationally criticize anyone who espouses what they might regard as a heinous principle. If, as seems to be the case, valid criticism supposes an objective or impartial standard, relativists cannot morally criticize anyone outside their own culture. Adolf Hitler's genocidal actions, so long as they are culturally accepted, are as morally legitimate as Mother Teresa's works of mercy. If Conventional Relativism is accepted, racism, genocide of unpopular minorities, oppression of the poor, slavery, and even the advocacy of war for its own sake are as equally moral as their opposites. And if a subculture decided that starting a nuclear war was somehow morally acceptable, we could not morally criticize these people. Any actual morality, whatever its content, is as valid as every other, and more valid than ideal moralities—since the latter aren't adhered to by any culture.

There are other disturbing consequences of ethical relativism. It seems to entail that reformers are always (morally) wrong since they go against the tide of cultural standards. William Wilberforce was wrong in the eighteenth century to oppose slavery; the British were immoral in opposing suttee in India (the burning of widows, which is now illegal in India). The early Christians were wrong in refusing to serve in the Roman army or to bow down to Caesar, since the majority in the Roman Empire believed that these two acts were moral duties. In fact, Jesus himself was immoral in breaking the law of His day by healing on the Sabbath day and by advocating the principles of the Sermon on the Mount, since it is clear that few in His time (or in ours) accepted them.

Yet we normally feel just the opposite, that the reformer is a courageous innovator who is right, who has the truth, against the mindless majority. Sometimes the individual must stand alone with the truth, risking social censure and persecution. . . . Yet if relativism is correct, the opposite is necessarily the case. Truth is with the crowd and error with the individual. . . .

There is an even more basic problem with the notion that morality is dependent on cultural acceptance for its validity. The problem is that the notion of a *culture* or *society* is notoriously difficult to define. This is especially so in a pluralistic society like our own where the notion seems to be vague with unclear boundary lines. One person may belong to several societies (subcultures) with different value emphases and arrangements of principles. A person may belong to the nation as a single society with certain values of patriotism, honor, courage, laws (including some which are controversial but have majority acceptance, such as the current law on abortion). But he or she may also belong to a church which opposes some of the laws of the State. He may also be an integral member of a socially mixed community where different principles hold sway, and he may belong to clubs and a family where still other rules are adhered to. Relativism would seem to tell us that where he is a member of societies with conflicting moralities he must be judged both wrong and not-wrong whatever he does. For example, if Mary is a U.S. citizen and a member of the Roman Catholic Church, she is wrong (qua Catholic) if she chooses to have an abortion and not-wrong (qua citizen of the U.S.A.) if she acts against the teaching of the Church on abortion. As a member of a racist university fraternity, KKK, John has no obligation to treat his fellow Black student as an equal, but as a member of the university community itself (where the principle of equal rights is accepted) he does have the obligation; but as a member of the surrounding community (which may reject the principle of equal rights) he again has no such obligation; but then again as a member of the nation at large (which accepts the principle) he is obligated to treat his fellow with respect. What is the morally right thing for John to do? The question no longer makes much sense in this moral Babel. It has lost its action-guiding function.

Perhaps the relativist would adhere to a principle which says that in such cases the individual may choose which group to belong to as primary. If Mary chooses to have an abortion, she is choosing to belong to the general society relative to that principle. And John must likewise choose among groups. The trouble with this option is that it seems to lead back to counter-intuitive results. If Murder Mike of Murder, Incorporated, feels like killing Bank President Ortcutt and wants to feel good about it, he identifies with the Murder, Incorporated society rather than the general public morality. Does this justify the killing? In fact, couldn't one justify anything simply by forming a small subculture that approved of it? Ted Bundy would be morally pure in raping and killing innocents simply by virtue of forming a little coterie. How large must the group be in order to be a legitimate subculture or society? Does it need ten or fifteen people? How about just three? Come to think about it, why can't my burglary partner and I found our own society with a morality of its own? Of course, if my partner dies, I could still claim that I was acting from an originally social set of norms. But why can't I dispense with the interpersonal agreements altogether and invent my own morality—since morality, on this view, is only an invention anyway? Conventionalist relativism seems to reduce to subjectivism. And subjectivism leads, as we have seen, to moral solipsism, to the demise of morality altogether. . . .

. . . I don't think you can stop the move from conventionalism to subjectivism. The essential force of the validity of the chosen moral principle is that it is dependent on choice. The conventionalist holds that it is the choice of the group, but why should I accept the group's silly choice, when my own is better (for me)? Why should anyone give such august authority to a culture of society? If this is all morality comes to, why not reject it altogether—even though one might want to adhere to its directives when others are looking in order to escape sanctions?

4. A Critique of Ethical Relativism

However, while we may fear the demise of morality, as we have known it, this in itself may not be a good reason for rejecting relativism. That is, for judging it false. Alas, truth may not always be edifying. But the consequences of this position are sufficiently alarming to prompt us to look carefully for some weakness in the relativist's argument. So let us examine the premises and conclusion listed at the beginning of this essay as the three theses of relativism.

1. *The Diversity Thesis.* What is considered morally right and wrong varies from society to society, so that there are no moral principles accepted by all societies.
2. *The Dependency Thesis.* All moral principles derive their validity from cultural acceptance.
3. *Ethical Relativism.* Therefore, there are no universally valid moral principles, objective standards which apply to all people everywhere and at all times.

Does any one of these seem problematic? Let us consider the first thesis, the diversity thesis, which we have also called cultural relativism. Perhaps there is not as much diversity as anthropologists like Sumner and Benedict suppose. One can also see great similarities between the moral codes of various cultures. E. O. Wilson has identified over a score of common features,[7] and before him Clyde Kluckhohn has noted much significant common ground between cultures.

> Every culture has a concept of murder, distinguishing this from execution, killing in war, and other "justifiable homicides." The notions of incest and other regulations upon sexual behavior, the prohibitions upon untruth under defined circumstances, of restitution and reciprocity, of mutual obligations between parents and children—these and many other moral concepts are altogether universal.[8]

Colin Turnbull's description of the sadistic, semidisplaced, disintegrating Ik in Northern Uganda supports the view that a people without principles of kindness, loyalty, and cooperation will degenerate into a Hobbesian state of nature.[9] But he has also produced evidence that underneath the surface of this dying society, there is a deeper moral code from a time when the tribe flourished, which occasionally surfaces and shows its nobler face.

On the other hand, there is enormous cultural diversity and many societies have radically different moral codes. Cultural relativism seems to be a fact, but, even if it is, it does not by itself establish the truth of ethical relativism. Cultural diversity in itself is neutral between theories. For the objectivist could concede complete cultural relativism, but still defend a form of universalism; for he or she could argue that some cultures simply lack correct moral principles.

On the other hand, a denial of complete cultural relativism (i.e., an admission of some universal principles) does not disprove ethical relativism. For even if we did find one or more universal principles, this would not prove that they had any objective status. We could still *imagine* a culture that was an exception to the rule and be unable to criticize it. So the first premise doesn't by itself imply ethical relativism and its denial doesn't disprove ethical relativism.

We turn to the crucial second thesis, the dependency thesis. Morality does not occur in a vacuum, but rather what is considered morally right or wrong must be seen in a context, depending on the goals, wants, beliefs, history, and environment of the society in question. We distinguished a weak and a strong thesis of dependency. The weak thesis says that the application of principles depends on the particular cultural predicament, whereas the strong thesis affirms that the principles themselves depend on that predicament. The nonrelativist can accept a certain relativity in the way moral principles are *applied* in various cultures, depending on beliefs, history, and environment. For example, a raw environment with scarce natural resources may justify the Eskimos' brand of euthanasia to the objectivist, who in another environment would consistently reject that practice. The members of a tribe in the Sudan throw their deformed children into the river because of their belief that such infants *belong* to the hippopotamus, the god of the river. We believe that they have a false belief about this, but the point is that the same principles of respect for property and respect for human life are operative in these contrary practices. They differ with us only in belief, not in substantive moral principle. This is an illustration of how nonmoral beliefs (e.g., deformed children belong to the hippopotamus) when applied to common moral principles (e.g., give to each his due) generate different actions in different cultures. In our own culture the difference in the nonmoral belief about the status of a fetus generates opposite moral prescriptions. The major difference between pro-choicers and pro-lifers is not whether we should kill persons but whether fetuses are really persons. It is a debate about the facts of the matter, not the principle of killing innocent persons.

So the fact that moral principles are weakly dependent doesn't show that ethical relativism is valid. In spite of this weak dependency on nonmoral factors, there could still be a set of general moral norms applicable to all cultures and even recognized in most, which are disregarded at a culture's own expense.

What the relativist needs is a strong thesis of dependency, that somehow all principles are essentially cultural inventions. But why should we choose to view morality this way? Is there anything to recommend the strong thesis over the weak thesis of dependency? The relativist may argue that in fact we don't have an obvious impartial standard from which to judge. "Who's to say which culture is right and which is wrong?" But this seems to be dubious. We can reason and perform thought experiments in order to make a case for one system over another. We may not be able to know with certainty that our moral beliefs are closer to the truth than those of another culture or those of others within our own culture, but we may be *justified* in believing that they are. If we can be closer to the truth regarding factual or scientific matters, why can't we be closer to the truth on moral matters? Why can't a culture be simply confused or wrong about its moral perceptions? Why can't we say that the society like the Ik which sees nothing wrong with enjoying watching its own children fall into fires is less moral in that regard than the culture that cherishes children and grants them protection and equal rights? To take such a stand is not to commit the fallacy of ethnocentricism, for we are seeking to derive principles through critical reason, not simply uncritical acceptance of one's own mores.

Many relativists embrace relativism as a default position. Objectivism makes no sense to them. I think this is Ladd and Harman's position, as the latter's quotation at the beginning of this article seems to indicate. Objectivism has insuperable problems, so the answer must be relativism. . . .

In conclusion I have argued (1) that cultural relativism (the fact that there are cultural differences regarding moral principles) does not entail ethical relativism (the thesis that there are no objectively valid universal moral principles) [and] (2) that the dependency thesis (that morality derives its legitimacy from individual cultural acceptance) is mistaken. . . .

So "Who's to judge what's right or wrong?" We are. We are to do so on the basis of the best reasoning we can bring forth, and with sympathy and understanding.[10]

Notes

1. Gilbert Harman, "Is There a Single True Morality?" in *Morality, Reason and Truth,* eds. David Copp and David Zimmerman (Rowman & Allenheld, 1984).
2. John Ladd, *Ethical Relativism* (Wadsworth, 1973).
3. Reported by the anthropologist Powers, *Tribes of California,* p. 178. Quoted in E. Westermarck, *Origin and Development of Moral Ideals* (London, 1906), p. 386. This work is a mine of examples of cultural diversity.
4. W. G. Sumner, *Folkways* (Ginn & Co., 1906), p. 76.
5. Ruth Benedict, *Patterns of Culture* (New American Library, 1934), p, 257.
6. elville Herskovits, *Cultural Relativism* (Random House, 1972).
7. E. O. Wilson, *On Human Nature* (Bantam Books, 1979), pp. 22–23.
8. Clyde Kluckhohn, "Ethical Relativity: Sic et Non," *Journal of Philosophy,* LII (1955).
9. Colin Turnbull, *The Mountain People* (New York: Simon & Schuster, 1972).
10. Bruce Russell, Morton Winston, Edward Sherline, and an anonymous reviewer made important criticisms on earlier versions of this article, issuing in this revision.

POSTSCRIPT

Is Moral Relativism Correct?

One important feature about this issue is that there is a difference between the well-known and widely recognized facts about moral diversity and the claim of moral relativism. Harman's claim goes beyond the observed facts about moral diversity. He claims that moral diversity can be *explained* by moral relativism; it's not identical with it. In fact, he admits that the existence of moral diversity doesn't by itself disprove moral absolutism.

Harman draws an analogy between physical (or Einsteinian) relativism and moral relativism. Just as Einstein has showed that there is no absolute motion, and something may be in motion according to one framework but not according to another, Harman suggests that there is no such thing as absolute good, but that something can be good according to one framework but not another.

If Harman is correct about good and bad (and right and wrong, etc.), then it is very important to be able to identify the *frameworks* that he says are involved. Note that these are not simply people's moral beliefs—as if believing that something is good would make it good! (Compare, for example, the idea of believing that something is in motion—the belief doesn't mean that it's really in motion.) Harman specifically rejects the idea of identifying the framework with a person's own values. If we did make such an identification, then—unless a person could be mistaken about his or her own values—we would all be right whenever we made moral claims. We'd be infallible when it comes to moral belief—but this is absurd. *Some* moral claims are mistaken. (One way to see this is to imagine that you held some moral belief in the past that you now regard as wrong; this is quite different from merely liking or disliking something, where your tastes could change without "right" and "wrong" coming into it at all.) Harman draws an analogy to law. The law is not infallible either. The view of "separate but equal" may have been the law in the past, but we see now that this is wrong, and we have changed our ways.

An objectivist like Pojman would want to focus on the part that says "we see that this is wrong." In order to see that something is wrong, it would have to be objectively wrong. Sometimes—-and civil rights may provide a good example—-we do see that something in the law needs to be changed. The Constitution, which is the highest law in the land, has been amended numerous times. There are several different possibilities as to what is going on when we amend the Constitution. One possibility is that things just come into fashion and go out of fashion. At one time, the Constitution allowed for slavery, for instance, and now it doesn't. Is slavery something that just came into fashion at one time and then passed out of fashion at another? A second possibility is that slavery was thought to be objectively wrong—and so egregiously wrong that it needed to be ruled out by the Constitution.

In some sense, Harman would be prepared for these considerations, since the Constitution could function similarly to his idea of a *framework*. He runs into a problem when we are changing frameworks (for example, when the Constitution is amended, or even when the Congress is just talking about the value of amending it). When we are "in between frameworks," as it were, relativism seems to make little sense.

Another difficulty comes about when we have a great number of frameworks, for example, as we do in a multicultural and pluralistic society. Here, any single individual may look at things in terms of religious, political, regional, generational, etc. frameworks. Someone may simultaneously belong to groups that use a number of frameworks. And not all of these frameworks will agree. Relativism seems to provide no way to get a handle on the kind of uncertainty that a person may have in choosing between the ways of his church, his family, his friends, his country, etc.

Strangely, it is just this kind of uncertainly in the face of diverse views that has cast doubt on the idea of moral objectivity, but moral relativism seems to fare no better.

Issues associated with moral relativism and absolutism, and the relation of all this to cultural variation and diversity, are quite complex. See Peter Kreeft, *A Refutation of Moral Relativism: Interviews with an Absolutist* (Ignatius Press, 1999); John Cook, *Morality and Cultural Differences* (Oxford University Press, 1999); Paul K. Moser and Thomas L. Carson, eds., *Moral Relativism: A Reader* (Oxford University Press, 2000); Neil Levy, *Moral Relativism: A Short Introduction* (OneWorld Publications, 2002); and Maria Baghramian, *Relativism* (Routledge, 2004; and Michael C. Brannigan, *Ethics across Cultures* (McGraw-Hill, 2005).

ISSUE 2

Does Morality Need Religion?

YES: C. Stephen Layman, from *The Shape of the Good: Christian Reflections on the Foundations of Ethics* (University of Notre Dame Press, 1991)

NO: John Arthur, from "Religion, Morality, and Conscience," in John Arthur, ed., *Morality and Moral Controversies,* 4th ed. (Prentice Hall, 1996)

ISSUE SUMMARY

YES: Philosopher C. Stephen Layman argues that morality makes the most sense from a theistic perspective and that a purely secular perspective is insufficient. The secular perspective, Layman asserts, does not adequately deal with secret violations, and it does not allow for the possibility of fulfillment of people's deepest needs in an afterlife.

NO: Philosopher John Arthur counters that morality is logically independent of religion, although there are historical connections. Religion, he believes, is not necessary for moral guidance or moral answers; morality is social.

There is a widespread feeling that morality and religion are connected. One view is that religion provides a ground for morality, so without religion there is no morality. Thus, a falling away from religion implies a falling away from morality.

Such thoughts have troubled many people. The Russian novelist Dostoyevsky (1821–1881) wrote, "If there is no God, then everything is permitted." Many Americans today also believe that religious faith is important. They often maintain that even if doctrines and dogmas cannot be known for certain, religion nevertheless leads to morality and good behavior. President Dwight D. Eisenhower is reputed to have said that everyone should have a religious faith but that it did not matter what that faith was. And many daily newspapers throughout the country advise their readers to attend the church or synagogue of their choice. Apparently, the main reason why people think it is important to subscribe to a religion is that only in this way will one be able to attain morality. If there is no God, then everything is permitted and there is moral chaos. Moral chaos can be played out in societies and, on a smaller scale, within the minds of individuals. Thus, if you do not believe in God, then you will confront moral chaos; you will be liable to permit (and permit yourself to do) anything, and you will have no moral bearings at all.

Such a view seems to face several problems, however. For example, what are we to say of the morally good atheist or of the morally good but completely nonreligious person? A true follower of the view that morality derives from religion might reply that we are simply begging the question if we believe that such people *could* be morally good. Such people might do things that are morally right and thus might *seem* good, the reply would go, but they would not be acting for the right reason (obedience to God). Such people would not have the same anchor or root for their seemingly moral attitudes that religious persons do.

Another problem for the view that links morality with religion comes from the following considerations: If you hold this view, what do you say of devoutly religious people who belong to religious traditions and who support moralities that are different from your own? If morality is indeed derived from religion, if different people are thus led to follow different moralities, and if the original religions are not themselves subject to judgment, then it is understandable how different people arrive at different moral views. But the views will still be different and perhaps even incompatible. If so, the statement that morality derives from religion must mean that one can derive *a* morality from *a* religion (and not that one derives morality itself from religion). The problem is that by allowing this variation among religions and moralities back into the picture, we seem to allow moral chaos back in, too.

The view that what God commands is good, what God prohibits is evil, and without divine commands and prohibitions nothing is either good or bad in itself is called the *divine command theory,* or the *divine imperative view.* This view resists the recognition of any source of good or evil that is not tied to criteria or standards of God's own creation. Such a recognition is thought to go against the idea of God's omnipotence. A moral law that applied to God but was not of God's own creation would seem to limit God in a way in which he cannot be limited. But, on the other hand, this line of thought (that no moral law outside of God's own making should apply to him) seems contrary to the orthodox Christian view that God is good. For if good means something in accordance with God's will, then when we say that God is good, we are only saying that he acts in accordance with his own will—and this just does not seem to be enough.

In the following selections, C. Stephen Layman argues that a religious perspective makes better sense of moral commitment than a secular perspective. Indeed, in his view, it is not even clear that a secular individual who followed the dictates of morality would be rational. John Arthur asserts that morality does not need a religious foundation at all and that morality is social.

YES

C. Stephen Layman

Ethics and the Kingdom of God

Why build a theory of ethics on the assumption that there is a God? Why not simply endorse a view of ethics along . . . secular lines . . . ? I shall respond to these questions in [two] stages. First, I contrast the secular and religious perspectives on morality. Second, I explain why I think the moral life makes more sense from the point of view of theism [belief in God] than from that of atheism. . . .

As I conceive it, the modern secular perspective on morality involves at least two elements. First, there is no afterlife; each individual human life ends at death. It follows that the only goods available to an individual are those he or she can obtain this side of death.[1]

Second, on the secular view, moral value is an *emergent* phenomenon. That is, moral value is "a feature of certain effects though it is not a feature of their causes" (as wetness is a feature of H_2O, but not of hydrogen or oxygen).[2] Thus, the typical contemporary secular view has it that moral value emerges only with the arrival of very complex nervous systems (viz., human brains), late in the evolutionary process. There is no Mind "behind the scenes" on the secular view, no intelligent Creator concerned with the affairs of human existence. As one advocate of the secular view puts it, "Ethics, though not consciously created [either by humans or by God], is a product of social life which has the function of promoting values common to the members of society."[3]

By way of contrast, the religious point of view (in my use of the phrase) includes a belief in God and in life after death. God is defined as an eternal being who is almighty and perfectly morally good. Thus, from the religious point of view, morality is not an emergent phenomenon, for God's goodness has always been in existence, and is not the product of nonmoral causes. Moreover, from the religious point of view, there are goods available after death. Specifically, there awaits the satisfaction of improved relations with God and with redeemed creatures.

It is important to note that, from the religious perspective, *the existence of God and life after death* are not independent hypotheses. If God exists, then at least two lines of reasoning lend support to the idea that death is not final.

From *The Shape of the Good: Christian Reflections on the Foundations of Ethics*, by Stephen Layman. Copyright © 1991 by the University of Notre Dame Press, Notre Dame, IN 46556.

While I cannot here scrutinize these lines of reasoning, I believe it will be useful to sketch them.[4] (1) It has often been noted that we humans seem unable to find complete fulfillment in the present life. Even those having abundant material possessions and living in the happiest of circumstances find themselves, upon reflection, profoundly unsatisfied. . . . [I]f this earthly life is the whole story, it appears that our deepest longings will remain unfulfilled. But if God is good, He surely will not leave our deepest longings unfulfilled provided He is able to fulfill them—at least to the extent that we are willing to accept His gracious aid. So, since our innermost yearnings are not satisfied in this life, it is likely that they will be satisfied after death.

(2) Human history has been one long story of injustice, of the oppression of the poor and weak by the rich and powerful. The lives of relatively good people are often miserable, while the wicked prosper. Now, if God exists, He is able to correct such injustices, though He does not correct all of them in the present life. But if God is also good, He will not leave such injustices forever unrectified. It thus appears that He will rectify matters at some point after death. This will involve benefits for some in the afterlife—it may involve penalties for others. (However, the . . . possibility of post-mortem punishment does not necessarily imply the possibility of hell as *standardly conceived.*)

We might sum up the main difference between the secular and religious views by saying that the only goods available from a secular perspective are *earthly* goods. Earthly goods include such things as physical health, friendship, pleasure, self-esteem, knowledge, enjoyable activities, an adequate standard of living, etc. The religious or theistic perspective recognizes these earthly goods *as good,* but it insists that there are non-earthly or *transcendent* goods. These are goods available only if God exists and there is life after death for humans. Transcendent goods include harmonious relations with God prior to death as well as the joys of the afterlife—right relations with both God and redeemed creatures.

[One secular] defense of the virtues amounts to showing that society cannot function well unless individuals have moral virtue. If we ask, "Why should we as individuals care about society?", the answer will presumably be along the following lines: "Individuals cannot flourish apart from a well-functioning society, *so morality pays for the individual.*"

This defense of morality raises two questions we must now consider. First, is it misguided to defend morality by an appeal to self-interest? Many people feel that morality and self-interest are fundamentally at odds: "If you perform an act because you see that it is in your interest to do so, then you aren't doing the right thing *just because it's right.* A successful defense of morality must be a defense of duty for duty's sake. Thus, the appeal to self-interest is completely misguided." Second, *does* morality really pay for the individual? More particularly, does morality always pay in terms of earthly goods? Let us take these questions up in turn.

(1) Do we desert the moral point of view if we defend morality on the grounds that it pays? Consider an analogy with etiquette. Why should one bother with etiquette? Should one do the well-mannered thing simply for its own sake? Do we keep our elbows off the table or refrain from belching just because these things are "proper"?

To answer this question we must distinguish between the *justification of an institution* and *the justification of a particular act within that institution.* (By 'institution' I refer to any system of activities specified by rules.) This distinction can be illustrated in the case of the game (institution) of baseball. If we ask a player why he performs a particular act during a game, he will probably give an answer such as, "To put my opponent out" or "To get a home run." These answers obviously would not be relevant if the question were, "Why play baseball at all?" Relevant answers to this second question would name some advantage for the individual player, e.g., "Baseball is fun" or "It's good exercise." Thus, a justification of the institution of baseball (e.g., "It's good exercise") is quite different from a justification of a particular act within the institution (e.g., "To get a home run").

Now let's apply this distinction to our question about etiquette. If our question concerns the justification of a particular act within the institution of etiquette, then the answer may reasonably be, in effect, "This is what's proper. This is what the rules of etiquette prescribe." . . .

But plainly there are deeper questions we can ask about etiquette. Who hasn't wondered, at times, what the point of the institution of etiquette is? Why do we have these quirky rules, some of which seem to make little sense? When these more fundamental questions concerning the entire institution of etiquette are being asked, it makes no sense to urge etiquette for etiquette's sake. What is needed is a description of the human *ends* the institution fulfills—ends which play a justificatory role similar to fun or good exercise in the case of baseball. And it is not difficult to identify some of these ends. For example, the rules of etiquette seem designed, in part, to facilitate social interaction; things just go more smoothly if there are agreed upon ways of greeting, eating, conversing, etc.

If anyone asks, "Why should I as an individual bother about etiquette?", an initial reply might be: "Because if you frequently violate the rules of etiquette, people will shun you." If anyone wonders why he should care about being shunned, we will presumably reply that good social relations are essential to human flourishing, and hence that a person is jeopardizing his own best interests if he places no value at all on etiquette. Thus, in the end, a defense of the institution of etiquette seems to involve the claim that the institution of etiquette *pays* for those who participate in it; it would not be illuminating to answer the question, "Why bother about etiquette?" by saying that etiquette is to be valued for its own sake.

Now, just as we distinguish between justifying the institution of etiquette (or baseball) and justifying a particular act within the institution, so we must distinguish between justifying the institution of morality and justifying a particular act within the institution. When choosing a particular course of action we may simply want to know what's right. But a more ultimate question also cries out for an answer: "What is the point of the institution of morality, anyway? Why should one bother with it?" It is natural to respond by saying that society cannot function well without morality, and individuals cannot flourish apart from a well-functioning society. In short, defending the institution of morality involves claiming that morality pays for the individual in the long run. It seems obscurantist to preach duty for duty's sake, once the more fundamental question about the point of the institution of morality has been raised.

But if morality is defended on the grounds that it pays, doesn't this distort moral motivation? Won't it mean that we no longer do things because they are right, but rather because they are in our self-interest? No. We must bear in mind our distinction between the reasons that justify a particular act within an institution and the reasons that justify the institution itself. A baseball player performs a given act in order to get on base or put an opponent out; he does not calculate whether this particular swing of the bat (or throw of the ball) is fun or good exercise. A well-mannered person is not constantly calculating whether a given act will improve her relations with others, she simply does "the proper thing." Similarly, even if we defend morality on the grounds that it pays, it does not follow that the motive for each moral act becomes, "It will pay" for we are not constantly thinking of the philosophical issues concerning the justification of the entire system of morality; for the most part we simply do things because they are right, honest, fair, loving, etc. Nevertheless, our willingness to plunge wholeheartedly into "the moral game" is apt to be vitiated should it become clear to us that the game does not pay.

At this point it appears that the institution of morality is justified only if it pays for the individuals who participate in it. For if being moral does not pay for individuals, it is difficult to see why they should bother with it. The appeal to duty for duty's sake is irrelevant when we are asking for a justification of the institution of morality itself.

(2) But we must now ask, "Does morality in fact pay?" There are at least four reasons for supposing that morality does not pay from a *secular* perspective. (a) One problem for the secular view arises from the fact that the moral point of view involves a concern for *all* human beings—or at least for all humans affected by one's actions. Thus, within Christian theology, the parable of the good Samaritan is well known for its expansion of the category of "my neighbor." But human societies seem able to get along well without extending full moral concern to all outsiders; this is the essence of tribal morality. Thus, explorers in the 1700s found that the Sioux Indians followed a strict code in dealing with each other, but regarded themselves as free to steal horses from the Crow. Later on, American whites repeatedly broke treaties with the American Indians in a way that would not have been possible had the Indians been regarded as equals. It is no exaggeration to say that throughout much of human history tribal morality has been the morality humans lived by.

And so, while one must agree . . . that the virtues are necessary for the existence of society, it is not clear that this amounts to anything more than a defense of tribal morality. . . . From a purely secular point of view, it is unclear why the scope of moral concern must extend beyond one's society—or, more precisely, why one's concern must extend to groups of people outside of one's society *who are powerless and stand in the way of things one's society wants*. Why should the members of a modern industrial state extend full moral consideration to a tiny Amazonian tribe? . . .

(b) A second problem for secular views concerns the possibility of secret violations of moral rules. What becomes of conscientiousness when one can break the rules in secret, without anyone knowing? After all, if I can break the rules in secret, I will not cause any social disharmony. Of course, there can be no breaking of the rules in secret if there is a God of the Christian type, who knows every human thought as well as every human act. But there are cases in which it is extraordinarily unlikely that any *humans* will discover one's rule breaking. Hence, from a secular perspective, there are cases in which secret violations of morality are possible.

Consider the following case. Suppose *A* has borrowed some money from *B*, but *A* discovers that *B* has made a mistake in his records. Because of the mistake, *B* believes that *A* has already paid the money back. *B* even goes out of his way to thank *A* for prompt payment on the loan. Let us further suppose that *B* is quite wealthy, and hence not in need of the money. Is it in *A*'s interest to pay the money back? Not paying the money back would be morally wrong; but would it be irrational, from a secular point of view? Not necessarily. Granted, it might be irrational in some cases, e.g., if *A* would have intense guilt feelings should he fail to repay the loan. But suppose *A* will not feel guilty because he really needs the money (and knows that *B* does not need it), and because he understands that secret violations belong to a special and rare category of action. Then, from a secular point of view, it is doubtful that paying the loan would be in *A*'s interest.

The point is not that theists never cheat or lie. Unfortunately they do. The point is rather that secret violations of morality arguably pay off from a secular point of view. And so, once again, it seems that there is a "game" that pays off better (in terms of earthly goods) than the relatively idealistic morality endorsed by the great ethicists, viz., one allowing secret "violations."

(c) Even supposing that morality pays for some people, does it pay for *everyone* on the secular view? Can't there be well-functioning societies in which some of the members are "moral freeloaders"? In fact, don't all actual societies have members who maintain an appearance of decency, but are in fact highly manipulative of others? How would one show, on secular grounds, that it is in the interest of these persons to be moral? Furthermore, according to psychiatrists, some people are highly amoral, virtually without feelings of guilt or shame. Yet in numerous cases these amoral types appear to be happy. These "successful egoists" are often intelligent, charming, and able to evade legal penalties for their unconventional behavior.[5] How could one show, on secular grounds, that it is in the interests of such successful egoists to be moral? They seem to find their amoral lives amply rewarding.

(d) Another problem from the secular perspective stems from the fact that in some cases morality demands that one risk death. Since death cuts one off from all earthly goods, what sense does it make to be moral (in a given case) if the risk of death is high?

This point must be stated with care. In many cases it makes sense, from a secular point of view, to risk one's life. For example, it makes sense if the risk is small and the earthly good to be gained is great; after all, one risks one's life driving to work. Or again, risking one's life makes sense from a secular point of view if failing to do so will probably lead to profound and enduring earthly unhappiness. Thus, a woman might take an enormous risk to save her child from an attacker. She might believe that she would be "unable to live with herself" afterward if she stood by and let the attacker kill or maim her child. Similarly, a man might be willing to die for his country, because he could not bear the dishonor resulting from a failure to act courageously.

But failing to risk one's life does not always lead to profound and enduring earthly unhappiness. Many soldiers play it safe in battle when risk taking is essential for victory; they may judge that victory is not worth the personal risks. And many subjects of ruthless tyrants entirely avoid the risks involved in resistance and reform. Though it may be unpleasant for such persons to find themselves regarded as cowards, this unpleasantness does not necessarily lead to profound and enduring earthly unhappiness. It seems strained to claim that what is commonly regarded as moral courage always pays in terms of earthly goods.

At this point it appears that the institution of morality cannot be justified from a secular point of view. For, as we have seen, the institution of morality is justified only if it pays (in the long run) for the individuals who participate in it. But if by "morality" we mean the relatively idealistic code urged on us by the great moralists, it appears that the institution of morality does not pay, according to the secular point of view. This is not to say that no moral code could pay off in terms of earthly goods; a tribal morality of some sort might pay for most people, especially if it were to include conventions which skirt the problems inherent in my "secret violation" and "risk of death" cases. But such a morality would be a far cry from the morality most of us actually endorse.

Defenders of secular morality may claim that these difficulties evaporate if we look at morality from an evolutionary point of view. The survival of the species depends on the sacrifice of individuals in some cases, and the end of morality is the survival of the species. Hence, it is not surprising that being highly moral will not always pay off for individuals.

This answer is confused for two reasons. First, even if morality does have survival value for the species, we have seen that this does not by itself justify the individual's involvement in the institution of morality. In fact, it does not justify such involvement if what is best for the species is not what is best for the individual member of the species. And I have been arguing that, from a secular point of view, the interests of the species and the individual diverge.

Second, while evolution might explain why humans *feel* obligated to make sacrifices, it is wholly unable to account for genuine moral obligation. If we did not feel obligated to make sacrifices for others, it might be that the species would have died out long ago. So, moral *feelings* may have survival value. However, *feeling obligated* is not the same thing as *being obligated*. . . . Thus, to show that moral feelings have survival value is not to show that there are any actual moral obligations at all. . . . The point is, the evolutionary picture does not require the existence of real obligations; it demands only the existence of moral feelings or beliefs. Moral feelings or beliefs would motivate action even if there were in actuality no moral obligations. For example, the belief that human life is sacred may very well have survival value even if human life is not sacred. Moral obligation, as opposed to moral feeling, is thus an unnecessary postulate from the standpoint of evolution.

At this point defenders of the secular view typically make one of two moves: (i) They claim that even if morality does not pay, there remain moral truths which we must live up to; or (ii) they may claim that morality pays in subtle ways which we have so far overlooked. Let us take these claims up in turn.

(i) It may be claimed that moral obligation is just a fact of life, woven into the structure of reality. Morality may not always pay, but certain moral standards remain true, e.g., "Lying is wrong" or "Human life is sacred." These are not made true by evolution or God, but are necessary truths, independent of concrete existence, like "1 + 1 = 2" or "There are no triangular circles."

There are at least three difficulties with this suggestion. First, assuming that there are such necessary truths about morality, why should we care about them or pay them any attention? We may grant that an act is correct from the moral point of view and yet wonder whether we have good reason to participate in the institution of morality. So, even if we grant that various statements of the form "One ought to do *X*" are necessarily true, this does not show that the institution of morality pays off. It just says that morality is a "game" whose rules are necessary truths. . . . To defend the institution of morality simply on the grounds that certain moral statements are necessarily true is to urge duty for duty's sake. And . . . this is not an acceptable defense of the institution of morality.

Second, the idea that some moral truths are necessary comports poorly with the usual secular account. As Mavrodes points out, necessary moral truths seem to be what Plato had in mind when he spoke about the Form of the Good. And Plato's view, though not contradicted by modern science, receives no support from it either. Plato's Form of the Good is not an emergent phenomenon, but is rather woven into the very structure of reality, independently of physical processes such as evolution. So, Plato's view is incompatible with the typically modern secular view that moral value is an emergent phenomenon, coming into existence with the arrival of the human nervous system. For this reason, Plato's views have "often been taken to be congenial . . . to a religious understanding of the world."[6]

Third, it is very doubtful that there are any necessary truths of the form "One ought to do *X*." We have seen that the institution of morality stands unjustified if participation in it does not pay (in the long run) for individuals. And why should we suppose that there are *any* necessary moral truths if the institution of morality is unjustified? . . . [S]tatements of the form "One ought to do *X*" are not *necessary* truths, though they may be true *if* certain conditions are met. . . . Hence, if there are any necessary moral truths, they appear to be conditional (if-then) in form: If certain conditions exist, one ought to do *X*. Among the conditions, as we have seen, is the condition that doing *X* pays for the individual in the long run. So, it is very doubtful that there are any necessary moral truths of the form "One ought to do *X*."[7] The upshot is that morality is partly grounded in those features of reality which guarantee that morality pays; and the secular view lacks the metaphysical resources for making such a guarantee. . . .

(ii) But some have claimed that, if we look closely at human psychology, we can see that morality does pay *in terms of earthly goods*. For example, Plato suggested that only a highly moral person could have harmony between the various elements of his soul (such as reason and desire). Others have claimed that being highly moral is the only means to inner satisfaction. We humans are just so constituted that violations of morality never leave us with a net gain. Sure, we may gain earthly goods of one sort or another by lying, stealing, etc., but these are always outweighed by inner discord or a sense of dissatisfaction with ourselves.

There are several problems with this. First, some may doubt that moral virtue is the best route to inner peace. After all, one may experience profound inner discord when one has done what is right. It can be especially upsetting to stand up for what is right when doing so is unpopular; indeed, many people avoid "making waves" precisely because it upsets their inner peace. . . .

Second, how good is the evidence that inner peace *always* outweighs the benefits achievable through unethical action? Perhaps guilt feelings and inner discord are a reasonable price to pay for certain earthly goods. If a cowardly act enables me to stay alive, or a dishonest act makes me wealthy, I may judge that my gains are worth the accompanying guilt feelings. A quiet conscience is not everything.

Third, if inner discord or a sense of dissatisfaction stems from a feeling of having done wrong, why not reassess my standards? Therapists are familiar with the phenomenon of false guilt. For example, a married woman may feel guilty for having sex with her spouse. The cure will involve enabling the patient to view sex as a legitimate means of expressing affection. The point is that just because I feel a certain type of act is wrong, it does not follow that the only route to inner peace is to avoid the action. I also have the option of revising my standards, which may enable me to pursue self-interested goals in a less inhibited fashion. Why drag along any unnecessary moral baggage? How could it be shown, on secular grounds, that it is in my interest to maintain the more idealistic standards endorsed by the great moralists? Certainly, some people have much less idealistic standards than others, and yet seem no less happy.

By way of contrast with the secular view, it is not difficult to see how morality might pay if there is a God of the Christian type. First, God loves all humans and wants all included in his kingdom. So, a tribal morality would violate his demands, and to violate his demands is to strain one's most important personal relationship. Second, there are no secret violations of morality if God exists. Since God is omniscient, willful wrongdoing of any sort will estrange the wrongdoer from God. Third, while earthly society may be able to function pretty well even though there exists a small number of "moral freeloaders," the freeloaders themselves are certainly not attaining harmonious relations with God. Accordingly, their ultimate fulfillment is in jeopardy. Fourth, death is the end of earthly life, but it is not the end of conscious existence, according to Christianity. Therefore, death does not end one's opportunity for personal fulfillment; indeed, if God is perfectly good and omnipotent, we can only assume that the afterlife will result in the fulfillment of our deepest needs—unless we willfully reject God's efforts to supply those needs.

So, it seems to me that the moral life makes more sense from a theistic perspective than from a secular perspective. Of course, I do not claim that I have proved the existence of God, and a full discussion of this metaphysical issue would take us too far from matters at hand.[8] But if I have shown that the moral life makes more sense from a theistic perspective than from a secular one, then I have provided an important piece of evidence in favor of the rationality of belief in God. Moreover, I believe that I have turned back one objection to the Christian teleological view, namely, the allegation that theism is unnecessary metaphysical baggage.

Notes

1. It can be argued that, even from a secular perspective, some benefits and harms are available after death. For example, vindicating the reputation of a deceased person may be seen as benefiting that person. See, for example, Thomas Nagel, *Mortal Questions* (London: Cambridge University Press, 1979), pp. 1–10. But even if we grant that these are goods for the deceased, it is obvious that, from the secular point of view, such post-mortem goods cannot be consciously enjoyed by the deceased. They are not available in the sense that he will never take pleasure in them.
2. George Mavrodes, "Religion and the Queerness of Morality," in *Rationality, Religious Belief, and Moral Commitment,* ed. Robert Audi and William J. Wainwright (Ithaca, N.Y.: Cornell University Press, 1986), p. 223.
3. Peter Singer, *Practical Ethics* (London: Cambridge University Press, 1970), p. 209.
4. For an excellent discussion of arguments for immortality, see William J. Wainwright, *Philosophy of Religion* (Belmont, Calif.: Wadsworth, 1988), pp. 99–111.
5. My source for these claims about "happy psychopaths" is Singer, *Practical Ethics,* pp. 214–216. Singer in turn is drawing from Hervey Cleckley, *The Mask of Sanity, (An Attempt to Clarify Some Issues About the So-Called Psychopathic Personality)*, 5th ed. (St. Louis, Mo.: E. S. Cleckley, 1988).
6. Mavrodes, "Religion and the Queerness of Morality," p. 224. I am borrowing from Mavrodes throughout this paragraph.
7. Those acquainted with modal logic may have a question here. By a principle of modal logic, if p is a necessary truth and p necessarily implies q, then q is a necessary truth. So, if it is necessarily true that "certain conditions are met" and necessarily true that "If they are met, one ought to X," then, "One ought to do X" is a necessary truth. But I assume it is not *necessarily true* that "certain conditions are met." In my judgment it would be most implausible to suppose, e.g., that "Morality pays for humans" is a necessary truth.
8. Two fine discussions of moral arguments for theism are Robert Merrihew Adams, "Moral Arguments for Theistic Belief," in *Rationality and Religious Belief,* ed. C. F. Delaney (Notre Dame, Ind.: University of Notre Dame Press, 1979), pp. 116–140, and J. L. Mackie, *The Miracle of Theism* (Oxford: Oxford University Press, 1982), pp. 102–118.

John Arthur

Religion, Morality, and Conscience

My first and prime concern in this paper is to explore the connections, if any, between morality and religion. I will argue that in fact religion is not necessary for morality. Yet despite the lack of any logical or other necessary connection, I will claim, there remain important respects in which the two are related. In the concluding section I will discuss the notion of moral conscience, and then look briefly at the various respects in which morality is "social" and the implications of that idea for moral education. First, however, I want to say something about the subjects: just what are we referring to when we speak of morality and of religion?

Morality and Religion

A useful way to approach the first question—the nature of morality—is to ask what it would mean for a society to exist without a social moral code. How would such people think and behave? What would that society look like? First, it seems clear that such people would never feel guilt or resentment. For example, the notions that I ought to remember my parent's anniversary, that he has a moral responsibility to help care for his children after the divorce, that she has a right to equal pay for equal work, and that discrimination on the basis of race is unfair would be absent in such a society. Notions of duty, rights, and obligations would not be present, except perhaps in the legal sense; concepts of justice and fairness would also be foreign to these people. In short, people would have no tendency to evaluate or criticize the behavior of others, nor to feel remorse about their own behavior. Children would not be taught to be ashamed when they steal or hurt others, nor would they be allowed to complain when others treat them badly. (People might, however, feel regret at a decision that didn't turn out as they had hoped; but that would only be because their expectations were frustrated, not because they feel guilty.)

Such a society lacks a moral code. What, then, of religion? Is it possible that a people lacking a morality would nonetheless have religious beliefs? It seems clear that it is possible. Suppose every day these same people file into their place of worship to pay homage to God (they may believe in many gods or in one all-powerful creator of heaven and earth). Often they can be heard praying to God for help in dealing with their problems and thanking Him for their good fortune. Frequently they give sacrifices to God, sometimes in the

From *Morality and Moral Controversies,* 4th ed., 1996, pp. 21–28. Copyright © 1996 by John Arthur. Reprinted by permission of Amy Shapiro, executor of the estate of John Arthur.

form of money spent to build beautiful temples and churches, other times by performing actions they believe God would approve such as helping those in need. These practices might also be institutionalized, in the sense that certain people are assigned important leadership roles. Specific texts might also be taken as authoritative, indicating the ways God has acted in history and His role in their lives or the lives of their ancestors.

To have a moral code, then, is to tend to evaluate (perhaps without even expressing it) the behavior of others and to feel guilt at certain actions when we perform them. Religion, on the other hand, involves beliefs in supernatural power(s) that created and perhaps also control nature, the tendency to worship and pray to those supernatural forces or beings, and the presence of organizational structures and authoritative texts. The practices of morality and religion are thus importantly different. One involves our attitudes toward various forms of behavior (lying and killing, for example), typically expressed using the notions of rules, rights, and obligations. The other, religion, typically involves prayer, worship, beliefs about the supernatural, institutional forms and authoritative texts.

We come, then, to the central question: What is the connection, if any, between a society's moral code and its religious practices and beliefs? Many people have felt that morality is in some way dependent on religion or religious truths. But what sort of "dependence" might there be? In what follows I distinguish various ways in which one might claim that religion is necessary for morality, arguing against those who claim morality depends in some way on religion. I will also suggest, however, some other important ways in which the two are related, concluding with a brief discussion of conscience and moral education.

Religious Motivation and Guidance

One possible role that religion might play in morality relates to motives people have. Religion, it is often said, is necessary so that people will DO right. Typically, the argument begins with the important point that doing what is right often has costs: refusing to shoplift or cheat can mean people go without some good or fail a test; returning a billfold means they don't get the contents. Religion is therefore said to be necessary in that it provides motivation to do the right thing. God rewards those who follow His commands by providing for them a place in heaven or by insuring that they prosper and are happy on earth. He also punishes those who violate the moral law. Others emphasize less self-interested ways in which religious motives may encourage people to act rightly. Since God is the creator of the universe and has ordained that His plan should be followed, they point out, it is important to live one's life in accord with this divinely ordained plan. Only by living a moral life, it is said, can people live in harmony with the larger, divinely created order.

The first claim, then, is that religion is necessary to provide moral motivation. The problem with that argument, however, is that religious motives are far from the only ones people have. For most of us, a decision to do the right thing (if that is our decision) is made for a variety of reasons: "What if

I get caught? What if somebody sees me—what will he or she think? How will I feel afterwards? Will I regret it?" Or maybe the thought of cheating just doesn't arise. We were raised to be a decent person, and that's what we are—period. Behaving fairly and treating others well is more important than whatever we might gain from stealing or cheating, let alone seriously harming another person. So it seems clear that many motives for doing the right thing have nothing whatsoever to do with religion. Most of us, in fact, do worry about getting caught, being blamed, and being looked down on by others. We also may do what is right just because it's right, or because we don't want to hurt others or embarrass family and friends. To say that we need religion to act morally is mistaken; indeed it seems to me that many of us, when it really gets down to it, don't give much of a thought to religion when making moral decisions. All those other reasons are the ones which we tend to consider, or else we just don't consider cheating and stealing at all. So far, then, there seems to be no reason to suppose that people can't be moral yet irreligious at the same time.

A second argument that is available for those who think religion is necessary to morality, however, focuses on moral guidance and knowledge rather than on people's motives. However much people may want to do the right thing, according to this view, we cannot ever know for certain what is right without the guidance of religious teaching. Human understanding is simply inadequate to this difficult and controversial task; morality involves immensely complex problems, and so we must consult religious revelation for help.

Again, however, this argument fails. First, consider how much we would need to know about religion and revelation in order for religion to provide moral guidance. Besides being sure that there is a God, we'd also have to think about which of the many religions is true. How can anybody be sure his or her religion is the right one? But even if we assume the Judeo-Christian God is the real one, we still need to find out just what it is He wants us to do, which means we must think about revelation.

Revelation comes in at least two forms, and not even all Christians agree on which is the best way to understand revelation. Some hold that revelation occurs when God tells us what he wants by providing us with His words: The Ten Commandments are an example. Many even believe, as evangelist Billy Graham once said, that the entire *Bible* was written by God using 39 secretaries. Others, however, doubt that the "word of God" refers literally to the words God has spoken, but believe instead that the *Bible* is an historical document, written by human beings, of the events or occasions in which God revealed Himself. It is an especially important document, of course, but nothing more than that. So on this second view revelation is not understood as *statements* made by God but rather as His *acts* such as leading His people from Egypt, testing Job, and sending His son as an example of the ideal life. The *Bible* is not itself revelation, it's the historical account of revelatory actions.

If we are to use revelation as a moral guide, then, we must first know what is to count as revelation—words given us by God, historical events, or both? But even supposing that we could somehow answer those questions, the problems of relying on revelation are still not over since we still must interpret that revelation. Some feel, for example, that the *Bible* justifies various forms of killing, including war and capital punishment, on the basis of such statements as "An eye for an eye." Others, emphasizing such sayings as "Judge not lest ye be judged" and "Thou shalt not kill," believe the *Bible* demands absolute pacifism. How are we to know which interpretation is correct? It is likely, of course, that the answer people give to such religious questions will be influenced in part at least by their own moral beliefs: if capital punishment is thought to be unjust, for example, then an interpreter will seek to read the *Bible* in a way that is consistent with that moral truth. That is not, however, a happy conclusion for those wishing to rest morality on revelation, for it means that their understanding of what God has revealed is itself dependent on their prior moral views. Rather than revelation serving as a guide for morality, morality is serving as a guide for how we interpret revelation.

So my general conclusion is that far from providing a short-cut to moral understanding, looking to revelation for guidance often creates more questions and problems. It seems wiser under the circumstances to address complex moral problems like abortion, capital punishment, and affirmative action directly, considering the pros and cons of each side, rather than to seek answers through the much more controversial and difficult route of revelation.

The Divine Command Theory

It may seem, however, that we have still not really gotten to the heart of the matter. Even if religion is not necessary for moral motivation or guidance, it is often claimed, religion is necessary in another more fundamental sense. According to this view, religion is necessary for morality because without God there could BE no right or wrong. God, in other words, provides the foundation or bedrock on which morality is grounded. This idea was expressed by Bishop R. C. Mortimer:

> "God made us and all the world. Because of that He has an absolute claim on our obedience. . . . From [this] it follows that a thing is not right simply because we think it is. It is right because God commands it."[1]

What Bishop Mortimer has in mind can be seen by comparing moral rules with legal ones. Legal statutes, we know, are created by legislatures; if the state assembly of New York had not passed a law limiting speed people can travel, then there would be no such legal obligation. Without the statutory enactments, such a law simply would not exist. Mortimer's view, the *divine command theory,* would mean that God has the same sort of relation to moral law as legislature has to statutes it enacts: without God's commands there would be no moral rules, just as without a legislature there would be no statutes.

Defenders of the divine command theory often add to this a further claim, that only by assuming God sits at the foundation of morality can we explain the objective difference between right and wrong. This point was forcefully argued by F. C. Copleston in a 1948 British Broadcasting Corporation radio debate with Bertrand Russell.

Copleston: . . . The validity of such an interpretation of man's conduct depends on the recognition of God's existence, obviously. . . . Let's take a look at the Commandant of the [Nazi] concentration camp at Belsen. That appears to you as undesirable and evil and to me too. To Adolf Hitler we suppose it appeared as something good and desirable. I suppose you'd have to admit that for Hitler it was good and for you it is evil.

Russell: No, I shouldn't go so far as that. I mean, I think people can make mistakes in that as they can in other things. If you have jaundice you see things yellow that are not yellow. You're making a mistake.

Copleston: Yes, one can make mistakes, but can you make a mistake if it's simply a question of reference to a feeling or emotion? Surely Hitler would be the only possible judge of what appealed to his emotions.

Russell: . . . You can say various things about that; among others, that if that sort of thing makes that sort of appeal to Hitler's emotions, then Hitler makes quite a different appeal to my emotions.

Copleston: Granted. But there's no objective criterion outside feeling then for condemning the conduct of the Commandant of Belsen, in your view. . . . The human being's idea of the content of the moral law depends certainly to a large extent on education and environment, and a man has to use his reason in assessing the validity of the actual moral ideas of his social group. But the possibility of criticizing the accepted moral code presupposes that there is an objective standard, that there is an ideal moral order, which imposes itself. . . . It implies the existence of a real foundation of God.[2]

Against those who, like Bertrand Russell, seek to ground morality in feelings and attitudes, Copleston argues that there must be a more solid foundation if we are to be able to claim truly that the Nazis were evil. God, according to Copleston, is able to provide the objective basis for the distinction, which we all know to exist, between right and wrong. Without divine commands at the root of human obligations, we would have no real reason for condemning the behavior of anybody, even Nazis. Morality, Copleston thinks, would then be nothing more than an expression of personal feeling.

To begin assessing the divine command theory, let's first consider this last point. Is it really true that only the commands of God can provide an objective basis for moral judgments? Certainly many philosophers have felt that morality rests on its own perfectly sound footing, be it reason, human nature, or natural sentiments. It seems wrong to conclude, automatically, that morality cannot rest on anything but religion. And it is also possible that morality doesn't have any foundation or basis at all, so that its claims should be ignored in favor of whatever serves our own self-interest.

In addition to these problems with Copleston's argument, the divine command theory faces other problems as well. First, we would need to say much more about the relationship between morality and divine commands. Certainly the expressions "is commanded by God" and "is morally required" do not *mean* the same thing. People and even whole societies can use moral concepts without understanding them to make any reference to God. And while it is true that God (or any other moral being for that matter) would tend to want others to do the right thing, this hardly shows that being right and being commanded by God are the same thing. Parents want their children to do the right thing, too, but that doesn't mean parents, or anybody else, can make a thing right just by commanding it!

I think that, in fact, theists should reject the divine command theory. One reason is what it implies. Suppose we were to grant (just for the sake of argument) that the divine command theory is correct, so that actions are right just because they are commanded by God. The same, of course, can be said about those deeds that we believe are wrong. If God hadn't commanded us not to do them, they would not be wrong.

But now notice this consequence of the divine command theory. Since God is all-powerful, and since right is determined solely by His commands, is it not possible that He might change the rules and make what we now think of as wrong into right? It would seem that according to the divine command theory the answer is "yes": it is theoretically possible that tomorrow God would decree that virtues such as kindness and courage have become vices while actions that show cruelty and cowardice will henceforth be the right actions. (Recall the analogy with a legislature and the power it has to change law.) So now rather than it being right for people to help each other out and prevent innocent people from suffering unnecessarily, it would be right (God having changed His mind) to create as much pain among innocent children as we possibly can! To adopt the divine command theory therefore commits its advocate to the seemingly absurd position that even the greatest atrocities might be not only acceptable but morally required if God were to command them.

Plato made a similar point in the dialogue *Euthyphro*. Socrates is asking Euthyphro what it is that makes the virtue of holiness a virtue, just as we have been asking what makes kindness and courage virtues. Euthyphro has suggested that holiness is just whatever all the gods love.

Socrates: Well, then, Euthyphro, what do we say about holiness? Is it not loved by all the gods, according to your definition?

Euthyphro: Yes.

Socrates: Because it is holy, or for some other reason?

Euthyphro: No, because it is holy.

Socrates: Then it is loved by the gods because it is holy: it is not holy because it is loved by them?

Euthyphro: It seems so.

Socrates: . . . Then holiness is not what is pleasing to the gods, and what is pleasing to the gods is not holy as you say, Euthyphro. They are different things.

Euthyphro: And why, Socrates?

Socrates: Because we are agreed that the gods love holiness because it is holy: and that it is not holy because they love it.[3]

This raises an interesting question: Why, having claimed at first that virtues are merely what is loved (or commanded) by the gods, would Euthyphro so quickly contradict this and agree that the gods love holiness *because* it's holy, rather than the reverse? One likely possibility is that Euthyphro believes that whenever the gods love something they do so with good reason, not without justification and arbitrarily. To deny this, and say that it is merely the gods' love that makes holiness a virtue, would mean that the gods have no basis for their attitudes, that they are arbitrary in what they love. Yet—and this is the crucial point—it's far from clear that a religious person would want to say that God is arbitrary in that way. If we say that it is simply God's loving something that makes it right, then what sense would it make to say God wants us to do right? All that could mean, it seems, is that God wants us to do what He wants us to do; He would have no reason for wanting it. Similarly "God is good" would mean little more than "God does what He pleases." The divine command theory therefore leads us to the results that God is morally arbitrary, and that His wishing us to do good or even God's being just mean nothing more than that God does what He does and wants whatever He wants. Religious people who reject that consequence would also, I am suggesting, have reason to reject the divine command theory itself, seeking a different understanding of morality.

This now raises another problem, however. If God approves kindness because it is a virtue and hates the Nazis because they were evil, then it seems that God discovers morality rather than inventing it. So haven't we then identified a limitation on God's power, since He now, being a good God, must love kindness and command us not to be cruel? Without the divine command theory, in other words, what is left of God's omnipotence?

But why, we may ask, is such a limitation on God unacceptable? It is not at all clear that God really can do anything at all. Can God, for example, destroy Himself? Or make a rock so heavy that He cannot lift it? Or create a universe which was never created by Him? Many have thought that God cannot do these things, but also that His inability to do them does not constitute a serious limitation on His power since these are things that cannot be done at all: to do them would violate the laws of logic. Christianity's most influential theologian, Thomas Aquinas, wrote in this regard that "whatever implies contradiction does not come within the scope of divine omnipotence, because it cannot have the aspect of possibility. Hence it is more appropriate to say that such things cannot be done than that God cannot do them."[4]

How, then, ought we to understand God's relationship to morality if we reject the divine command theory? Can religious people consistently maintain their faith in God the Creator and yet deny that what is right is right because He commands it? I think the answer to this is "yes." Making cruelty good is not like making a universe that wasn't made, of course. It's a moral limit on God rather than a logical one. But why suppose that God's limits are only logical?

One final point about this. Even if we agree that God loves justice or kindness because of their nature, not arbitrarily, there still remains a sense in which God could change morality even having rejected the divine command theory. That's because if we assume, plausibly I think, that morality depends in part on how we reason, what we desire and need, and the circumstances in which we find ourselves, then morality will still be under God's control since God could have constructed us or our environment very differently. Suppose, for instance, that he created us so that we couldn't be hurt by others or didn't care about freedom. Or perhaps our natural environment were created differently, so that all we have to do is ask and anything we want is given to us. If God had created either nature or us that way, then it seems likely our morality might also be different in important ways from the one we now think correct. In that sense, then, morality depends on God whether or not one supports the divine command theory.

"Morality Is Social"

I have argued here that religion is not necessary in providing moral motivation or guidance, and against the divine command theory's claim that God is necessary for there to be morality at all. In this last section, I want first to look briefly at how religion and morality sometimes *do* influence each other. Then I will consider the development of moral conscience and the important ways in which morality might correctly be thought to be "social."

Nothing I have said so far means that morality and religion are independent of each other. But in what ways are they related, assuming I am correct in claiming morality does not *depend* on religion? First, of course, we should note the historical influence religions have had on the development of morality as well as on politics and law. Many of the important leaders of the abolitionist and civil rights movements were religious leaders, as are many current members of the pro-life movement. The relationship is not, however, one-sided: morality has also influenced religion, as the current debate within the Catholic church over the role of women, abortion, and other social issues shows. In reality, then, it seems clear that the practices of morality and religion have historically each exerted an influence on the other.

But just as the two have shaped each other historically, so, too, do they interact at the personal level. I have already suggested how people's understanding of revelation, for instance, is often shaped by morality as they seek the best interpretations of revealed texts. Whether trying to understand a work of art, a legal statute, or a religious text, interpreters regularly seek to understand them in the best light—to make them as good as they can be, which requires that they bring moral judgment to the task of religious interpretation and understanding.

The relationship can go the other direction as well, however, as people's moral views are shaped by their religious training and beliefs. These relationships between morality and religion are often complex, hidden even from ourselves, but it does seem clear that our views on important moral issues, from sexual morality and war to welfare and capital punishment, are often influenced by our religious outlook. So not only are religious and moral practices and understandings historically linked, but for many religious people the relationship extends to the personal level—to their understanding of moral obligations as well as their sense of who they are and their vision of who they wish to be.

Morality, then, is influenced by religion (as is religion by morality), but morality's social character extends deeper even than that, I want to argue. First, of course, we possess a socially acquired language within which we think about our various choices and the alternatives we ought to follow, including whether a possible course of action is the right thing to do. Second, morality is social in that it governs relationships among people, defining our responsibilities to others and theirs to us. Morality provides the standards we rely on in gauging our interactions with family, lovers, friends, fellow citizens, and even strangers. Third, morality is social in the sense that we are, in fact, subject to criticism by others for our actions. We discuss with others what we should do, and often hear from them concerning whether our decisions were acceptable. Blame and praise are a central feature of morality.

While not disputing any of this, John Dewey has stressed another, less obvious aspect of morality's social character. Consider then the following comments regarding the origins of morality and conscience in an article he titled "Morality Is Social":

> In language and imagination we rehearse the responses of others just as we dramatically enact other consequences. We foreknow how others will act, and the foreknowledge is the beginning of judgment passed on action. We know *with* them; there is conscience. An assembly is formed within our breast which discusses and appraises proposed and performed acts. The community without becomes a forum and tribunal within, a judgment-seat of charges, assessments and exculpations. Our thoughts of our own actions are saturated with the ideas that others entertain about them. . . . Explicit recognition of this fact is a prerequisite of improvement in moral education. . . . Reflection is morally indispensable.[5]

To appreciate fully the role of society in shaping morality and influencing people's sense of responsibility, Dewey is arguing, requires appreciating the fact that to think from the moral point of view, as opposed to the selfish one, for instance, means rejecting our private, subjective perspective in favor of the view of others, envisioning how they might respond to various choices we might make. Far from being private and unrelated to others, moral conscience is in that sense "public." To consider a decision from the moral perspective, says Dewey, requires that we envision an "assembly of others" that is "formed within our breast." In that way, our moral conscience cannot be sharply distinguished from our nature as social beings since conscience invariably brings with it, or constitutes, the perspective of the other. "Is this right?" and "What would this look like were I to have to defend it to others?" are not entirely separable questions.[6]

It is important not to confuse Dewey's point here, however. He is *not* saying that what is right is finally to be determined by the reactions of actually existing other people, or even by the reaction of society as a whole. What is right or fair can never be finally decided by a vote, and might not meet the approval of any specific others. But what then might Dewey mean in speaking of such an "assembly of others" as the basis of morality? The answer is that rather than actual people or groups, the assembly Dewey envisions is hypothetical or "ideal." The "community without" is thus transformed into a "forum and tribunal within, a judgment seat of charges, assessments and exculpations." So it is through the powers of our imagination that we can meet our moral responsibilities and exercise moral judgment, using these powers to determine what morality requires by imagining the reaction of Dewey's "assembly of others."

Morality is therefore *inherently* social, in a variety of ways. It depends on socially learned language, is learned from interactions with others, and governs our interactions with others in society. But it also demands, as Dewey put it, that we know "with" others, envisioning for ourselves what their points of view would require along with our own. Conscience demands we occupy the positions of others.

Viewed in this light, God would play a role in a religious person's moral reflection and conscience since it is unlikely a religious person would wish to exclude God from the "forum and tribunal" that constitutes conscience. Rather, for the religious person conscience would almost certainly include the imagined reaction of God along with the reactions of others who might be affected by the action. Other people are also important, however, since it is often an open question just what God's reaction would be; revelation's meaning, as I have argued, is subject to interpretation. So it seems that for a religious person morality and God's will cannot be separated, though the connection between them is not the one envisioned by defenders of the divine command theory.

Which leads to my final point, about moral education. If Dewey is correct, then it seems clear there is an important sense in which morality not only can be taught but must be. Besides early moral training, moral thinking depends on our ability to imagine others' reactions and to imaginatively put ourselves into their shoes. "What would somebody (including, perhaps, God) think if this got out?" expresses more than a concern with being embarrassed or punished; it is also the voice of conscience and indeed of morality itself. But that would mean, thinking of education, that listening to others, reading about what others think and do, and reflecting within ourselves about our actions and whether we could defend them to others are part of the practice of morality itself. Morality cannot exist without the broader, social perspective introduced by others, and this social nature ties it, in that way, with education and with public discussion, both actual and imagined. "Private" moral reflection taking place independent of the social world would be no moral reflection at all; and moral education is not only possible, but essential.

Notes

1. R. C. Mortimer, *Christian Ethics* (London: Hutchinson's University Library, 1950), pp. 7–8.
2. This debate was broadcast on the "Third Program" of the British Broadcasting Corporation in 1948.

3. Plato, *Euthyphro,* tr. H. N. Fowler (Cambridge MA: Harvard University Press, 1947).
4. Thomas Aquinas, *Summa Theologica,* Part I, Q.25, Art. 3.
5. John Dewey, "Morality Is Social" in *The Moral Writings of John Dewey,* revised edition, ed. James Gouinlock (Amherst, NY: Prometheus Books, 1994), pp. 182–184.
6. Obligations to animals raise an interesting problem for this conception of morality. Is it wrong to torture animals only because other *people* could be expected to disapprove? Or is it that the animal itself would disapprove? Or, perhaps, duties to animals rest on sympathy and compassion while human moral relations are more like Dewey describes, resting on morality's inherently social nature and on the dictates of conscience viewed as an assembly of others?

POSTSCRIPT

Does Morality Need Religion?

As Arthur notes, some of the earliest—and indeed some of the best—arguments on this issue can be found in Plato's dialogue *Euthyphro,* which was written in the fourth century B.C. His arguments were in terms of Greek religious practices and Greek gods, but we can reformulate the points and elaborate on the arguments in monotheistic terms.

One key dilemma in the original Greek version asks us to consider whether holy things (i) are holy because they please the gods or (ii) please the gods because they are holy. In monotheistic terms, the dilemma would be whether holy things (i) are holy because they please God or (ii) please God because they are holy. The question can then be broadened and the dilemma posed in terms of good things in general. We then ask whether good things are (i) good because God wills them or (ii) willed by God because they are good.

Plato believed that the gods love what is holy because it is holy (i.e., he believed the second option above), just as Christians have traditionally believed that God wills good things because they are good. Traditionally, a contrast is drawn between God, an infinite and all-good being who always wills the good, and humans, finite beings who are not all-good and do not always will the good.

We might also consider a parallel dilemma concerning truths. Are things true because God knows them, or does God know them because they are true? The traditional view is that God is all-knowing. God knows all truths because they are truths (and no truths lie outside divine knowledge), whereas people do not know all truths (and many truths lie outside human knowledge).

Nevertheless, there has also been in Christianity a tradition that the almighty power of God is not to be constrained by anything—even if we imagine that what constrains God are good things. This view holds that God creates not only good things but the very fact that a good thing (such as honesty) is good while another thing (such as false witness against your neighbor) is not. Thus, in this view, God in his power determines what is good and what is bad.

These topics are further discussed in Glenn Tinder, "Can We Be Good Without God? On the Political Meaning of Christianity," *The Atlantic Monthly* (December 1989); Richard J. Mouw, *The God Who Commands: A Study in Divine Command Ethics* (University of Notre Dame Press, 1990); E. M. Adams, *Religion and Cultural Freedom* (Temple University Press, 1993); D. Z. Phillips, ed., *Religion and Morality* (St. Martin's Press, 1996); and Paul Chamberlain, *Can We Be Good Without God? A Conversation About Truth, Morality, Culture, and a Few Other Things That Matter* (InterVarsity Press, 1996).

Internet References . . .

National Abortion and Reproductive Rights Action League

This is the home page of the National Abortion and Reproductive Rights Action League (NARAL), an organization that works to promote reproductive freedom and dignity for women and their families.

http://www.naral.org/index.cfm

Pro-Life Action League

This site is pro-life with respect to abortion, but some of the links also concern euthanasia and related topics.

www.prolifeaction.org/

Pro-Life News

This site contains many links to news items and information on abortion, euthanasia, etc.

http://www.lifenews.com/

Literature on Cloning and Reproductive Technologies

This *Ethics Updates* site contains many links to articles, interviews, associations, and other resources that are concerned with cloning and reproductive technologies.

http://ethics.acused.edu/applied/bioethics/index.asp

UNIT 2

Gender, Sex, and Reproduction

Humans are sexual, reproductive, social beings. Given this fact, it is imperative to have some idea of what is socially acceptable and what is not, as well as what is expected of males and females, and what is not.

The issues in this section do not presuppose that there is anything morally questionable about sex itself, but they do raise questions about how, in today's society, we should think about sex roles and matters of sex and reproduction.

- Is Abortion Immoral?
- Must Sex Involve Commitment?
- Is It Right to Prohibit Same-Sex Marriage?
- Should Human Cloning Be Banned?

ISSUE 3

Is Abortion Immoral?

YES: Don Marquis, from "Why Abortion Is Immoral," *The Journal of Philosophy* (April 1989)

NO: Jane English, from "Abortion and the Concept of a Person," *Canadian Journal of Philosophy* (October 1975)

ISSUE SUMMARY

YES: Professor of philosophy Don Marquis argues that abortion is generally wrong for the same reason that killing an innocent adult human being is generally wrong: it deprives the individual of a future that he or she would otherwise have.

NO: Philosopher Jane English (1947–1978) asserts that there is no well-defined line dividing persons from nonpersons. She maintains that both the conservative and the liberal positions are too extreme and that some abortions are morally justifiable and some are not.

Abortion is a divisive topic, and discussions can easily become polarized. Here we will briefly consider some of the biological facts associated with abortion and review some relevant historical and legal matters. The selections themselves will then look at the moral issues raised by abortion.

Conception occurs when the spermatozoon of a male unites with the ovum of a female. The single cell thus formed is called a zygote. In a normal pregnancy, this zygote will multiply into several cells, travel through the fallopian tube, enter the uterus, and implant itself in the uterine wall. When implantation is complete, one to two weeks after fertilization (as the original conception is also called), we can say that the pregnancy is established and that the zygote has become an embryo. Once the placenta and umbilical cord are established, the embryo takes nourishment by means of these from the blood of the pregnant woman and quickly grows primitive limbs and organs. At eight weeks from conception, the first brain waves can be detected and the embryo is now called a fetus. So-called quickening, the first felt spontaneous movement of the fetus, occurs at around 14 or 15 weeks. The threshold of viability (the point at which the fetus can be kept alive outside the uterus) is dependent upon many factors, especially the development of the cardiopulmonary system. Depending on the level of available medical technology, viability can be reached sometime between 20 and 28 weeks. Birth generally takes place about 38 to 40 weeks after conception, although here too there is significant variation.

There are other possibilities once the spermatozoon and ovum unite. The fertilized ovum, for example, might never be implanted in the wall of the uterus and might be expelled uneventfully, and even without notice, from the body. Or the zygote might implant itself somewhere other than inside the uterus, resulting in an ectopic pregnancy. The embryo will not grow properly outside the uterus, and this kind of pregnancy can be dangerous to the mother. (In the case of an ectopic pregnancy, the Roman Catholic Church will permit an abortion to save the pregnant woman's life.) Another possibility is that the pregnancy will develop normally for a while but then end in miscarriage; this is sometimes called a spontaneous abortion.

The historic *Roe v. Wade* case, decided in 1973 by the U.S. Supreme Court in a split decision of 7–2, ruled that the nineteenth-century Texas statutes against abortion were unconstitutional. The Court divided the normal pregnancy into three trimesters and ruled as follows:

> For the stage prior to approximately the end of the first trimester, the abortion decision and its effectuation must be left to the medical judgment of the pregnant woman's attending physician. For the stage subsequent to approximately the end of the first trimester, the State, in promoting its interest in the health of the mother, may, if it chooses, regulate the abortion procedure in ways that are reasonably related to maternal health. For the stages subsequent to viability, the State, in promoting its interest in the potentiality of human life, may, if it chooses, regulate, and even proscribe, abortion except where it is necessary, in appropriate medical judgment, for the preservation of the life or health of the mother. (410 U.S.113, 93 S. Ct. 705 [1973])

Before *Roe v. Wade,* some states permitted abortion only if a woman's life was in danger; abortion for any other reason or consideration was illegal and punishable by law. *Roe v. Wade* ruled that states do not have the right to regulate abortion procedures in any way during the first trimester of pregnancy. It is important to note that neither the Supreme Court nor the Texas statutes said anything about the relation of the woman to the fetus (or embryo) or about the reasons a woman might have for seeking an abortion.

In the following selections, Don Marquis constructs a secular argument to show that abortion is immoral. He focuses not on the present status of the fetus, but on the future status. This avoids the divisive question of whether or not the fetus is a person. Jane English counters that this question has no determinate answer. In her view, neither the standard conservative position nor the standard liberal position adequately addresses the issue of abortion.

YES

Don Marquis

Why Abortion Is Immoral

The view that abortion is, with rare exceptions, seriously immoral has received little support in the recent philosophical literature. No doubt most philosophers affiliated with secular institutions of higher education believe that the anti-abortion position is either a symptom of irrational religious dogma or a conclusion generated by seriously confused philosophical argument. The purpose of this essay is to undermine this general belief. This essay sets out an argument that purports to show, as well as any argument in ethics can show, that abortion is, except possibly in rare cases, seriously immoral, that it is in the same moral category as killing an innocent adult human being.

The argument is based on a major assumption. Many of the most insightful and careful writers on the ethics of abortion—such as Joel Feinberg, Michael Tooley, Mary Anne Warren, H. Tristram Engelhardt, Jr., L. W. Sumner, John T. Noonan, Jr., and Philip Devine[1]—believe that whether or not abortion is morally permissible stands or falls on whether or not a fetus is the sort of being whose life it is seriously wrong to end. The argument of this essay will assume, but not argue, that they are correct.

Also, this essay will neglect issues of great importance to a complete ethics of abortion. Some anti-abortionists will allow that certain abortions, such as abortion before implantation or abortion when the life of a woman is threatened by a pregnancy or abortion after rape, may be morally permissible. This essay will not explore the casuistry of these hard cases. The purpose of this essay is to develop a general argument for the claim that the overwhelming majority of deliberate abortions are seriously immoral.

A sketch of standard anti-abortion and pro-choice arguments exhibits how those arguments possess certain symmetries that explain why partisans of those positions are so convinced of the correctness of their own positions, why they are not successful in convincing their opponents, and why, to others, this issue seems to be unresolvable. An analysis of the nature of this standoff suggests a strategy for surmounting it.

Consider the way a typical anti-abortionist argues. She will argue or assert that life is present from the moment of conception or that fetuses look like babies or that fetuses possess a characteristic such as a genetic code that is both

From *Journal of Philosophy,* vol. 86, no. 4, April 1989. Copyright © 1989 by Journal of Philosophy, Inc. Reprinted by permission.

necessary and sufficient for being human. Anti-abortionists seem to believe that (1) the truth of all of these claims is quite obvious, and (2) establishing any of these claims is sufficient to show that abortion is morally akin to murder.

A standard pro-choice strategy exhibits similarities. The pro-choicer will argue or assert that fetuses are not persons or that fetuses are not rational agents or that fetuses are not social beings. Pro-choicers seem to believe that (1) the truth of any of these claims is quite obvious, and (2) establishing any of these claims is sufficient to show that an abortion is not a wrongful killing.

In fact, both the pro-choice and the anti-abortion claims do seem to be true, although the "it looks like a baby" claim is more difficult to establish the earlier the pregnancy. We seem to have a standoff. How can it be resolved?

As everyone who has taken a bit of logic knows, if any of these arguments concerning abortion is a good argument, it requires not only some claim characterizing fetuses, but also some general moral principle that ties a characteristic of fetuses to having or not having the right to life or to some other moral characteristic that will generate the obligation or the lack of obligation not to end the life of a fetus. Accordingly, the arguments of the anti-abortionist and the pro-choicer need a bit of filling in to be regarded as adequate.

Note what each partisan will say. The anti-abortionist will claim that her position is supported by such generally accepted moral principles as "It is always prima facie seriously wrong to take a human life" or "It is always prima facie seriously wrong to end the life of a baby." Since these are generally accepted moral principles, her position is certainly not obviously wrong. The pro-choicer will claim that her position is supported by such plausible moral principles as "Being a person is what gives an individual intrinsic moral worth" or "It is only seriously prima facie wrong to take the life of a member of the human community." Since these are generally accepted moral principles, the pro-choice position is certainly not obviously wrong. Unfortunately, we have again arrived at a standoff.

Now, how might one deal with this standoff? The standard approach is to try to show how the moral principles of one's opponent lose their plausibility under analysis. It is easy to see how this is possible. On the one hand, the anti-abortionist will defend a moral principle concerning the wrongness of killing which tends to be broad in scope in order that even fetuses at an early stage of pregnancy will fall under it. The problem with broad principles is that they often embrace too much. In this particular instance, the principle "It is always prima facie wrong to take a human life" seems to entail that it is wrong to end the existence of a living human cancer-cell culture, on the grounds that the culture is both living and human. Therefore, it seems that the anti-abortionist's favored principle is too broad.

On the other hand, the pro-choicer wants to find a moral principle concerning the wrongness of killing which tends to be narrow in scope in order that fetuses will *not* fall under it. The problem with narrow principles is that they often do not embrace enough. Hence, the needed principles such as "It is prima facie seriously wrong to kill only persons" or "It is prima facie wrong to kill only rational agents" do not explain why it is wrong to kill infants or young children or the severely retarded or even perhaps the severely mentally ill. Therefore, we seem again to have a standoff. The anti-abortionist charges, not unreasonably, that pro-choice principles concerning killing are too narrow to be acceptable; the pro-choicer charges, not unreasonably, that anti-abortionist principles concerning killing are too broad to be acceptable.

Attempts by both sides to patch up the difficulties in their positions run into further difficulties. The anti-abortionist will try to remove the problem in her position by reformulating her principle concerning killing in terms of human beings. Now we end up with: "It is always prima facie seriously wrong to end the life of a human being." This principle has the advantage of avoiding the problem of the human cancer-cell culture counterexample. But this advantage is purchased at a high price. For although it is clear that a fetus is both human and alive, it is not at all clear that a fetus is a human *being*. There is at least something to be said for the view that something becomes a human being only after a process of development, and that therefore first trimester fetuses and perhaps all fetuses are not yet human beings. Hence, the anti-abortionist, by this move, has merely exchanged one problem for another.[2]

The pro-choicer fares no better. She may attempt to find reasons why killing infants, young children, and the severely retarded is wrong which are independent of her major principle that is supposed to explain the wrongness of taking human life, but which will not also make abortion immoral. This is no easy task. Appeals to social utility will seem satisfactory only to those who resolve not to think of the enormous difficulties with a utilitarian account of the wrongness of killing and the significant social costs of preserving the lives of the unproductive.[3] A pro-choice strategy that extends the definition of 'person' to infants or even to young children seems just as arbitrary as an anti-abortion strategy that extends the definition of 'human being' to fetuses. Again, we find symmetries in the two positions and we arrive at a standoff.

There are even further problems that reflect symmetries in the two positions. In addition to counterexample problems, or the arbitrary application problems that can be exchanged for them, the standard anti-abortionist principle "It is prima facie seriously wrong to kill a human being," or one of its variants, can be objected to on the grounds of ambiguity. If 'human being' is taken to be a *biological* category, then the anti-abortionist is left with the problem of explaining why a merely biological category should make a moral difference. Why, it is asked, is it any more reasonable to base a moral conclusion on the number of chromosomes in one's cells than on the color of one's skin?[4] If 'human being', on the other hand, is taken to be a *moral* category, then the claim that a fetus is a human being cannot be taken to be a premise in the anti-abortion argument, for it is precisely what needs to be established. Hence, either the anti-abortionist's main category is a morally irrelevant, merely biological category, or it is of no use to the anti-abortionist in establishing (noncircularly, of course) that abortion is wrong.

Although this problem with the anti-abortionist position is often noticed, it is less often noticed that the pro-choice position suffers from an analogous problem. The principle "Only persons have the right to life" also suffers from an ambiguity. The term 'person' is typically defined in terms of psychological characteristics, although there will certainly be disagreement concerning which characteristics are most important. Supposing that this matter can be settled, the pro-choicer is left with the problem of explaining why *psychological* characteristics should make a *moral* difference. If the pro-choicer should attempt to deal with this problem by claiming that an explanation is not necessary, that in fact we do treat such a cluster of psychological properties as having moral significance, the sharp-witted anti-abortionist should have a ready response. We do treat being both living and human as having moral significance. If it is legitimate for the pro-choicer to demand that the anti-abortionist provide an explanation of the connection between the biological character of being a human being and the wrongness of being killed (even though people accept this connection), then it is legitimate for the anti-abortionist to demand that the pro-choicer provide an explanation of the connection between psychological criteria for being a person and the wrongness of being killed (even though that connection is accepted).[5] . . .

[T]he pro-choicer cannot any more escape her problem by making person a purely moral category than the anti-abortionist could escape by the analogous move. For if person is a moral category, then the pro-choicer is left without the resources for establishing (noncircularly, of course) the claim that a fetus is not a person, which is an essential premise in her argument. Again, we have both a symmetry and a standoff between pro-choice and anti-abortion views.

Passions in the abortion debate run high. There are both plausibilities and difficulties with the standard positions. Accordingly, it is hardly surprising that partisans of either side embrace with fervor the moral generalizations that support the conclusions they preanalytically favor, and reject with disdain the moral generalizations of their opponents as being subject to inescapable difficulties. It is easy to believe that the counterexamples to one's own moral principles are merely temporary difficulties that will dissolve in the wake of further philosophical research, and that the counterexamples to the principles of one's opponents are . . . straightforward. . . . This might suggest to an impartial observer (if there are any) that the abortion issue is unresolvable.

There is a way out of this apparent dialectical quandary. The moral generalizations of both sides are not quite correct. The generalizations hold for the most part, for the usual cases. This suggests that they are all *accidental* generalizations, that the moral claims made by those on both sides of the dispute do not touch on the *essence* of the matter.

This use of the distinction between essence and accident is not meant to invoke obscure metaphysical categories. Rather, it is intended to reflect the rather atheoretical nature of the abortion discussion. If the generalization a partisan in the abortion dispute adopts were derived from the reason why ending the life of a human being is wrong, then there could not be exceptions to that generalization unless some special case obtains in which there are even more powerful countervailing reasons. Such generalizations would not be merely accidental generalizations; they would point to, or be based upon, the essence of the wrongness of killing, what it is that makes killing wrong. All this suggests that a necessary condition of resolving the abortion controversy is a more theoretical account of the wrongness of killing. After all, if we merely believe, but do not understand, why killing adult human beings such as ourselves is wrong, how could we conceivably show that abortion is either immoral or permissible?

In order to develop such an account, we can start from the following unproblematic assumption concerning our own case: it is wrong to kill *us*. Why is it wrong? . . .

What primarily makes killing wrong is neither its effect on the murderer nor its effect on the victim's friends and relatives, but its effect on the victim. The loss of one's life is one of the greatest losses one can suffer. The loss of one's life deprives one of all the experiences, activities, projects, and enjoyments that would otherwise have constituted one's future. Therefore, killing someone is wrong, primarily because the killing inflicts (one of) the greatest possible losses on the victim. To describe this as the loss of life can be misleading, however. The change in my biological state does not by itself make killing me wrong. The effect of the loss of my biological life is the loss to me of all those activities, projects, experiences, and enjoyments which would otherwise have constituted my future personal life. These activities, projects, experiences, and enjoyments are either valuable for their own sakes or are means to something else that is valuable for its own sake. Some parts of my future are not valued by me now, but will come to be valued by me as I grow older and as my values and capacities change. When I am killed, I am deprived both of what I now value which would have been part of my future personal life, but also what I would come to value. Therefore, when I die, I am deprived of all of the value of my future. Inflicting this loss on me is ultimately what makes killing me wrong. This being the case, it would seem that what makes killing *any* adult human being prima facie seriously wrong is the loss of his or her future.[6] . . .

The claim that what makes killing wrong is the loss of the victim's future is directly supported by two considerations. In the first place, this theory explains why we regard killing as one of the worst of crimes. Killing is especially wrong, because it deprives the victim of more than perhaps any other crime. In the second place, people with AIDS or cancer who know they are dying believe, of course, that dying is a very bad thing for them. They believe that the loss of a future to them that they would otherwise have experienced is what makes their premature death a very bad thing for them. A better theory of the wrongness of killing would require a different natural property associated with killing which better fits with the attitudes of the dying. What could it be?

The view that what makes killing wrong is the loss to the victim of the value of the victim's future gains additional support when some of its implications are examined. In the first place, it is incompatible with the view that it is wrong to kill only beings who are biologically human. It is possible that there exists a different species from another planet whose members have a future like ours. Since having a future like that is what makes killing someone wrong, this theory entails that it would be wrong to kill members of such a species. Hence, this theory is opposed to the claim that only life that is biologically human has great moral worth, a claim which many anti-abortionists have seemed to adopt. This opposition, which this theory has in common with personhood theories, seems to be a merit of the theory.

In the second place, the claim that the loss of one's future is the wrong-making feature of one's being killed entails the possibility that the futures of some actual nonhuman mammals on our own planet are sufficiently like ours that it is seriously wrong to kill them also. Whether some animals do have the same right to life as human beings depends on adding to the account of the wrongness of killing some additional account of just what it is about my future or the futures of other adult human beings which makes it wrong to kill us. No such additional account will be offered in this essay. Undoubtedly, the provision of such an account would be a very difficult matter. Undoubtedly, any such account would be quite controversial. Hence, it surely should not reflect badly on this sketch of an elementary theory of the wrongness of killing that it is indeterminate with respect to some very difficult issues regarding animal rights.

In the third place, the claim that the loss of one's future is the wrong-making feature of one's being killed does not entail, as sanctity of human life theories do, that active euthanasia is wrong. Persons who are severely and incurably ill, who face a future of pain and despair, and who wish to die will not have suffered a loss if they are killed. It is, strictly speaking, the value of a human's future which makes killing wrong in this theory. This being so, killing does not necessarily wrong some persons who are sick and dying. Of course, there may be other reasons for a prohibition of active euthanasia, but that is another matter. Sanctity-of-human-life theories seem to hold that active euthanasia is seriously wrong even in an individual case where there seems to be good reason for it independently of public policy considerations. This consequence is most implausible, and it is a plus for the claim that the loss of a future of value is what makes killing wrong that it does not share this consequence.

In the fourth place, the account of the wrongness of killing defended in this essay does straightforwardly entail that it is prima facie seriously wrong to kill children and infants, for we do presume that they have futures of value. Since we do believe that it is wrong to kill defenseless little babies, it is important that a theory of the wrongness of killing easily account for this. Personhood theories of the wrongness of killing, on the other hand, cannot straightforwardly account for the wrongness of killing infants and young children.[7] Hence, such theories must add special ad hoc accounts of the wrongness of killing the young. The plausibility of such ad hoc theories seems to be a function of how desperately one wants such theories to work. The claim that the primary wrong-making feature of a killing is the loss to the victim of the value of its future accounts for the wrongness of killing young children and infants directly; it makes the wrongness of such acts as obvious as we actually think it is. This is a further merit of this theory. Accordingly, it seems that this value of a future-like-ours theory of the wrongness of killing shares strengths of both sanctity-of-life and personhood accounts while avoiding weaknesses of both. In addition, it meshes with a central intuition concerning what makes killing wrong.

The claim that the primary wrong-making feature of a killing is the loss to the victim of the value of its future has obvious consequences for the ethics of abortion. The future of a standard fetus includes a set of experiences, projects, activities, and such which are identical with the futures of adult human beings and are identical with the futures of young children. Since the reason that is sufficient to explain why it is wrong to kill human beings after the time of birth is a reason that also applies to fetuses, it follows that abortion is prima facie seriously morally wrong. . . .

How complete an account of the wrongness of killing does the value of a future-like-ours account have to be in order that the wrongness of abortion is a consequence? This account does not have to be an account of the necessary conditions for the wrongness of killing. Some persons in nursing homes may lack valuable human futures, yet it may be wrong to kill them for other reasons. Furthermore, this account does not obviously have to be the sole reason killing is wrong where the victim did have a valuable future. This analysis claims only that, for any killing where the victim did have a valuable future like ours, having that future by itself is sufficient to create the strong presumption that the killing is seriously wrong. . . .

In this essay, it has been argued that the correct ethic of the wrongness of killing can be extended to fetal life and used to show that there is a strong presumption that any abortion is morally impermissible. If the ethic of killing adopted here entails, however, that contraception is also seriously immoral, then there would appear to be a difficulty with the analysis of this essay.

But this analysis does not entail that contraception is wrong. Of course, contraception prevents the actualization of a possible future of value. Hence, it follows from the claim that futures of value should be maximized that contraception is prima facie immoral. This obligation to maximize does not exist, however; furthermore, nothing in the ethics of killing in this paper entails that it does. The ethics of killing in this essay would entail that contraception is wrong only if something were denied a human future of value by contraception. Nothing at all is denied such a future by contraception, however. . . .

At the time of contraception, there are hundreds of millions of sperm, one (released) ovum and millions of possible combinations of all of these. There is no actual combination at all. Is the subject of the loss to be a merely possible combination? Which one? This alternative does not yield an actual subject of harm either. Accordingly, the immorality of contraception is not entailed by the loss of a future-like-ours argument simply because there is no nonarbitrarily identifiable subject of the loss in the case of contraception.

The purpose of this essay has been to set out an argument for the serious presumptive wrongness of abortion subject to the assumption that the moral permissibility of abortion stands or falls on the moral status of the fetus. Since a fetus possesses a property, the possession of which in adult human beings is sufficient to make killing an adult human being wrong, abortion is wrong. This way of dealing with the problem of abortion seems superior to other approaches to the ethics of abortion, because it rests on an ethics of killing which is close to self-evident, because the crucial morally relevant property clearly applies to fetuses, and because the argument avoids the usual equivocations on 'human life', 'human being', or 'person'. The argument rests neither on religious claims nor on Papal dogma. It is not subject to the objection of "speciesism." Its soundness is compatible with the moral permissibility of euthanasia and contraception. It deals with our intuitions concerning young children.

Finally, this analysis can be viewed as resolving a standard problem—indeed, *the* standard problem—concerning the ethics of abortion. Clearly, it is wrong to kill adult human beings. Clearly, it is not wrong to end the life of some arbitrarily chosen single human cell. Fetuses seem to be like arbitrarily chosen human cells in some respects and like adult humans in other respects. The problem of the ethics of abortion is the problem of determining the fetal property that settles this moral controversy. The thesis of this essay is that the problem of the ethics of abortion, so understood, is solvable.

Notes

1. Feinberg, "Abortion," in *Matters of Life and Death: New Introductory Essays in Moral Philosophy,* Tom Regan, ed. (New York: Random House, 1986), pp. 256–293; Tooley, "Abortion and Infanticide," *Philosophy and Public Affairs,* II, 1 (1972): 37–65; Tooley, *Abortion and Infanticide* (New York: Oxford, 1984); Warren, "On the Moral and Legal Status of Abortion," *The Monist,* I.VII, 1 (1973): 43–61; Engelhardt, "The Ontology of Abortion," *Ethics,* I, XXXIV, 3 (1974): 217–234; Sumner, *Abortion and Moral Theory* (Princeton: University Press, 1981); Noonan, "An Almost Absolute Value in History," in *The Morality of Abortion: Legal and Historical Perspectives,* Noonan, ed. (Cambridge: Harvard, 1970); and Devine, *The Ethics of Homicide* (Ithaca: Cornell, 1978).
2. For interesting discussions of this issue, see Warren Quinn, "Abortion: Identity and Loss," *Philosophy and Public Affairs,* XIII, 1 (1984): 24–54; and Lawrence C. Becker, "Human Being: The Boundaries of the Concept," *Philosophy and Public Affairs,* IV, 4 (1975): 334–359.
3. For example, see my "Ethics and the Elderly: Some Problems," in Stuart Spicker, Kathleen Woodward, and David Van Tassel, eds., *Aging and the Elderly: Humanistic Perspectives in Gerontology* (Atlantic Highlands, NJ: Humanities, 1978), pp. 341–355.
4. See Warren, *op. cit.,* and Tooley, "Abortion and Infanticide."
5. This seems to be the fatal flaw in Warren's treatment of this issue.
6. I have been most influenced on this matter by Jonathan Glover, *Causing Death and Saving Lives* (New York: Penguin, 1977), ch. 3; and Robert Young, "What Is So Wrong with Killing People?" *Philosophy,* LIV, 210 (1979): 515–528.
7. Feinberg, Tooley, Warren, and Engelhardt have all dealt with this problem.

Jane English

Abortion and the Concept of a Person

The abortion debate rages on. Yet the two most popular positions seem to be clearly mistaken. Conservatives maintain that a human life begins at conception and that therefore abortion must be wrong because it is murder. But not all killings of humans are murders. Most notably, self-defense may justify even the killing of an innocent person.

Liberals, on the other hand, are just as mistaken in their argument that since a fetus does not become a person until birth, a woman may do whatever she pleases in and to her own body. First, you cannot do to as you please with your own body if it affects other people adversely.[1] Second, if a fetus is not a person, that does not imply that you can do to it anything you wish. Animals, for example, are not persons, yet to kill or torture them for no reason at all is wrong.

At the center of the storm has been the issue of just when it is between ovulation and adulthood that a person appears on the scene. Conservatives draw the line at conception, liberals at birth. In this paper I first examine our concept of a person and conclude that no single criterion can capture the concept of a person and no sharp line can be drawn. Next I argue that if a fetus is a person, abortion is still justifiable in many cases; and if a fetus is not a person, killing it is still wrong in many cases. To a large extent, these two solutions are in agreement. I conclude that our concept of a person cannot and need not bear the weight that the abortion controversy has thrust upon it.

The several factions in the abortion argument have drawn battle lines around various proposed criteria for determining what is and what is not a person. For example, Mary Anne Warren[2] lists five features (capacities for reasoning, self-awareness, complex communication, etc.) as her criteria for personhood and argues for the permissibility of abortion because a fetus falls outside this concept. Baruch Brody[3] uses brain waves. Michael Tooley[4] picks having-a-concept-of-self as his criterion and concludes that infanticide and abortion are justifiable, while the killing of adult animals is not. On the other side, Paul Ramsey[5] claims a certain gene structure is the defining characteristic. John Noonan[6] prefers conceived-of-humans and presents counterexamples to various other candidate criteria. For instance, he argues against viability as the criterion because the newborn and infirm would then be nonpersons, since

From *Canadian Journal of Philosophy,* vol. 5. no. 2, October 1975, pp. 233–243. Copyright © 1975 by Canadian Journal of Philosophy. Reprinted by permission of University of Calgary Press.

they cannot live without the aid of others. He rejects any criterion that calls upon the sorts of sentiments a being can evoke in adults on the grounds that this would allow us to exclude other races as nonpersons if we could just view them sufficiently unsentimentally.

These approaches are typical: foes of abortion propose sufficient conditions for personhood which fetuses satisfy, while friends of abortion counter with necessary conditions for personhood which fetuses lack. But these both presuppose that the concept of a person can be captured in a straitjacket of necessary and/or sufficient conditions.[7] Rather, "person" is a cluster of features, of which rationality, having a self concept and being conceived of humans are only part.

What is typical of persons? Within our concept of a person we include, first, certain biological factors: descended from humans, having a certain genetic makeup, having a head, hands, arms, eyes, capable of locomotion, breathing, eating, sleeping. There are psychological factors: sentience, perception, having a concept of self and of one's own interests and desires, the ability to use tools, the ability to use language or symbol systems, the ability to joke, to be angry, to doubt. There are rationality factors: the ability to reason and draw conclusions, the ability to generalize and to learn from past experience, the ability to sacrifice present interests for greater gains in the future. There are social factors: the ability to work in groups and respond to peer pressure, the ability to recognize and consider as valuable the interests of others, seeing oneself as one among "other minds," the ability to sympathize, encourage, love, the ability to evoke from others the responses of sympathy, encouragement, love, the ability to work with others for mutual advantage. Then there are legal factors: being subject to the law and protected by it, having the ability to sue and enter contracts, being counted in the census, having a name and citizenship, the ability to own property, inherit, and so forth.

Now the point is not that this list is incomplete, or that you can find counterinstances to each of its points. People typically exhibit rationality, for instance, but someone who was irrational would not thereby fail to qualify as a person. On the other hand, something could exhibit the majority of these features and still fail to be a person, as an advanced robot might. There is no single core of necessary and sufficient features which we can draw upon with the assurance that they constitute what really makes a person; there are only features that are more or less typical.

This is not to say that no necessary or sufficient conditions can be given. Being alive is a necessary condition for being a person, and being a U.S. Senator is sufficient. But rather than falling inside a sufficient condition or outside a necessary one, a fetus lies in the penumbra region where our concept of a person is not so simple. For this reason I think a conclusive answer to the question whether a fetus is a person is unattainable.

Here we might note a family of simple fallacies that proceed by stating a necessary condition for personhood and showing that a fetus has that characteristic. This is a form of the fallacy of affirming the consequent. For example, some have mistakenly reasoned from the premise that a fetus is human (after all, it is a human fetus rather than, say, a canine fetus), to the conclusion that it is a human. Adding an equivocation on "being," we get the fallacious argument that since a fetus is something both living and human, it is a human being.

Nonetheless, it does seem clear that a fetus has very few of the above family of characteristics, whereas a newborn baby exhibits a much larger proportion of them—and a two-year-old has even more. Note that one traditional antiabortion argument has centered on pointing out the many ways in which a fetus resembles a baby. They emphasize its development ("It already has ten fingers . . .") without mentioning its dissimilarities to adults (it still has gills and a tail). They also try to evoke the sort of sympathy on our part that we only feel toward other persons ("Never to laugh . . . or feel the sunshine?"). This all seems to be a relevant way to argue, since its purpose is to persuade us that a fetus satisfies so many of the important features on the list that it ought to be treated as a person. Also note that a fetus near the time of birth satisfies many more of these factors than a fetus in the early months of development. This could provide reason for making distinctions among the different stages of pregnancy, as the U.S. Supreme Court has done.[8]

Historically, the time at which a person has been said to come into existence has varied widely. Muslims date personhood from fourteen days after conception. Some medievals followed Aristotle in placing ensoulment at forty days after conception for a male fetus and eighty days for a female fetus.[9] In European common law since the seventeenth century, abortion was considered the killing of a person only after quickening, the time when a pregnant woman first feels the fetus move on its own. Nor is this variety of opinions surprising. Biologically, a human being develops gradually. We shouldn't expect there to be any specific time or sharp dividing point when a person appears on the scene.

For these reasons I believe our concept of a person is not sharp or decisive enough to bear the weight of a solution to the abortion controversy. To use it to solve that problem is to clarify *obscurum per obscurius* [to clarify what is obscure by what is more obscure].

Next let us consider what follows if a fetus is a person after all. Judith Jarvis Thomson's landmark article, "A Defense of Abortion,"[10] correctly points out that some additional argumentation is needed at this point in the conservative argument to bridge the gap between the premise that a fetus is an innocent person and the conclusion that killing it is always wrong. To arrive at this conclusion, we would need the additional premise that killing an innocent person is always wrong. But killing an innocent person is sometimes permissible, most notably in self-defense. Some examples may help draw out our intuitions or ordinary judgments about self-defense.

Suppose a mad scientist, for instance, hypnotized innocent people to jump out of the bushes and attack innocent passers-by with knives. If you are so attacked, we agree you have a right to kill the attacker in self-defense, if killing him is the only way to protect your life or to save yourself from serious injury. It does not seem to matter here that the attacker is not malicious but himself an innocent pawn, for your killing of him is not done in a spirit of retribution but only in self-defense.

How severe an injury may you inflict in self-defense? In part this depends upon the severity of the injury to be avoided: you may not shoot someone merely to avoid having your clothes torn. This might lead one to the mistaken conclusion that the defense may only equal the threatened injury in severity; that to avoid death you may kill, but to avoid a black eye you may only inflict a black eye or the equivalent. Rather, our laws and customs seem to say that you may create an injury somewhat, but not enormously, greater than the injury to be avoided. To fend off an attack whose outcome would be as serious as rape, a severe beating or the loss of a finger, you may shoot; to avoid having your clothes torn, you may blacken an eye. . . .

Some cases of pregnancy present a parallel situation. Though the fetus is itself innocent, it may pose a threat to the pregnant woman's well-being, life prospects or health, mental or physical. If the pregnancy presents a slight threat to her interests, it seems self-defense cannot justify abortion. But if the threat is on a par with a serious beating or the loss of a finger, she may kill the fetus that poses such a threat, even if it is an innocent person. If a lesser harm to the fetus could have the same defensive effect, killing it would not be justified. It is unfortunate that the only way to free the woman from the pregnancy entails the death of the fetus (except in very late stages of pregnancy). Thus a self-defense model supports Thomson's point that the woman has a right only to be freed from the fetus, not a right to demand its death.[11] . . .

Thanks to modern technology, the cases are rare in which pregnancy poses as clear a threat to a woman's bodily health as an attacker brandishing a switchblade. How does self-defense fare when more subtle, complex and long-range harms are involved?

To consider a somewhat fanciful example, suppose you are a highly trained surgeon when you are kidnapped by the hypnotic attacker. He says he does not intend to harm you but to take you back to the mad scientist who, it turns out, plans to hypnotize you to have a permanent mental block against all your knowledge of medicine. This would automatically destroy your career which would in turn have a serious adverse impact on your family, your personal relationships and your happiness. It seems to me that if the only way you can avoid this outcome is to shoot the innocent attacker, you are justified in so doing. You are defending yourself from a drastic injury to your life prospects. I think it is no exaggeration to claim that unwanted pregnancies (most obviously among teenagers) often have such adverse life-long consequences as the surgeon's loss of livelihood.

Several parallels arise between various views on abortion and the self-defense model. Let's suppose further that these hypnotized attackers only operate at night, so that it is well known that they can be avoided completely by the considerable inconvenience of never leaving your house after dark. One view is that since you could stay home at night, therefore if you go out and are selected by one of these hypnotized people, you have no right to defend yourself. This parallels the view that abstinence is the only acceptable way to avoid pregnancy. Others might hold that you ought to take along some defense such as Mace which will deter the hypnotized person without killing him, but that if this defense fails, you are obliged to submit to the resulting injury, no matter how severe it is. This parallels the view that contraception is all right but abortion is always wrong, even in cases of contraceptive failure.

A third view is that you may kill the hypnotized person only if he will actually kill you, but not if he will only injure you. This is like the position that abortion is permissible only if it is required to save a woman's life. Finally we have the view that it is all right to kill the attacker, even if only to avoid a very slight inconvenience to yourself and even if you knowingly walked down the very street where all these incidents have been taking place without taking along any Mace or protective escort. If we assume that a fetus is a person, this is the analogue of the view that abortion is always justifiable, "on demand."

The self-defense model allows us to see an important difference that exists between abortion and infanticide, even if a fetus is a person from conception. Many have argued that the only way to justify abortion without justifying infanticide would be to find some characteristic of personhood that is acquired at birth. Michael Tooley, for one, claims infanticide is justifiable because the really significant characteristics of person[hood] are acquired some time after birth. But all such approaches look to characteristics of the developing human and ignore the relation between the fetus and the woman. What if, after birth, the presence of an infant or the need to support it posed a grave threat to the woman's sanity or life prospects? She could escape this threat by the simple expedient of running away. So a solution that does not entail the death of the infant is available. Before birth, such solutions are not available because of the biological dependence of the fetus on the woman. Birth is the crucial point not because of any characteristics the fetus gains, but because after birth the woman can defend herself by a means less drastic than killing the infant. Hence self-defense can only be used to justify abortion without necessarily thereby justifying infanticide.

On the other hand, supposing a fetus is not after all a person, would abortion always be morally permissible? Some opponents of abortion seem worried that if a fetus is not a full-fledged person, then we are justified in treating it in any way at all. However, this does not follow. Nonpersons do get some consideration in our moral code, though of course they do not have the same rights as persons have (and in general they do not have moral responsibilities), and though their interests may be overridden by the interests of persons. Still, we cannot just treat them in any way at all.

Treatment of animals is a case in point. It is wrong to torture dogs for fun or to kill wild birds for no reason at all. It is wrong Period, even though dogs and birds do not have the same rights persons do. However, few people think it is wrong to use dogs as experimental animals, causing them considerable suffering in some cases, provided that the resulting research will probably bring discoveries of great benefit to people. And most of us think it all right to kill birds for food or to protect our crops. People's rights are different from the consideration we give to animals, then, for it is wrong to experiment on people, even if others might later benefit a great deal as a result of their suffering. You might volunteer to be a subject, but this would be supererogatory; you certainly have a right to refuse to be a medical guinea pig.

But how do we decide what you may or may not do to nonpersons? This is a difficult problem, one for which I believe no adequate account exists. You do not want to say, for instance, that torturing dogs is all right whenever the sum of its effects on people is good—when it doesn't warp the sensibilities of the torturer so much that he mistreats people. If that were the case, it would be all right to torture dogs if you did it in private, or if the torturer lived on a desert island or died soon afterward, so that his actions had no effect on people. This is an inadequate account, because whatever moral consideration animals get, it has to be indefeasible, too. It will have to be a general proscription of certain actions, not merely a weighing of the impact on people on a case-by-case basis. . . .

An ethical theory must operate by generating a set of sympathies and attitudes toward others which reinforces the functioning of . . . moral principles. Our prohibition against killing people operates by means of certain moral sentiments including sympathy, compassion and guilt. But if these attitudes are to form a coherent set, they carry us further; we tend to perform supererogatory actions, and we tend to feel similar compassion toward person-like nonpersons.

It is crucial that psychological facts play a role here. Our psychological constitution makes it the case that for our ethical theory to work, it must prohibit certain treatment of nonpersons which are significantly person-like. If our moral rules allowed people to treat some person-like nonpersons in ways we do not want people to be treated, this would undermine the system of sympathies and attitudes that makes the ethical system work. . . . Thus it makes sense that it is those animals whose appearance and behavior are most like those people that get the most consideration in our moral scheme.

It is because of "coherence of attitudes," I think, that the similarity of a fetus to a baby is very significant. A fetus one week before birth is so much like a newborn baby in our psychological space that we cannot allow any cavalier treatment of the former while expecting full sympathy and nurturative support for the latter. Thus, I think that antiabortion forces are indeed giving their strongest arguments when they point to the similarities between a fetus and a baby, and when they try to evoke our emotional attachment to and sympathy for the fetus. An early horror story from New York about nurses who were expected to alternate between caring for six-week premature infants and disposing of viable 24-week aborted fetuses is just that—a horror story. These beings are so much alike that no one can be asked to draw a distinction and treat them so very differently.

Remember, however, that in the early weeks after conception, a fetus is very much unlike a person. It is hard to develop these feelings for a set of genes which doesn't yet have a head, hands, beating heart, response to touch or the ability to move by itself. Thus it seems to me that the alleged "slippery slope" between conception and birth is not so very slippery. In the early stages of pregnancy, abortion can hardly be compared to murder for psychological reasons, but in the latest stages it is psychologically akin to murder.

Another source of similarity is the bodily continuity between fetus and adult. Bodies play a surprisingly central role in our attitudes toward persons. One has only to think of the philosophical literature on how far physical identity suffices for personal identity or Wittgenstein's remark that the best picture of the human soul is the human body. Even after death, when all agree the body is no longer a person, we will observe elaborate customs of respect for the human body; like people who torture dogs, necrophiliacs are not to be trusted with people.[12] So it is appropriate that we show respect to a fetus as the body continuous with the body of the person. This is a degree of resemblance to persons that animals cannot rival. . . .

Even if a fetus is not a person, abortion is not always permissible, because of the resemblance of a fetus to a person. I agree with Thomson that it would be wrong for a woman who is seven months pregnant to have an abortion just to avoid having to postpone a trip to Europe. In the early months of pregnancy when the fetus hardly resembles a baby at all, then, abortion is permissible whenever it is in the interests of the pregnant woman or her family. The reasons would only need to outweigh the pain and inconvenience of the abortion itself. In the middle months, when the fetus comes to resemble a person, abortion would be justifiable only when the continuation of the pregnancy or the birth of the child would cause harms—physical, psychological, economic or social—to the woman. In the late months of pregnancy, even on our current assumption that a fetus is not a person, abortion seems to be wrong except to save a woman from significant injury or death.

The Supreme Court has recognized similar gradations in the alleged slippery slope stretching between conception and birth. To this point, the present paper has been a discussion of the moral status of abortion only, not its legal status. In view of the great physical, financial and sometimes psychological costs of abortion, perhaps the legal arrangement most compatible with the proposed moral solution would be the absence of restrictions, that is, so-called abortion "on demand."

So I conclude, first, that application of our concept of a person will not suffice to settle the abortion issue. After all, the biological development of a human being is gradual. Second, whether a fetus is a person or not, abortion is justifiable early in pregnancy to avoid modest harms and seldom justifiable late in pregnancy except to avoid significant injury or death.[13]

Notes

1. We also have paternalistic laws which keep us from harming our own bodies even when no one else is affected. Ironically, antiabortion laws were originally designed to protect pregnant women from a dangerous but tempting procedure.
2. Mary Anne Warren, "On the Moral and Legal Status of Abortion," *Monist* 57 (1973), p. 55.
3. Baruch Brody, "Fetal Humanity and the Theory of Essentialism," in Robert Baker and Frederick Elliston, eds., *Philosophy and Sex* (Buffalo, N. Y., 1975).
4. Michael Tolley, "Abortion and Infanticide," *Philosophy and Public Affairs* 2 (1982).
5. Paul Ramsey, "The Morality of Abortion," in James Rachels, ed., *Moral Problems* (New York, 1971).
6. John Noonan, "Abortion and the Catholic Church: A Summary History," *Natural Law Forum* 12 (1967), pp. 125–131.

7. Wittgenstein has argued against the possibility of so capturing the concept of a game, *Philosophical Investigations* (New York, 1958), § 66.
8. Not because the fetus is partly a person and so has some of the rights of persons, but rather because of the rights of person-like nonpersons. This I discuss . . . below.
9. Aristotle himself was concerned, however, with the different question of when the soul takes form. For historical data, see Jimmye Kimmey, "How the Abortion Laws Happened," *Ms.* 1 (April 1973), pp. 48ff, and John Noonan, *loc. cit.*
10. J. J. Thomson, "A Defense of Abortion," *Philosophy and Public Affairs* 1 (1971).
11. *Ibid.,* p. 62.
12. On the other hand, if they can be trusted with people, then our moral customs are mistaken. It all depends on the facts of psychology.
13. I am deeply indebted to Larry Crocker and Arthur Kuflik for their constructive comments.

POSTSCRIPT

Is Abortion Immoral?

Whether or not a fetus can be considered a person is often at the center of the abortion issue. Marquis, however, does not find that a direct approach to this question breaks the deadlock that is characteristic of many discussions of the morality of abortion. Instead he argues that the effect of aborting a fetus, which is the loss of that fetus's future experiences, is the reason why abortion is immoral. Marquis considers this loss of future experiences to be the reason why killing adult human beings is wrong, and he carries the logic over to fetuses.

English also does not consider the question, Is a fetus a person? to be a key one, because, first, even if the fetus is *not* a person, this does not imply that we may do anything to it that we like. Second, even if it *is* a person, this does not mean that abortion may always be ruled out. Not only is the question not decisive, English asserts, but it has no *right* answer. She does not mean that there really is a right answer but we do not know it; she means instead that our concepts (including the concept of a person) do not have clear boundaries. Likewise, we might ask, when does a baby become a child? Again, there is no right answer. The problem is not that babies turn into children without our being able to catch them in the act. There is no right answer because the concepts in our language (such as *baby* and *child*) do not have sharply defined boundaries. Thus, when we ask whether or not a fetus is a person, instead of finding out that it is or is not, we find out that it has some of the features of a person but that it lacks other features.

Judith Jarvis Thomson, in her ground-breaking article "In Defense of Abortion," *Philosophy and Public Affairs* (Fall 1971), argues that, from the premise that the fetus is a person with a right to life, it does not follow that a woman cannot disconnect herself from it and terminate an unwanted pregnancy. Suppose, she says, that you wake up one day to find yourself medically attached to a famous violinist who would die if you detached yourself. A violinist is a person and has a right to life. Does it then follow, asks Thomson, that you may not detach yourself from this unwanted arrangement?

Further readings on this issue are Joel Feinberg, *The Problem of Abortion,* 2d ed. (Wadsworth, 1984); Laurence Tribe, *Abortion: The Clash of Absolutes* (W. W. Norton, 1990); Bonnie Steinbock, *Life Before Birth: The Moral and Legal Status of Embryos and Fetuses* (Oxford University Press, 1992); Frances Myrna Kamm, *Creation and Abortion: An Essay in Moral and Legal Philosophy* (Oxford University Press, 1992); Robert M. Baird and Stuart E. Rosenbaum, eds., *The Ethics of Abortion: Pro-Life vs. Pro-Choice,* 2d ed. (Prometheus Books, 1993); Eva R. Rubin, ed., *The Abortion Controversy: A Documentary History* (Greenwood Press, 1994); Bhavani Sitaraman, *The Middleground: The American Public and the Abortion*

Debate (Garland, 1994); Laurie Shrage, *Moral Dilemmas of Feminism: Prostitution, Adultery, and Abortion* (Routledge, 1994); Ian Shapiro, ed., *Abortion: The Supreme Court Decisions* (Hackett, 1995); Peter Korn, *Lovejoy: A Year in the Life of an Abortion Clinic* (Atlantic Monthly Press, 1996); Patrick Lee, *Abortion and Unborn Human Life* (Catholic University of America Press, 1996); Janet Hadley, *Abortion: Between Freedom and Necessity* (Temple University Press, 1996); Eileen McDonagh, *Breaking the Abortion Deadlock: From Choice to Consent* (Oxford University Press, 1996); Kathy Rudy, *Beyond Pro-Life and Pro-Choice: Moral Diversity in the Abortion Debate* (Beacon Press, 1997); Donald T. Critchlow, ed., *The Politics of Abortion in Historical Perspective* (Pennsylvania State Press, 1996); Katha Pollitt, "Abortion in American History," *The Atlantic Monthly* (May 1997); and Louis Pojman and Francis Beckwith, eds., *The Abortion Controversy: 25 Years After Roe v. Wade: A Reader,* 2d ed. (Wadsworth Publishing Company, 1998).

On RU-486 (sometimes called the "abortion pill"), see Janice G. Raymond, Renate Klein, and Lynette J. Dumble, *RU 486: Myths, Misconceptions, and Morals* (Institute on Women and Technology, 1991), and Lawrence Ladder, *A Private Matter: RU-486 and the Abortion Crisis* (Prometheus Books, 1995).

A CD-ROM on abortion is J. Douglas Butler, ed., *Abortion and Reproductive Rights* (J. Douglas Butler, Inc., 1997).

Recent publications include Lawrence Becker et al., eds., *Encyclopedia of Ethics,* 2d ed. (Routledge, 2002); Edwin C. Hui, *At the Beginning of Life: Dilemmas in Theological Bioethics* (InterVarsity Press, 2002); David Boonin, *A Defense of Abortion* (Cambridge University Press, 2002); and Laurie J. Shrage, *Abortion and Social Responsibility: Depolarizing the Debate* (Oxford University Press, 2003).

ISSUE 4

Must Sex Involve Commitment?

YES: Vincent C. Punzo, from *Reflective Naturalism* (Macmillan, 1969)

NO: Alan H. Goldman, from "Plain Sex," *Philosophy and Public Affairs* (Spring 1977)

ISSUE SUMMARY

YES: Philosopher Vincent C. Punzo maintains that the special intimacy of sex requires a serious commitment that is for the most part not required in other human activities.

NO: Philosopher Alan H. Goldman argues for a view of sex that is completely separate from any cultural or moral ideology that might be attached to it.

For many people, sex and morality are interconnected. Some complain that talk about sex, such as in sex education classes, is worse than worthless—it is downright corrupt—if it is divorced from talk about morality. Yet, with the exception of specialized concepts such as sexual harassment, most contemporary moral philosophers have very little to say about sex. In part, this may be due to the modern idea that many traditional beliefs about sex are steeped in superstitious, prejudiced, or misguided views that are in need of scientific correction.

In the traditional thought of ancient and medieval times, the stage of the world contains a large backdrop that is intended to make sense of the place of humans in the world. Ancient Greek philosophers created metaphysical theories and medieval theologians created religious theories to explain the role and purpose of humankind. According to both ancient and medieval views, humans are different from animals and thought to possess traits beyond the physical, which ground this difference. However, the modern and scientific view is that humans have no special metaphysical or supernatural standing above animals. Humans are simply a part of nature. This is not an attempt to provide another backdrop, but instead an attempt to eliminate all backdrops, so that people can be viewed in a more realistic manner. This view supports the idea that sexual urges are simply a part of our nature.

Consider a different example. Eating habits are also considered to be a part of our nature, but traditionalists would remind us that we have to eat the correct foods from a nutritional standpoint. We have to direct our eating habits with reason—we cannot simply eat whatever we feel like whenever we want to. Traditionalists view eating as something beyond the process of digestion. Sexual intercourse has its own physical processes, and, like eating, also involves more than just the physical. Sex involves the use of self-control and reason.

Modernists may argue that in many ways the analogy with eating fails. In the past, eating habits were only minimally affected by superstitious or false ideas, whereas sexual practices were greatly affected.

What we are left with today are elements of ancient, medieval, and modern thought. When it comes to sex, it is clear that modern scientific views have a contribution to make; but it is not clear whether we can simply do away with all previous ideas about sex.

In the following selections, Vincent C. Punzo argues for the view that sex, since it involves the highest level of human intimacy, must involve commitment. Alan H. Goldman counters that a concept of "plain sex" helps us to understand sex for what it is—something that does not need moral ideas attached to it.

YES

Vincent C. Punzo

Morality and Human Sexuality

If one sees man's moral task as being simply that of not harming anyone, that is if one sees this task in purely negative terms, he will certainly not accept the argument to be presented in the following section. However, if one accepts the notion of the morality of aspiration, if one accepts the view that man's moral task involves the positive attempt to live up to what is best in man, to give reality to what he sees to be the perfection of himself as a human subject, the argument may be acceptable.

Sexuality and the Human Subject

[Previous discussion] has left us with the question as to whether sexual intercourse is a type of activity that is similar to choosing a dinner from a menu. The question is of utmost significance in that one's view of the morality of premarital intercourse seems to depend on the significance that one gives to the sexual encounter in human life. Those such as [John] Wilson and [Eustace] Chesser who see nothing immoral about the premarital character of sexual intercourse seem to see sexual intercourse as being no different from myriad of other purely aesthetic matters. This point is seen in Chesser's questioning of the reason for demanding permanence in the relationship of sexual partners when we do not see such permanence as being important to other human relationships.[1] It is also seen in his asking why we raise a moral issue about premarital coition when two people may engage in it, with the resulting social and psychological consequences being no different than if they had gone to a movie.[2]

Wilson most explicitly makes a case for the view that sexual intercourse does not differ significantly from other human activities. He holds that people think that there is a logical difference between the question "Will you engage in sexual intercourse with me?" and the question, "Will you play tennis with me?" only because they are influenced by the acquisitive character of contemporary society.[3] Granted that the two questions may be identical from the purely formal perspective of logic, the ethician must move beyond this perspective to a consideration of their content. Men and women find themselves involved in many different relationships: for example, as buyer-seller, employer-employee, teacher-student, lawyer-client, and partners or competitors in certain games such as tennis or bridge. Is there any morally significant

From *Reflective Naturalism,* by Vincent C. Punzo, 1969, pp. 193–196, 198–200. Copyright © 1969 by Pearson Education. Reprinted by permission of Pearson Education, Inc., Upper Saddle River, NJ.

difference between these relationships and sexual intercourse? We cannot examine all the possible relationships into which a man and woman can enter, but we will consider the employer-employee relationship in order to get some perspective on the distinctive character of the sexual relationship.

A man pays a woman to act as his secretary. What rights does he have over her in such a situation? The woman agrees to work a certain number of hours during the day taking dictation, typing letters, filing reports, arranging appointments and flight schedules, and greeting clients and competitors. In short, we can say that the man has rights to certain of the woman's services or skills. The use of the word "services" may lead some to conclude that this relationship is not significantly different from the relationship between a prostitute and her client in that the prostitute also offers her "services."

It is true that we sometimes speak euphemistically of a prostitute offering her services to a man for a sum of money, but if we are serious about our quest for the difference between the sexual encounter and other types of human relationships, it is necessary to drop euphemisms and face the issue directly. The man and woman who engage in sexual intercourse are giving their bodies, the most intimate physical expression of themselves, over to the other. Unlike the man who plays tennis with a woman, the man who has sexual relations with her has literally entered her. A man and woman engaging in sexual intercourse have united themselves as intimately and as totally as is physically possible for two human beings. Their union is not simply a union of organs, but is as intimate and as total a physical union of two selves as is possible of achievement. Granted the character of this union, it seems strange to imply that there is no need for a man and woman to give any more thought to the question of whether they should engage in sexual intercourse than to the question of whether they should play tennis.

In opposition to Wilson, I think that it is the acquisitive character of our society that has blinded us to the distinction between the two activities. Wilson's and Chesser's positions seem to imply that exactly the same moral considerations ought to apply to a situation in which a housewife is bartering with a butcher for a few pounds of pork chops and the situation in which two human beings are deciding whether sexual intercourse ought to be an ingredient of their relationship. So long as the butcher does not put his thumb on the scale in the weighing process, so long as he is truthful in stating that the meat is actually pork, so long as the woman pays the proper amount with the proper currency, the trade is perfectly moral. Reflecting on sexual intercourse from the same sort of economic perspective, one can say that so long as the sexual partners are truthful in reporting their freedom from contagious venereal diseases and so long as they are truthful in reporting that they are interested in the activity for the mere pleasure of it or to try out their sexual techniques, there is nothing immoral about such activity. That in the one case pork chops are being exchanged for money whereas in the other the decision concerns the most complete and intimate merging of one's self with another makes no difference to the moral evaluation of the respective cases.

It is not surprising that such a reductionistic outlook should pervade our thinking on sexual matters, since in our society sexuality is used to sell everything from shave cream to underarm deodorants, to soap, to mouthwash, to cigarettes, and to automobiles. Sexuality has come to play so large a role in our commercial lives that it is not surprising that our sexuality should itself come to be treated as a commodity governed by the same moral rules that govern any other economic transaction.

Once sexuality is taken out of this commercial framework, once the character of the sexual encounter is faced directly and squarely, we will come to see that Doctor Mary Calderone has brought out the type of questions that ought to be asked by those contemplating the introduction of sexual intercourse into their relationships: "How many times, and how casually, are you willing to invest a portion of your total self, and to be the custodian of a like investment from the other person, without the sureness of knowing that these investments are being made for keeps?"[4] These questions come out of the recognition that the sexual encounter is a definitive experience, one in which the physical intimacy and merging involves also a merging of the nonphysical dimensions of the partners. With these questions, man moves beyond the negative concern with avoiding his or another's physical and psychological harm to the question of what he is making of himself and what he is contributing to the existential formation of his partner as a human subject.

If we are to make a start toward responding to Calderone's questions we must cease talking about human selfhood in abstraction. The human self is an historical as well as a physical being. He is a being who is capable of making at least a portion of his past an object of his consciousness and thus is able to make this past play a conscious role in his present and in his looking toward the future. He is also a being who looks to the future, who faces tomorrow with plans, ideals, hopes, and fears. The very being of a human self involves his past and his movement toward the future. Moreover, the human self is not completely shut off in his own past and future. Men and women are capable of consciously and purposively uniting themselves in a common career and venture. They can commit themselves to sharing the future with another, sharing it in all its aspects—in its fortunes and misfortunes, in its times of happiness and times of tragedy. Within the lives of those who have so committed themselves to each other, sexual intercourse is a way of asserting and confirming the fullness and totality of their mutual commitment.

Unlike those who have made such a commitment and who come together in the sexual act in the fullness of their selfhood, those who engage in premarital sexual unions and who have made no such commitment act as though they can amputate their bodily existence and the most intimate physical expression of their selfhood from their existence as historical beings. Granting that there may be honesty on the verbal level in that two people engaging in premarital intercourse openly state that they are interested only in the pleasure of the activity, the fact remains that such unions are morally deficient because they lack existential integrity in that there is a total merging and union on a physical level, on the one hand, and a conscious decision not to unite any other dimension of themselves, on the other hand. Their sexual union thus involves a "depersonalization" of their bodily existence, an attempt to cut off the most intimate physical expression of their respective selves from their very selfhood. The mutual agreement of premarital sex partners is an agreement to merge with the other not as a self, but as a body which one takes unto oneself, which one possesses in a most intimate and total fashion for one's own pleasure or designs, allowing the other to treat oneself in the same way. It may be true that no physical or psychological harm may result from such unions, but such partners have failed to existentially incorporate human sexuality, which is at the very least the most intimate physical expression of the human self, into the character of this selfhood.

In so far as premarital sexual unions separate the intimate and total physical union that is sexual intercourse from any commitment to the self in his historicity, human sexuality, and consequently the human body, have been fashioned into external things or objects to be handed over totally to someone else, whenever one feels that he can get possession of another's body, which he can use for his own purposes.[5] The human body has thus been treated no differently from the pork chops spoken of previously or from any other object or commodity, which human beings exchange and haggle over in their day-to-day transactions. One hesitates to use the word that might be used to capture the moral value that has been sacrificed in premarital unions because in our day the word has taken on a completely negative meaning at best, and, at worst, it has become a word used by "sophisticates" to mock or deride certain attitudes toward human sexuality. However, because the word "chastity" has been thus abused is no reason to leave it in the hands of those who have misrepresented the human value to which it gives expression.

The chaste person has often been described as one intent on denying his sexuality. The value of chastity as conceived in this section is in direct opposition to this description. It is the unchaste person who is separating himself from his sexuality, who is willing to exchange human bodies as one would exchange money for tickets to a baseball game—honestly and with no commitment of self to self. Against this alienation of one's sexuality from one's self, an alienation that makes one's sexuality an object, which is to be given to another in exchange for his objectified sexuality, chastity affirms the integrity of the self in his bodily and historical existence. The sexuality of man is seen as an integral part of his subjectivity. Hence, the chaste man rejects depersonalized sexual relations as a reduction of man in his most intimate physical being to the status of an object or pure instrument for another. He asserts that man is a subject and end in himself, not in some trans-temporal, nonphysical world, but in the historical-physical world in which he carries on his moral task and where he finds his fellow man. He will not freely make of himself in his bodily existence a thing to be handed over to another's possession, nor will he ask that another treat his own body in this way. The total physical intimacy of sexual intercourse will be an expression of total union with the other self on all levels of their beings. Seen from this perspective, chastity is one aspect of man's attempt to attain existential integrity, to accept his body as a dimension of his total personality.

In concluding this section, it should be noted that I have tried to make a case against the morality of premarital sexual intercourse even in those cases in which the partners are completely honest with each other. There is reason to question whether the complete honesty, to which those who see nothing immoral in such unions refer, is as a matter of fact actually found very often among premarital sex partners. We may well have been dealing with textbook cases which present these unions in their best light. One may be pardoned for wondering whether sexual intercourse often occurs under the following conditions: "Hello, my name is Josiah. I am interested in having a sexual experience with you. I can assure you that I am good at it and that I have no communicable disease. If it sounds good to you and if you have taken the proper contraceptive precautions, we might have a go at it. Of course, I want to make it clear to you that I am interested only in the sexual experience and that I have no intention of making any long-range commitment to you." If those, who defend the morality of premarital sexual unions so long as they are honestly entered into, think that I have misrepresented what they mean by honesty, then they must specify what they mean by an honest premarital union. . . .

Marriage as a Total Human Commitment

The preceding argument against the morality of premarital sexual unions was not based on the view that the moral character of marriage rests on a legal certificate or on a legal or religious ceremony. The argument was not directed against "preceremonial" intercourse, but against premarital intercourse. Morally speaking, a man and woman are married when they make the mutual and total commitment to share the problems and prospects of their historical existence in the world. Although marriages are not to be identified with ceremonies, the words used in marriage ceremonies have captured the character of marriage in the promise which the partners make to each other to join their lives "for better, for worse, for richer, for poorer, in sickness and in health, till death do us part."

. . . The commitment that constitutes marriage is a total commitment of one person to another person of the opposite sex. To understand the character of such commitment, it is necessary to know something about the being of those involved in the commitment; for if it is to be truly total, the commitment must be as rich as the being of those who have made it. It is at this point that the historical character of the human self's existence becomes important. A total commitment to another means a commitment to him in his historical existence. Such a commitment is not simply a matter of words or of feelings, however strong. It involves a full existential sharing on the part of two beings of the burdens, opportunities, and challenges of their historical existence.

Granted the importance that the character of their commitment to each other plays in determining the moral quality of a couple's sexual encounter, it is clear that there may be nothing immoral in the behavior of couples who engage in sexual intercourse before participating in the marriage ceremony. For example, it is foolish to say that two people who are totally committed to each other and who have made all the arrangements to live this commitment are immoral if they engage in sexual intercourse the night before the marriage ceremony. Admittedly this position can be abused by those who have made a purely verbal commitment, a commitment which will be carried out in some vague and ill-defined future. At some time or other, they will unite their two lives totally by setting up house together and by actually undertaking the task of meeting the economic, social, legal, medical responsibilities that are involved in living this commitment. Apart from the reference to a vague and amorphous future time when they will share the full responsibility for each other, their commitment presently realizes itself in going to dances, sharing a box of popcorn at Saturday night movies, and sharing their bodies whenever they can do so without taking too great a risk of having the girl become pregnant.

Having acknowledged that the position advanced in this section can be abused by those who would use the word "commitment" to rationalize what is an interest only in the body of the other person, it must be pointed out that neither the ethician nor any other human being can tell two people whether they actually have made the commitment that is marriage or are mistaking a "warm glow" for such a commitment. There comes a time when this issue falls out of the area of moral philosophy and into the area of practical wisdom. . . .

The characterization of marriage as a total commitment between two human beings may lead some to conclude that the marriage ceremony is a wholly superfluous affair. It must be admitted that people may be morally married without having engaged in a marriage ceremony. However, to conclude from this point that the ceremony is totally meaningless is to lose sight of the social character of human beings. The couple contemplating marriage do not exist in a vacuum, although there may be times when they think they do. Their existences reach out beyond their union to include other human beings. By making their commitment a matter of public record, by solemnly expressing it before the law and in the presence of their respective families and friends and, if they are religious people, in the presence of God and one of his ministers, they sink the roots of their commitment more deeply and extensively in the world in which they live, thus taking steps to provide for the future growth of their commitment to each other. The public expression of this commitment makes it more fully and more explicitly a part of a couple's lives and of the world in which they live.

Notes

1. Eustace Chesser, *Unmarried Love* (New York: Pocket Books, 1965), p. 29.
2. *Op. cit.,* pp. 35–36; see also p. 66.
3. John Wilson, *Logic and Sexual Morality* (Baltimore, Md.: Penguin Books, 1965), p. 67, note 1.
4. Mary Steichen Calderone, "The Case for Chastity," *Sex in America,* ed. by Henry Anatole Grunwald (New York: Bantam Books, 1964), p. 147.
5. The psychoanalyst Rollo May makes an excellent point in calling attention to the tendency in contemporary society to exploit the human body as if it were only a machine. Rollo May, "The New Puritanism," *Sex in America,* pp. 161–164.

Alan H. Goldman

Plain Sex

Several recent articles on sex herald its acceptance as a legitimate topic for analytic philosophers (although it has been a topic in philosophy since Plato). One might have thought conceptual analysis unnecessary in this area; despite the notorious struggles of judges and legislators to define pornography suitably, we all might be expected to know what sex is and to be able to identify at least paradigm sexual desires and activities without much difficulty. Philosophy is nevertheless of relevance here if for no other reason than that the concept of sex remains at the center of moral and social consciousness in our, and perhaps any, society. Before we can get a sensible view of the relation of sex to morality, . . . social regulation, and marriage, we require a sensible analysis of the concept itself; one which neither understates its animal pleasure nor overstates its importance within a theory or system of value. I say "before," but the order is not quite so clear, for questions in this area, as elsewhere in moral philosophy, are both conceptual and normative at the same time. Our concept of sex will partially determine our moral view of it, but as philosophers we should formulate a concept that will accord with its proper moral status. What we require here, as elsewhere, is "reflective equilibrium," a goal not achieved by traditional and recent analyses together with their moral implications. Because sexual activity, like other natural functions such as eating or exercising, has become imbedded in layers of cultural, moral, and superstitious superstructure, it is hard to conceive it in its simplest terms. But partially for this reason, it is only by thinking about plain sex that we can begin to achieve this conceptual equilibrium.

I shall suggest here that sex continues to be misrepresented in recent writings, at least in philosophical writings, and I shall criticize the predominant form of analysis which I term "means-end analysis." Such conceptions attribute a necessary external goal or purpose to sexual activity, whether it be reproduction, the expression of love, simple communication, or interpersonal awareness. They analyze sexual activity as a means to one of these ends, implying that sexual desire is a desire to reproduce, to love or be loved, or to communicate with others. All definitions of this type suggest false views of the relation of sex to . . . morality by implying that sex which does not fit one of these models or fulfill one of these functions is in some way deviant or incomplete.

From *Philosophy and Public Affairs,* vol. 6, no. 3, Spring 1977, pp. 267–275, 280–281, 283. Copyright © 1977 by Philosophy and Public Affairs Journal. Reprinted by permission of Wiley-Blackwell.

The alternative, simpler analysis with which I will begin is that sexual desire is desire for contact with another person's body and for the pleasure which such contact produces; sexual activity is activity which tends to fulfill such desire of the agent. Whereas Aristotle and [others] were correct in holding that pleasure is normally a byproduct rather than a goal of purposeful action, in the case of sex this is not so clear. The desire for another's body is, principally among other things, the desire for the pleasure that physical contact brings. On the other hand, it is not a desire for a particular sensation detachable from its causal context, a sensation which can be derived in other ways. This definition in terms of the general goal of sexual desire appears preferable to an attempt to more explicitly list or define specific sexual activities, for many activities such as kissing, embracing, massaging, or holding hands may or may not be sexual, depending upon the context and more specifically upon the purposes, needs, or desires into which such activities fit. The generality of the definition also represents a refusal (common in recent psychological texts) to overemphasize orgasm as the goal of sexual desire or genital sex as the only norm of sexual activity. . . .

Central to the definition is the fact that the goal of sexual desire and activity is the physical contact itself, rather than something else which this contact might express. By contrast, what I term "means-end analyses" posit ends which I take to be extraneous to plain sex, and they view sex as a means to these ends. Their fault lies not in defining sex in terms of its general goal, but in seeing plain sex as merely a means to other separable ends. I term these "means-end analyses" for convenience, although "means-separable-end analyses," while too cumbersome, might be more fully explanatory. The desire for physical contact with another person is a minimal criterion for (normal) sexual desire, but is both necessary and sufficient to qualify normal desire as sexual. Of course, we may want to express other feelings through sexual acts in various contexts; but without the desire for the physical contact in and for itself, or when it is sought for other reasons, activities in which contact is involved are not predominantly sexual. Furthermore, the desire for physical contact in itself, without the wish to express affection or other feelings through it, is sufficient to render sexual the activity of the agent which fulfills it. Various activities with this goal alone, such as kissing and caressing in certain contexts, qualify as sexual even without the presence of genital symptoms of sexual excitement. The latter are not therefore necessary criteria for sexual activity. . . .

Our definition of sex in terms of the desire for physical contact may appear too narrow in that a person's personality, not merely her or his body, may be sexually attractive to another, and in that looking or conversing in a certain way can be sexual in a given context without bodily contact. Nevertheless, it is not the contents of one's thoughts per se that are sexually appealing, but one's personality as embodied in certain manners of behavior. Furthermore, if a person is sexually attracted by another's personality, he or she will desire not just further conversation, but actual sexual contact. While looking at or conversing with someone can be interpreted as sexual in given contexts it is so when intended as preliminary to, and hence parasitic upon, elemental sexual interest. Voyeurism or viewing a pornographic movie qualifies as a sexual activity, but only as an imaginative substitute for the real thing (otherwise a deviation from the norm as expressed in our definition). The same is true of masturbation as a sexual activity without a partner.

That the initial definition indicates at least an ingredient of sexual desire and activity is too obvious to argue. We all know what sex is, at least in obvious cases, and do not need philosophers to tell us. My preliminary analysis is meant to serve as a contrast to what sex is not, at least, not necessarily. I concentrate upon the physically manifested desire for another's body, and I take as central the immersion in the physical aspect of one's own existence and attention to the physical embodiment of the other. One may derive pleasure in a sex act from expressing certain feelings to one's partner or from awareness of the attitude of one's partner, but sexual desire is essentially desire for physical contact itself: it is a bodily desire for the body of another that dominates our mental life for more or less brief periods. Traditional writings were correct to emphasize the purely physical or animal aspect of sex; they were wrong only in condemning it. This characterization of sex as an intensely pleasurable physical activity and acute physical desire may seem to some to capture only its barest level. But it is worth distinguishing and focusing upon this least common denominator in order to avoid the false views of sexual morality . . . which emerge from thinking that sex is essentially something else.

One common position views sex as essentially an expression of love or affection between the partners. It is generally recognized that there are other types of love besides sexual, but sex itself is taken as an expression of one type, sometimes termed "romantic" love.[1] Various factors again ought to weaken this identification. First, there are other types of love besides that which it is appropriate to express sexually, and "romantic" love itself can be expressed in many other ways. I am not denying that sex can take on heightened value and meaning when it becomes a vehicle for the expression of feelings of love or tenderness, but so can many other usually mundane activities such as getting up early to make breakfast on Sunday, cleaning the house, and so on. Second, sex itself can be used to communicate many other emotions besides love, and, as I will argue below, can communicate nothing in particular and still be good sex.

On a deeper level, an internal tension is bound to result from an identification of sex, which I have described as a physical-psychological desire, with love as a long-term, deep emotional relationship between two individuals. As this type of relationship, love is permanent, at least in intent, and more or less exclusive. A normal person cannot deeply love more than a few individuals even in a lifetime. We may be suspicious that those who attempt or claim to love many love them weakly if at all. Yet, fleeting sexual desire can arise in relation to a variety of other individuals one finds sexually attractive. It may even be, as some have claimed, that sexual desire in humans naturally seeks variety, while this is obviously false of love. For this reason, monogamous sex, even if justified, almost always represents a sacrifice or the exercise of self-control on the part of the spouses, while monogamous love generally does not. There is no such thing as casual love in the sense in which I intend the term "love." It may occasionally happen that a spouse falls deeply in love with someone else (especially when sex is conceived in terms of love), but this is relatively rare in comparison to passing sexual desires for others; and while the former often indicates a weakness or fault in the marriage relation, the latter does not.

If love is indeed more exclusive in its objects than is sexual desire, this explains why those who view sex as essentially an expression of love would again tend to hold a repressive or restrictive sexual ethic. . . . [T]here may be good reasons for reserving the total commitment of deep love to the context of marriage and family—the normal personality may not withstand additional divisions of ultimate commitment and allegiance. There is no question that marriage itself is best sustained by a deep relation of love and affection; and even if love is not naturally monogamous, the benefits of family units to children provide additional reason to avoid serious commitments elsewhere which weaken family ties. It can be argued similarly that monogamous sex strengthens families by restricting and at the same time guaranteeing an outlet for sexual desire in marriage. But there is more force to the argument that recognition of a clear distinction between sex and love in society would help avoid disastrous marriages which result from adolescent confusion of the two when sexual desire is mistaken for permanent love, and would weaken damaging jealousies which arise in marriages in relation to passing sexual desires. The love and affection of a sound marriage certainly differs from the adolescent romantic variety, which is often a mere substitute for sex in the context of a repressive sexual ethic.

In fact, the restrictive sexual ethic tied to the means-end analysis in terms of love . . . has failed to be consistent. At least, it has not been applied consistently, but forms part of the double standard which has curtailed the freedom of women. The inconsistency in the sexual ethic typically attached to the sex-love analysis, according to which it has generally been taken with a grain of salt when applied to men, is simply another example of the impossibility of tailoring a plausible moral theory in this area to a conception of sex which builds in conceptually extraneous factors.

I am not suggesting here that sex ought never to be connected with love or that it is not a more significant and valuable activity when it is. Nor am I denying that individuals need love as much as sex and perhaps emotionally need at least one complete relationship which encompasses both. Just as sex can express love and take on heightened significance when it does, so love is often naturally accompanied by an intermittent desire for sex. But again love is accompanied appropriately by desires for other shared activities as well. What makes the desire for sex seem more intimately connected with love is the intimacy which is seen to be a natural feature of mutual sex acts. Like love, sex is held to lay one bare psychologically as well as physically. Sex is unquestionably intimate, but beyond that the psychological toll often attached may be a function of the restrictive sexual ethic itself, rather than a legitimate apology for it. The intimacy involved in love is psychologically consuming in a generally healthy way, while the psychological tolls of sexual relations, often including embarrassment as a correlate of intimacy, are too often the result of artificial sexual ethics and taboos. The intimacy involved in both love and sex is insufficient in any case in light of previous points to render a means-end analysis in these terms appropriate.

. . . To the question of what morality might be implied by my analysis, the answer is that there are no moral implications whatever. Any analysis of sex which imputes a moral character to sex acts in themselves is wrong for that reason. There is no morality intrinsic to sex, although general moral rules apply to the treatment of others in sex acts as they apply to all human relations. We can speak of a sexual ethic as we can speak of a business ethic, without implying that business in itself is either moral or immoral or that special rules are required to judge business practices which are not derived from rules that apply elsewhere as well. Sex is not in itself a moral category, although like business it invariably places us into relations with others in which moral rules apply. It gives us opportunity to do what is otherwise recognized as wrong, to harm others, deceive them or manipulate them against their wills. Just as the fact that an act is sexual in itself never renders it wrong or adds to its wrongness if it is wrong on other grounds (sexual acts towards minors are wrong on other grounds, as will be argued below), so no wrong act is to be excused because done from a sexual motive. If a "crime of passion" is to be excused, it would have to be on grounds of temporary insanity rather than sexual context (whether insanity does constitute a legitimate excuse for certain actions is too big a topic to argue here). Sexual motives are among others which may become deranged, and the fact that they are sexual has no bearing in itself on the moral character, whether negative or exculpatory, of the actions deriving from them. Whatever might be true of war, it is certainly not the case that all's fair in love or sex.

Our first conclusion regarding morality and sex is therefore that no conduct otherwise immoral should be excused because it is sexual conduct, and nothing in sex is immoral unless condemned by rules which apply elsewhere as well. The last clause requires further clarification. Sexual conduct can be governed by particular rules relating only to sex itself. But these precepts must be implied by general moral rules when these are applied to specific sexual relations or types of conduct. The same is true of rules of fair business, ethical medicine, or courtesy in driving a car. In the latter case, particular acts on the road may be reprehensible, such as tailgating or passing on the right, which seem to bear no resemblance as actions to any outside the context of highway safety. Nevertheless their immorality derives from the fact that they place others in danger, a circumstance which, when avoidable, is to be condemned in any context. This structure of general and specifically applicable rules describes a reasonable sexual ethic as well. To take an extreme case, rape is always a sexual act and it is always immoral. A rule against rape can therefore be considered an obvious part of sexual morality which has no bearing on nonsexual conduct. But the immorality of rape derives from its being an extreme violation of a person's body, of the right not to be humiliated, and of the general moral prohibition against using other persons against their wills, not from the fact that it is a sexual act.

The application elsewhere of general moral rules to sexual conduct is further complicated by the fact that it will be relative to the particular desires and preferences of one's partner (these may be influenced by and hence in some sense include misguided beliefs about sexual morality itself). This means that there will be fewer specific rules in the area of sexual ethics than in other areas of conduct, such as driving cars, where the relativity of preference is irrelevant to the prohibition of objectively dangerous conduct. More reliance will have to be placed upon the general moral rule, which in this area holds simply that the preferences, desires, and interests of one's partner or potential partner ought to be taken into account. This rule is certainly not specifically formulated to govern sexual relations; it is a form of the central principle of morality itself. But when applied to sex, it prohibits certain actions, such as molestation of children, which cannot be categorized as violations of the rule without at the same time being classified as sexual. I believe this last case is the closest we can come to an action which is wrong *because* it is sexual, but even here its wrongness is better characterized as deriving from the detrimental effects such behavior can have on the future emotional and sexual life of the naive victims, and from the fact that such behavior therefore involves manipulation of innocent persons without regard for their interests. Hence, this case also involves violation of a general moral rule which applies elsewhere as well. . . .

I suggested earlier that in addition to generating confusion regarding the rightness or wrongness of sex acts, false conceptual analyses of the means-end form cause confusion about the value of sex to the individual. My account recognizes the satisfaction of desire and the pleasure this brings as the central psychological function of the sex act for the individual. Sex affords us a paradigm of pleasure, but not a cornerstone of value. For most of us it is not only a needed outlet for desire but also the most enjoyable form of recreation we know. Its value is nevertheless easily mistaken by being confused with that of love, when it is taken as essentially an expression of that emotion. Although intense, the pleasures of sex are brief and repetitive rather than cumulative. They give value to the specific acts which generate them, but not the lasting kind of value which enhances one's whole life. The briefness of these pleasures contributes to their intensity (or perhaps their intensity makes them necessarily brief), but it also relegates them to the periphery of most rational plans for the good life.

By contrast, love typically develops over a long term relation; while its pleasures may be less intense and physical, they are of more cumulative value. The importance of love to the individual may well be central in a rational system of value. And it has perhaps an even deeper moral significance relating to the identification with the interests of another person, which broadens one's possible relationships with others as well. Marriage is again important in preserving this relation between adults and children, which seems as important to the adults as it is to the children in broadening concerns which have a tendency to become selfish. Sexual desire, by contrast, is desire for another which is nevertheless essentially self-regarding. Sexual pleasure is certainly a good for the individual, and for many it may be necessary in order for them to function in a reasonably cheerful way. But it bears little relation to those other values just discussed, to which some analyses falsely suggest a conceptual connection. . . .

The position I have taken in this paper against those concepts is not totally new. Something similar to it is found in Freud's view of sex, which of course was genuinely revolutionary, and in the body of writings deriving from

Freud to the present time. But in his revolt against romanticized and repressive conceptions, Freud went too far—from a refusal to view sex as merely a means to a view of it as the end of all human behavior, although sometimes an elaborately disguised end. This pansexualism led to the thesis (among others) that repression was indeed an inevitable and necessary part of social regulation of any form, a strange consequence of a position that began by opposing the repressive aspects of the means-end view. Perhaps the time finally has arrived when we can achieve a reasonable middle ground in this area, at least in philosophy if not in society.

Note

1. Even Bertrand Russell, whose writing in this area was a model of rationality, at least for its period, tends to make this identification and to condemn plain sex in the absence of love: "sex intercourse apart from love has little value, and is to be regarded primarily as experimentation with a view to love." *Marriage and Morals* (New York: Bantam, 1959), p. 87.

POSTSCRIPT

Must Sex Involve Commitment?

It is clear that Punzo and Goldman differ fundamentally in their approach to sex and commitment. Goldman maintains that a concept of "plain sex" can be used to view sex without cultural and moral ideology. Punzo's approach counters the idea that an important human concept like sex can be separated from ideology.

A further question is whether men and women regard this issue in different ways. Traditionally, there has been a cultural demand that commitment is required before engaging in sex. However, a "double standard" exists that lets men practice sex in the absence of commitment without cultural disapproval. On the other hand, women are more likely to be viewed as "immoral" if they engage in sex without commitment. If the double standard is to be replaced by a unified standard, should this be one that includes commitment?

Sources relevant to this topic include Russell Vannoy, *Sex Without Love: A Philosophical Exploration* (Prometheus Books, 1981); G. Sidney Buchanan, *Morality, Sex and the Constitution: A Christian Perspective on the Power of Government to Regulate Private Sexual Conduct Between Consenting Adults* (University Press of America, 1985); G. Frankson, *Sex and Morality* (Todd & Honeywell, 1987); Joseph Monti, *Arguing About Sex: The Rhetoric of Christian Sexual Morality* (State University of New York Press, 1995); John Marshall Townsend, *What Women Want—What Men Want: Why the Sexes Still See Love and Commitment so Differently* (Oxford University Press, 1998); and J. Gordon Muir, *Sex, Politics, and the End of Morality* (Pentland Press, 1998).

ISSUE 5

Is It Right to Prohibit Same-Sex Marriage?

YES: Jeff Jordan, "Is It Wrong to Discriminate on the Basis of Homosexuality?" *Journal of Social Philosophy,* vol. 26, no. 1 (Spring 1995)

NO: David Boonin, "Same-Sex Marriage and the Argument from Public Disagreement," *Journal of Social Philosophy,* vol. 30, no. 2 (Summer 1999)

ISSUE SUMMARY

YES: Philosopher Jeff Jordan defends the claim that there are situations in which it is morally permissible to discriminate against homosexuals, i.e., to treat homosexuals unfavorably. There is a public dilemma (or a clash of views) concerning the moral status of homosexuality and, unless something of overriding importance—such as human rights—is at stake, the government should refrain from favoring one side by publicly recognizing same-sex marriage.

NO: Philosopher David Boonin argues directly against Jordan that his argument is unsuccessful. He uses Jordan's argument to address some of the questions that seem to lie, unanswered, in the background of this issue: In particular, is it correct that homosexuality is immoral? Do people have a right to marry only certain other people? Is opposition to same-sex marriage comparable to opposition to interracial marriage?

Homosexuality exists in all known human societies, and also among some animals. This, however, has not prevented homosexual behavior from being condemned by virtually all world religions. In some societies, this behavior exists in a hidden, socially unacceptable way; in others, it has been tolerated and even highly esteemed. (The variation here among both existing and historical societies is amazingly wide-ranging.)

Homosexuality is receiving more acceptance in our society. One way this can be seen is in the extension of insurance and other benefits to same-sex "domestic partners." But whereas married heterosexuals can state that they are indeed legally married, homosexual couples generally cannot. The status of homosexual relationships is somewhat unclear as far as the law is concerned. Of course, heterosexuals sometimes have unmarried sexual relationships too—but is that type of relationship the heterosexual counterpart of unmarried homosexual relationships? In a way, it is, but in a way, it isn't. For, at the very least, heterosexual marriage is a recognized possibility, while homosexual marriage is often not. Whereas an unmarried heterosexual relationship is one that could involve marriage, an unmarried homosexual relationship generally cannot. As it is, only a few states recognize same-sex marriage, while several states have specifically ruled it out. There is a great social divide here.

For us, one question that may lie behind issues of same-sex marriage is whether or not homosexuality is immoral. If it is, then it is hard to see why society should support same-sex marriage. Many arguments do aim to show that homosexuality is indeed immoral, but this is much more difficult to demonstrate than many people suppose. Part of the problem is that heterosexuals often know very little about homosexuality and rely upon stereotypical thinking or feelings rather than on facts and logic. But if a successful argument could be made here, then any ground for same-sex marriage would be destroyed.

One argument that is sometimes made does not directly address the morality of homosexuality, but raises practical problems such as the spread of AIDS. Same-sex marriage, however, would probably decrease the spread of AIDS, as homosexuals would presumably indulge in less promiscuous sexual behavior and would tend to become involved in much more stable relationships.

But opponents of same-sex marriage often worry about where (and how) we are to draw the line between two-person same-sex marriage and other forms of marriage such as polygamous marriage. One idea is that we have here a kind of "slippery slope" argument to the effect that if same-sex marriage is allowed, then there is nothing to keep us from sliding farther down this slippery slope and allowing such things as polygamous marriage, incestuous marriage, and so on—at least if this is what the parties to the marriage want. This form of argument depends on just how slippery the slope is. Here, one must face the question: Is it really true that there will be no principled place to stop and draw the line? Won't society be able to articulate some relevant principles? Opponents to same-sex marriage would agree that there are indeed principled lines to be drawn—but would say that on one side of the line we have heterosexual marriages and on the other we have everything else.

In the following selection, Jeff Jordan makes the case that society should prohibit same-sex marriage. The argument is not particularly religiously based, but it does acknowledge that the major monotheistic religions have traditionally prohibited same-sex marriages. David Boonin then takes issue with the argument of Jordan, and examines his conclusion, his premises, and some of the background considerations that do not seem to be explicitly mentioned. One positive feature of both authors is that they deal with the issue in a careful and logical way rather than emotionally.

YES

Jeff Jordan

Is It Wrong to Discriminate on the Basis of Homosexuality?

Much like the issue of abortion in the early 1970s, the issue of homosexuality has exploded to the forefront of social discussion. Is homosexual sex on a moral par with heterosexual sex? Or is homosexuality in some way morally inferior? Is it wrong to discriminate against homosexuals—to treat homosexuals in less favorable ways than one does heterosexuals? Or is some discrimination against homosexuals morally justified? These questions are the focus of this essay.

In what follows, I argue that there are situations in which it is morally permissible to discriminate against homosexuals because of their homosexuality. That is, there are some morally relevant differences between heterosexuality and homosexuality which, in some instances, permit a difference in treatment. The issue of marriage provides a good example. While it is clear that heterosexual unions merit the state recognition known as marriage, along with all the attendant advantages—spousal insurance coverage, inheritance rights, ready eligibility of adoption—it is far from clear that homosexual couples ought to be accorded that state recognition.

The argument of this essay makes no claim about the moral status of homosexuality per se. Briefly put, it is the argument of this essay that the moral impasse generated by conflicting views concerning homosexuality, and the public policy ramifications of those conflicting views justify the claim that it is morally permissible, in certain circumstances, to discriminate against homosexuals.[1]

1. The Issue

The relevant issue is this: does homosexuality have the same moral status as heterosexuality? Put differently, since there are no occasions in which it is morally permissible to treat heterosexuals unfavorably, whether because they are heterosexual or because of heterosexual acts, are there occasions in which it is morally permissible to treat homosexuals unfavorably, whether because they are homosexuals or because of homosexual acts?

A negative answer to the above can be termed the "parity thesis." The parity thesis contends that *homosexuality has the same moral status as*

From *Journal of Social Philosophy,* vol. 26, no. 1, Spring 1995, pp. 39–52 (excerpts). Copyright © 1995 by Journal of Social Philosophy. Reprinted by permission of Wiley-Blackwell.

heterosexuality. If the parity thesis is correct, then it would be immoral to discriminate against homosexuals because of their homosexuality. An affirmative answer can be termed the "difference thesis" and contends that there are morally relevant differences between heterosexuality and homosexuality which justify a difference in moral status and treatment between homosexuals and heterosexuals. The difference thesis entails that *there are situations in which it is morally permissible to discriminate against homosexuals. . . .*

A word should be said about the notion of discrimination. To discriminate against X means treating X in an unfavorable way. The word "discrimination" is not a synonym for "morally unjustifiable treatment." Some discrimination is morally unjustifiable; some is not. For example, we discriminate against convicted felons in that they are disenfranchised. This legal discrimination is morally permissible even though it involves treating one person unfavorably different from how other persons are treated. The difference thesis entails that there are circumstances in which it is morally permissible to discriminate against homosexuals.

2. An Argument for the Parity Thesis

One might suppose that an appeal to a moral right, the right to privacy, perhaps, or the right to liberty, would provide the strongest grounds for the parity thesis. Rights talk, though sometimes helpful, is not very helpful here. If there is reason to think that the right to privacy or the right to liberty encompasses sexuality (which seems plausible enough), it would do so only with regard to private acts and not public acts. Sexual acts performed in public (whether heterosexual or homosexual) are properly suppressible. It does not take too much imagination to see that the right to be free from offense would soon be offered as a counter consideration by those who find homosexuality morally problematic. Furthermore, how one adjudicates between the competing rights claims is far from clear. Hence, the bald appeal to a right will not, in this case anyway, take one very far.

Perhaps the strongest reason to hold that the parity thesis is true is something like the following:

1. Homosexual acts between consenting adults harm no one. And,
2. respecting persons' privacy and choices in harmless sexual matters maximizes individual freedom. And,
3. individual freedom should be maximized. But,
4. discrimination against homosexuals, because of their homosexuality, diminishes individual freedom since it ignores personal choice and privacy. So,
5. the toleration of homosexuality rather than discriminating against homosexuals is the preferable option since it would maximize individual freedom. Therefore,
6. the parity thesis is more plausible than the difference thesis.

Premise (2) is unimpeachable: if an act is harmless and if there are persons who want to do it and who choose to do it, then it seems clear that respecting the choices of those people would tend to maximize their freedom.[2] Step (3) is also beyond reproach: since freedom is arguably a great good and since there does not appear to be any ceiling on the amount of individual freedom—no "too much of a good thing"—(3) appears to be true.

At first glance, premise (1) seems true enough as long as we recognize that if there is any harm involved in the homosexual acts of consenting adults, it would be harm absorbed by the freely consenting participants. This is true, however, only if the acts in question are done in private. Public acts may involve more than just the willing participants. Persons who have no desire to participate, even if only as spectators, may have no choice if the acts are done in public. A real probability of there being unwilling participants is indicative of the public realm and not the private. However, where one draws the line between private acts and public acts is not always easy to discern, it is clear that different moral standards apply to public acts than to private acts.[3]

If premise (1) is understood to apply only to acts done in private, then it would appear to be true. The same goes for (4): discrimination against homosexuals for acts done in private would result in a diminishing of freedom. So (1)–(4) would lend support to (5) only if we understand (1)–(4) to refer to acts done in private. Hence, (5) must be understood as referring to private acts; and, as a consequence, (6) also must be read as referring only to acts done in private.

With regard to acts which involve only willing adult participants, there may be no morally relevant difference between homosexuality and heterosexuality. In other words, acts done in private. However, acts done in public add a new ingredient to the mix; an ingredient which has moral consequence. Consequently, the argument (1)–(6) fails in supporting the parity thesis. The argument (1)–(6) may show that there are some circumstances in which the moral status of homosexuality and heterosexuality are the same, but it gives us no reason for thinking that this result holds for all circumstances.[4]

3. Moral Impasses and Public Dilemmas

Suppose one person believes that X is morally wrong, while another believes that X is morally permissible. The two people, let's stipulate, are not involved in a semantical quibble; they hold genuinely conflicting beliefs regarding the moral status of X. If the first person is correct, then the second person is wrong; and, of course, if the second person is right, then the first must be wrong. This situation of conflicting claims is what we will call an "impasse." Impasses arise out of moral disputes. Since the conflicting parties in an impasse take contrary views, the conflicting views cannot all be true, nor can they all be false.[5] Moral impasses may concern matters only of a personal nature, but moral impasses can involve public policy. An impasse is likely to have public policy ramifications if large numbers of people hold the conflicting views, and the conflict involves matters which are fundamental to a person's moral identity (and, hence, from a practical point of view, are probably irresolvable) and it involves acts done in public. Since not every impasse has public policy ramifications, one can mark off "public dilemma" as a special case of moral impasses: those moral impasses that have public policy consequences. Public dilemmas, then, are impasses located in the public square. Since they have public policy ramifications and since they arise from impasses, one side or another of the dispute will have its views implemented as public policy. Because of the public policy ramifications, and also because social order is sometimes threatened by the volatile parties involved in the impasse, the state has a role to play in resolving a public dilemma.

A public dilemma can be actively resolved in two ways.[6] The first is when the government allies itself with one side of the impasse and, by state coercion and sanction, declares that side of the impasse the correct side. The American Civil War was an example of this: the federal government forcibly ended slavery by aligning itself with the Abolitionist side of the impasse.[7] Prohibition is another example. The 18th Amendment and the Volstead Act allied the state with the Temperance side of the impasse. State mandated affirmative action programs provide a modern example of this. This kind of resolution of a public dilemma we can call a "resolution by declaration." The first of the examples cited above indicates that declarations can be morally proper, the right thing to do. The second example, however, indicates that declarations are not always morally proper. The state does not always take the side of the morally correct; nor is it always clear which side is the correct one.

The second way of actively resolving a public dilemma is that of accommodation. An accommodation in this context means resolving the public dilemma in a way that gives as much as possible to all sides of the impasse. A resolution by accommodation involves staking out some middle ground in a dispute and placing public policy in that location. The middle ground location of a resolution via accommodation is a virtue since it entails that there are no absolute victors and no absolute losers. The middle ground is reached in order to resolve the public dilemma in a way which respects the relevant views of the conflicting parties and which maintains social order. The Federal Fair Housing Act and, perhaps, the current status of abortion (legal but with restrictions) provide examples of actual resolutions via accommodation.[8]

In general, governments should be, at least as far as possible, neutral with regard to the disputing parties in a public dilemma. Unless there is some overriding reason why the state should take sides in a public dilemma—the protection of innocent life, or abolishing slavery, for instance—the state should be neutral, because no matter which side of the public dilemma the state takes, the other side will be the recipient of unequal treatment by the state. A state which is partial and takes sides in moral disputes via declaration, when there is no overriding reason why it should, is tyrannical. Overriding reasons involve, typically, the protection of generally recognized rights.[9] In the case of slavery, the right to liberty; in the case of protecting innocent life, the right involved is the negative right to life. If a public dilemma must be actively resolved, the state should do so (in the absence of an overriding reason) via accommodation and not declaration since the latter entails that a sizable number of people would be forced to live under a government which "legitimizes" and does not just tolerate activities which they find immoral. Resolution via declaration is appropriate only if there is an overriding reason for the state to throw its weight behind one side in a public dilemma.

Is moral rightness an overriding reason for a resolution via declaration? What better reason might there be for a resolution by declaration than that it is the right thing to do? Unless one is prepared to endorse a view that is called "legal moralism"—that immorality alone is a sufficient reason for the state to curtail individual liberty—then one had best hold that moral rightness alone is not an overriding reason. Since some immoral acts neither harm nor offend nor violate another's rights, it seems clear enough that too much liberty would be lost if legal moralism were adopted as public policy.[10] . . .

4. Conflicting Claims on Homosexuality

The theistic tradition, Judaism and Christianity and Islam, has a clear and deeply entrenched position on homosexual acts: they are prohibited. Now it seems clear enough that if one is going to take seriously the authoritative texts of the respective religions, then one will have to adopt the views of those texts, unless one wishes to engage in a demythologizing of them with the result that one ends up being only a nominal adherent of that tradition.[11] As a consequence, many contemporary theistic adherents of the theistic tradition, in no small part because they can read, hold that homosexual behavior is sinful. Though God loves the homosexual, these folk say, God hates the sinful behavior. To say that act X is a sin entails that X is morally wrong, not necessarily because it is harmful or offensive, but because X violates God's will. So, the claim that homosexuality is sinful entails the claim that it is also morally wrong. And, it is clear, many people adopt the difference thesis just because of their religious views: because the Bible or the Koran holds that homosexuality is wrong, they too hold that view.

Well, what should we make of these observations? We do not, for one thing, have to base our moral conclusions on those views, if for no other reason than not every one is a theist. If one does not adopt the religion-based moral view, one must still respect those who do; they cannot just be dismissed out of hand.[12] And, significantly, this situation yields a reason for thinking that the difference thesis is probably true. Because many religious people sincerely believe homosexual acts to be morally wrong and many others believe that homosexual acts are not morally wrong, there results a public dilemma.[13]

The existence of this public dilemma gives us reason for thinking that the difference thesis is true. It is only via the difference thesis and not the parity thesis, that an accommodation can be reached. Here again, the private/public distinction will come into play.

To see this, take as an example the issue of homosexual marriages. A same-sex marriage would be a public matter. For the government to sanction same-sex marriages—to grant the recognition and reciprocal benefits which attach to marriage—would ally the government with one side of the public dilemma and against the adherents of religion-based moralities. . . .

Of course, some would respond here that by not sanctioning same-sex marriages the state is, and historically has been, taking sides to the detriment of homosexuals. There is some truth in this claim. But one must be careful here. The respective resolutions of this issue—whether the state should recognize and sanction same-sex marriages—do not have symmetrical implications. The asymmetry of this issue is a function of the private/public distinction and the fact that marriage is a public matter. If the state sanctions same-sex marriages, then there is no accommodation available. In that event, the religion-based morality proponents are faced with a public, state sanctioned matter which they find seriously immoral. This would be an example of a resolution via declaration. On the other hand, if the state does not sanction same-sex marriages, there is an accommodation available: in the public realm the state sides with the religion-based moral view, but the state can tolerate private homosexual acts. That is, since homosexual acts are not essentially public acts; they can be, and historically have been, performed in private. The state, by not sanctioning same-sex marriages is acting in the public realm, but it can leave the private realm to personal choice.[14]

5. The Argument From Conflicting Claims

It was suggested in the previous section that the public dilemma concerning homosexuality, and in particular whether states should sanction same-sex marriages, generates an argument in support of the difference thesis. The argument, again using same-sex marriages as the particular case, is as follows:

7. There are conflicting claims regarding whether the state should sanction same-sex marriages. And,
8. this controversy constitutes a public dilemma. And,
9. there is an accommodation possible if the state does not recognize same-sex marriages. And,
10. there is no accommodation possible if the state does sanction same-sex marriages. And,
11. there is no overriding reason for a resolution via declaration. Hence,
12. the state ought not sanction same-sex marriages. And,
13. the state ought to sanction heterosexual marriages. So,
14. there is at least one morally relevant case in which discrimination against homosexuals, because of their homosexuality, is morally permissible. Therefore,
15. the difference thesis is true.

Since proposition (14) is logically equivalent to the difference thesis, then, if (7)–(14) are sound, proposition (15) certainly follows.

Premises (7) and (8) are uncontroversial. Premises (9) and (10) are based on the asymmetry that results from the public nature of marriage. Proposition (11) is based on our earlier analysis of the argument (1)–(6). Since the strongest argument in support of the parity thesis fails, we have reason to think that there is no overriding reason why the state ought to resolve the public dilemma via declaration in favor of same-sex marriages. We have reason, in other words, to think that (11) is true.

Proposition (12) is based on the conjunction of (7)–(11) and the principle that, in the absence of an overriding reason for state intervention via declaration, resolution by accommodation is the preferable route. Proposition (13) is just trivially true. So, given the moral difference mentioned in (12) and (13), proposition (14) logically follows.

6. Two Objections Considered

The first objection to the argument from conflicting claims would contend that it is unsound because a similar sort of argument would permit discrimination against some practice which, though perhaps controversial at some earlier time, is now widely thought to be morally permissible. Take mixed-race marriages, for example. The opponent of the argument from conflicting claims could argue that a similar argument would warrant prohibition against mixed-race marriages. If it does, we would have good reason to reject (7)–(14) as unsound.

There are three responses to this objection. The first response denies that the issue of mixed-race marriages is in fact a public dilemma. It may have been so at one time, but it does not seem to generate much, if any, controversy today. Hence, the objection is based upon a faulty analogy.

The second response grants for the sake of the argument that the issue of mixed-race marriages generates a public dilemma. But the second response points out that there is a relevant difference between mixed-race marriages and same-sex marriages that allows for a resolution by declaration in the one case but not the other. As evident from the earlier analysis of the argument in support of (1)–(6), there is reason to think that there is no overriding reason for a resolution by declaration in support of the parity thesis. On the other hand, it is a settled matter that state protection from racial discrimination is a reason sufficient for a resolution via declaration. Hence, the two cases are only apparently similar, and, in reality, they are crucially different. They are quite different because, clearly enough, if mixed-race marriages do generate a public dilemma, the state should use resolution by declaration in support of such marriages. The same cannot be said for same-sex marriages. . . .

The third response to the first objection is that the grounds of objection differ in the respective cases: one concerns racial identity; the other concerns behavior thought to be morally problematic. A same-sex marriage would involve behavior which many people find morally objectionable; a mixed-race marriage is objectionable to some, not because of the participants' behavior, but because of the racial identity of the participants. It is the race of the marriage partners which some find of primary complaint concerning mixed-race marriages. With same-sex marriages, however, it is the behavior which is primarily objectionable. To see this latter point, one should note that, though promiscuously Puritan in tone, the kind of sexual acts that are likely involved in a same-sex marriage are objectionable to some, regardless of whether done by homosexuals or heterosexuals.[15] So again, there is reason to reject the analogy between same-sex marriages and mixed-race marriages. Racial identity is an immutable trait and a complaint about mixed-race marriages necessarily involves, then, a complaint about an immutable trait. Sexual behavior is not an immutable trait and it is possible to object to same-sex marriages based on the behavior which would be involved in such marriages. Put succinctly, the third response could be formulated as follows: objections to mixed-race marriages necessarily involve objections over status, while objections to same-sex marriages could involve objections over behavior. Therefore, the two cases are not analogues. . . .

The second objection to the argument from conflicting claims can be stated so: if homosexuality is biologically based—if it is inborn[16]—then how can discrimination ever be justified? If it is not a matter of choice, homosexuality is an immutable trait which is, as a consequence, morally permissible. Just as it would be absurd to hold someone morally culpable for being of a certain race, likewise it would be absurd to hold someone morally culpable for being a homosexual. Consequently, according to this objection, the argument from conflicting claims "legitimizes" unjustifiable discrimination.

But this second objection is not cogent, primarily because it ignores an important distinction. No one could plausibly hold that homosexuals act by some sort of biological compulsion. If there is a biological component involved in sexual identity, it would incline but it would not compel. Just because one naturally (without any choice) has certain dispositions, is not in itself a morally cogent reason for acting upon that disposition. Most people are naturally selfish, but it clearly does not follow that selfishness is in any way permissible on that account. Even if it is true that one has a predisposition to do X as a matter of biology and not as a matter of choice, it does not follow that doing X is morally permissible. For example, suppose that pyromania is an inborn predisposition. Just because one has an inborn and, in that sense, natural desire to set fires, one still has to decide whether or not to act on that desire.[17] The reason that the appeal to biology is specious is that it ignores the important distinction between being a homosexual and homosexual acts. One is status; the other is behavior. Even if one has the status naturally, it does not follow that the behavior is morally permissible, nor that others have a duty to tolerate the behavior.

But, while moral permissibility does not necessarily follow if homosexuality should turn out to be biologically based, what does follow is this: in the absence of a good reason to discriminate between homosexuals and heterosexuals, then, assuming that homosexuality is inborn, one ought not discriminate between them. . . . The argument from conflicting claims, however, provides a good reason which overrides this presumption.

7. A Second Argument for the Difference Thesis

A second argument for the difference thesis, similar to the argument from conflicting claims, is what might be called the "no-exit argument." This argument is based on the principle that:

> A. no just government can coerce a citizen into violating a deeply held moral belief or religious belief.

Is (A) plausible? It seems to be since the prospect of a citizen being coerced by the state into a practice which she finds profoundly immoral appears to be a clear example of an injustice. Principle (A), conjoined with there being a public dilemma arising over the issue of same-sex marriages, leads to the observation that if the state were to sanction same-sex marriages, then persons who have profound religious or moral objections to such unions would be legally mandated to violate their beliefs since there does not appear to be any feasible "exit right" possible with regard to state sanctioned marriage. An exit right is an exemption from some legally mandated practice, granted to a person or group, the purpose of which is to protect the religious or moral integrity of that person or group. Prominent examples of exit rights include conscientious objection and military service, home-schooling of the young because of some religious concern, and property used for religious purposes being free from taxation.

It is important to note that marriage is a public matter in the sense that, for instance, if one is an employer who provides health care benefits to the spouses of employees, one must provide those benefits to any employee who is married. Since there is no exit right possible in this case, one would be coerced, by force of law, into subsidizing a practice one finds morally or religiously objectionable.[18]

In the absence of an exit right, and if (A) is plausible, then the state cannot morally force persons to violate deeply held beliefs that are moral or religious in nature. In particular, the state morally could not sanction same-sex marriages since this would result in coercing some into violating a deeply held religious conviction.

8. A Conclusion

It is important to note that neither the argument from conflicting claims nor the no-exit argument licenses wholesale discrimination against homosexuals. What they do show is that some discrimination against homosexuals, in this case refusal to sanction same-sex marriages, is not only legally permissible but also morally permissible. The discrimination is a way of resolving a public policy dilemma that accommodates, to an extent, each side of the impasse and, further, protects the religious and moral integrity of a good number of people. In short, the arguments show us that there are occasions in which it is morally permissible to discriminate on the basis of homosexuality.[19]

Notes

1. The terms "homosexuality" and "heterosexuality" are defined as follows. The former is defined as sexual feelings or behavior directed toward individuals of the same sex. The latter, naturally enough, is defined as sexual feelings or behavior directed toward individuals of the opposite sex.

   Sometimes the term "gay" is offered as an alternative to "homosexual." Ordinary use of "gay" has it as a synonym of a male homosexual (hence, the common expression, "gays and lesbians"). Given this ordinary usage, the substitution would lead to a confusing equivocation. Since there are female homosexuals, it is best to use "homosexual" to refer to both male and female homosexuals, and reserve "gay" to signify male homosexuals, and "lesbian" for female homosexuals in order to avoid the equivocation.

2. This would be true even if the act in question is immoral.
3. The standard answer is, of course, that the line between public and private is based on the notion of harm. Acts which carry a real probability of harming third parties are public acts.
4. For other arguments supporting the moral parity of homosexuality and heterosexuality, see Richard Mohr, *Gays/Justice: A Study of Ethics, Society and Law* (NY: Columbia, 1988); and see Michael Ruse, "The Morality of Homosexuality" in *Philosophy and Sex,* eds. R. Baker & F. Elliston (Buffalo, NY: Prometheus Books, 1984), pp. 370–390.
5. Perhaps it would be better to term the disputing positions "contradictory" views rather than "contrary" views.
6. Resolutions can also be passive in the sense of the state doing nothing. If the state does nothing to resolve the public dilemma, it stands pat with the status quo, and the public dilemma is resolved gradually by sociological changes (changes in mores and in beliefs).
7. Assuming, plausibly enough, that the disputes over the sovereignty of the Union and concerning states' rights were at bottom disputes about slavery.
8. The Federal Fair Housing Act prohibits discrimination in housing on the basis of race, religion, and sex. But it does not apply to the rental of rooms in single-family houses, or to a building of five units or less if the owner lives in one of the units. See 42 U.S.C. Section 3603.
9. Note that overriding reasons involve *generally recognized* rights. If a right is not widely recognized and the state nonetheless uses coercion to enforce it, there is a considerable risk that the state will be seen by many or even most people as tyrannical.
10. This claim is, perhaps, controversial. For a contrary view see Richard George, *Making Men Moral* (Oxford: Clarendon Press, 1993).
11. See, for example, Leviticus 18:22,21:3; and Romans 1:22–32; and Koran IV:13
12. For an argument that religiously-based moral views should not be dismissed out of hand, see Stephen Carter, *The Culture of Disbelief: How American Law and Politics Trivialize Religious Devotion* (NY: Basic Books, 1993).
13. Two assumptions are these: that the prohibitions against homosexuality activity are part of the religious doctrine and not just an extraneous addition; second, that if X is part of one's religious belief or religious doctrine, then it is morally permissible to hold X. Though this latter principle is vague, it is, I think, clear enough for our purposes here (I ignore here any points concerning the rationality of religious belief in general, or in particular cases).
14. This point has implications for the moral legitimacy of sodomy laws. One implication would be this: the private acts of consenting adults should not be criminalized.
15. Think of the sodomy laws found in some states which criminalize certain sexual acts, whether performed by heterosexuals or homosexuals.
16. There is some interesting recent research which, though still tentative, strongly suggests that homosexuality is, at least in part, biologically based.

See Simon LeVay, *The Sexual Brain* (Cambridge, MA: MIT Press, 1993), pp. 120–122; and J.M. Bailey & R.C. Pillard "A Genetic Study of Male Sexual Orientation" *Archives of General Psychiatry* 48 (1991): 1089–1096; and C. Burr, "Homosexuality and Biology" *The Atlantic* 271/3 (March, 1993): 64; and D. Hamer, S. Hu, V. Magnuson, N. Hu, A. Pattatucci, "A Linkage Between DNA Markers on the X Chromosome and Male Sexual Orientation" *Science* 261 (16 July 1993): 321–327; and see the summary of this article by Robert Pool, "Evidence for Homosexuality Gene" *Science* 261 (16 July 1993): 291–292.

17. I do not mean to suggest that homosexuality is morally equivalent or even comparable to pyromania.
18. Is the use of subsidy here inappropriate? It does not seem so since providing health care to spouses, in a society where this is not legally mandatory, seems to be more than part of a salary and is a case of providing supporting funds for a certain end.
19. I thank David Haslett, Kate Rogers, Louis Pojman, and Jim Fieser for helpful and critical comments.

David Boonin

Same-Sex Marriage and the Argument from Public Disagreement

Most arguments against same-sex marriage rest at least in part on claims about the moral status of homosexuality: claims to the effect that homosexual behavior is morally objectionable in itself, or that homosexuals as a class are predisposed to commit acts (such as infidelity or child molestation) that are morally objectionable on independent grounds. In "Is It Wrong to Discriminate on the Basis of Homosexuality?" Jeff Jordan claims to produce an argument against same-sex marriage that makes no such assumptions.[1] Rather than relying on claims about the morality of homosexuality per se, Jordan attempts to show that it is morally permissible for the state to refuse to sanction same-sex marriages by appealing to the fact that marriage is a public rather than private institution, and that there is widespread public disagreement about the moral status of homosexuality. I will begin by presenting a brief summary of Jordan's principal argument for this claim and will then argue that it should be rejected for three distinct reasons: the argument itself is unsound, it is subject to a *reductio ad absurdum* that Jordan fails to overcome, and, contrary to Jordan's claim, it does in fact depend on claims about the morality of homosexuality, claims that stand in need of support and that Jordan has not defended.

I

Jordan begins by defining an "impasse" over the moral status of *x* as a situation in which people hold "genuinely conflicting beliefs regarding the moral status of *x*, and a "public dilemma" as an impasse that has "public policy consequences." In cases of genuine public dilemmas, the state will have to act in a way that has some implications with respect to *x*, and as a result will not be able to fully satisfy the interests of everyone on both sides of the impasse. When it does so by putting its power and authority squarely on one side of the impasse, as in the case of the federal government's forcibly ending slavery, it in effect "declares that side of the impasse the correct side," and Jordan refers to this as "resolution by declaration." When it finds a way to stake out some kind of middle ground "in a way that gives as much as possible to all sides of

From *Journal of Social Philosophy,* vol. 30, no. 2, Summer 1999, pp. 251–259. Copyright © 1999 by Journal of Social Philosophy. Reprinted by permission of Wiley-Blackwell.

the impasse," it ensures that "there are no absolute victors and no absolute losers" in the impasse and that the views of all sides are respected. Jordan refers to this as "resolution by accommodation," and cites abortion as a possible example (pornography might be another): the government permits its use, but restricts its availability. Jordan then argues, quite plausibly, that whenever a public dilemma must be actively resolved, the state should institute a resolution by accommodation rather than by declaration, unless there is an "overriding reason" that it should take sides, where such reasons typically involve "the protection of generally recognized rights."

With this general framework in place, Jordan then makes the following claims about same-sex marriage in particular: First, there is a moral impasse over the question of whether or not homosexual acts are morally permissible. Many people think that they are and many think that they are not. Second, whereas engaging in homosexual conduct in itself is essentially a private matter, entering into a relationship of marriage is essentially a public one. Marriage involves a public recognition of a personal relationship between two people and people who are married become eligible for various sorts of public benefits that are unavailable to unmarried couples. As a result, the debate over same-sex marriage represents not merely a moral impasse, but a public dilemma. Third, for the government to sanction same-sex marriage is for it to resolve this public dilemma by declaration in favor of one side of the dispute, in a way that leaves no room for accommodation. If it does this, then members of one segment of the population "are faced with a public, state sanctioned matter which they find seriously immoral." But, fourth, if the state instead refuses to sanction same-sex marriage, this counts as a resolution by accommodation, provided that the state permits private homosexual acts between consenting adults. If it does this, then each side of the impasse gets some but not all of what it wants and thus neither side is an absolute victor or loser. Fifth, and finally, there is no overriding reason for the state to take sides in this dispute. What is at stake is not comparable to what is at stake in those cases, such as the abolition of slavery, where there is plainly reason for the state to resolve the issue by declaration.

If these five claims are correct, and if Jordan's general framework is defensible, the result is that the state should refuse to sanction same-sex marriages. We can represent the argument as follows:

P1 If (a) there is a public dilemma about *x*, *and* (b) resolution of the dilemma by accommodation is possible, *and* (c) there is no overriding reason to prefer resolution of the dilemma by declaration, *then* (d) the state should resolve the public dilemma about *x* by accommodation.
P2 There is a public dilemma about same-sex marriage.
P3 It is possible for the state to resolve the dilemma by accommodation if it refuses to sanction same-sex marriage (provided that it permits private homosexual acts between consenting adults).
P4 It is not possible for the state to resolve the dilemma by accommodation if it sanctions same-sex marriage (since that amounts to resolving the dilemma by declaration and leaves no room for accommodation).
P5 There is no overriding reason for the state to resolve the dilemma by declaration.

C The state should refuse to sanction same-sex marriage (provided that it permits private homosexual acts between consenting adults).

At the end of his paper, Jordan characterizes the thesis this argument is meant to defend as one on which it is "morally permissible" for the state to refuse to sanction same-sex marriages, but this puts things far too modestly. If Jordan's argument is successful, it shows not merely that it would be *permissible* for the state to do this, but that this is what the state in fact *ought* to do. Indeed, if the argument is successful, it is difficult to see how one could avoid the conclusion that it would be positively *wrong* for the state to sanction same-sex marriages, because it would be wrong for it, in general, to fully favor one side of a moral dispute over another without a compelling reason for doing so. So a good deal is at stake if Jordan's argument is successful.

But I want now to show that Jordan's argument is not successful. In section II, I will argue that one of the argument's premises is importantly ambiguous, and that either way of resolving the ambiguity renders two of the other premises false. In section III, I will argue that the argument is undermined by a reductio ad absurdum objection that Jordan tries, but fails, to overcome. And in section IV, I will argue that, contrary to Jordan's characterization of the argument, it does, in fact, presuppose a particular and contentious claim about the moral status of homosexuality.

II

Let me begin by raising a question about P2: the claim that there is a public dilemma about same-sex marriage. On the face of it, this might seem to be the clearest and least problematic of all of the premises in Jordan's argument. If anything at all about same-sex marriage is uncontroversial it is the fact that it is controversial. But what, exactly, does the claim made by P2 mean? Jordan, remember, defines a public dilemma as a special case of a moral impasse, and a moral impasse as a situation in which people "hold genuinely conflicting beliefs regarding the moral status of *x*." The question is: in the case of the public dilemma about same-sex marriage, what does the *x* stand for?

There are two possibilities: it can stand for acts of homosexual behavior, or it can stand for acts of participating in a same-sex marriage. Jordan at one point speaks of "*the* public dilemma concerning homosexuality, and in particular whether states should sanction same-sex marriages", as if there is a single subject of dispute here, but these are in fact two distinct subjects of disagreement. The former concerns the moral permissibility of certain forms of sexual behavior, regardless of whether the people who engage in them are generally heterosexual or homosexual in their orientation. The latter concerns the moral permissibility of granting certain forms of social recognition and public benefits to same-sex couples, regardless of whether or not they engage in such (or any) sexual behavior.[2]

Suppose that the genuinely conflicting beliefs that generate the dilemma referred to in P2 are beliefs regarding the moral status of acts of participating in a same-sex marriage. This seems to be the most natural interpretation, since the dilemma itself is about same-sex marriage and since a dilemma is simply a special case of an impasse, which is itself a case of conflicting beliefs about something. If this is what is meant by P2, then P3 and P4 are false. P3 says that if the state refuses to sanction same-sex marriages, then it resolves the public dilemma by accommodation (provided that it permits private homosexual acts between consenting adults). If we conflate the two distinct questions about private acts and public benefits into one issue, and think of it as "the" dispute over homosexuality, then this seems plausible enough. Each side gets some of what it wants, and neither side gets all of what it wants. But if the conflict is over the permissibility of same-sex *marriage* in particular, as opposed to about the complex cluster of issues relating to homosexuality taken as a whole, then this is no accommodation at all. It is simply a declaration that one side of the debate is entirely correct (those who oppose same-sex marriages) and the other side entirely incorrect (those who support them). It is as if one were to join together the distinct but related debates about whether or not the government should fund the arts and whether or not it should ban violent pornography, announce that the government will permit violent pornography but will not subsidize it, and declare that "the" debate in question had been settled in a way that accommodates both sides. This would not be a resolution by accommodation of one dilemma, but rather a resolution by declaration of two distinct but related dilemmas.

On this understanding of P2, P4 is also false, for similar but distinct reasons. P4 says that if the state sanctions same-sex marriage, then it resolves the public dilemma by declaration and leaves no room for accommodation. But if the dilemma is over same-sex marriage rather than over same-sex sex, this too is incorrect. If accommodation is reached in controversies such as that over pornography or abortion by permitting but discouraging the controversial practice, then the same would hold here as well. The state could sanction same-sex marriage, but make it more difficult to obtain a same-sex marriage license than to obtain an opposite-sex marriage license. For example, it could require proof that a homosexual couple had been engaged for two years before obtaining a same-sex marriage license, but not require such proof from heterosexual couples, or require extensive premarital counseling, or charge a greater licensing fee. And it could discourage homosexuals from marrying in other ways, such as by taxing married homosexuals at a higher rate (higher than married heterosexuals and/or higher than unmarried homosexuals), or making it more difficult for them to obtain divorces or to adopt children than it is for heterosexual couples.

None of these suggestions will be fully satisfactory to defenders of same-sex marriage, of course. What they demand is marriage for homosexuals that is on an equal footing with marriage for heterosexuals. Nor will any of these proposals be fully satisfactory to opponents of same-sex marriage. What they demand is that there be no such thing as same-sex marriage. But that is precisely the point. If Jordan is correct that dilemmas of this sort should be resolved by accommodation, and if the dilemma is understood to be one over marriage and not over sex, then following a proposal that is fully satisfactory to neither side is exactly what his argument demands that we do. As in other such cases, the state should find a way to allow those who wish to engage in the disputed behavior to engage in it while at the same time expressing society's disapproval or at least lack of approval of the behavior in question.

Suppose, on the other hand, that the genuinely conflicting beliefs that generate the dilemma referred to in P2 are beliefs regarding the moral status of acts of homosexual behavior. This seems to be what Jordan typically has in mind when he introduces his argument. When he supports the contention that there exists a public dilemma that needs some sort of resolution, for example, he cites the fact that "[t]he theistic tradition, Judaism and Christianity and Islam, has a clear and deeply entrenched position on homosexual *acts:* they are prohibited". And he concludes his argument for the claim by saying that "[b]ecause many religious people sincerely believe homosexual *acts* to be morally wrong and many others believe that homosexual *acts* are not morally wrong, there results a public dilemma".

But if the genuinely conflicting beliefs that generate the dilemma referred to in P2 are beliefs regarding the moral status of acts of homosexual behavior, then P3 and P4 are again false, for different but parallel reasons. If the state sanctions same-sex marriage, it does not resolve the conflicting beliefs about the moral permissibility of acts of homosexual behavior in a way that leaves no room for accommodation. For example, the state could recognize both same-sex and opposite-sex marriage and make it illegal to have homosexual intercourse outside of such a relation while legal to have heterosexual intercourse outside of such a relation. This would have the effect of permitting but restricting the form of behavior whose moral status is the subject of genuinely conflicting beliefs. So if the conflicting beliefs referred to in P2 concern the permissibility of acts of homosexual behavior, then P4 is false. Similarly, if the state refuses to sanction same-sex marriage and permits private homosexual acts between consenting adults, it does not resolve the conflicting beliefs about the moral permissibility of acts of homosexual behavior by accommodation. Rather, it simply declares that one side of the conflict is the correct side, namely, the side that believes that such acts are permissible. Doing so thus renders P3 false as well. So either way that we specify the meaning of the claim made in P2, the argument as a whole proves to be unsound.

III

A second objection to Jordan's argument takes the form of a reductio ad absurdum: if the state should refuse to sanction same-sex marriage because it is the subject of a moral impasse, then it should also refuse to sanction mixed-race marriage on the same ground. But the claim that the state should refuse to sanction mixed-race marriage is surely intolerable. So, therefore, is Jordan's argument. Jordan provides three responses to this objection, but none of them are satisfactory.

His first response is that unlike the issue of same-sex marriage, the issue of mixed-race marriages "does not seem to generate much, if any, controversy today." On this account, there is no such public dilemma in the first place, and so it does not matter that Jordan's position would justify forbidding mixed-race marriage if there were. This response is unsuccessful for two reasons. First, it is not at all clear that there is no such dilemma about mixed-race marriage. In many communities in the South, at least, there remains substantial opposition to interracial *dating,* let alone interracial marriage. And although such opposition is traditionally associated with white racists, there is a more recent and hardly less heated controversy within the black community in all parts of the country about whether or not black men, in particular, have an obligation to marry black women.[3] Second, and more importantly, even if Jordan is right that there is no longer a moral impasse on this issue, this response makes the impermissibility of laws forbidding mixed-race marriage contingent on this fact. And surely such laws were impermissible even when many racists supported them.

Jordan's second response to the mixed-race objection is to say that even if it does represent a public dilemma, it is one in which there is an overriding reason in favor of resolution by declaration. The reason is that "it is a settled matter that state protection from racial discrimination is a reason sufficient for a resolution via declaration" while the same is not true of protection from discrimination according to sexual orientation. This response fails for the simple reason that a law banning mixed-race marriages does not discriminate against people on racial grounds. It says that *every* person, regardless of race, is free to marry anyone else of his or her race, and that *every* person, regardless of race, is prohibited from marrying anyone else of some other race. A white person who falls in love with a black person is adversely affected in just the same way as is [a]black person who falls in love with a white person. And since every black–white couple consists of one black person and one white person, the total number of blacks and whites who are adversely affected in this way is the same. As a result, a law recognizing mixed-race marriage does not protect anyone from racial discrimination that would occur without such a law.

A law forbidding same-sex marriage, it is worth noting, is fundamentally different in this respect. It says that a heterosexual man can marry any member of the sex he is attracted to while a homosexual man can marry any member of the sex he is *not* attracted to, and that a heterosexual man is forbidden to marry any member of the sex that he is not attracted to while a homosexual man is forbidden to marry any member of the sex that he *is* attracted to. This law does discriminate by sexual orientation, since all of the people who are adversely affected by it (at least directly) are homosexuals. And thus a law recognizing same-sex marriage does protect people from discrimination on the basis of sexual orientation that would otherwise occur without such a law. In short, laws banning mixed-race marriage treat people of all races equally while laws banning same-sex marriage do not treat people of all sexual orientations equally. So Jordan has failed to show that there is an overriding reason for the state to resolve the mixed-race marriage issue by declaration that does not also apply to the case of same-sex marriages. Indeed, if anything, he has pointed to an overriding reason to resolve the same-sex marriage issue by declaration that does not apply to the mixed-race marriage issue.

Jordan's final response to the mixed-race marriage objection turns on his attempt to identify a second disanalogy between the two cases: "A same-sex marriage would involve behavior which many people find morally objectionable; a mixed-race marriage is objectionable to some, not because of the participants' behavior, but because of the racial identity of the participants." And since objections based on a person's identity are different from objections based on a person's behavior, it does not follow from the fact that the objection to mixed-race marriage should be overruled by a resolution by declaration that the objection to same-sex marriage should also be overruled in this manner.

This response must be rejected because it rests on a misdescription of the view held by those who object to mixed-race marriage. It is not that they object to the *identity* of the individuals involved. White racists need not have anything against blacks marrying other blacks, and black separatists surely have nothing against white people marrying other whites. It is not the identity of the individuals that they object to, but the act they perform: the act of weakening the purity of the race, or of violating the obligation to put one's own community first. In this sense, they are no different from the antihomosexual people Jordan describes: they say they object not to what homosexuals are, but to what they do.

IV

I have argued that Jordan's argument is unsound, and I have argued that it is subject to an important objection by reductio ad absurdum. In doing this, I have accepted Jordan's claim that if his argument succeeds, it does so without depending on any claims about the moral status of homosexuality. I want to conclude by questioning this claim.

I do so by raising a question about the one premise about same-sex marriage that I have to this point set aside. This is the claim made by P5 that there is no overriding reason for the state to resolve the public dilemma about same-sex marriage by declaration. Jordan does not provide specific criteria for distinguishing overriding reasons from less weighty ones, but his comment that they typically involve "the protection of generally recognized rights" seems to me sufficient for my purposes. The claim that a right is a generally recognized one can be taken in two distinct ways. In the case of the United States prior to the Civil War, for example, there is one sense in which the right not to be enslaved was a generally recognized one. If you tried to enslave a white person during this period, it would have been generally recognized that you were violating his rights. But there is another sense in which the right not to be enslaved was not generally recognized, since it was not generally recognized that it was enjoyed by all people regardless of race.

Now if a right must be generally recognized in this second sense in order for there to be an overriding reason for the state to take sides in a public dilemma, then Jordan will be unable to account for the fact that the morally right thing for the state to do was to abolish slavery. Indeed, if this is what is needed in order for there to be an overriding reason for the state to so act, then P5 will be vacuous: if a right is generally recognized in this sense, there will for that very reason be no public dilemma about it. So the argument can only succeed if the rights that suffice to underwrite an overriding reason in P5 are ones that are widely agreed to be held by most people, even if many people refrain from attributing them to all people. And this is what creates the final problem with Jordan's argument. For surely it is widely agreed that most people have a right to marry whomever they wish, and to have their marriage publicly recognized. Suppose that the government announced that, starting tomorrow, the state would no longer sanction marriages between heterosexual Jews. For purposes of taxes, child custody, property ownership, next-of-kin visitation rights, and so on, there would no longer be a distinction between married heterosexual Jewish couples and pairs of Jewish people of opposite sexes who happen to live in the same dwelling. Most people would regard this as outrageous. And although I am sympathetic toward those who complain that the language of rights is too often stretched beyond reason, I suspect that most people would object to the edict by saying that it violated a very commonly recognized right, the right of consenting adults to marry whomever they please and to have their marriages publicly recognized. But if it is generally recognized that this is a right that most people have, even if it is not generally recognized that this is a right that all people have, then this is sufficient to establish that there is an overriding reason to resolve the dilemma by declaration in favor of same-sex marriage. It is not sufficient only if there is some morally relevant difference between homosexuals and heterosexuals, just as it would not be sufficient if there were some morally relevant difference between Jews and non-Jews.

Now I do not mean to suggest that this argument provides anything like a conclusive resolution of the debate about same-sex marriage. It is simply the first step that then leaves open any number of responses that might be given to undermine the claim that if heterosexuals have the right to marry whomever they please then so do homosexuals. My point here is simply that it is very difficult to see how any such response could succeed in vindicating P5 without at some point depending at least in part on the claim that there is a morally relevant difference between homosexuals and heterosexuals or between homosexual and heterosexual relationships. This is precisely the sort of argument that Jordan's argument was meant to avoid. And this suggests that even if his argument were not subject to the objections I have presented in the previous two sections, it would still prove incapable of accomplishing the task it set out to accomplish.

Notes

1. *Journal of Social Philosophy,* 25, no. 1 (Spring 1995), reprinted in Robert M. Baird and Stuart E. Rosenbaum, eds., *Same-Sex Marriage: The Moral and Legal Debate* (Amherst, NY: Prometheus Books, 1997), 72–83. . . .
2. It is also worth noting that from the mere claim that a certain kind of behavior is morally impermissible, it does not follow that the state should not sanction marriages between people who engage in such behavior. There are genuinely conflicting moral beliefs about the permissibility of abortion, contraception, pornography, sexual promiscuity, and the use of animals in medical research, to name but a few, but there is no parallel conflict over whether or not the state should sanction marriages between

pornographers, animal researchers, people who use contraception or perform abortion, or who have long and varied sexual histories.

3. That this debate cannot be easily dismissed is shown by Charles W. Mills, "Do Black Men Have a Moral Duty to Marry Black Women?" *Journal of Social Philosophy,* 25th Anniversary Special Issue (1994), 131–53.

POSTSCRIPT

Is It Right to Prohibit Same-Sex Marriage?

Marriage has rather surprisingly changed over time. For example, both now and in the past (as recorded in the Old Testament, for example), there are cases of men with several wives—indeed, King Solomon is said to have had 700 wives and 300 concubines! More recently, interracial marriages have been banned, and then later allowed, in several states. Currently, civil unions for homosexuals are available in Vermont, and several American and Canadian jurisdictions are considering, or have already performed, gay marriages. Meanwhile, there is much heated discussion among both elected lawmakers and the public at large.

Generally, we want to live in a society that is not tied to a specific religion—for we want to recognize diversity and to grant freedom of religion—but we don't want to live in a society that has no specific values; nor do we want to live in a society that allows people to do whatever they want. (We can't allow absolute freedom because we want to maintain some rights against people who are not allowed to transgress those rights.) Hence, we need to draw some lines. The question is whether we should include same-sex marriage inside the line or not.

One general approach that is often recognized by both proponents and opponents of gay marriage is what might be called *liberalism* (in the classical sense): liberalism recognizes that individuals have rights, and that those rights should extend as far as possible until they start to interfere with the rights of other individuals. Classical liberalism is also committed to refraining from endorsing controversial conceptions of the good—it is neutral in this respect. For example, if some people prefer to spend their time reading literary classics (and this is part of *their* conception of "the good"), while other people spend their time playing video games (and this is part of *their* conception of "the good"), the government is not to say that one group of people has the correct conception of the good—it is to remain neutral and let the different parties pursue happiness along the paths that they themselves determine (as long as no rights are violated).

It might seem that classical liberalism must automatically support same-sex marriage. After all, the parties to the marriage are acting according to their own conception of the good, and they are not violating anyone else's rights. But Jeff Jordan has argued that there are several different models of marriage, and that a state endorsement of same-sex marriage *would* endorse one of these as right. So in recognizing same-sex marriage, the state wouldn't be neutral. It would be illiberal. Jonathan Rauch, on the other hand, has argued that the institution of marriage exerts a powerful stabilizing force and contributes to the well-being of society, and is something that *should* be recognized.

This issue is not only about gay rights and the social acceptance of gays, but also about our idea of marriage. It is worthwhile examining Jordan's models and his argumentation to see exactly what is acceptable and what is not.

Relevant literature here includes David Moats, *Civil War: A Battle for Gay Marriage* (Harcourt, 2004); George Chauncey, *Why Marriage? The History Shaping Today's Debate over Gay Equality* (Basic Books, 2004); Evan Wolfson, *Why Marriage Matters: America, Equality, and Gay People's Right to Marry* (Simon & Schuster, 2004); and the TFP Committee on American Issues, *Defending a Higher Law: Why We Must Resist Same-Sex "Marriage" and the Homosexual Movement* (The American Society for the Defense of Tradition, Family and Property, 2004).

ISSUE 6

Should Human Cloning Be Banned?

YES: Michael J. Sandel, from "The Ethical Implications of Human Cloning," *Perspectives in Biology and Medicine* (Spring 2005)

NO: John A. Robertson, from "Human Cloning and the Challenge of Regulation," *The New England Journal of Medicine* (July 9, 1998)

ISSUE SUMMARY

YES: Political philosopher Michael J. Sandel argues that much of the talk about cloning revolves around a few limited concepts (e.g., rights, autonomy, and the supposed unnaturalness of asexual reproduction) that are inadequate and fail to express what is really wrong with cloning. We need, Instead, to address fundamental questions about our stance toward nature.

NO: Law professor John A. Robertson maintains that there should not be a complete ban on human cloning but that regulatory policy should be focused on ensuring that it is performed in a responsible manner.

The issue of human cloning requires careful consideration. Each person is believed to be uniquely valuable. Also, many prefer to differentiate humans from animals. If it is accepted that the same technology that allows for the cloning of sheep can also be applied to the cloning of humans, both of these ideas are brought into question. In light of animal cloning, the existence of humans seems to be based on the very same biological processes that exist in sheep and other animals. And if there can be such a thing as human cloning, what happens to the idea that we are all unique? What happens to the idea that we all have our individual lives to lead, and that each person is responsible for his or her own choices?

Moreover, cloning can change ideas about reproduction. In cloning, no male is required. Consider the case of Dolly, the sheep cloned from the cell of an adult ewe. An egg cell, taken from a female sheep, had its nucleus removed; this was replaced with the nucleus of a cell taken from another female sheep. Then the result was implanted and grew in the uterus of a third female sheep, who eventually gave birth to Dolly. Normally, a newborn has genetic input from both the father's side and the mother's side, with the mother supplying the egg cell. But the original egg cell that was used in Dolly's case contributed almost nothing in this regard. The nucleus from the cell of the other sheep contained virtually all of the genetic input for Dolly.

Identical twins are familiar cases of human beings who, like clones, share a common genetic input. When environmental factors connected with identical twins are closely the same, and when they have similar clothes, haircut, etc., they can be difficult to tell apart. But when the environmental factors that impinge on their lives are quite different—as in the case of twins separated at birth—the twins can be quite different in obvious physical ways.

Physical aspects such as height have both genetic and environmental inputs; two people with the same genetic input can have quite different heights if environmental conditions (e.g., their diets) are different.

In some ways, clones are like identical twins, but in many cases there would be far less resemblance between clones than between identical twins, since they would be subject to very different environmental factors. Being conceived and born at different times—perhaps years or even decades apart from each other—they may have radically different environmental input.

Human cloning can be seen as beneficial. Cloning may provide another way for people to utilize technological assistance in reproduction. For example, a couple who could not have children naturally might consider a range of options, including cloning. Some maintain that is a relatively innocent use of human cloning, and can benefit those who are infertile.

Some object to cloning by citing other possible scenarios. Suppose a person wanted numerous clones of himself or herself. Suppose a sports star desired a clone who would then be expected to achieve greatness in sports. Suppose parents wanted a replacement for a child that they had lost, or want a child who could serve as a bone marrow or organ donor. These cases may give some pause, since the motivation for cloning appears to be questionable.

To counter this argument, it is stated that proper regulation would prevent these types of scenarios from occurring. Instead, cloning would be performed only under the correct circumstances, and would promote individual happiness.

In the following selections, Michael Sandel argues that there is something deeply wrong with human cloning. What is wrong goes beyond questions of rights, autonomy, and cloning's supposed "unnaturalness." It involves our fundamental attitudes toward nature and human existence. John A. Robertson counters that human cloning, if properly regulated, need not and would not be sinister. Properly regulated, human cloning should be permitted.

YES

Michael J. Sandel

The Ethical Implications of Human Cloning

In this essay, I will consider the ethics of reproductive and therapeutic cloning. But I want also to advance a more general claim: that the cloning issue, and related debates about genetic engineering, will change the way philosophers think about their subject. Much of the debate about cloning and genetic engineering is conducted in the familiar language of autonomy, consent, and individual rights. Defenders of "liberal eugenics" argue that parents should be free to enhance the genetic traits of their children for the sake of improving their life prospects (Agar 1999; Buchanan et al. 2000; Dworkin 2000). Ronald Dworkin, for example argues that there is nothing wrong with the ambition "to make the lives of future generations of human beings longer and more full of talent and hence achievement." In fact, he maintains, the principle of ethical individualism makes such efforts obligatory (Dworkin 2000, p. 452). Many opponents of cloning and genetic engineering also invoke the language of autonomy and rights. For example, Jurgen Habermas (2003) worries that even favorable genetic enhancements may impair the autonomy and individuality of children by pointing them toward particular life choices, hence violating their right to choose their life plans for themselves.

But talk of autonomy and rights does not address the deepest questions posed by cloning. In order to grapple with the ethical implications of cloning and genetic engineering, we need to confront questions largely lost from view in the modern world—questions about the moral status of nature and about the proper stance of human beings toward the given world. Since questions such as these verge on theology, or at least involve a certain view of the best way for human beings to live their lives, modern philosophers and political theorists tend to shrink from them. But our new powers of biotechnology make these questions unavoidable.

In the United States today, no federal law prohibits human cloning, either for purposes of reproduction or for purposes of biomedical research. This is not because most people favor reproductive cloning. To the contrary, public opinion and almost all elected officials oppose it. But there is strong disagreement about whether to permit cloning for biomedical research. And the opponents of cloning for biomedical research have so far been unwilling to support a separate ban on reproductive cloning, as Britain has enacted. Because of this stalemate, no federal ban on cloning has been enacted.

From *Perspectives in Biology and Medicine,* vol. 48, no. 2, Spring 2005, pp. 241–247. Copyright © 2005 by Johns Hopkins University Press. Reprinted by permission.

The Ethics of Reproductive Cloning

I turn first to the ethics of reproductive cloning, and then to cloning for biomedical research. The case for banning human reproductive cloning is not difficult to make, at least for now. Most scientists agree that it is unsafe and likely to lead to serious abnormalities and birth defects. But suppose that, one day, producing a baby through cloning were no more risky than natural reproduction. Many believe—and I agree—that it would still be ethically objectionable. But it is not easy to say why.

The autonomy argument against cloning is not persuasive, for it wrongly implies that, absent a genetically designing parent, children can choose their physical characteristics for themselves. But none of us has a right to choose our genetic inheritance. The alternative to a cloned or genetically enhanced child is not an autonomous one, but a child at the mercy of the genetic lottery.

Some argue that cloning is wrong because it departs from natural, sexual procreation (Kass and Wilson 1998). But this objection also fails to reach the heart of the matter. What makes reproductive cloning morally troubling is that its primary purpose is to create children of a certain kind. In this respect, it is similar to other forms of genetic engineering by which parents seek to choose the traits of their children—sex, eye color, perhaps one day even their intellectual attributes, athletic prowess, and musical ability. Although a few eccentric narcissists might aspire to create genetic replicas of themselves, the real market for designer children lies elsewhere, in the desire of parents to produce children with genetic traits superior to their own.

The desire to control the genetic characteristics of one's offspring points to the heart of the ethical issue. The moral problem with reproductive cloning lies not in its asexual character, but in its assault on the understanding of children as gifts rather than possessions, or projects of our will, or vehicles for our happiness.

It might be replied that cloning and genetic engineering are in principle no different from other ways in which parents go to great lengths to produce children of a certain kind, or "designer children." But rather than giving us reason to embrace cloning, this observation may give us reason to worry about existing practices of childrearing.

What is most troubling about human cloning and bioengineering is not that they represent a radical departure, but that they carry to full expression troubling tendencies already present in our culture, especially in the way we regard and treat children. We have already traveled some distance down the path of regarding children as vehicles for our own ambitions or fulfillment. Consider the chilling discrepancy in sex ratios in China, South Korea, and parts of India, where boys now outnumber girls by up to 30% (Eberstadt 2002). But think also of the enormous pressure parents put on children in the United States and many other Western societies to qualify for admission to the best schools—not only at the university level, but even, in Manhattan at least, at the preschool level. Sometimes, the drive to produce successful children begins even earlier. The Harvard college newspaper recently carried an advertisement from a couple seeking an egg donor. They did not want just any egg donor.

The ad specified that the donor should be attractive, athletic, at least 5 feet, 10 inches tall, and with a college entrance exam score of 1400 or above. For an egg from a donor meeting these stringent qualifications, the couple was offering a payment of $50,000 (Kolata 1999).

The notion that the project of mastery and choice is subject to certain limits is at odds with the spirit of contemporary liberalism. That is why many who are uneasy with human cloning try to cast their objections in the language of autonomy and rights, arguing that choosing the traits of one's children, by cloning or otherwise, violates their rights. The European Assembly has maintained, for example, that human cloning is wrong because it is a violation of human rights. But the language of rights misses the point. The problem is not that parents usurp the autonomy of the child they design: it is not as if the child could otherwise choose her gender, height, and eye color for herself. The problem lies in the hubris of the designing parents, in their drive to master the mystery of birth. Even if this hubris does not make parents tyrants to their children, it disfigures the relation of parent and child. It deprives the parents of the humility and enlarged human sympathies that an openness to the unbidden "otherness" of our progeny can cultivate.

Like the autonomy objection, the argument that focuses on the asexual character of reproductive cloning misses the point. Understood simply as a departure from sexual procreation, cloning would not represent a serious threat. Sex will survive perfectly well on its own—without the help of federal legislation. By contrast, the sense of life as a gift we cannot summon or control is fragile and vulnerable. In the face of the Promethean drive to mastery that animates modern societies, an appreciation of the giftedness of life is in constant need of support.

The Ethics of Cloning for Biomedical Research

I turn now to the ethics of cloning for biomedical research. It is here that the greatest disagreement prevails. The U.S. Senate is split between those who want to ban all cloning and those who want to ban reproductive cloning but not cloning for stem cell research and regenerative medicine. (For the American debate on cloning, see President's Council 2002.) As in the case of reproductive cloning, the concepts of autonomy and rights cannot by themselves resolve the moral question. In order to assess the moral permissibility of cloning for stem cell research, we need to determine the moral status of the early embryo. If the six-day, pre-implantation embryo (or blastocyst) is morally equivalent to a person, then it is wrong to extract stem cells from it, even for the sake of curing devastating diseases such as Parkinson's, Alzheimer's, or diabetes. If the embryo is a person, then not only should all therapeutic cloning be banned, so also should all embryonic stem cell research.

Before turning to the moral status of the embryo, I would like to consider one influential argument against cloning for biomedical research that stops short of opposing embryonic stem cell research as such. Some opponents of research cloning, troubled by the deliberate creation of embryos for research, support embryonic stem cell research, provided it uses "spare" embryos left over from fertility clinics (Sandel 2002). Since in vitro fertilization (IVF) clinics (at least in the United States) create many more fertilized eggs than are ultimately implanted, some argue that there is nothing wrong with using those spares for research: if excess embryos would be discarded anyway, why not use them (with donor consent) for potentially life-saving research?

This seems to be a sensible distinction. But on closer examination, it does not hold up. The distinction fails because it begs the question whether the "spare" embryos should be created in the first place. If it is immoral to create and sacrifice embryos for the sake of curing or treating devastating diseases, why isn't it also objectionable to create and discard spare IVF embryos in the course of treating infertility? Or, to look at the argument from the opposite end, if the creation and sacrifice of embryos in IVF is morally acceptable, why isn't the creation and sacrifice of embryos for stem cell research also acceptable? After all, both practices serve worthy ends, and curing diseases such as Parkinson's, is at least as important as enabling infertile couples to have genetically related children.

Of course, bioethics is not only about ends, but also about means. Those who oppose creating embryos for research argue that doing so is exploitative and fails to accord embryos the respect they are due. But the same argument could be made against fertility treatments that create excess embryos bound for destruction. In fact, a recent study found that some 400,000 frozen embryos are languishing in American fertility clinics, with another 52,000 in the United Kingdom and 71,000 in Australia (Wade 2003).

If my argument is correct, it shows only that stem cell research on IVF spares and on embryos created for research (whether natural or cloned) are morally on a par. This conclusion can be accepted by people who hold very different views about the moral status of the embryo. If cloning for stem cell research violates the respect the embryo is due, then so does stem cell research on IVF spares, and so does any version of IVF that creates and discards excess embryos. If, morally speaking, these practices stand or fall together, it remains to ask whether they stand or fall. And that depends on the moral status of the embryo.

The Moral Status of the Embryo

There are three possible ways of conceiving the moral status of the embryo: as a thing, as a person, or as something in between. To regard an embryo as a mere thing, open to any use we may desire or devise, is, it seems to me, to miss its significance as nascent human life. One need not regard an embryo as a full human person in order to believe that it is due a certain respect. Personhood is not the only warrant for respect: we consider it a failure of respect when a thoughtless hiker carves his initials in an ancient sequoia, not because we regard the sequoia as a person, but because we consider it a natural wonder worthy of appreciation and awe—modes of regard inconsistent with treating it as a billboard or defacing it for the sake of petty vanity. To respect the old growth forest does not mean that no tree may ever be felled or harvested for human purposes. Respecting the forest may be consistent with using it. But the purposes should be weighty and appropriate to the wondrous nature of the thing.

One way to oppose a degrading, objectifying stance toward nascent human life is to attribute full personhood to the embryo. I will call this the "equal moral status" view. One way of assessing this view is to play out its full implications, in order to assess their plausibility. Consider the following hypothetical: a fire breaks out in a fertility clinic, and you have time to save either a five-year-old girl or a tray of 10 embryos. Would it be wrong to save the girl?[1]

A further implication of the equal moral status view is that harvesting stem cells from a six-day-old blastocyst is as morally abhorrent as harvesting organs from a baby. But is it? If so, the penalty provided in the proposed U.S. anti-cloning legislation—a $1 million fine and 10 years in prison—is woefully inadequate. If embryonic stem cell research is morally equivalent to yanking organs from babies, it should be treated as a grisly form of murder, and the scientist who performs it should face life imprisonment or the death penalty.

A further source of difficulty for the equal moral status view lies in the fact that, in natural pregnancies, at least half of all embryos either fail to implant or are otherwise lost. It might be replied that a high rate of infant mortality does not justify infanticide. But the way we respond to the natural loss of embryos or even early miscarriages suggests that we do not regard these events as the moral or religious equivalent of infant mortality. Otherwise, wouldn't we carry out the same burial rituals for the loss of an embryo that we observe for the death of a child?

The conviction that the embryo is a person derives support not only from certain religious doctrines but also from the Kantian assumption that the moral universe is divided in binary terms: everything is either a person, worthy of respect, or a thing, open to use. But this dualism is overdrawn.

The way to combat the instrumentalizing impulse of modern technology and commerce is not to insist on an all-or-nothing ethic of respect for persons that consigns the rest of life to a utilitarian calculus. Such an ethic risks turning every moral question into a battle over the bounds of personhood. We would do better to cultivate a more expansive appreciation of life as a gift that commands our reverence and restricts our use. Human cloning to create designer babies is the ultimate expression of the hubris that marks the loss of reverence for life as a gift. But stem cell research to cure debilitating disease, using six-day-old blastocysts, cloned or uncloned, is a noble exercise of our human ingenuity to promote healing and to play our part in repairing the given world.

Those who warn of slippery slopes, embryo farms, and the commodification of ova and zygotes are right to worry but wrong to assume that cloning for biomedical research necessarily opens us to these dangers. Rather than ban stem cell cloning and other forms of embryo research, we should allow it to proceed subject to regulations that embody the moral restraint appropriate to the mystery of the first stirrings of human life. Such regulations should include licensing requirements for embryo research projects and fertility clinics, restrictions on the commodification of eggs and sperm, and measures to prevent proprietary interests from monopolizing access to stem cell lines. This approach, it seems to me, offers the best hope of avoiding the wanton use of nascent human life and making these biomedical advances a blessing for health rather than an episode in the erosion of our human sensibilities.

Note

1. I am indebted to George Annas for this hypothetical (see Annas 1989).

References

Agar, N. 1999. Liberal eugenics. In *Bioethics,* ed. H. Kuhse and P. Singer. Oxford: Blackwell.

Annas, G.J. 1989. A French homunculus in a Tennessee court. *Hastings Cent Rep* 19(6): 20–22.

Buchanan, A., et al. 2000. *From chance to choice: Genetics and justice.* Cambridge: Cambridge Univ. Press.

Dworkin, R. 2000. Playing God: Genes, clones, and luck. In *Sovereign virtue: The theory and practice of equality,* 427–52. Cambridge: Harvard Univ. Press.

Eberstadt, N. 2002. Testimony to President's Council on Bioethics, Oct. 17. . . .

Habermas, J. 2003. *The future of human nature.* Cambridge, UK: Polity Press.

Kass, L. R., and J. Q. Wilson. 1998. *The ethics of human cloning.* Washington, DC:AEI Press.

Kolata, G. 1999. $50,000 offered to tall, smart egg donor. *NY Times,* March 3.

President's Council on Bioethics. 2002. *Human cloning and human dignity: The report of the President's Council on Bioethics.* Washington, DC: President's Council on Bioethics. Repr. New York: Public Affairs, 2002. . . .

Sandel, M.J. 2002. The anti-cloning conundrum. *NY Times,* May 28.

Wade, N. 2003. Clinics hold more embryos than had been thought. *NY Times,* May 9.

John A. Robertson

Human Cloning and the Challenge of Regulation

The birth of Dolly, the sheep cloned from a mammary cell of an adult ewe, has initiated a public debate about human cloning. Although cloning of humans may never be clinically feasible, discussion of the ethical, legal, and social issues raised is important. Cloning is just one of several techniques potentially available to select, control, or alter the genome of offspring.[1–3] The development of such technology poses an important social challenge: how to ensure that the technology is used to enhance, rather than limit, individual freedom and welfare.

A key ethical question is whether a responsible couple, interested in rearing healthy offspring biologically related to them, might ethically choose to use cloning (or other genetic-selection techniques) for that purpose. The answer should take into account the benefits sought through the use of the techniques and any potential harm to offspring or to other interests.

The most likely uses of cloning would be far removed from the bizarre or horrific scenarios that initially dominated media coverage.[4] Theoretically, cloning would enable rich or powerful persons to clone themselves several times over, and commercial entrepreneurs might hire women to bear clones of sports or entertainment celebrities to be sold to others to rear. But current reproductive techniques can also be abused, and existing laws against selling children would apply to those created by cloning.

There is no reason to think that the ability to clone humans will cause many people to turn to cloning when other methods of reproduction would enable them to have healthy children. Cloning a human being by somatic-cell nuclear transfer, for example, would require a consenting person as a source of DNA, eggs to be enucleated and then fused with the DNA, a woman who would carry and deliver the child, and a person or couple to raise the child. Given this reality, cloning is most likely to be sought by couples who, because of infertility, a high risk of severe genetic disease, or other factors, cannot or do not wish to conceive a child.

Several plausible scenarios can be imagined. Rather than use sperm, egg, or embryo from anonymous donors, couples who are infertile as a result of gametic insufficiency might choose to clone one of the partners. If the husband were the source of the DNA and the wife provided the egg that received

From *The New England Journal of Medicine,* vol. 339, no. 2, July 9, 1998, pp. 119–121. Copyright © 1998 by Massachusetts Medical Society. All rights reserved. Reprinted by permission.

the nuclear transfer and then gestated the fetus, they would have a child biologically related to each of them and would not need to rely on anonymous gamete or embryo donation. Of course, many infertile couples might still prefer gamete or embryo donation or adoption. But there is nothing inherently wrong in wishing to be biologically related to one's children, even when this goal cannot be achieved through sexual reproduction.

A second plausible application would be for a couple at high risk of having offspring with a genetic disease.[5] Couples in this situation must now choose whether to risk the birth of an affected child, to undergo prenatal or preimplantation diagnosis and abortion or the discarding of embryos, to accept gamete donation, to seek adoption, or to remain childless. If cloning were available, however, some couples, in line with prevailing concepts of kinship, family, and parenting, might strongly prefer to clone one of themselves or another family member. Alternatively, if they already had a healthy child, they might choose to use cloning to create a later-born twin of that child. In the more distant future, it is even possible that the child whose DNA was replicated would not have been born healthy but would have been made healthy by gene therapy after birth.

A third application relates to obtaining tissue or organs for transplantation. A child who needed an organ or tissue transplant might lack a medically suitable donor. Couples in this situation have sometimes conceived a child coitally in the hope that he or she would have the correct tissue type to serve, for example, as a bone marrow donor for an older sibling.[6, 7] If the child's disease was not genetic, a couple might prefer to clone the affected child to be sure that the tissue would match.

It might eventually be possible to procure suitable tissue or organs by cloning the source DNA only to the point at which stem cells or other material might be obtained for transplantation, thus avoiding the need to bring a child into the world for the sake of obtaining tissue.[8] Cloning a person's cells up to the embryo stage might provide a source of stem cells or tissue for the person cloned. Cloning might also be used to enable a couple to clone a dead or dying child so as to have that child live on in some closely related form, to obtain sufficient numbers of embryos for transfer and pregnancy, or to eliminate mitochondrial disease.[5]

Most, if not all, of the potential uses of cloning are controversial, usually because of the explicit copying of the genome. As the National Bioethics Advisory Commission noted, in addition to concern about physical safety and eugenics, somatic-cell cloning raises issues of the individuality, autonomy, objectification, and kinship of the resulting children.[5] In other instances, such as the production of embryos to serve as tissue banks, the ethical issue is the sacrifice of embryos created solely for that purpose.

Given the wide leeway now granted couples to use assisted reproduction and prenatal genetic selection in forming families, cloning should not be rejected in all circumstances as unethical or illegitimate. The manipulation of embryos and the use of gamete donors and surrogates are increasingly common. Most fetuses conceived in the United States and Western Europe are now screened for genetic or chromosomal anomalies. Before conception, screening to identify carriers of genetic diseases is widespread.[9] Such practices also deviate from conventional notions of reproduction, kinship, and medical treatment of infertility, yet they are widely accepted.

Despite the similarity of cloning to current practices, however, the dissimilarities should not be overlooked. The aim of most other forms of assisted reproduction is the birth of a child who is a descendant of at least one member of the couple, not an identical twin. Most genetic selection acts negatively to identify and screen out unwanted traits such as genetic disease, not positively to choose or replicate the genome as in somatic-cell cloning.[3] It is not clear, however, why a child's relation to his or her rearing parents must always be that of sexually reproduced descendant when such a relationship is not possible because of infertility or other factors. Indeed, in gamete donation and adoption, although sexual reproduction is involved, a full descendant relation between the child and both rearing parents is lacking. Nor should the difference between negative and positive means of selecting children determine the ethical or social acceptability of cloning or other techniques. In both situations, a deliberate choice is made so that a child is born with one genome rather than another or is not born at all.

Is cloning sufficiently similar to current assisted-reproduction and genetic-selection practices to be treated similarly as a presumptively protected exercise of family or reproductive liberty?[10] Couples who request cloning in the situations I have described are seeking to rear healthy children with whom they will have a genetic or biologic tie, just as couples who conceive their children sexually do. Whether described as "replication" or as "reproduction," the resort to cloning is similar enough in purpose and effects to other reproduction and genetic-selection practices that it should be treated similarly. Therefore, a couple should be free to choose cloning unless there are compelling reasons for thinking that this would create harm that the other procedures would not cause.[10]

The concern of the National Bioethics Advisory Commission about the welfare of the clone reflects two types of fear. The first is that a child with the same nuclear DNA as another person, who is thus that person's later-born identical twin, will be so severely harmed by the identity of nuclear DNA between them that it is morally preferable, if not obligatory, that the child not be born at all.[5] In this case the fear is that the later-born twin will lack individuality or the freedom to create his or her own identity because of confusion or expectations caused by having the same DNA as another person.[5, 11]

This claim does not withstand the close scrutiny that should precede interference with a couple's freedom to bear and rear biologically related children.[10] Having the same genome as another person is not in itself harmful, as widespread experience with monozygotic twins shows. Being a twin does not deny either twin his or her individuality or freedom, and twins often have a special intimacy or closeness that few non-twin siblings can experience.[12] There is no reason to think that being a later-born identical twin resulting from cloning would change the overall assessment of being a twin.

Differences in mitochondria and the uterine and childhood environment will undercut problems of similarity and minimize the risk of overidentification with the first twin. A clone of Smith may look like Smith, but he or she will not be Smith and will lack many of Smith's phenotypic characteristics. The effects of having similar DNA will also depend on the length of time before the second twin is born, on whether the twins are raised together, on whether they are informed that they are genetic twins, on whether other people are so informed, on the beliefs that the rearing parents have about genetic influence on behavior, and on other factors. Having a previously born twin might in some circumstances also prove to be a source of support or intimacy for the later-born child.

The risk that parents or the child will overly identify the child with the DNA source also seems surmountable. Would the child invariably be expected to match the phenotypic characteristics of the DNA source, thus denying the second twin an "open future" and the freedom to develop his or her own identity?[5, 11, 13] In response to this question, one must ask whether couples who choose to clone offspring are more likely to want a child who is a mere replica of the DNA source or a child who is unique and valued for more than his or her genes. Couples may use cloning in order to ensure that the biologic child they rear is healthy, to maintain a family connection in the face of gametic infertility, or to obtain matched tissue for transplantation and yet still be responsibly committed to the welfare of their child, including his or her separate identity and interests and right to develop as he or she chooses.

The second type of fear is that parents who choose their child's genome through somatic-cell cloning will view the child as a commodity or an object to serve their own ends.[5] We do not view children born through coital or assisted reproduction as "mere means" just because people reproduce in order to have company in old age, to fulfill what they see as God's will, to prove their virility, to have heirs, to save a relationship, or to serve other selfish purposes.[14] What counts is how a child is treated after birth. Self-interested motives for having children do not prevent parents from loving children for themselves once they are born.

The use of cloning to form families in the situations I have described, though closely related to current assisted-reproduction and genetic-selection practices, does offer unique variations. The novelty of the relation—cloning in lieu of sperm donation, for example, produces a later-born identical twin raised by the older twin and his spouse—will create special psychological and social challenges. Can these challenges be successfully met, so that cloning produces net good for families and society? Given the largely positive experience with assisted-reproduction techniques that initially appeared frightening, cautious optimism is justified. We should be able to develop procedures and guidelines for cloning that will allow us to obtain its benefits while minimizing its problems and dangers.

In the light of these considerations, I would argue that a ban on privately funded cloning research is unjustified and likely to hamper important types of research.[8] A permanent ban on the cloning of human beings, as advocated by the Council of Europe and proposed in Congress, is also unjustified.[15, 16] A more limited ban—whether for 5 years, as proposed by the National Bioethics Advisory Commission and enacted in California, or for 10 years, as in the bill of

Senator Dianne Feinstein (D-Calif.) and Senator Edward M. Kennedy (D-Mass.) that is now before Congress—is also open to question.[5, 17, 18] Given the early state of cloning science and the widely shared view that the transfer of cloned embryos to the uterus before the safety and efficacy of the procedure has been established is unethical, few responsible physicians are likely to offer human cloning in the near future.[5] Nor are profit-motivated entrepreneurs, such as Richard Seed, likely to have many customers for their cloning services until the safety of the procedure is demonstrated.[19] A ban on human cloning for a limited period would thus serve largely symbolic purposes. Symbolic legislation, however, often has substantial costs.[20, 21] A government-imposed prohibition on privately funded cloning, even for a limited period, should not be enacted unless there is a compelling need. Such a need has not been demonstrated.

Rather than seek to prohibit all uses of human cloning, we should focus our attention on ensuring that cloning is done well. No physician or couple should embark on cloning without careful thought about the novel relational issues and child-rearing responsibilities that will ensue. We need regulations or guidelines to ensure safety and efficacy, fully informed consent and counseling for the couple, the consent of any person who may provide DNA, guarantees of parental rights and duties, and a limit on the number of clones from any single source.[10] It may also be important to restrict cloning to situations where there is a strong likelihood that the couple or individual initiating the procedure will also rear the resulting child. This principle will encourage a stable parenting situation and minimize the chance that cloning entrepreneurs will create clones to be sold to others.[22] As our experience grows, some restrictions on who may serve as a source of DNA for cloning (for example, a ban on cloning one's parents) may also be defensible.[10]

Cloning is important because it is the first of several positive means of genetic selection that may be sought by families seeking to have and rear healthy, biologically related offspring. In the future, mitochondrial transplantation, germ-line gene therapy, genetic enhancement, and other forms of prenatal genetic alteration may be possible.[3, 23, 24] With each new technique, as with cloning, the key question will be whether it serves important health, reproductive, or family needs and whether its benefits outweigh any likely harm. Cloning illustrates the principle that when legitimate uses of a technique are likely, regulatory policy should avoid prohibition and focus on ensuring that the technique is used responsibly for the good of those directly involved. As genetic knowledge continues to grow, the challenge of regulation will occupy us for some time to come.

References

1. Silver LM. Remaking Eden: cloning and beyond in a brave new world. New York: Avon Books, 1997.
2. Walters L, Palmer JG. The ethics of human gene therapy. New York: Oxford University Press, 1997.
3. Robertson JA. Genetic selection of offspring characteristics. Boston Univ Law Rev 1996;76:421–82.

4. Begley S. Can we clone humans? Newsweek. March 10, 1997:53–60.
5. Cloning human beings: report and recommendations of the National Bioethics Advisory Commission. Rockville, Md.: National Bioethics Advisory Commission, June 1997.
6. Robertson JA. Children of choice: freedom and the new reproductive technologies. Princeton, N.J.: Princeton University Press, 1994.
7. Kearney W, Caplan AL. Parity for the donation of bone marrow: ethical and policy considerations. In: Blank RH, Bonnicksen AL, eds. Emerging issues in biomedical policy: an annual review. Vol. 1. New York: Columbia University Press, 1992:262–85.
8. Kassirer JP, Rosenthal NA. Should human cloning research be off limits? N Engl J Med 1998;338:905–6.
9. Holtzman NA. Proceed with caution: predicting genetic risks in the recombinant DNA era. Baltimore: Johns Hopkins University Press, 1989.
10. Robertson JA. Liberty, identity, and human cloning. Texas Law Rev 1998; 77:1371–456.
11. Davis DS. What's wrong with cloning? Jurimetrics 1997;38:83–9.
12. Segal NL. Behavioral aspects of intergenerational human cloning: what twins tell us. Jurimetrics 1997;38:57–68.
13. Jonas H. Philosophical essays: from ancient creed to technological man. Englewood Cliffs, N.J.: Prentice-Hall, 1974:161.
14. Heyd D. Genethics: moral issues in the creation of people. Berkeley: University of California Press, 1992.
15. Council of Europe. Draft additional protocol to the Convention on Human Rights and Biomedicine on the prohibition of cloning human beings with explanatory report and Parliamentary Assembly opinion (adopted September 22, 1997). XXXVI International Legal Materials 1415 (1997).
16. Human Cloning Prohibition Act, H.R. 923, S. 1601 (March 5, 1997).
17. Act of Oct. 4, 1997, ch. 688, 1997 Cal. Legis. Serv. 3790 (West, WESTLAW through 1997 Sess.).
18. Prohibition on Cloning of Human Beings Act, S. 1602, 105th Cong. (1998).
19. Stolberg SG. A small spark ignites debate on laws on cloning humans. New York Times. January 19, 1998:A1.
20. Gusfield J. Symbolic crusade: status politics and the American temperance movement. Urbana: University of Illinois Press, 1963.
21. Wolf SM. Ban cloning? Why NBAC is wrong. Hastings Cent Rep 1997;27(5):12.
22. Wilson JQ. The paradox of cloning. The Weekly Standard. May 26, 1997:23–7.
23. Zhang J, Grifo J, Blaszczyk A, et al. In vitro maturation of human preovulatory oocytes reconstructed by germinal vesicle transfer. Fertil Steril 1997; 68:Suppl:S1. abstract.
24. Bonnicksen AL. Transplanting nuclei between human eggs: implications for germ-line genetics. Politics and the Life Sciences. March 1998:3–10.

POSTSCRIPT

Should Human Cloning Be Banned?

The social and legal debates about cloning are appropriate because the technology is so fundamentally groundbreaking. Although no human beings have as yet been cloned, note that, as much as Sandel and Robertson disagree in the preceding readings, neither would think it advisable for human cloning to proceed in a totally free and unregulated way.

One problem that might seem small at first but is quite serious is that we do not have a good way of assimilating the new ideas of cloning into our vocabulary and thought. For example, we think of a baby as having both a father and a mother. But a clone would be made from a single person. The clone and the single original person would both have the same set of genes. This set of genes comes from the parents of the original person, who are also the parents, as viewed from one biological standpoint, of the clone. So, this creates a situation in which people can have children when they are very old (or possibly even after their death). Moreover, if the original person and the clone share the same genes, then they seem like identical twins. But they could be of vastly different ages; in fact, one of the "twins" could be an adoptive parent of the other. Thus, for example, if Mr. and Mrs. Jones decide to use Mrs. Jones's egg—but replaced with the nucleus of a cell from Mr. Jones, Mr. Jones could be considered as both father and twin brother of Baby Jones. In addition, we are confused about who the mother is here: it looks like it's Mrs. Jones, since she gave birth, but it also looks like it's the mother of Mr. Jones, since she provided maternal genetic input to Mr. Jones's cells. And what of Baby Jones? Is Baby Jones the child of Mr. and Mrs. Jones—or perhaps a delayed twin of Mr. Jones? Our kinship concepts do not seem to apply, probably because these concepts were developed along other lines, long before cloning was ever imagined.

Some say that the fact that cloning doesn't fit into our normal system for making sense of family relationships is due to the fact that cloning upsets the system in a fundamental way. But others say that the fact that our traditional vocabulary is inadequate to the situation only shows that we are unprepared for this new situation, not that human cloning should be totally banned.

For the original bioethics report discussed by Robertson, see *Cloning Human Beings: Report and Recommendations of the National Bioethics Advisory Commission* (Gem Publications, 1998). A variety of views about cloning can be found in Gregory E. Pence, *Who's Afraid of Human Cloning?* (Rowman & Littlefield, 1998); Glenn McGee, ed., *The Human Cloning Debate* (Berkeley Hills Books, 1998); James C. Hefley and Lane P. Lester, *Human Cloning: Playing God or Scientific Progress?* (Fleming H. Revell, 1998); Gregory E. Pence, ed., *Flesh of My Flesh: The Ethics of Cloning Humans: A Reader* (Rowman & Littlefield, 1998); Martha Nussbaum and Cass R. Sunstein eds., *Clones and Clones: Facts and Fantasies About Human Cloning* (W. W. Norton, 1998); Lori B. Andrews, *The Clone Age: Adventures in the New World of Reproductive Technology* (Henry Holt, 1999); Michael C. Brannigan, ed., *Ethical Issues in Human Cloning: Cross-Disciplinary Perspectives* (Seven Bridges Press, 2000); Leon R. Kass, *Human Cloning and Human Dignity: The Report of the President's Council on Bioethics* (Public Affairs, 2002); Ian Wilmut and Roger Highfield, *After Dolly: The Promise and Perils of Cloning* (2007); and Aaron D. Levine, *Cloning: A Beginner's Guide* (Oneworld Publications, 2007).

Internet References . . .

Drugs

The Drug Reform Coordination Network (DRCN) sponsors this site of links to drug policy organizations and studies.

http://druglibrary.org

The Drug Enforcement Administration's Web site contains numerous useful links.

http://www.dea.gov/

Affirmative Action

A collection of sites dealing with affirmative action has been posted by Yahoo! at:

http://dir.yahoo.com/society_and_culture/

issues_and_causes/affirmative_action/

Punishment and the Death Penalty

This *Ethics Updates* site contains discussion forums, court decisions, statistical resources, and Internet resources on the death penalty.

http://ethics.sandiego.edu/Applied/DeathPenalty/index.asp

Gun Control and Gun Rights

Numerous links regarding gun control and gun rites are on the following sites:

http://www.guncite.com/

http://jurist.law.pitt.edu/gunlaw.htm

Euthanasia and End-of-Life Decisions

This *Ethics Updates* site contains discussion questions, court decisions, statistical resources, and Internet resources on euthanasia and physician-assisted suicide.

http://ethics.sandiego.edu/Applied/Euthanasia/index.asp

UNIT 3

Law and Society

Living in groups is part of the social nature of human beings. And this requires that we have laws or rules that govern our behavior and interpersonal interactions. Morality and shared values can be positive tools for social living. One presupposition in a democratic society is that social differences must be settled by open discussion, argument, and persuasion—not by force. The issues in this section include some that have strongly divided our own society and some that currently challenge existing social institutions and practices.

- Is Cloning Pets Ethically Justified?
- Should Congress Allow the Buying and Selling of Human Organs?
- Should Drugs Be Legalized?
- Is Gambling Immoral?
- Is Affirmative Action Fair?
- Should Licensing for Handguns Be More Restrictive?
- Should the Death Penalty Be Abolished?
- Is Torture Ever Justified?
- Is Physician-Assisted Suicide Wrong?

ISSUE 7

Is Cloning Pets Ethically Justified?

YES: Autumn Fiester, from "Creating Fido's Twin," *Hastings Center Report* (July/August 2005)

NO: Hilary Bok, from "Cloning Companion Animals Is Wrong," *Journal of Applied Animal Welfare Science* (vol. 5, no. 3, 2002)

ISSUE SUMMARY

YES: Autumn Fiester argues in support of cloning animals (in particular, people's pets). She emphasizes the point that pet owners really care about their pets. One result of this is that they spend large amounts of money on veterinary care for their pets. Cloning their pets could serve as a useful extension of this idea—and also serve as a positive demonstration of society in general that individual pets have intrinsic value and cannot simply be replaced by new pets.

NO: Hilary Bok argues that cloning pets is immoral first of all because it causes great harm to animals. The animal that results from cloning, for example, is much more likely to have physical defects than the animal from which it was cloned. Moreover, the process of cloning itself necessarily involves harm to other animals (e.g., the animal that will carry the new pet to term). Finally, the end result simply does not provide pet owners with what they were looking for.

The idea of cloning pets rather than human beings raises some interesting questions for both issues. If there is virtually nothing different between human beings and pets, then the answers to the questions in the issues should be the same. If there is a difference in the answers, then some further explanation should be given in order to show that two different answers are required.

But even if we just consider cloning pets, many questions are raised. For one thing, there are factual (empirical, often scientific) questions about what exactly a clone of a pet is. So, for example, we might wonder about the extent, if any, that it is true to think that having a clone of your beloved pet dog Fido is a way of having Fido live on—or, admitting that he died, but bringing him back to life—or having Fido as a puppy all over again—or an exercise in nostalgia perhaps, harkening back to days when Fido was your faithful companion. But further, if it is true (as I think we can all agree) that cloning Fido does not bring him back to life, suppose that a certain percentage of pet owners think that this is indeed the case and want to have the cloning done. In general, even if we can establish the actual truth with respect to factual and scientific matters, does it make a difference that pet owners might not be aware of the truth—or might be in a state of denial? Then there are further questions associated with the fact that some people have more money and resources than others, and might stand to benefit by the use of this cloning, while others, whose relationship with their pets is no different from that in the first group, are nevertheless unable to take advantage of this technology. Moreover, we might wonder whether the newly cloned pets (for example, Fido II) would be done a disservice since their owners might expect them to be just like the original Fido.

Note that the idea of cloning pets seems to be a special case, different from cloning other sorts of animals. We might think that the idea of cloning cows, for example, doesn't give us much pause, because of all the milk (and possibly meat) that they can provide, the benefits are widespread and clear. Anyway, that's the reason most people raise cows in the first place. The situation is similar in the case of animals (such as rats) cloned for scientific or medical research. If cloning animals in this context can provide researchers with important data or even cures for cancer, heart disease, etc., then again the benefit is widespread and clear. Of course, people who support the idea of animal rights might say that the benefits *to us* are clear—but the animals suffer. I think we should put this thought aside, at least for the moment, although it may arise again in the course of the argument about cloning pets. The key point for us right now is that these animals (both the agricultural kind and the laboratory kind) can contribute to human welfare as a whole, whereas the cloning of pets seems to benefit pet owners exclusively. So, whereas we can point to a general benefit (even if it is a benefit *for us*) that we derive from agricultural and laboratory animals, the point here is that these benefits are based on the animals' inpact on human beings in general, while cloning pets seems to benefit only certain private individuals.

Many of these issues arose in the case of the Missyplicity Project, for example. Here, wealthy owners of a dog named Missy spent millions of dollars in an attempt to clone her. Various scientific breakthroughs in the Missyplicity Project allowed the formation of a commercial enterprise, Genetic Savings and Clone, which aimed to clone pets. The following essays discuss these points, both in general, and with specific reference to the Missyplicity Project and the commercial enterprise that grew from it. First, Autumn Fiester argues that pet cloning is indeed ethically justified; Hilary Bok argues that it is wrong.

YES

Autumn Fiester

Creating Fido's Twin: Can Pet Cloning Be Ethically Justified?

Commercial pet cloning—currently cats only—is now available from the firm Genetic Savings and Clone for the small price of $30,000. In December 2004, a nine-week-old cat clone was delivered to its owner, the first of six customers waiting for the identical twin of a beloved pet.[1] "Little Nicky," as he's known, has stirred up a great deal of ethical controversy, with more to come as the firm expands to dog cloning. . . .

For many, the cloning of companion animals seems morally suspect in a way that the cloning of animals for agricultural purposes or for biomedical research does not. In judging the ethics of cloning animals that will be healthier to eat or will advance science or medicine, there is a natural argument to be made that the technique will serve the greater human good. But in the case of pet cloning, there is really no analogous argument, however wonderful the original "Missy," the mixed-breed dog whose owner funded the now-famous Missyplicity Project at Texas A&M to make pet cloning possible. Cloned companion animals will not significantly enhance general human well-being. In balancing the cost to animals against the possible benefit to humans, the ethics of pet cloning seems to be a simple equation: a concern for animal welfare equals an anti-cloning stance.

But what if there were benefits to animals, and what if these benefits outweighed the pain and suffering they endure from cloning research and procedures? Then there would be an argument in favor of pet cloning at least as strong as those offered for cloning conducted for agriculture or medical research. The idea of animals suffering for *animal* benefit makes a tidy moral case that just might justify the practice.

Of course, making this case will be a challenge given the serious anti-cloning objections raised by animal advocacy organizations and cloning critics. But the benefit to animals that I will consider is this: the practice of pet cloning—like advanced veterinary care such as transplants, neurosurgery, orthopedics, and psychopharmaceuticals—might improve the public's perception of the moral status of companion animals because it puts animals in the category of being worthy of a very high level of expense and concern. Something that warrants this level of commitment and investment seems valuable

From *Hastings Center Report,* vol. 35, no. 4, July–August 2005, pp. 34–39. Copyright © 2005 by The Hastings Center. Reprinted by permission of Hastings Center and the author.

intrinsically, not merely instrumentally, and this change in the public's perception could have far-reaching benefits for all animals.

Of course, even if this controversial claim is true—that pet cloning might contribute to an increase in the public's esteem for companion animals—it can justify pet cloning only for those who already find some forms of animal cloning morally acceptable. My case rests on the premise that some types of cloning are morally justified by the benefits that will result from them. People opposed in principle to all forms of animal cloning—for example, because this type of biotechnology is "playing God" or because animals should never be used in research—will not accept this consequentialist starting point. The most straightforward way to make the point is this: we can talk about justifying pet cloning only on the assumption that animal cloning for clearly important ends—like medical or pharmaceutical advances—is morally permissible. If one rejects those types of cloning, the argument about pet cloning cannot get off the ground.

The Anti-Cloning Case

Critics of pet cloning typically offer three objections: (1) the cloning process causes animals to suffer; (2) widely available pet cloning could have bad consequences for the overwhelming numbers of unwanted companion animals; and, (3) companies that offer pet cloning are deceiving and exploiting grieving pet owners.

Animal Suffering Animal welfare advocates have been quick to point out the cost of animal cloning to the animals involved in the procedures.[2] A large body of literature documents high rates of miscarriage, stillbirth, early death, genetic abnormalities, and chronic diseases among the first cloned animals. These problems occur against a backdrop of what in cloning science is called "efficiency," the percentage of live offspring from the number of transferred embryos. The efficiency of animal cloning has typically been about 1 to 2 percent, meaning that of every one hundred embryos implanted in surrogate animals, ninety-eight or ninety-nine fail to produce live offspring.[3] Given the invasive techniques used to implant the embryos in the surrogate, these numbers represent a certain amount of suffering on the part of the donor animals: for every one or two live animals, one hundred eggs must be harvested and one hundred embryos implanted. In the experiments conducted to clone "CC" the calico cat, one hundred and eighty-eight eggs were harvested, eighty-seven cloned embryos were transferred into eight female cats, two of the females became pregnant, and one live kitten was born.[4]

Further, of the live clones born, many have experienced compromised health status or early death. In one study of cloned pigs, researchers reported a 50% mortality rate for the live offspring, with five out of ten dying between three and one hundred and thirty days of age from ailments including chronic diarrhea, congestive heart failure, and decreased growth rate.[5] A study published last year showed that cloned mice experience early death due to liver failure and lung problems.[6] Another study showed that cloned mice had a high tendency to morbid obesity.[7]

Cloning scientists respond that both efficiency rates and health outcomes are radically improving, and that we can reasonably expect in the very near future to see fewer animals involved in the cloning process and better health status for the clones that are born.[8] Although the process that produced "CC" was inefficient, there were no kittens born with compromised health status. Research on cloned cattle published last year showed that once the animals survived infancy, they had no health problems when compared with non-clones.[9] Genetics Savings and Clone claims that it has pioneered a new cloning technique that not only improves the health status of clones but greatly increases cloning efficiency, achieving pregnancy loss rates on par with those of breeders.[10] Although information is limited, the company claims that six healthy kittens have been born with no deformities. If this proves to be true, then the animal suffering caused by the process is limited to that of the surrogate mothers. There aren't even any donor animals involved, since the company uses eggs harvested from ovaries purchased from spay clinics. And the suffering of the surrogates is surely not greater than that of cats who "donate" kidneys for feline kidney transplants, a practice that has not received widespread criticism on grounds of inordinate feline suffering.[11]

Unwanted Pets A second objection to pet cloning is that there are millions of unwanted pets in the United States. How can we justify the creation of designer companion animals when so many wonderful animals languish in shelters? This is the main argument behind the Humane Society's anticloning position. Says Senior Vice President Wayne Pacelle, "The Humane Society of the United States opposes pet cloning because it is dangerous for the animals involved, it serves no compelling social purpose, and it threatens to add to the pet overpopulation problem. It doesn't sit well with us to create animals through such extreme and experimental means when there are so many animals desperate for homes."[12] To be sure, the data on the number of companion animals euthanized in American shelters are sobering. The 2001 Human Society report on the state of animals in the United States found that four to six million dogs and cats were euthanized in shelters in 2001.[13] These figures do not include the millions of stray animals in the country: the ASPCA estimates that 70 million stray dogs and cats live in the United States.[14]

But what is the connection between the sorry state of unwanted companion animals in this country and the anti-pet-cloning stance? Surely one cannot hold that no new animals ought to be intentionally created until all shelter animals are adopted. Anticloners would then have bigger fish to fry than pet cloning—namely, the breeders and puppy farms that produce millions of dogs and cats each year. By comparison, pet cloning, even if it becomes a viable industry, will produce only trivial numbers of animals.

Critics of pet cloning say that pet owners who are so devoted to their animal companions that they would spend thousands of dollars to clone one are precisely the type of adoptive parents who could save an already-existing animal's life through pet adoption, sparing one more dog or cat from euthanasia.[15] But why should a person devoted to a particular animal be more obligated than anyone else to save others of that same species? Being a parent doesn't obligate me more than childless folks to help parentless children. Critics will say this comparison is outrageous. We can't compare animals and children. But for the pet owner willing to clone a deceased pet, there *is* one analogy between a child and a companion animal: you can't substitute or exchange one for another. Pet owners grieving a lost animal see their animal as unique and irreplaceable, so they can't just go to a shelter and get any old animal as a replacement pet. Naturally, this invites the third criticism, which we will discuss below, that this clone *isn't* actually the original pet. But the point is that what these pet owners are after cannot be found in a shelter or purchased from a breeder.

What about the money involved? Isn't there something wrong with spending $30,000 on an animal? Perhaps so, but the problem certainly isn't limited to pet cloning—think of race horses, for example. And if the charge is really that pet cloning is a frivolous use of money that could be better spent on noble causes, then this is just a universal attack on all luxury goods. It doesn't make pet cloning any morally worse than boat-buying.

Exploitation and Deception But what about the concern that pet owners are being tricked into believing that they are getting Fido back, when in truth, Fido and the clone could be as different as any identical twins? There are two separate charges here: one is about false advertising or exploitation on the part of the cloning firm; the other is about the pet owner's self-deception.

Take the cloning firm first. Opponents argue that grieving pet owners are deceived by companies like Genetic Savings and Clone into believing that cloning is a way of resurrecting a deceased and beloved pet. They argue that the business of pet cloning assumes genetic determinism—that genes alone determine all physical and behavioral characteristics—which is false. For example, criticizing the practice of companion animal cloning, bioethicist David Magnus argues, "The people who want this are spending huge sums of money to get their pet immortalized or to guarantee they're getting a pet exactly like the one they had before—and it's simply not possible."[16] If pet cloning firms are contributing to this false belief, then they are engaging in a type of fraud and are certainly exploiting the grief of the devoted pet owner. Genetic Savings and Clone argues that they have an informed consent process that educates clients about the environmental and in utero factors that influence personality and behavior—maybe even physical characteristics. But whatever policies need to be put in place to make sure the owner has realistic expectations, how cloning firms market pet cloning and educate potential customers does not bear on the moral legitimacy of pet cloning itself. There is a clear need to regulate this emerging industry to ensure truth in advertising, but that could be achieved without eliminating the product.

As for the self-deception of the pet owner, this is a psychological, not an ethical concern. Again, Magnus:

> I can completely sympathize with people who become so attached to their pet that they want to bring it back at any cost, but there is nothing that can bring that animal back. Attempting to do so is unhealthy.

> It's trying to pretend that death doesn't exist, which speaks to a larger symptom in our culture of not dealing with death. It's better to just move on.[17]

There are two responses here. First, if the customers don't feel betrayed or deceived (and indeed, they do not) and are satisfied with their investment and comforted by the clone's existence, then it is hard to get this psychological concern going. Second, this argument assumes that there is no good reason to clone a pet unless one *were* deceived[18]—and this is false. The bereft pet owner might know full well that the clone will be nothing more than a genetic twin, and the decision to clone might be merely an attempt to preserve something important from the original animal, rather than *resurrect* it. In the human context, we think of offspring this way. We say things like, "I am so glad my son had children before he died." For animals that were neutered at an early age, who have no offspring, it is perfectly rational to desire the genetic "starting blocks" Fido had, even under complete comprehension that this animal will not be Fido. Wanting to get as close as possible to the original animal is not irrational. In the absence of immortality, genetic identity is the next best thing.

Pet Cloning and "Rising Status"

Now consider an argument in favor of pet cloning: pet cloning may change common views of what in philosophy is called the "moral status" of animals. The fact that companion animals are deemed worthy recipients of this level of effort and expense might encourage people to view animals as having intrinsic value and uniqueness.

The public's perception of the value of animals is not fixed. In fact, the public's estimation of animals' status is arguably rising fast. Getting at perceptions of animal status is difficult, but consider some of the following facts: a 2001 ABC News poll found that 41 percent of Americans believe that animals go to heaven,[19] and a May 2003 Gallup poll found that a full 33 percent of Americans are at least somewhat supportive of an all-out ban on medical research involving laboratory animals.[20] Attitudes among pet owners are even more interesting. For example, a 1999 survey by the American Animal Hospital Association found that 84 percent of pet owners refer to themselves as their pet's "mommy" or "daddy," 63 percent celebrate the pet's birthday, and 72 percent of married respondents greet their pet first when they return home.[21] There are also more pet owners now than ever before; 62 percent of households in the United States own pets in 2005,[22] up from 50 percent in 1975.[23]

The dramatic shift in the status of American pets can also be seen in the resources devoted to them. Americans spent over $30 billion on small animal companions in 2003,[24] a 10 percent increase over 2002 spending,[25] and two and a half times the spending levels of 1978 (in adjusted dollars, Americans spent $11 billion in 1978 vs. $30 billion today).[26] A large part of this figure represents a surge in veterinary service spending: Americans are spending more not only on routine care for companion animals, but on specialty care as well, reflecting a change in priorities and values. For example, pain management expenditures have increased 275 percent in the last six years.[27] Pet owners are now investing in pain control medicines for animals that would have been euthanized a decade ago.

These figures represent what has been called the "pet as family" trend.[28] While it is difficult to empirically document that these figures correspond to an increase in status of companion animals, experts in the field believe they do. Robert Gilbert, associate dean for clinical programs at Cornell Hospital for Animals, describes pet owners' attitudes toward pets as somewhat like parents' attitudes toward children; when he started practicing veterinary medicine in 1977, "a pet was a pet."[29] Thomas Cusick, president of the American Animal Hospital Association, declares, "Pets are clearly becoming an integral part of the American family, enjoying much of the same attention, care, and treatment that is given to a child or spouse."[30]

There is also anecdotal evidence that those who don't own pets are beginning to acknowledge and adopt the changing attitudes of their pet-owning friends and relatives. It is no longer appropriate, for example, to say to a grieving pet owner, "What's the fuss about? Just get another pet." News of an ill pet now engenders concern and sympathy.

The argument I want to advance is that the treatment of companion animals by their caretakers alters what the public in general thinks about them. Attitudes toward companion animals are heavily influenced by the dominant view and mainstream practice (indeed it is the majority of Americans who currently have pets).

More specifically, I want to offer a hypothesis about one mechanism by which this kind of cultural change takes place, namely, that the routinization of certain practices and expenses on the part of pet owners normalizes that behavior, which affects the general view of what care animals deserve; and this in turn enhances the public's estimation of the value of companion animals because it encourages the public to view animals as entities worthy enough to merit this attention and care. One of the most significant influences on the public's perceptions is the effort expended to improve the health and extend the lives of companion animals. Pet cloning is just the extreme form of pet owners' attempts to extend the life (in this case, in the form of the genome) of a beloved animal.

Advanced veterinary care is the paradigm case. Veterinary services are the fastest-growing segment of the companion animal industry, increasing at an annual rate of 4.7 percent, with current expenditures pegged at close to $8 billion.[31] As noted earlier, much of the spending increase is directed at services unheard of a few decades ago. Veterinary medicine has specialized into surgery, dermatology, ophthalmology, orthopedics, neurology, oncology, and even transplant surgery. At a price estimated to be between $5,000 and $15,000 (plus $50–$150 per month in immunosuppressant drugs for life), one's dog or cat can receive a renal transplant at one of the country's new transplant centers.[32] Kidney transplants are still rare, but many other specialty services are not, including x-rays, psychopharmaceuticals, and insulin therapy.

As each new procedure or service is incorporated into veterinary care, pet owners' acceptance of the new standard of care alters the overall public's attitude toward those procedures. No longer seen as a bizarre or exorbitant waste of money and resources, the new procedure starts to seem entirely warranted. Think of the public's attitude toward now commonplace treatments, such as daily shots of insulin, arthritis medicines, corrective surgery for orthopedic problems, or antianxiety medicines. These expenses easily exceed the original price of the animal, but few people would now tell a pet owner to cut her losses and buy a new pet. What is happening to the public's attitude toward companion animals if these advance treatments seem like reasonable measures and expenses to protect animal lives and well-being? At a minimum, the normalization of advanced veterinary care indicates the public's recognition of the "irreplaceability" for the pet owner of one animal with some other. We no longer think of companion animals as disposable or interchangeable, despite the ready supply of homeless animals.

Of course, this argument may suffer from the classic "chicken or the egg" question: is the attention given to animals raising public perceptions of animals' status, or is the perception of animals' status rising independently of the actions of pet owners? In fact, it can go both ways. To the pet owner, the intrinsic value of the companion animal is already recognized, which is why she expends the resources and energy to treat the animal. To someone observing that practice, the effect is to affirm or alter the perception of value that companion animals have—or ought to have. So while only a handful of people may value their pets enough to go through the expense of an organ transplant, the effect of employing "pet organ transplants" is much more widespread. As this type of practice becomes reasonable, it becomes a statement about the intrinsic value and worth of its recipients.

It is plausible that pet cloning will have a parallel effect. Pet cloning makes the statement that one's companion animal is so important that it is worth trying to come as close as possible to preserving it by investing in a genetic twin. The hypothesis is that when pet cloning is seen as a rational, justifiable activity for pet owners as a response to the (impending) death of an animal, the societal effect—as with advanced veterinary care—will be to enhance the companion animal's position on the moral map through the public's recognition that these entities have high value.

One possible rejoinder is that the dignity and uniqueness of the original pet is degraded by an attempt to obtain a clone. Believing that we can replace a companion animal with its clone demonstrates that animals are, in fact, mere objects, not at all like children, and the effect of widespread use of pet cloning will be to downgrade animals' status, not raise it. But whether pet cloning will have this effect will depend on how society interprets it. A pet-cloning-as-mass-production view will undoubtedly reinforce the idea that companion animals are replaceable consumer goods, and this will have a deleterious effect on perceptions of their status. In the cloning-as-solace view as I have described above, however, companion animal cloning will be seen as a tribute to the value of the original animal. There are parents who desperately want to clone their lost children.[33] Pet owners, mirroring their feelings, are making a statement about both the animal's immeasurable value and the level of loss and grief they feel at its death. Whatever one thinks of human cloning, no one argues that the parents who request it don't assign the highest possible worth to the deceased child; the sentiment to clone is a testimony to the parents' belief in the infinite value of that unique person. If this becomes widely understood, the cloning-as-solace interpretation may indeed win out.

If pet cloning bolsters even slightly a perception that companion animals have intrinsic value, then the positive consequences for companion animals will far outweigh the minimal suffering the animals undergo through the cloning process. The rising status of companion animals has already begun to translate into laws that offer more protection for them, including changes in the designation of pet owners to "animal guardians" in some areas.[34] If companion animals' status continues to rise, and if pet cloning contributes at all to that trend, then there is an argument for the moral legitimacy of pet cloning.

References

1. P. Fimrite, "Cat Has 10 Lives, Thanks to $50,000 Cloning," *San Francisco Chronicle,* December 23, 2004.
2. See H. Bok, "Cloning Animals Is Wrong," *Journal of Applied Animal Welfare Science* 5, no. 3 (2002), 233–38.
3. A. Coleman, "Somatic Cell Nuclear Transfer in Mammals: Progress and Application," *Cloning* 1 (1999), 185–200. See also L. Paterson, "Somatic Cell Nuclear Transfer (Cloning) Efficiency." . . .
4. T. Shin et al., "Cell Biology: A Cat Cloned by Nuclear Transplantation," *Nature* 415 (2002): 859.
5. A.B. Carter, "Phenotyping of Transgenic Cloned Pigs," *Cloning and Stem Cells* 4 (2002): 131–45.
6. N. Ogonuki et al., "Early Death of Mice Cloned from Somatic Cells," *Nature Genetics* 30 (2002): 253–54.
7. K. Tamashiro, "Cloned Mice Have an Obese Phenotype Not Transmitted to Their Offspring," *Nature Genetics* 8 (2002): 262–67.
8. *Nature Biotechnology* recently published a metareview of the health status of clones from prior studies, and it reports that 77 percent of cloned animals showed no developmental abnormalities throughout the period of follow-up, although the percentage of healthy clones ranged from 20 percent to 100 percent across the studies. J.B. Cibelli et al. "The Health Profile of Cloned Animals," *Nature Biotechnology* 20 (2002), 13–14.
9. C. Yang, X.C. Tian, and X. Yang, "Serial Bull Cloning by Somatic Cell Nuclear Transfer," *Nature Biotechnology* 22 (2004), 693–94.
10. M. Fox, "Company Says It Cloned Copy Cats," Reuters, August 5, 2004; Fimrite, "Cat Has 10 Lives."
11. Of course, the obvious objection to this comparison is that the kidneys are harvested to save the life of another cat, whereas the animals who suffer through egg harvesting and embryo implantation are not saving an existing cat but creating an entirely new (unneeded) one. But what is in question here is the amount of suffering—not the justification for it.
12. Humane Society of the United States, "Cat Cloning Is Wrong-Headed," February 14, 2002. . . .

13. P.G. Irwin, "Overview: The State of Animals in 2001," in *The State of Animals 2001,* ed. D.J. Salem and A.N. Rowan (Washington, D.C.: Humane Society Press, 2001).
14. American Society for the Prevention of Cruelty to Animals, "Annual Shelter Statistics." . . .
15. The pet owners most likely to request a clone of a deceased pet are those who originally adopted pets from shelters, because these animals are often mixed-breed animals whose personality traits or other features cannot be generated by conventional breeding. It was the owner of a mixed-breed dog, "Missy," that funded the now-famous Missyplicity Project at Texas A&M, which resulted in the cloning of "CC" the cat. But the owner of Missy chose to invest $3.7 million in trying to create Missy's twin; he did not invest the $3.7 million in improving the lives of shelter animals, the original source of Missy herself. . . .
16. M. Shiels, "Carbon Kitty's $50,000 Price Tag," *BBC News,* April 27, 2004.
17. Fimrite, "Cat Has 10 Lives."
18. Magnus reaches this conclusion: "There is no good reason why anybody would do this." Fimrite, "Cat Has 10 Lives."
19. The Roper Center For Public Opinion Research, "Do You Think Animals Go to Heaven When They Die or Only People Go to Heaven?" ABC News/ BeliefNet Poll (June 2001). . . .
20. The Roper Center For Public Opinion Research, "Banning All Medical Research on Laboratory Animals," Gallup Poll (May, 2003). . . .
21. American Animal Hospital Association, Pet Owner Survey, 1999. . . .
22. American Pet Products Manufacturers Association, "APPMA Survey Finds Pet Ownership Continues Growth Trend in U.S." . . .
23. C.W. Schwabe et al., *Veterinary Medicine and Human Health,* third ed. (Baltimore, Md.: Williams & Wilkins Co, 1976).
24. DVM News Magazine, "Pet Spending to Top $37 Billion by '08." . . .
25. S. Aschoff, "Pet RX," *Floridian,* June 10, 2003.
26. Schwabe et al., *Veterinary Medicine and Human Health.*
27. Aschoff, "Pet RX."
28. J.E. Brody. "V.I.P. Medical Treatment Adds Meaning to Dog's (or Cat's) Life," *New York Times,* August 14, 2001: Section F; Page 4; Column 2.
29. J.E. Brody. "V.I.P. Medical Treatment Adds Meaning to Dog's (or Cat's) Life," *New York Times,* August 14, 2001.
30. American Veterinary Medical Association, "Survey Says: Owners Taking Good Care of Their Pets," *Journal of the American Veterinary Medical Association.* . . .
31. *DVM News Magazine,* "Pet Spending to Top $37 Billion by '08." . . .
32. L. Copeland. "Transplant Offers Hope for a Tabby; With Kidney Comes 2nd Chance at 9 Lives," *Washington Post,* March 14, 1999. Also B. Bilger, "The Last Meow," *New Yorker,* September 8, 2003, at 46. Donor cats are taken from local shelters and research labs, and the owners of the transplantee must agree to adopt the donor (p. 49).

33. Offering a pro-pet cloning argument in no way commits me to a pro-human cloning argument, although I can understand the powerful sentiments that would drive a parent to desire the ability to clone a beloved child. The difference is that we can accept a sacrifice in animal lives (we euthanize them, we experiment on them, and we eat them) that we cannot accept in human lives. But if human cloning could be guaranteed never to result in a birth defect, stillbirth, or compromised health status of a child, the debate about human cloning would be quite different.
34. *CBS Evening News,* "Legal Relationship Between Pets and Their Owners," CBS News Transcripts, Aug. 7, 2000; B. Pool, "In West Hollywood, Pets Are Part of the Family," *Los Angeles Times,* February 22, 2001; "Pet Owners in San Francisco Become 'Pet Guardians,'" *The San Diego Union Tribune,* March 1, 2001; and "Students Make History by Helping to Draft & Pass Animal Rights Legislation," *News from General Assembly,* September 26, 2001. . . .

Hilary Bok

Cloning Companion Animals Is Wrong

In principle, I have nothing against cloning either nonhuman animals or humans. If cloning were as safe as natural procreation and if those who chose to clone themselves or others completely understood cloning (in particular, how clones are related to their originals), I would not worry about cloning being tantamount to, in Hawthorne's words, "playing God" or "cheating death" (Hawthorne, 2002 . . .). I would view it simply as a complicated and expensive way of producing an identical twin born at a different time and from a different mother than the original. In fact, however, neither of these things is true. Cloning is not safe, and it is not widely understood. Nonetheless, I suppose that some extremely compelling reason might justify our cloning animals. However, there is no such justification for the Missyplicity Project.

Suffering and Complications

Cloning causes animals to suffer. Egg donors must have their ovaries artificially stimulated with hormone treatments and their eggs surgically harvested. Given the unusually high rates of late-term miscarriages and high birth weights among clones, the surrogate mothers are at greater risk of dying or suffering serious complications than animals who become pregnant naturally. The clones, themselves, however, suffer the most serious problems: They are much more likely than other animals to be miscarried, have birth defects, develop serious illnesses, and die prematurely.

Hawthorne (2002 . . .) acknowledges that this is "the ethical issue of greatest concern" (p. 229) raised by animal cloning. However, he greatly understates its seriousness. He claims, for instance, that 20% of cattle clones detectable in utero experience some sort of physical problem resulting in miscarriages, early deaths, or later health problems. In fact, to go by the published reports of cloning surveyed by the National Academy of Sciences (2002) in its recent report on cloning, the numbers are much higher: Of at least 242 pregnancies from cloned adult cattle cells, at least 174 were miscarried. Of the 68 calves born alive, only 42 were still alive at the time of publication, and investigators reported that 5 of those had significant health

From *Journal of Applied Animal Welfare Science,* vol. 5, no. 3, July 2002, pp. 233–238. Copyright © 2002 by ASPCA and Society & Animals Forum. Reprinted by permission of Taylor & Francis Group via Rightslink.

problems other than high birth weight. This means that the number of cattle clones detectable in utero who go on to experience serious health problems is not 20% but at least 85%.

In a recent study, Ogonuki et al. (2002) compared the lifespan of 12 cloned mice, 7 genetically matched, naturally conceived mice, and 6 mice produced by a process of spermatid injection performed under the same laboratory conditions as the cloning but resulting in natural conception. Eight hundred days after their birth, 10 of 12 cloned mice had died, compared with 1 of the 7 mice conceived naturally and 2 of the 6 produced by spermatid injection. Autopsies performed on 6 of the cloned mice revealed that all had severe pneumonia, 4 had necrotic livers, and 2 had tumors. In addition, the cloned mice had reduced immune system function, which the researchers believed might account for their pneumonia. Here again, the number of clones with serious health problems is much higher than Hawthorne (2002 . . .) suggests: In Ogonuki et al.'s study, two thirds of the animals who were born alive died prematurely as a result of physical problems associated with their being clones.

Real Problems, Unknown Solutions

Hawthorne (2002 . . .) suggests that these problems may be species specific and that researchers do not know whether dogs and cats will exhibit them. This is disingenuous. It is true that researchers do not yet know what problems cloned dogs and cats might have. No one has yet cloned a dog, and it is too early to tell whether the one cloned cat in existence will develop the kinds of health problems seen in other species. We do know, however, that these problems have turned up in every other species cloned, including goats. Therefore, there is every reason to expect that they will turn up in cats and dogs as well.

Hawthorne also suggests that some test yet to be developed might detect abnormalities prior to implantation. It seems extremely unlikely that in the foreseeable future someone will develop a reliable preimplantation test for problems with gene expression comprehensive enough to ensure that the clones we produce will be healthy. The number of genes whose expression would have to be tested is enormous, and researchers do not now understand the effects of various possible differences in their expression on an animal's subsequent development. In addition, many of these genes are not active before implantation; therefore, it is unclear how one could test their expression at that stage. For these reasons, it is unlikely that such a test will be developed in the near future.

In the meantime, cloned animals will continue to suffer serious health problems at much higher rates than other animals of the same species. Some will be suffocated when their lungs do not inflate, some will be poisoned because of liver or kidney failure, and some will be eaten away by cancer. Some will die from heart failure, and some will have only such "minor" problems as gross obesity or premature arthritis. Almost all clones will suffer and die, and they will do so, not because of some natural illness or misfortune but because researchers have chosen to bring them into existence using a process that is not understood well enough to use safely.

Of course, the only way researchers can learn enough about cloning cats and dogs to do it safely is by trying and learning from their mistakes. This, however, does not justify conducting this process of trial and error on the bodies of dogs and cats, absent some reason to think that learning how to clone dogs and cats is worth the cost in animal suffering. One must ask whether enabling humans to clone their pets is important enough to justify the considerable suffering involved in learning how to do so.

Why Clone Pets?

As the caregiver for two cats, I can easily understand why persons who do not understand what cloning involves might be tempted to clone their pets. Pet owners love their pets. When an animal one loves dies, the most natural thing in the world is to want that animal back. Just as a parent whose child has died is unlikely to be comforted by the thought that there are plenty of other children waiting for adoption, most grieving pet owners are not consoled by the thought that they can always adopt another dog or cat. This is not because pet owners are unduly sentimental or confused about the differences between pets and children. It is because, like parents, they love individuals, and adopting another dog or cat will not replace the individual they have loved and lost.

Cloning is not a way of bringing back the animal one loves. That is the point of loving an individual: Not even an exact replica can be the particular being one loves. Still, to a grieving pet owner an exact replica might seem to be the next best thing, and some pet owners might think that cloning could produce one. This misconception is easy to remove: One need only point out that clones will not have the same memories as their originals and that because their upbringing and environment will differ, their behavior and temperament will differ as well.

However, even after this mistake is corrected, one might still think that cloned animals will be identical to their originals in all respects except those that depend on environment and upbringing. One might, that is, think that although a clone of one's dog will not be a copy of that dog as an adult, the clone, when born, will be identical to the newborn puppy who grew up to be that dog. This is, I think, what many of those who are interested in cloning their pets believe. Unfortunately, they are wrong. Cloning produces animals who are genetically identical to their originals. However, genetic identity is not, and does not ensure, physical identity; the difference between the two is extremely significant.

The genes in an adult animal's somatic cells are programmed not for directing embryonic development but for directing the activities of skin cells, liver cells, and so forth. If researchers tried to clone a cat by inducing one skin cell to divide without reprogramming its DNA, they would end up not with a kitten but with, at best, a kitten-sized mass of skin cells. That mass would be genetically identical to the original cat but, presumably, would not be what the owners had in mind when they asked to clone the cat. To produce not a mass of skin cells but a kitten, the skin cell's DNA needs to be reprogrammed.

To produce a kitten largely, although not entirely, similar to the kitten the cat once was, researchers would have to reprogram the cat's DNA to exactly the state it was in when that cat was a fertilized egg.

In practice, it is extraordinarily unlikely that any animal's DNA can be reprogrammed perfectly. Tens of thousands of genes might need reprogramming, and researchers do not know what they all are, let alone what would count as their correct expression. Nor is it known in most cases, what contribution they make to an animal's subsequent development. Moreover, although the word *reprogramming* might suggest the existence of easily manipulable switches that could be reset one by one, in practice reprogramming is a messy and haphazard process that is neither understood nor controllable.

For these reasons, the likelihood that every gene will be reset correctly is minute. Some problems with reprogramming might be benign. Others might be so serious that any fetus who has them will be miscarried. There is, however, a middle group: problems serious enough to create significant physical differences between clones and their originals but not serious enough to prevent those clones from being born at all. Given the number of such mistakes that it is possible to make and the impossibility in practice of screening for any appreciable number of them, clones probably will differ in unpredictable and potentially significant respects from their originals.

Consider in this light that 85% of cattle clones detected in utero are miscarried, die prematurely, or suffer serious health problems. As far as is known, these cattle were cloned from healthy adults whose lungs, livers, and kidneys did not malfunction; who were born without serious cardiac problems or joint irregularities; and who did not have juvenile diabetes or severe anemia. All these problems appeared among their clones. This indicates three things. First, that clones are genetically identical to their originals does not mean that they will be physically identical to them. Second, the differences between clones and their originals will involve not only relatively unimportant things like coat coloring but also crucial ones like whether their hearts work. Third, these differences are not rare or anomalous: They are the norm.

Cloning, then, is not a way for a pet owner to acquire, say, a puppy just like the puppy who grew up to be his or her dog. It is a way of acquiring a dog who is genetically identical to that dog, but who is much more likely to have major physical defects that cause real suffering and require serious medical care. Moreover, even if that dog is lucky enough not to have serious health problems, he or she is likely to differ from his or her original in subtler ways. In particular, there is no reason to think that the genes that underlie a dog's temperament are less likely than other genes to be reprogrammed incorrectly and, therefore, no reason to think that cloned dogs will necessarily share their originals' temperament and disposition. If pet owners want to get dogs similar to ones who have died, they are much more likely to succeed by adopting puppies of the same breed with similar dispositions than by cloning their pets.

The one goal pet owners might accomplish by cloning their pets is to make it possible for the genes of spayed, neutered, or otherwise infertile pets to be passed on to another generation. Although many clones have serious physical defects because these defects result mostly from problems with gene expression rather than with the genes themselves, clones are unlikely to pass these defects on to their offspring (Tamashiro et al., 2002). Cloning might make sense, then, as a very complicated way of reversing a spaying or neutering operation one had come to regret.

Although a pet owner might achieve this goal through cloning, it is clearly immoral. To clone a dog for this reason is to subject other dogs to hormonal treatments to stimulate their ovaries; surgically harvest their eggs; create hundreds of fetuses; implant them in dogs who will risk unusually dangerous pregnancies; and finally, bring into existence a clone who probably will suffer serious health problems, just to make it possible for this dog to have puppies genetically related to one's original pet. This would display great callousness toward the suffering of animals and a willingness to sacrifice their interests to one's whims.

If the arguments above are sound, then people who want to clone their pets must be either mistaken about what cloning is or immoral. In the first case, it would be wrong of the Missyplicity Project to take advantage of their misconceptions, especially at the expense of other animals. In the second, it would be wrong for the Missyplicity Project to collude in their wrongdoing. In no case is it morally justifiable either to clone one's pet or to enable others to clone theirs.

References

Hawthorne, L. (2002). A project to clone companion animals. *Journal of Applied Animal Welfare Science,* 5, 227–229.

National Academy of Sciences: Committee on Science, Engineering, and Public Policy (2002). *Scientific and medical aspects of human reproductive cloning* (Appendix B). Washington, DC: National Academy Press.

Ogonuki, N., Inove, K., Yamamoto, Y., Noguchi, Y., Tanemura, K., Suzuki, O., et al. (2002, February 11). Early death of mice cloned from somatic cells. *Nature Genetics* [Advance on-line publication]. . . .

Tamashiro, K. L. K., Wakayama, T., Akutsu, H., Yamazaki, Y., Lachey, J. L., Wortman, M. D., et al. (2002). Cloned mice have an obese phenotype not transmitted to their offspring. *Nature Medicine, 8,* 262–267.

POSTSCRIPT

Is Cloning Pets Ethically Justified?

The Missyplicity Project (and the related commercial enterprise called Genetic Savings and Clone) can be a fascinating case study in animal cloning. See the online sources at http://www.the-scientist.com, http://en.wikipedia.org, http://www.mindfully.org, and http://www.pamperedpuppy.com.

As for the idea of cloning pets in general, it is remarkable that some people have immediate reactions that are highly positive, while others have immediate reactions that are highly negative. This suggests that emotions play a great role in the way we think about this. To some extent, we can transcend emotional reactions and try to gain a rational view of the matter. Yet, this raises some additional questions because we wonder whether, if emotion is totally removed, this issue can still be appreciated for what it is. Indeed, pet owners can feel such strong emotional bonds with their pets. Nevertheless, even if emotions are allowed a place here, it is undeniable that it is also worthwhile to attend to scientific and factual matters about cloning. Some relevant sources here are http://www.ornl.gov and http://en.wikipedia.org.

A couple of factors still remain though. First, even though cloning is sometimes discussed in the abstract—as if all the kinks with the procedure had been worked out—there are several severe problems with cloning: It is highly inefficient, often requiring hundreds of implantations in order to generate even one live birth, and even if the clone is successfully born, clones are often subject to serious disease and a shorter-than-normal lifespan. The trouble with discussion that ignores these problems and proceeds as if everything were fine is that these problems may never be solved. There is often a great optimism surrounding discussions of cloning yet problems remain.

Another source of unease is that there is a gap between the two kinds of people who are (or would be) most closely involved with pet cloning: the scientists and the pet owners. Scientists may have accurate ideas about what cloning is, but it is far from clear that pet owners have accurate ideas. For example, pet owners might think that the newly cloned animals will be guaranteed to have the same dispositions and behavioral traits (and perhaps even the same memories) as the original pet. Pet owners may have established emotional bonds here that prevent them from seeing (or acknowledging) the truth. "Idealized" discussion of pet cloning often overlooks this fact, since in the ideal case, everyone knows (and fully acknowledges) the facts.

For further reading, see "Pet Cloning Misses Point," *The Register-Guard*, Eugene, Oregon (February 20, 2002). Pet cloning is also discussed by John Kilner, *Basic Questions in Genetics, Stem Cell Research and Cloning* (Kregel, 2003) and Hwa A. Lim, *Multiplicity Yours* (World Scientific, 2006).

ISSUE 8

Should Congress Allow the Buying and Selling of Human Organs?

YES: Lewis Burrows, from "Selling Organs for Transplantation," *The Mount Sinai Journal of Medicine* (September 2004)

NO: James F. Childress, from "Should Congress Allow the Buying and Selling of Human Organs? No," *Insight on the News* (May 7, 2001)

ISSUE SUMMARY

YES: Lewis Burrows, M.D., begins with the observation that the need for organs far outstrips the supply: each year, hundreds of patients die while waiting for transplants. Burrows argues that payment to the donor (or payment to the donor's family, in cases in which the donor is deceased) would increase the supply of organs, regulations could restrain possible abuses, and a payment-for-organs system could meet relevant medical ethical principles.

NO: James F. Childress, professor of ethics and professor of medical education, argues that a free market would cause the loss of important altruistic motivations and would turn organs into commodities; moreover, such an untried market might make fewer—not more—organs available.

Some facts are important for the proper appreciation of this issue. First, the supply of organs is vastly lower than the demand. This is so not only in the United States, but on a worldwide basis. In America, people who need a new kidney have to be put on a waiting list. In the meantime, they may be able to use a dialysis machine. Receiving dialysis is a noncurative procedure, which must be performed on a regular basis—often three times a week for several hours. Unless people who need new kidneys receive them, the dialysis machine must become a regular part of their lives—forever. Second, when an organ such as a kidney is transplanted into someone selected for transplantation, numerous parties receive compensation for the services they render. Thousands of dollars are paid to physicians and hospitals and others; but donors must be *donors:* they must *give* the organ and must not receive any compensation of any kind, except perhaps a small amount for their time or for their own expenses. (Since 1984 and the passage of the National Organ Transplant Act, it has been a federal offense to buy or sell organs.)

Many people think that there is something wrong, perhaps something distasteful, with buying or selling an organ. By contrast, *donating* an organ is often regarded as an extremely worthy—perhaps heroic—act. But also, to *receive* an organ through transplantation is thought to be extremely beneficial, not distasteful or shameful at all. A donor can give a kidney to a recipient, and both of them will be thought well of. But we tend to look askance at a situation in which money changes hands.

And yet, from one point of view, it seems only fair for the person who gives up a kidney to be compensated for doing so. Everyone else involved in the transplant situation seems to be benefited or compensated. But the donor is supposed to be motivated by pure altruism and not at all by money. This works well when the donor and the recipient are close relations. It is not infrequent for transplantations to occur between family members. (What parent would not give a kidney to a son or daughter who desperately needed one?) But there remains the problem of the general societal lack of organs for transplantation.

In the first of the two selections below, Dr. Lewis Burrows first argues that there should indeed be a (regulated) market for organs. (He speaks, first of all, about kidneys, but suggests that there may also be possibilities for liver, lung, and pancreas transplantation. And if the donor is deceased, the scope for transplantation of organs may be wider still.) This, he claims, would greatly increase the supply. Then, on the other side of the issue, James F. Childress argues against all forms of buying and selling organs; he emphasizes the values that would be lost if there were to be such a market, and he casts doubt on the idea that a market in human organs really would increase the supply. According to Childress, instead of establishing a market in organs—which would likely put a damper on donations—donations and the altruistic motivation that generally lies behind them should be actively encouraged.

YES

Lewis Burrows

Selling Organs for Transplantation

Living donor organ transplantation is the only field of medicine in which two individuals are intimately involved: the donor and the recipient. It is also the only field of medicine in which altruistic giving of oneself is the basis of the medical practice. I have been asked to address a very specific aspect of this process, that is, living organ donation for financial remuneration. No other subject in the transplant experience is as controversial. Many of those involved in the field—surgeons, physicians, social scientists, ethicists, and theologians—have expressed an opinion on this issue.

As a result of impressive gains in this field, organ recipients now have a significant chance for both long-term survival and a reasonable quality of life. These successes have led nearly 80,000 individuals to opt for transplantation as a form of therapy. Unfortunately, the number of organs available has lagged far behind the demand. Every year thousands die while waiting for the gift of life that an organ transplant could provide.

In the case of cadaveric giving, the family of the brain-dead person is asked to donate. There is a serious shortfall in cadaveric organ donations, with only 40–60% of U.S. families consenting to organ recovery. Countries that have adopted the doctrine of "presumed consent" (such as Spain, Austria, and Belgium) have a much higher rate of organ recovery. In these countries, families can "opt out" of donation; if they do not, the organs of deceased family members can be used for transplantation. In most of the rest of the world, families have to "opt in" before organs can be used for transplantation. "Presumed consent" countries that require "opting out" obtain more than 40 donations per million population, as contrasted with half that amount elsewhere. The lower rate is obviously not adequate for meeting current needs.

The number and rate of donations have reached a plateau and leveled off following the enforcement of lower speed limits for automobiles and the introduction of seat belt laws. It is said that donation is a middle class, suburban phenomenon; those groups donate at a somewhat higher rate than others. Why is the rate of donation lower among the poor and in the big cities? We truly do not know. Education, family cohesiveness, trust in medicine, and moral and religious sensibility may all play important roles.

In light of the gap between organ need and organ donation, we are beginning to consider various forms of financial incentives to families as a stimulant for donation (1, 2). I am not referring to the token $399 that the state of

From *Mount Sinai Journal of Medicine,* vol. 71, no. 4, September 2004, pp. 251–254. Copyright © 2004 by Mt. Sinai School of Medicine. Reprinted by permission of Wiley-Blackwell.

Pennsylvania has offered for funeral expenses. That amount would hardly pay for a plain pine coffin. Nor am I referring to the more than $10,000 state income tax credit that the Wisconsin senate approved in January 2004 (3). That incentive would be of little use to the poor. I am referring to a substantial amount, to be included in the financial transactions that occur during the transplant process.

Organ transplantation involves payments of large sums of money. Huge sums go to the hospitals, the transplant surgeons, the physicians, the ancillary staffs and the insurance companies. And most of the money actually goes to the pharmaceutical industry. Many millions of dollars flow into their coffers for the immunosuppressants, antihypertensives, antibiotics, anticholesterols, antacids, and so on, that recipients routinely receive in the course of their treatments. The only people who are not being remunerated are the families of the donors. They alone are being asked to be altruistic.

Just try to do a transplant today on an uninsured patient. I can assure you, the patient will not get through the front door. Medicaid will pay for dialysis treatment of an uninsured alien. But Medicaid will not pay for his or her transplant.

What would be the harm of providing a payment to the donating family of, let's say, $20,000? A liver transplant can cost upward of $300,000, a heart transplant $200,000, and a kidney transplant more than $100,000. In kidney transplantation, even the insurance company would benefit from the payment, since they would no longer have to pay for dialysis therapy.

The most controversial remuneration of all is payment to a living donor who has no relationship to the recipient. Because of the organ shortage, most centers in this country accept the donations of living donors who are related, or emotionally related (for example, a spouse or a friend) as the source of transplant organs. In situations where there is an obvious relationship between the donor and recipient, people find no violation of ethical principles. In spite of the inherent risks of donating a kidney or a segment of liver, and the pressures and emotions related to the desire to save a loved one, these organ donations are found acceptable.

But, what of the donor who has no obvious relationship to the recipient? What should we say of someone who only wants to donate an organ to someone with the means to pay for it, perhaps out of financial desperation? About twenty years ago, a foreign-born nephrologist at our institution offered me the opportunity to perform more than two hundred kidney transplants each year. He proposed bringing donor-recipient pairs from his country to our hospital for the surgery. I was to be paid a sizable sum. The apparently wealthy recipients would pay all the involved expenses, and each donor would receive approximately $2,000 for his or her kidney. Apparently, $2,000 was then a substantial sum for a poor person in his country. According to my nephrologist friend, that amount of money would change the donor's life and the standing of his family for generations. Yet even aside from the legal considerations. I rejected the offer outright, because it included no assurance of the donor receiving adequate long-term aftercare. I also felt a sense of revulsion at the idea of a poor, desperate individual peasant being used in this manner by some wealthy businessman or aristocrat.

Nowadays, this form of commercialism is prevalent in the Third World, where either there are no laws prohibiting these transactions or existing laws are not enforced. I shall not address those practices. Instead I want to consider payment for organ donation in an ideal situation. I want to consider the situation where the donor and recipient are carefully selected and carefully matched, and where the operation is well controlled. The donor would be offered long-term care, and the recipient would pay the donor a significant sum. There would be no "middle-men" or brokers involved, and the allocation process would be carefully controlled by the national or regional organ allocation mechanism. Under such circumstances, would it be ethically acceptable for one individual to use another for his own survival and well-being? Would the infliction of pain and suffering on one individual be justified by the benefit to another individual? Should someone with the financial wherewithal be allowed to purchase transplant priority? Does allowing such financial transactions undermine what has been a truly altruistic practice? Would payment to living donors inevitably undermine the public's faith in the process?

Let us examine the proposal in light of the ethical principles involved, to see if they would be violated. But first, I would like to rule out several factors that would be inconsistent with the organ exchange ideal that I imagine:

1. **The donor comes from a country where aftercare is deficient or unavailable.** Such a situation would subject the donor to an unacceptable risk of harm and would therefore exceed a reasonable balance of harms and benefits.
2. **Third-party brokers, profiteers, or entrepreneurs are involved in the transaction.** Removing any portion of the transplant process from the oversight of medical professionals would remove it from the fiduciary relationship that assures that the donor's life and health would be safeguarded. And commercialism introduces possibilities of exploitation and conflict of interest.
3. **The donor does not truly understand the nature of the donation and the potential risks involved.** Evaluation of the donor by an impartial psychiatrist would be a crucial element in assuring that the donor is making an informed choice that reflects personal values and priorities.
4. **There are bidding wars for organs.** The assurance of donor and recipient safety must be a crucial feature of living donor transplantation. Organ auctions could compromise long-term safety or lead to unexpected and untoward outcomes of living donor transplantation. Auctions can only assure price compatibility between buyer and seller. While the selling price should be set high enough to elicit donors, the larger process must take into account the costs of long-term care and emergencies such as primary non-function of the transplanted organ, or organ rejection. Because the transplantation community has the ultimate responsibility for the careful management of these situations, the transplant community must have oversight of any financial exchange.

I would like to summarize the considerations that incline me to accept payment to organ donors in the ideal situation.

1. **Autonomy.** Certainly the donor and the recipient have the right to proceed if those involved in their care are assured that they have freely accepted the transaction with a complete understanding of the risks and benefits involved.
2. **Beneficence.** Both the donor and the recipient stand to gain from their contract, as does everyone else on the waiting list below the recipient. All of the others waiting for a cadaveric organ will benefit by moving up a notch in the process.
3. **The "do no harm" principle (*primum nolle nocere*).** There is obviously some harm done to the donor in the surgery involved in organ donation. There is also the immediate exposure to surgical risks, and the certain disfigurement and loss of an organ. Also there are possible long-term consequences of organ loss. These risks of harm are so well defined in the kidney transplant experience that donors can be assured that the risks, both long- and short-term, are minimal. The risks associated with the liver, lung and pancreas donation process are not as well defined. Perhaps this element of uncertainty justifies a moratorium on these donations until the risks can be carefully assessed in well-controlled clinical studies.
4. **Justice.** I am less confident about whether an ideal organ payment system will conform to the basic principle of fair and equitable distribution of benefits and burdens. The main benefit of payments for organ procurement would go to relatively privileged individuals. They would get transplant organs more readily than others, in addition to all the other privileges that accrue to the wealthy (e.g., better homes, health care, service, etc.). Yet no one else would be harmed by the paid organ donation, unless there is a general loss of faith in the donation process, with a fall in the rate of altruistic giving. This is an empirical question that can only be answered by a trial.

It is clear that I have changed my position somewhat, on this form of donation. I have accepted the libertarian thesis that selling one's organs does not necessarily violate the right of self-determination, and should fall within the protected privacy of free individuals on the basis of the principle of autonomy. I have also been persuaded by pragmatic and utilitarian considerations—the current system is failing, and the benefits for all recipients of an increase in available organs outweigh most objections.

Of course, I would insist on controls. The donor must be healthy, both physically and mentally, as determined by competent physicians and psychiatrists who are not directly involved in the transplant process. We must be assured that the donor fully understands the risks involved and must sign a statement demonstrating true informed consent. Paid donors must be guaranteed long-term medical care and life insurance for themselves and their families in the event that complications occur. The transplant should be controlled by medical professionals and medical agencies that are intimately involved in transplantation and that can administer the process with due care and impartiality.

I offer a final personal note. I am not entirely pleased that I have had to reach this decision. I would certainly prefer that an ample source of cadaveric organs be available to those in need. Available organs would allow us to avoid the dilemmas of living organ donors and paid donations. But for the time being, while my patients are dying for want of an organ, I have accepted this libertarian, utilitarian approach. We do not live in ivory towers. In life, we have to make hard decisions and accept the consequences when all of our options have serious flaws.

References

1. Arnold R, Bartlett S, Bernat J, et al. Financial incentives for cadaver organ donation: an ethical reappraisal. Transplantation 2002; 73(8):1361–1367.
2. Delmonico FL, Arnold R, Scheper-Hughes N, et al. Ethical incentives—not payment—for organ donation. N Engl J Med 2002; 346(25):2002–2005.
3. Napolitano J. Wisconsin senate approves tax deduction for organ donors. N Y Times 2004 Jan 23; A:12.

James F. Childress

Should Congress Allow the Buying and Selling of Human Organs?

A Free Market Would Reduce Donations and Would Commodify the Human Body

The number of patients awaiting an organ transplant exceeded 75,000 in late March [2001]. Yet in 1999, the last year for which there are complete figures, there only were 21,655 transplants with organs from 4,717 living donors and 5,859 from cadavers (many of which provided more than one organ). Organ donation continues to fall further and further behind the demand for organs, and new initiatives have failed to reduce the gap. In this situation, why shouldn't we turn to the free market to increase the supply of transplantable organs, which can save lives and improve the quality of life?

Buying or selling an organ isn't always morally wrong. We don't, and shouldn't, always condemn those who sell or purchase an organ. We can understand why someone might do so. But should we change our laws to permit sales of organs and even enforce contracts to sell organs? Should we turn away from a system of gifts to a market in organs?

Our society has very strong reasons not to allow the transfer of organs from the living or the dead for money. In presenting these reasons, it is useful to separate the acquisition of organs from their distribution. Normally, acquisition and distribution go together. However, if those who need organs had to purchase them directly, then the poor would end up selling organs to the rich—a distribution that would strike many as unfair. Thus, let's assume that the government or a private organization under government regulation will purchase organs and then distribute them in a fair and equitable way. I'll call this an "organ-procurement market."

Such a market could target living donors or cadaveric sources of organs. I use the term "sources" because those who sell their organs are not donors, they are sellers or vendors. Let's begin with cadaveric organs removed after an individual's death.

The main argument for rescinding the federal prohibition on the sale of organs is based on utility—allowing the sale of organs would increase their supply. But would a market actually increase the number of cadaveric organs for transplantation? Despite the claims of market fundamentalists, we simply

From *Insight on the News,* May 7, 2001, pp. 41, 43. Copyright © 2001. Reprinted by permission of News World Communications. All rights reserved.

do not know whether a market would reduce the scarcity of organs, in contrast to many other goods. And we have good reasons to be skeptical.

Indeed, I will argue, we shouldn't legalize a market in organ procurement because it probably would be ineffective, perhaps counterproductive (in reducing donations and possibly even the overall number of organs available for transplantation) and likely change our attitudes and practices by commodifying the human body and its parts. Furthermore, it is unnecessary to take this route, with all its problems, because we can make the system of donation effective without such ethical risks.

It would be unwise to move away from a system of donation unless we have good evidence that a market actually would increase the supply of organs. After all, organ donations provide a substantial (though insufficient) number of organs. Some evidence against a potential market's effectiveness in cadaveric organ procurement comes from the reasons people now give for not signing donor cards. One proponent of the market contends that people now fail to donate "because of inertia, mild doubts about their preferences, a slight distaste for considering the subject or the inconvenience involved in completing or carrying a donor card." If these reasons for nondonation were the only ones, a market in cadaveric organ procurement probably would work. In fact, however, opinion polls indicate that fears of being declared dead prematurely or having one's death hastened in order to provide organs seriously inhibit many from signing donor cards.

The fears and distrust that limit organ donation would render utterly ineffective a system of organ procurement based on sales. A futures market—whereby individuals contract now for delivery of organs upon their deaths—is the most defensible because people sell their own, not others', organs. However, if people at present are reluctant to sign donor cards because they fear they may not receive proper care in the hospital, imagine their fears about accepting money for the delivery of usable organs upon their deaths. Once they have signed the contract, all that remains for its fulfillment is their death. And a regulated market would not eliminate their fears. After all, such fears persist in our regulated system of organ donation.

Critics often contend that allowing sales of organs would turn bodies and parts into commodities. Such commodification could lead us to think about and treat dead bodies in merely instrumental terms, thereby damaging important social values. In addition, many claim, commodification could damage and even reduce altruism. A market in organs would drive out, or very substantially reduce, organ donations, in part because it would redefine acts of donating organs. No longer would donors provide the "gift of life"—they instead would donate the equivalent of the market value of the organs provided.

In short, market defenders have not proposed an effective system to obtain additional cadaveric organs. Not only would a procurement market probably be ineffective, it could be counterproductive and have other social costs. Its financial costs would not be negligible. Furthermore, the system of donation has features, including its connection with altruism, that make it ethically preferable, other things being equal. And we can make our system of express donation more effective.

It works fairly well now. For example, according to some estimates, the acts of cadaveric-organ donation in 1999 represented close to half of the patients who died in circumstances where their organs could be salvaged for transplantation (usually following brain death). It might be possible, and desirable, to expand the categories of potential donors to include many who die according to cardiopulmonary standards. Beyond expanding the criteria of donor eligibility, we need to work to make effective the recently adopted policy of required referral. This policy mandates referral to an organ-procurement organization that can then ask the family about organ donation.

Programs to educate the public about organ donation must attend to attitudes of distrust and mistrust, not merely to the tremendous need for organs. It is difficult to alter those attitudes, but increasing the public's understanding of brain death certainly is one way to proceed.

The public's willingness to donate cadaveric organs generally presupposes trust not only in the society's criteria and procedures for determining death, but in its criteria for fairly and effectively distributing donated organs as well. In addition, the provision of access to basic health care for everyone would create a sense of solidarity that dramatically could increase organ donation, but that vision is a distant one.

I salute the decisions in some states to give the decedent's signed donor card priority over family objections, but it is even more important to educate individuals as members of families. They need to share their decisions with their families and consider their roles as potential donors of a family member's organs. Donor cards may be a useful mechanism to stimulate such conversations, but in and of themselves they are too individualistic, legalistic and formalistic. The process of intrafamilial communication is more important.

Society also provides various incentives for organ donation, such as by recognizing and honoring donors in various ways. Would it be possible to offer some financial incentives without crossing over into a market for organ procurement? Consider the following: As a regular expression of its gratitude for organ donation, society could cover the decedent's funeral expenses up to a certain amount, perhaps $1,000 or more. In this way, the community would recognize with gratitude the decedent's and/or the family's act of donation and also pay respects to the donor or source of the organs by sharing in the disposition of his/her final remains.

Any proposal for such "rewarded gifting" will require careful scrutiny, in part because organ donation is such a highly sensitive area, marked by complex beliefs, symbols, attitudes, sentiments and practices, some of them religious in nature. But a carefully conceived pilot experiment, such as providing death benefits—as Pennsylvania has discussed—may be justifiable. However, it may infringe current laws. In any event, it requires the utmost caution because of its risks. One risk is that it will be perceived as purchasing organs rather than as expressing gratitude and providing incentives for donation.

I have focused on cadaveric organs, but what about a market in organ procurement from living individuals? Such a market probably would be more effective than a futures market in cadaveric organs—more individuals probably would be willing to part with a kidney, especially with reduced risks from kidney removal and with generous compensation. However, the social risk of commodification—of treating living human bodies and their parts as commodities—is very troubling. In addition, the risks of coercion and exploitation, especially of poor people, are substantial. The assertion of a moral right to sell a kidney against the legal prohibition of such a sale is not persuasive; we have good reasons, based on concerns about commodification, coercion and exploitation, to reject such sales as incompatible with our moral vision of the kind of society to which we aspire.

Vigorous efforts along the paths I have indicated should obviate the need to adopt a market in organ procurement, whether from living or cadaveric sources. We have little reason to believe that a futures market will be effective in obtaining cadaveric organs and considerable reason to worry about the risks and social costs of such a market, as well as a market for living organ procurement. We should just say "no" to both markets.

POSTSCRIPT

Should Congress Allow the Buying and Selling of Human Organs?

This is a difficult issue to discuss. One of the difficulties is fairly straightforward. We need to know the medical facts about kidneys and other organs. In the case of kidneys, we are born with two, but we need only one kidney to survive. (And the form of survival here is not just marginal or borderline. Approximately 98 percent of life insurance companies do not charge a higher premium for people with only one kidney.) If your kidneys don't function properly, and you are unable to receive a transplanted kidney, it may be possible to survive through the use of a kidney dialysis machine—but this requires attachment to such a machine for several hours at a time, several times a week. The use of the machine does not *cure* or solve the problem; it merely "purifies" your blood, removing some of the unwanted products and chemicals, while saving what's useful. However, since the fundamental problem is never cured this way, you must return to the machine in about two days for several hours' more purification—and the process never ends. But if you could have a kidney transplant, and your body didn't reject it, then the kidney could do the blood purifying, and you wouldn't have to use the dialysis machine anymore. Hence, the great need for a functioning kidney.

But at this point, we encounter another problem in dealing with this issue. There is a certain feeling of ghoulishness associated with the buying and selling of human organs. It might be nice, we think, for a good friend or family member to *donate* a kidney—and perhaps it is even somewhat noble—but the buying and selling of human organs threatens to turn them into mere commodities. Childress even suggests that if kidneys can be bought and sold, and have a market value, then there will be fewer donations. This would occur because what used to be *donations* of kidneys would simply be superseded by the market; under a market system, if the good friend or relative wanted to help the person on the dialysis machine, all that would be required is money or a loan. Childress wants to encourage donation, not a market. But as Burrows points out, the supply of donated kidneys falls far short of the demand. And these are the conditions that most favor a market solution.

Recent publications that address this issue are Patrick Waldron, "You Gave Me a New Life: St. Charles Gymnastics Coach Receives Kidney Donation from Her Co-Worker," *Daily Herald* (Arlington Heights, IL, July 2, 2004); James Stacey Taylor, *Stakes and Kidneys: Why Markets in Human Body Parts Are Morally Imperative* (Ashgate, 2005); Mark J. Cherry, *Kidney for Sale by Owner: Human Organs, Transplantation, and the Market* (Georgetown University

Press, 2005); Lesley A Sharp, *Bodies, Commodities, and Biotechnologies: Death, Mourning, and Scientific Desire in the Realm of Human Organ Transfer* (Columbia University Press, 2006); Rohan J. Hardcastle, *Law and the Human Body: Property Rights, Ownership and Control* (Hart Publishing, 2007); and Donna Dickenson, *Body Shopping: The Economy Fuelled by Flesh and Blood* (Oneworld Publications, 2008).

ISSUE 9

Should Drugs Be Legalized?

YES: Meaghan Cussen and Walter Block, from "Legalize Drugs Now! An Analysis of the Benefits of Legalized Drugs," *American Journal of Economics and Sociology* (July 2000)

NO: Drug Enforcement Administration, from "Speaking Out Against Drug Legalization," http://www.DEA.gov (May 2003)

ISSUE SUMMARY

YES: Meaghan Cussen (a student in economics) and Walter Block (her economics professor) argue that the legalization of drugs would provide many sorts of benefits (e.g., crime would fall, the quality of life in inner cities would rise, and taxpayers would no longer have to pay for an unwinnable "war on drugs"). Moreover, the legalization of drugs would promote the American the value of liberty.

NO: The Drug Enforcement Administration presents the case that drugs are illegal for good reason—they are harmful. If the legalization proponents were heeded, we as a society would be much worse off. We should be concentrating harder on fighting drug use and drug trafficking, where there is significant progress.

No one can deny that the use of psychoactive substances has a great impact on society today—from the health effects of cigarettes to the criminal activity of street-corner crack dealers. In many ways, the greatest impact is from the smuggling, trafficking, and consumption of illegal drugs. These practices inevitably lead to bribery, violent crime, babies born addicted to drugs such as crack, and a host of other social ills.

In recent years, there has been a "war on drugs" that is supposed to address (if not solve) these problems. Since the problems still exist, and the war on drugs has been going on now for some time, critics might wonder how effective the war is. Severe critics would say that the so-called war on drugs isn't working at all and that it's time to try another approach.

Some have called for the legalization of drugs. If drugs were legal, proponents say, their sale and use could be regulated and controlled. The government would be able to raise revenue through taxation (instead of having huge drug profits go to organized crime), the quality and quantity of the drugs could be officially monitored, and much street crime could be eliminated. On the other hand, even after legalization, there would still be many drug addicts (and perhaps even more of them), "crack babies," and other victims of drug use.

Proponents of drug legalization must offer a realistic plan for the legal market they propose. At least two elements should be addressed. First, what exactly is meant by legalization? Substances that are legal are not necessarily available at all times to everyone. Alcohol, for example, is a legal substance, but when and where and to whom it may be sold are all regulated by federal and local authorities. And some currently legal drugs are available only by prescription. Second, some further clarification is needed about what is meant by drugs. Talk about drugs can be very vague. Caffeine and nicotine are common drugs, but since they are already legal, we might say that we are considering here only illegal drugs. But why are some drugs legal and others illegal in the first place?

Twentieth-century (alcohol) Prohibition is one of the useful test cases that some people appeal to—while we obviously cannot experiment with changing the legal status of a drug for a limited time to see what would happen, Prohibition is a historical reality. We can check the historical record to see what happened when alcohol was prohibited. Prohibition became effective on January 16, 1920, and was repealed December 5, 1933. During this time, the Constitution was amended to outlaw "the manufacture, sale, or the transportation of intoxicating liquors within . . . the United States." Also outlawed were all import and export of these items. During Prohibition, many of the problems that we now associate with the modern drug world existed: smuggling, official corruption, murder, large amounts of money being made by violent criminals, and organized criminal networks. Members of the public could, with a little effort—and in some cases with very little effort—buy and consume the very products that were against the law. And what was bought on the black market had no guarantees with respect to health or safety.

In the following selections, Meaghan Cussen and Walter Block and the Drug Enforcement Agency present radically different cases. Cussen and Block argue that government programs that are meant to control the use of certain substances are misguided; in fact, these efforts are themselves responsible for much drug-related crime; and, for both drug users and the general public, many benefits would follow from the legalization of drugs. On the other hand, the Drug Enforcement Administration argues that it is the drugs themselves that are harmful, and that much progress and success have been achieved by fighting drug use. Drug legalization, they say, would be much more problematic than legalization proponents admit and would certainly lead to an increase in drug abuse and drug addiction. Social ills would follow in the wake of drug legalization.

YES

Meaghan Cussen and Walter Block

Legalize Drugs Now! An Analysis of the Benefits of Legalized Drugs

Abstract: The legalization of drugs would prevent our civil liberties from being threatened any further, it would reduce crime rates, reverse the potency effect, improve the quality of life in the inner cities, prevent the spread of disease, save the taxpayer money, and generally benefit both individuals and the community as a whole. Our arguments are based on a basic appreciation of the benefits provided by voluntary exchange and the role markets play in coordinating human activities. Legalizing drugs would eliminate many inconsistencies, guarantee freedoms, and increase the effectiveness of the government's anti-drug beliefs. The present war on drugs has not and will not produce a decisive victory. We advocate a new approach to this important social problem.

Drug dealers are a thing of the past. Violent crimes and theft are greatly reduced. Drug-related shoot-outs are unheard of. The streets of America begin to "clean up." Communities pull themselves together. Youths and adults once involved in crime rings are forced to seek legitimate work. Deaths due to infected intravenous needles and poisonous street drugs are eliminated. Taxpayers are no longer forced to pay $10,000,000,000 to fund drug-related law enforcement. The $80,000,000,000 claimed by organized crime and drug rings will now go to honest workers (Ostrowski 1993, pp. 203–205). What policy change will bring about such good news? The legalization of drugs! Both practically and philosophically speaking, addictive drugs should be legalized.

I. Basic Constitutional Rights

Many argue that drug prohibition protects addicts from themselves by exerting parental control over their behavior. This government-enforced control, the anti-drug laws, strictly monitors addicts' treatment of their own bodies. For example, the government decides that it wants to protect Fred Brown from destroying his body. The government, therefore, outlaws narcotics and, in effect, takes control of Fred's body. Under the United States Constitution and the anti-slavery laws, this hegemony should not happen. The guiding principles of the United States, iterated both in the Declaration of Independence and the

From *American Journal of Economics & Sociology,* vol. 59, no. 3, July 2000, pp. 525–536. Copyright © 2000 by American Journal of Economics & Sociology, Inc. Reprinted by permission of Wiley-Blackwell.

Constitution, protect Fred's basic civil liberties to "pursue his own happiness" as long as he doesn't infringe on others' rights to life and property. With prohibition, Fred no longer has this constitutional right. He no longer controls his own body. Regulation has stripped him of his civil liberty. Fred's role of "owner of his own body" is taken away from him. This has in effect made him a slave.

Are we being hysterical in categorizing present drug law as a form of servitude? No, our drug laws amount to partial slavery. We must all question the practices of roadblocks, strip-searches, urine tests, locker searches, and money laundering laws. Philosophically speaking, drug prohibition severely threatens our civil liberties and is inconsistent with the anti-slavery philosophy and the founding documents of the United States. The legalization of drugs would give a basic civil liberty back to U.S. citizens, by granting them control over their own bodies.

II. Free Trade

Free trade benefits all parties. It can be assumed that if drugs were legalized, and thus were a part of the market, both the buyer and the seller would gain. Each time a trade occurs, the welfare of both parties is improved. If Joe sold you his shirt for $10, he would benefit because he obviously values the $10 more than the shirt. If he didn't, he would not have traded it. You would also gain from the trade because you obviously value the shirt more than you do the $10. If you didn't, then you would not have agreed to the deal. Free trade in the drug market works the same way. If Joe sells you marijuana for $10, he gains because he values the money more, and you gain because you value the drugs more. Whether or not another person *thinks you should* value the drugs more is not the question. That third party is not involved in the trade. The amount of pleasure the drug brings you is your motivation for buying it. Trade is a positive-sum game. Both parties gain, at least in the ex ante sense.

It cannot be denied that certain third parties will be offended by the drug transaction, on moral or ethical grounds. However, try to find any transaction that does not offend at least one person. Many people object to the sale of alcohol, cigarettes, birth control or animal products, but their feelings or beliefs do not stop these items from being sold. Marxists object to *any* market transactions because they see commercial activity as necessarily exploitative. There is obviously no pleasing everyone when it comes to market transactions. In our free enterprise economy, however, anyone who participates in the market will benefit from it. ". . . For all third parties who say they will be aggrieved by a legalized drug trade, there will be many more benefiting from the reduction in crime" (Block 1993). "A third party can verbally oppose any given trade. But that opposition cannot be revealed through market choices in the same way that trade between the two parties indicates a positive evaluation of the transaction" (Block 1996, p. 434). Free trade of all goods contributes to the number of those who gain. In a free market economy, everybody has opportunity to participate in the market, and therefore, equal opportunity to gain in a positive sum transaction.

Not only would the legalization of drugs protect basic freedoms and lead to individual benefit through free trade, but it would also bring enormous benefits to society as a whole. The first and most important societal benefit is a reduction in crime.

III. Reductions in Crime

When addictive drugs are made legal, crime will decrease substantially, for four main reasons. First, the lowered price of narcotics will eliminate the theft and murder associated with their high prices. When drugs are legalized, law-abiding businesspeople will no longer be deterred by the illegality of drug commerce and will become willing to enter the market. With this increase of supply, assuming a less than proportional increase in demand, the price of narcotics will fall. Addicts who were formerly forced to steal, murder, and engage in illegal employment to earn enough money for their habits will be able to afford the lower prices. Therefore, these types of drug-related crimes will decrease.

Second, substance-related disputes such as gang wars and street violence will be reduced. Dealers will be able to use the courts to settle their disputes instead of taking the law into their own hands. Violations of rights within the drug business will be resolved through the judicial system, thereby decreasing gang violence, and saving the many innocent lives that often get caught in the crossfire.

Third, the drug business creates great profits for cartels. Cartels are often international organizations, many of which support terrorism and add to violent crime in America. If the narcotics market were open, drug revenues would be equally distributed by free-market forces, and would have less of a chance of supporting terrorist organizations, crime rings, and cartel activity and profit.

Finally, and most obviously, with transport, sale, and possession legalized, formerly illegal activities will now become society-approved business transactions. Crime, an act that breaks the law, and in its very insurrectional essence leads to societal instability, will be greatly reduced through the legalization of the inevitable activity of drug transactions.

The prohibition of alcohol in the 1920s provides us with a perfect case in point. The high crime rates during this decade were due to the existence of the black market, spawned from the government-enforced illegalization of alcohol. The black market led to the formation of major crime rings. The underground market for alcohol grew and led many profit-hungry entrepreneurs into a risky lifestyle of crime. Many were jailed due to transport, sale, and possession.

When Prohibition ended, alcohol-related crime ceased. The profit balloon driven by the limited supply of the illegal substance was deflated. The black market disappeared, along with all of the illegal activity associated with it. Crime rings were forced to disband and seek other means of income. How many crime rings exist today for the selling of alcohol? The answer is none. The reason is legalization.

In contrast, drug-related crime is skyrocketing. As Ostrowski (1993, p. 209) notes, "The President's Commission on Organized Crime estimates a total of seventy drug market murders yearly in Miami alone. Based on that figure and FBI data, a reasonable nationwide estimate would be at least 750 murders a year. Recent estimates from New York and Washington are even higher." Anyone who questions whether prohibition is responsible for violence should note the relative peace that prevails in the alcohol and legal drug markets.

IV. The Potency Effect

The end of prohibition also brought the end of the dangerous potency effect. During Prohibition, it was in the best interests of the sellers to carry more potent forms of alcohol. Hence, an alcohol dealer would be more likely to carry vodka and other hard liquor instead of beer and wine because of hard liquor's greater value (per unit of volume). Therefore, people began drinking vodka and other hard liquor, which because of their high potency are more dangerous than beer and wine. Alcohol-related deaths increased. This horrific result is known as the potency effect.

Fifty years after the repeal of Prohibition, the potency effect has been reversed. The average per capita consumption of alcohol has fallen to its lowest level ever (Hamid 1993, p. 184). In fact, people have begun switching to weaker alcohol alternatives, such as wine coolers and nonalcoholic beer. The legalization of alcohol reversed the potency effect. The legalization of drugs will do the same.

For example, the risks involved in transporting marijuana, a low-potency drug, for the purpose of sale are extremely high. It is in the best interests of the dealer to carry more potent, thus more expensive, drugs, which is why he or she will be more likely to carry cocaine because of its greater value (per unit of volume). Because cocaine is more potent, it is also more dangerous. Addicts face increased health risks when using cocaine as opposed to using marijuana. These health risks grow as potency increases. Stronger and more dangerous drugs such as crack, "ice," and PCP are substituted for the weaker, relatively safer drugs. The results are often deadly.

V. Health Benefits

The legalization of drugs would eliminate serious health risks by assuring market-driven high quality substances and the availability of clean needles. Prohibition in the 1920s created a market for cheap versions of alcoholic products, such as bathtub gin. Alcohol was diluted or adulterated in often dangerous ways. Needless deaths occurred because of the poor quality of the product. So is drug prohibition worth the health risks? Fly-by-night goods cannot always be trusted. If narcotics were legalized, purity could be all but guaranteed. Drugstores, held accountable by customers, would deliver safe products. Brand names would bring competition into the market and assure safer, better products. Doctors would now be able to monitor the drug use of seriously addicted patients. Poor quality would be a thing of the past.

In addition, clean needles would be readily available. Drug vendors and health care organizations would be able to provide clean needles for their customers and patients, respectively. Today, needles are shared because they are difficult to obtain. About twenty-five percent of AIDS cases are contracted through the sharing of intravenous needles (Boaz 1990, p. 3). Legalizing drugs would eliminate this problem. "In Hong Kong, where needles are available in drugstores, as of 1987 there were no cases of AIDS among drug users" (ibid).

When was the last time you heard of a diabetic contracting AIDS from contaminated needles? If insulin were prohibited, this situation would surely change for the worse.

VI. Societal Benefits

Illegal drug sale creates a destructive atmosphere. When a criminal culture emerges, a community is torn apart. A booming black market fosters a large criminal presence. Casual recreational users are forced to come in contact with criminals to make their purchases, as prohibition makes it impossible to make a legal transaction. Additionally, basically good citizens often deal with and, unfortunately, become influenced by, the criminals of the area (Boaz 1990, p. 2).

Inner-city youths, surrounded by the booming black market, are influenced by the sheer amount of money dealers make and often fall into a life of crime (Boaz 1990, p. 2). These youths often see themselves as having the choice of remaining in poverty, earning "chump change," or pursuing a life of crime and making thousands of dollars a week. Which do you think all too many young people will choose?

The black market presence often leads to the corruption of police officers and public officials. Police, on average, make $35,000 a year. When they arrest the denizens of the drug world who make ten times that amount, it is often difficult not to be tempted into a life of crime.

> Drug corruption charges have been leveled against FBI agents, police officers, prison guards, U.S. customs inspectors, even prosecutors. In 1986, in New York City's 77th Precinct, twelve police officers were arrested for stealing and selling drugs. Miami's problem is worse. In June 1986, seven officers there were indicted for using their jobs to run a drug operation that used murders, threats, and bribery. Add to that two dozen other cases of corruption in the last three years in Miami alone (Ostrowski 1993, pp. 296–207).

We must question a policy that so frequently turns police officers into the very outlaws they are authorized to bring to justice. We must question a policy that leads to the enormous success of those willing to break the laws of our society. We must question a policy that leaves a criminal profession in a position of great influence over our youth and other honest citizens. Milton Friedman put it best when he wrote, "Drugs are a tragedy for addicts. But criminalizing their use converts the tragedy into a disaster for society, for users and non-users alike" (Friedman 1989a).

VII. Prohibit the Crime, Not the Drug

The laws of the United States prohibit violent acts against other citizens. This is consistent with the founding principles of our nation, which allow each free individual to pursue life, liberty, and happiness. The laws of United States should not prohibit the intake of narcotics that only have an immediate effect on the individual consumer. If I ingest a drug, I am doing possible harm only to myself, and no other. If I subsequently act violently on account of my altered state of mind, only then am I doing harm to others. It is the subsequent action that is harmful, not the drug taking itself. Since I am responsible for my actions, I should be arrested and punished only when I am violent. Alcohol is legal even though people commit rapes, murders, beatings, and other violent crimes when they are drunk. Yet if a person commits these crimes when intoxicated, he or she is held responsible for them. A mere substance should not and does not serve as an excuse for the violent acts. The ingestion of alcohol is not illegal per se. The same standard should be applied to the use of presently illegal drugs.

It should also be noted that every narcotic does not turn the user into a crazed, enraged lunatic capable of all sorts of violent crimes. In fact, it is just the opposite. Most drugs induce lethargy. Remember that opium, now illegal, was used quite often in England, China, and the United States, and tended to induce stupor. The use of traditional opiates did not render users violent. In fact, no drug is "as strongly associated with violent behavior as is alcohol. According to Justice Department statistics, 54 percent of all jail inmates convicted of violent crimes in 1983 reported having just used alcohol just prior to committing their offense" (Nadelmann 1989, p. 22). This statistic renders the prohibition of drugs rather than alcohol a legal inconsistency.

VIII. Save the U.S. Taxpayer Money

According to the U.S. Department of Justice, federal, state, and local governments currently spend over $20 billion per year on drug enforcement. In 1992, there were more than one million arrests for drug law violations. In 1993, sixty percent of the seventy-seven thousand federal prisoners were incarcerated for drug-related crimes (Miron and Zweibel 1995, p. 176). Jails are crowded and large amounts of tax dollars are being spent on enforcement efforts that only aggravate the problem. We can add to this sum the amount of money spent on research and medical care for those infected with AIDS and other diseases caused by needle sharing.

With legalization, the tax dollars spent on enforcement would be saved. The availability of clean needles would reduce the rate of AIDS infections, and would consequently reduce the amount of money spent on medical care, to say nothing of the reduction in human misery.

IX. Don't Help Inflate Criminals' Profit Balloons

If we continue with the same anti-drug policies, we are only helping drug lords get richer. Each time a bust occurs and a shipment is captured and destroyed, the criminals benefit. The seizure reduces supply and takes out one or more black market participants. According to the laws of supply and demand, with a decrease in drug supply, black market prices will rise, creating a larger profit for suppliers. So, every time we think we are winning a battle in the war, we are really strengthening the enemy rather than weakening it. The way to win is not by fighting the alligators, but by draining their swamp (Block 1993, p. 696). It is better to ruin drug lords' businesses by deflating the profit balloon than by acting in a way (i.e., prohibition) that only benefits them. "By taking the profits out of [drugs], we could at one fell swoop do more to reduce their power than decades of fighting them directly" (Holloway, p. 6).

At present, governmental control of the drug lords, while minuscule, is as effective as it will ever be in any sector of society (Thornton 1991). Just think, even in jails, where the lives of residents are completely controlled by the government, drugs still have not been eliminated. If the government cannot even control the drug trade within its own house, how can it expect to control it within the entire nation? Are we to imprison the whole citizenry in an attempt? Legalization will takes the profits out of the narcotics industry.

X. Elasticity of Demand for Drugs

Many believe the elasticity of demand for narcotics is very high. If drugs are legalized and their prices fall, the amount purchased will increase by a large amount. This is not the case. In fact, the elasticity of demand for drugs in general is very low for three main reasons. First, narcotics are seen as necessities for drug users, not luxuries. "While one might severely reduce demand for [luxuries] in the face of an increased price, or even give it up entirely in the extreme, this does not apply to [necessities]" (Block 1993, p. 696). This behavioral pattern indicates that drugs are indeed low elasticity goods. In fact, there is really no good reason to assume that many Americans would suddenly start to ingest or inject narcotics even if given the legal opportunity.

Second, most people recognize the danger of drugs and will avoid them no matter what the price. Third, if drugs are made legal, they will no longer have to be pushed. If they are sold over the counter to adults, criminals will no longer have to pawn these goods off on innocent youths. Competition will be high and dealers will have no reason to resort to this extreme measure. Certainly, market competition will occur which may result in advertisements' targeting particular age groups. However, this would have a negligible effect compared to drug pushers' current youth-targeted tactics.

Finally, we should realize that legalization would cause potency to fall. With normalized supply, people will begin purchasing weaker, safer drugs. This normalized supply, along with the low elasticity of demand for narcotics, will lead to only a small increase in consumption.

XI. Government Regulations

A main driver of anti-drug legislation is the concern that government would be sanctioning an immoral and destructive activity, viewed as sinful in many eyes of the population. However, the legalization of drugs does not mean that government and society would sanction their use. Alcohol and cigarettes are legal but we have pretty successful campaigns against these substances. Gossiping and burping are also legal, but you never see a government sponsored advertisement advocating catty behavior or belching in public. Are we as a society to prohibit automobile racing, extreme skiing, the ingestion of ice cream and fried foods because they may have a detrimental effect on human health? No. Dangers associated with these activities cannot be measured. ". . . Such inherently unquantifiable variables cannot be measured, much less weighed against each other. Interpersonal comparison of utility is incompatible with valid economic analysis" (Block 1996, p. 435). We cannot allow such legal inconsistencies to take place.

Legalizing drugs would eliminate these inconsistencies, guarantee freedoms, and increase the efficiency and effectiveness of the government's anti-drug beliefs. If drugs were legalized, taxes could be cut, with the elimination of government expenditures on enforcement. All of the money saved could be used to promote anti-drug campaigns. Private organizations could take over the tasks of inspecting and regulating. A minimum age of twenty-one would be mandated for the consumption of drugs. Transactions would take place in a drugstore, with upstanding suppliers. Drugs could safely be administered, with clean needles, in hospitals where medical professionals could monitor and rehabilitate the addicted. MADD (Mothers Against Drunk Driving) is a good example of a successful anti-substance abuse campaign. Private, nonprofit groups like this one could help in the fight against drug abuse.

Currently, we are not by any means winning the war on drugs. Our futile attempts at enforcement only exacerbate the problem. We need to de-escalate the war rather than continue fighting the over twenty-three million adult Americans who are obviously determined to enjoy themselves as they see fit (Boaz 1990, p. 5). We must also remember that those that need to be deterred the most, the hard-core drug users, are the least likely to be stopped (Ostrowski 1993, p. 205). Our law enforcement is not working to contain and control the very people the anti-drug laws are designed to control. The war on drugs has done little to reduce narcotics use in the United States and has thus proved counterproductive (Holloway, p. 6). Philosophically and practically speaking, drugs should be legalized. This act would prevent our civil liberties from being threatened, reduce crime rates, reverse the potency effect, improve the quality of life in inner cities, prevent the spread of disease, save the taxpayer money, and generally benefit both individuals and society as a whole.

References

Block, Walter. (1993). "Drug Prohibition: A Legal and Economic Analysis." *Journal of Business Ethics* 12: 689–700.

———. (1996). "Drug Prohibition and Individual Virtue." *Review of Political Economy.* Volume 8, November: 433–436.

Boaz, David. (1990). "The Consequences of Prohibition." In *The Crisis of Drug Prohibition.* Washington, D.C.: Cato Institute.

Friedman, Milton. (1989a). "An Open Letter to Bill Bennett." *Wall Street Journal,* September 7.

Hamid, Ansley. (1993). "To the Editor of the Commentary." In *Drugs in America: The Reference Shelf* (New York: H.W. Wilson) 65 (4): 181–184.

Holloway, Jason and Walter Block. (1998). "Should Drugs Be Legalized?" In *West Coast Libertarian* April: 6–7.

Miron, Jeffrey and Jeffrey Zweibel. (1995). "The Economic Case Against Drug Prohibition." *Journal of Economic Perspectives* 9 (4): 175–192.

Nadelmann, E. (1989). "The Case for Legalization," *Washington Post,* October 8.

Ostrowski, James (1993) [1990]. "Has the Time Come to Legalize Drugs?" *USA Today Magazine* 119 (July 1990): Reprinted in *Drugs in America: The Reference Shelf* (New York: H.W. Wilson) 65 (4): 203–212.

Thornton, M. (1991). *The Economics of Prohibition.* Salt Lake City: The University of Utah Press.

Speaking Out Against Drug Legalization

A Message from the Drug Enforcement Administration

In many circles, U.S. drug policy is under attack. It is being criticized primarily by those who favor a legalization agenda. It is also being challenged by those who encourage certain trends in European drug policy, like decriminalization of drug use, "harm reduction" programs, and distinctions between hard and soft drugs.

Proponents of legalization are spending huge amounts of money to encourage a greater tolerance for drug use. A number of states have passed referendums to permit their residents to use drugs for a variety of reasons. The citizens who vote in these referendums too often have to rely on the information—or rather, misinformation—being presented by the sponsors of these expensive campaigns to legalize drugs.

This [publication], *Speaking Out Against Drug Legalization,* is designed to cut through the fog of misinformation with hard facts. The ten factual assertions, taken together, present an accurate picture of America's experience with drug use, the current state of the drug problem, and what might happen if America chooses to adopt a more permissive policy on drug abuse. . . .

Summary of the Top Ten Facts on Legalization

Fact 1: We have made significant progress in fighting drug use and drug trafficking in America. Now is not the time to abandon our efforts.

The Legalization Lobby claims that the fight against drugs cannot be won. However, overall drug use is down by more than a third in the last twenty years, while cocaine use has dropped by an astounding 70 percent. Ninety-five percent of Americans do not use drugs. This is success by any standards.

Fact 2: A balanced approach of prevention, enforcement, and treatment is the key in the fight against drugs.

A successful drug policy must apply a balanced approach of prevention, enforcement and treatment. All three aspects are crucial. For those who end up hooked on drugs, there are innovative programs, like Drug Treatment Courts,

From U.S. Department of Justice, Drug Enforcement Administration, January 2000.

that offer non-violent users the option of seeking treatment. Drug Treatment Courts provide court supervision, unlike voluntary treatment centers.

Fact 3: Illegal drugs are illegal because they are harmful.
There is a growing misconception that some illegal drugs can be taken safely. For example, savvy drug dealers have learned how to market drugs like Ecstasy to youth. Some in the Legalization Lobby even claim such drugs have medical value, despite the lack of conclusive scientific evidence.

Fact 4: Smoked marijuana is not scientifically approved medicine. Marinol, the legal version of medical marijuana, is approved by science.
According to the Institute of Medicine, there is no future in smoked marijuana as medicine. However, the prescription drug Marinol—a legal and safe version of medical marijuana which isolates the active ingredient of THC—has been studied and approved by the Food & Drug Administration as safe medicine. The difference is that you have to get a prescription for Marinol from a licensed physician. You can't buy it on a street corner, and you don't smoke it.

Fact 5: Drug control spending is a minor portion of the U.S. budget. Compared to the social costs of drug abuse and addiction, government spending on drug control is minimal.
The Legalization Lobby claims that the United States has wasted billions of dollars in its anti-drug efforts. But for those kids saved from drug addiction, this is hardly wasted dollars. Moreover, our fight against drug abuse and addiction is an ongoing struggle that should be treated like any other social problem. Would we give up on education or poverty simply because we haven't eliminated all problems? Compared to the social costs of drug abuse and addiction—whether in taxpayer dollars or in pain and suffering—government spending on drug control is minimal.

Fact 6: Legalization of drugs will lead to increased use and increased levels of addiction. Legalization has been tried before, and failed miserably.
Legalization has been tried before—and failed miserably. Alaska's experiment with Legalization in the 1970s led to the state's teens using marijuana at more than twice the rate of other youths nationally. This led Alaska's residents to vote to re-criminalize marijuana in 1990.

Fact 7: Crime, violence, and drug use go hand-in-hand.
Crime, violence and drug use go hand in hand. Six times as many homicides are committed by people under the influence of drugs, as by those who are looking for money to buy drugs. Most drug crimes aren't committed by people trying to pay for drugs; they're committed by people on drugs.

Fact 8: Alcohol has caused significant health, social, and crime problems in this country, and legalized drugs would only make the situation worse.
The Legalization Lobby claims drugs are no more dangerous than alcohol. But drunk driving is one of the primary killers of Americans. Do we want our bus

drivers, nurses, and airline pilots to be able to take drugs one evening, and operate freely at work the next day? Do we want to add to the destruction by making drugged driving another primary killer?

Fact 9: Europe's more liberal drug policies are not the right model for America.

The Legalization Lobby claims that the "European Model" of the drug problem is successful. However, since legalization of marijuana in Holland, heroin addiction levels have tripled. And Needle Park seems like a poor model for America.

Fact 10: Most non-violent drug users get treatment, not jail time.

The Legalization Lobby claims that America's prisons are filling up with users. Truth is, only about 5 percent of inmates in federal prison are there because of simple possession. Most drug criminals are in jail—even on possession charges—because they have plea-bargained down from major trafficking offences or more violent drug crimes.

Fact 1: We have made significant progress in fighting drug use and drug trafficking in America. Now is not the time to abandon our efforts.

- Legalization advocates claim that the fight against drugs has not been won and is, in fact, unconquerable. They frequently state that people still take drugs, drugs are widely available, and that efforts to change this are futile. They contend that legalization is the only workable alternative.
- The facts are to the contrary to such pessimism. On the demand side, the U.S. has reduced casual use, chronic use and addiction, and prevented others from even starting using drugs. Overall drug use in the United States is down by *more than a third* since the late 1970s. That's 9.5 million people fewer using illegal drugs. We've reduced cocaine use by an astounding 70% during the last 15 years. That's 4.1 million fewer people using cocaine.
- Almost two-thirds of teens say their schools are drug-free, according to a new survey of teen drug use conducted by The National Center on Addiction and Substance Abuse (CASA) at Columbia University. This is the first time in the seven-year history of the study that a majority of public school students report drug-free schools. . . .
- There is still much progress to make. There are still far too many people using cocaine, heroin and other illegal drugs. In addition, there are emerging drug threats like **Ecstasy** and **methamphetamine.** But the fact is that our current policies balancing prevention, enforcement, and treatment have kept drug usage outside the scope of acceptable behavior in the U.S.
- To put things in perspective, less than 5 percent of the population uses illegal drugs of any kind. Think about that: More than 95 percent of Americans do not use drugs. How could anyone but the most hardened pessimist call this a losing struggle? . . .

- Progress does not come overnight. America has had a long, dark struggle with drugs. It's not a war we've been fighting for 20 years. We've been fighting it for 120 years. In 1880, many drugs, including opium and cocaine, were legal. We didn't know their harms, but we soon learned. We saw the highest level of drug use ever in our nation, per capita. There were over 400,000 opium addicts in our nation. That's twice as many per capita as there are today. And like today, we saw rising crime with that drug abuse. But we fought those problems by passing and enforcing tough laws and by educating the public about the dangers of these drugs. And this vigilance worked—by World War II, drug use was reduced to the very margins of society. And that's just where we want to keep it. With a 95 percent success rate—bolstered by an effective, three-pronged strategy combining education/prevention, enforcement, and treatment—we shouldn't give up now.

Fact 2: A balanced approach of prevention, enforcement, and treatment is the key in the fight against drugs.

- Over the years, some people have advocated a policy that focuses narrowly on controlling the supply of drugs. Others have said that society should rely on treatment alone. Still others say that prevention is the only viable solution. As the 2002 National Drug Strategy observes, "What the nation needs is an honest effort to integrate these strategies."
- Drug treatment courts are a good example of this new balanced approach to fighting drug abuse and addiction in this country. These courts are given a special responsibility to handle cases involving drug-addicted offenders through an extensive supervision and treatment program. Drug court programs use the varied experience and skills of a wide variety of law enforcement and treatment professionals: judges, prosecutors, defense counsels, substance abuse treatment specialists, probation officers, law enforcement and correctional personnel, educational and vocational experts, community leaders and others—all focused on one goal: to help cure addicts of their addiction, and to keep them cured. . . .

Fact 3: Illegal drugs are illegal because they are harmful.

- There is a growing misconception that some illegal drugs can be taken safely—with many advocates of legalization going so far as to suggest it can serve as medicine to heal anything from headaches to bipolar diseases. Today's drug dealers are savvy businessmen. They know how to market to kids. They imprint Ecstasy pills with cartoon characters and designer logos. They promote parties as safe and alcohol-free. Meanwhile, the drugs can flow easier than water. Many young people believe the new "club drugs," such as Ecstasy, are safe, and tablet testing at raves has only fueled this misconception.
- Because of the new marketing tactics of drug promoters, and because of a major decline in drug use in the 1990s, there is a growing perception

among young people today that drugs are harmless. A decade ago, for example, 79 percent of 12th graders thought regular marijuana use was harmful; only 58 percent do so today. Because peer pressure is so important in inducing kids to experiment with drugs, the way kids perceive the risks of drug use is critical. There always have been, and there continues to be, real health risks in using illicit drugs. . . .

Marijuana

- Drug legalization advocates in the United States single out marijuana as a different kind of drug, unlike cocaine, heroin, and methamphetamine. They say it's less dangerous. . . . However, as many people are realizing, marijuana is not as harmless as some would have them believe. Marijuana is far more powerful than it used to be. In 2000, there were six times as many emergency room mentions of marijuana use as there were in 1990, despite the fact that the number of people using marijuana is roughly the same. In 1999, a record 225,000 Americans entered substance abuse treatment primarily for marijuana dependence, second only to heroin—and not by much.
- At a time of great public pressure to curtail tobacco because of its effects on health, advocates of legalization are promoting the use of marijuana. Yet, according to the National Institute on Drug Abuse, "Studies show that someone who smokes five joints per week may be taking in as many cancer-causing chemicals as someone who smokes a full pack of cigarettes every day." Marijuana contains more than 400 chemicals, including the most harmful substances found in tobacco smoke. For example, smoking one marijuana cigarette deposits about four times more tar into the lungs than a filtered tobacco cigarette.
- Those are the long-term effects of marijuana. The short-term effects are also harmful. They include: memory loss, distorted perception, trouble with thinking and problem solving, loss of motor skills, decrease in muscle strength, increased heart rate, and anxiety. Marijuana impacts young people's mental development, their ability to concentrate in school, and their motivation and initiative to reach goals. And marijuana affects people of all ages: Harvard University researchers report that the risk of a heart attack is five times higher than usual in the hour after smoking marijuana.

Fact 4: Smoked marijuana is not scientifically approved medicine. Marinol, the legal version of medical marijuana, *is* approved by science.

- Medical marijuana already exists. It's called Marinol.
- A pharmaceutical product, Marinol, is widely available through prescription. It comes in the form of a pill and is also being studied by researchers for suitability via other delivery methods, such as an inhaler or patch. The active ingredient of Marinol is synthetic THC, which has been found to relieve the nausea and vomiting associated with chemotherapy for cancer patients and to assist with loss of appetite with AIDS patients.

- Unlike smoked marijuana—which contains more than 400 different chemicals, including most of the hazardous chemicals found in tobacco smoke—Marinol has been studied and approved by the medical community and the Food and Drug Administration (FDA), the nation's watchdog over unsafe and harmful food and drug products. Since the passage of the 1906 Pure Food and Drug Act, any drug that is marketed in the United States must undergo rigorous scientific testing. The approval process mandated by this act ensures that claims of safety and therapeutic value are supported by clinical evidence and keeps unsafe, ineffective, and dangerous drugs off the market. . . .

Fact 5: Drug control spending is a minor portion of the U.S. budget. Compared to the social costs of drug abuse and addiction, government spending on drug control is minimal.

- Legalization advocates claim that the United States has spent billions of dollars to control drug production, trafficking, and use, with few, if any, positive results. As shown in previous [sections], the results of the American drug strategy have been positive indeed—with a 95 percent rate of Americans who do *not* use drugs. If the number of drug abusers doubled or tripled, the social costs would be enormous.

Social Costs

- . . . Legalization would result in skyrocketing costs that would be paid by American taxpayers and consumers. Legalization would significantly increase drug use and addiction—and all the social costs that go with it. With the removal of the social and legal sanctions against drugs, many experts estimate the user population would at least double. For example, a 1994 article in the *New England Journal of Medicine* stated that it was probable, that if cocaine were legalized, the number of cocaine addicts in America would increase from 2 million to at least 20 million.
- Drug abuse drives some of America's most costly social problems—including domestic violence, child abuse, chronic mental illness, the spread of AIDS, and homelessness. Drug treatment costs, hospitalization for long-term drug-related disease, and treatment of the consequences of family violence burden our already strapped health care system. In 2000, there were more than 600,000 hospital emergency department drug episodes in the United States. Health care costs for drug abuse alone were about $15 billion. . . .
- Legalizers fail to mention the hidden consequences of legalization. . . .
- Advocates also argue that legalization will lower prices. But that raises a dilemma: If the price of drugs is low, many more people will be able to afford them and the demand for drugs will explode. For example, the cost of cocaine production is now as low as $3 per gram. At a market price of, say, $10 a gram, cocaine could retail for as little as ten cents a hit. That means a young person could buy six hits of cocaine for the price of a candy bar. On the other hand, if legal drugs are priced

too high, through excise taxes, for example, illegal traffickers will be able to undercut it.

- Advocates of legalization also argue that the legal market could be limited to those above a certain age level, as it is for alcohol and cigarettes. . . . But teenagers today have found many ways to circumvent the age restrictions, whether by using false identification or by buying liquor and cigarettes from older friends. According to the 2001 National Household Survey on Drug Abuse, approximately 10.1 million young people aged 12–20 reported past month alcohol use (28.5 percent of this age group). Of these, nearly 6.8 million (19 percent) were binge drinkers. With drugs, teenagers would have an additional outlet: the highly organized illegal trafficking networks that exist today and that would undoubtedly concentrate their marketing efforts on young people to make up for the business they lost to legal outlets.

Costs to the Taxpayer

- . . . Legalization advocates fail to note the skyrocketing social and welfare costs, not to mention the misery and addiction, that would accompany outright legalization of drugs.
- Legalizers also fail to mention that, unless drugs are made available to children, law enforcement will still be needed to deal with the sale of drugs to minors. In other words, a vast black market will still exist. Since young people are often the primary target of pushers, many of the criminal organizations that now profit from illegal drugs would continue to do so.
- Furthermore, it is reasonable to assume that the health and societal costs of drug legalization would also increase exponentially. Drug treatment costs, hospitalization for long-term drug-related diseases, and treatment of family violence would also place additional demands on our already overburdened health system. More taxes would have to be raised to pay for an American health care system already bursting at the seams. . . .

Fact 6: Legalization of drugs will lead to increased use and increased levels of addiction. Legalization has been tried before, and failed miserably.

- Legalization proponents claim, absurdly, that making illegal drugs legal would not cause more of these substances to be consumed, nor would addiction increase. They claim that many people can use drugs in moderation and that many would choose not to use drugs, just as many abstain from alcohol and tobacco now. Yet how much misery can already be attributed to alcoholism and smoking? Is the answer to just add more misery and addiction? . . .

The Alaska Experiment and Other Failed Legalization Ventures

- The consequences of legalization became evident when the Alaska Supreme Court ruled in 1975 that the state could not interfere with an adult's possession of marijuana for personal consumption in the home.

The court's ruling became a green light for marijuana use. Although the ruling was limited to persons 19 and over, teens were among those increasingly using marijuana. According to a 1988 University of Alaska study, the state's 12- to 17-year-olds used marijuana at more than twice the national average for their age group. Alaska's residents voted in 1990 to recriminalize possession of marijuana, demonstrating their belief that increased use was too high a price to pay.

- By 1979, after 11 states decriminalized marijuana and the Carter administration had considered federal decriminalization, marijuana use shot up among teenagers. That year, almost 51 percent of 12th graders reported they used marijuana in the last 12 months. By 1992, with tougher laws and increased attention to the risks of drug abuse, that figure had been reduced to 22 percent, *a 57 percent decline*. . . .
- When legalizers suggest that easy access to drugs *won't* contribute to greater levels of addiction, they aren't being candid. The question isn't whether legalization will increase addiction levels—it will—it's whether we care or not. The compassionate response is to do everything possible to prevent the destruction of addiction, not make it easier.

Fact 7: Crime, violence, and drug use go hand-in-hand.

- Proponents of legalization have many theories regarding the connection between drugs and violence. Some dispute the connection between drugs and violence, claiming that drug use is a *victimless crime* and users are putting only themselves in harm's way and therefore have the right to use drugs. Other proponents of legalization contend that if drugs were legalized, crime and violence would decrease, believing that it is the illegal nature of drug production, trafficking, and use that fuels crime and violence, rather than the violent and irrational behavior that drugs themselves prompt.
- Yet, under a legalization scenario, a black market for drugs would still exist. And it would be a vast black market. If drugs were legal for those over 18 or 21, there would be a market for everyone under that age. People under the age of 21 consume the majority of illegal drugs, and so an illegal market and organized crime to supply it would remain—along with the organized crime that profits from it. After Prohibition ended, did the organized crime in our country go down? No. It continues today in a variety of other criminal enterprises. Legalization would not put the cartels out of business; cartels would simply look to other illegal endeavors. . . .
- The greatest weakness in the logic of legalizers is that the violence associated with drugs is simply a product of drug trafficking. That is, if drugs were legal, then most drug crime would end. But most violent crime is committed not because people want to buy drugs, but because people are on drugs. Drug use changes behavior and exacerbates criminal activity, and there is ample scientific evidence that demonstrates the links between drugs, violence, and crime. Drugs often cause people to do things they wouldn't do if they were rational and free of the influence of drugs. . . .

- For experts in the field of crime, violence, and drug abuse, there is no doubt that there is a connection between drug use and violence. As Joseph A. Califano, Jr., of the National Center on Addiction and Substance Abuse at Columbia University stated, "Drugs like marijuana, heroin and cocaine are not dangerous because they are illegal; they are illegal because they are dangerous." . . .

Fact 8: Alcohol has caused significant health, social, and crime problems in this country, and legalized drugs would only make the situation worse.

- Drugs are far more addictive than alcohol. According to Dr. Mitchell Rosenthal, director of Phoenix House, only 10 percent of drinkers become alcoholics, while up to 75 percent of regular illicit drug users become addicted. . . .

Fact 9: Europe's more liberal drug policies are not the right model for America.

- Over the past decade, European drug policy has gone through some dramatic changes toward greater liberalization. The Netherlands, considered to have led the way in the liberalization of drug policy, is only one of a number of West European countries to relax penalties for marijuana possession. Now several European nations are looking to relax penalties on all drugs—including cocaine and heroin—as Portugal did in July 2001, when minor possession of all drugs was decriminalized. . . .
- The Netherlands has led Europe in the liberalization of drug policy. "Coffee shops" began to emerge throughout the Netherlands in 1976, offering marijuana products for sale. Possession and sale of marijuana are not legal, but coffee shops are permitted to operate and sell marijuana under certain restrictions, including a limit of no more than 5 grams sold to a person at any one time, no alcohol or hard drugs, no minors, and no advertising. In the Netherlands, it is illegal to sell or possess marijuana products. So coffee shop operators must purchase their marijuana products from illegal drug trafficking organizations.
- Apparently, there has been some public dissatisfaction with the government's policy. Recently the Dutch government began considering scaling back the quantity of marijuana available in coffee shops from 5 to 3 grams.
- Furthermore, drug abuse has increased in the Netherlands. From 1984 to 1996, marijuana use among 18–25 year olds in Holland increased twofold. Since legalization of marijuana, heroin addiction levels in Holland have tripled and perhaps even quadrupled by some estimates.
- The increasing use of marijuana is responsible for more than increased crime. It has widespread social implications as well. The head of Holland's best-known drug abuse rehabilitation center has described what the new drug culture has created: The strong form of marijuana that most of the young people smoke, he says, produces "a chronically

passive individual—someone who is lazy, who doesn't want to take initiatives, doesn't want to be active—the kid who'd prefer to lie in bed with a joint in the morning rather than getting up and doing something.". . .

- The United Kingdom has also experimented with the relaxation of drug laws. Until the mid-1960s, British physicians were allowed to prescribe heroin to certain classes of addicts. . . . Many addicts chose to boycott the program and continued to get their heroin from illicit drug distributors. The British Government's experiment with controlled heroin distribution . . . resulted in, at a minimum, a 30-fold increase in the number of addicts in ten years.
- Switzerland has some of the most liberal drug policies in Europe. In [the] late 1980s, Zurich experimented with what became known as Needle Park, where addicts could openly purchase drugs and inject heroin without police intervention. Zurich became the hub for drug addicts across Europe, until the experiment was ended, and "Needle Park" was shut down.
- Many proponents of drug legalization or decriminalization claim that drug use will be reduced if drugs were legalized. However, history has not shown this assertion to be true. According to an October 2000 CNN report, marijuana, the illegal drug most often decriminalized, is "continuing to spread in the European Union, with one in five people across the 15-state bloc having tried it at least once."
- It's not just marijuana use that is increasing in Europe. According to the *2001 Annual Report on the State of the Drugs Problem in the European Union,* there is a Europe-wide increase in cocaine use. . . .
- Drug policy also has an impact on general crime. In a 2001 study, the British Home Office found violent crime and property crime increased in the late 1990s in every wealthy country except the United States.

Fact 10: Most non-violent drug users get treatment, not just jail time.

- There is a myth in this country that U.S. prisons are filled with drug users. This assertion is simply not true. Actually, only 5 percent of inmates in *federal* prison on drug charges are incarcerated for drug possession. In our *state* prisons, it's somewhat higher—about 27% of drug offenders. In New York, which has received criticism from some because of its tough Rockefeller drug laws, it is estimated that 97% of drug felons sentenced to prison were charged with sale or intent to sell, not simply possession. In fact, first time drug offenders, even sellers, typically do not go to prison. . . .

Policy Shift to Treatment

- There has been a shift in the U.S. criminal justice system to provide treatment for non-violent drug users with addiction problems, rather than incarceration. The criminal justice system actually serves as the largest referral source for drug treatment programs.
- Any successful treatment program must also require accountability from its participants. Drug treatment courts are a good example

of combining treatment with such accountability. These courts are given a special responsibility to handle cases involving drug-addicted offenders through an extensive supervision and treatment program. Drug treatment court programs use the varied experience and skills of a wide variety of law enforcement and treatment professionals: judges, prosecutors, defense counsels, substance abuse treatment specialists, probation officers, law enforcement and correctional personnel, educational and vocational experts, community leaders and others—all focused on one goal: to help cure addicts of their addiction, and to keep them cured.

- Drug treatment courts are working. Researchers estimate that more than 50 percent of defendants convicted of drug possession will return to criminal behavior within two to three years. Those who graduate from drug treatment courts have far lower rates of recidivism, ranging from 2 to 20 percent. . . .

POSTSCRIPT

Should Drugs Be Legalized?

Cussen and Block state that governmental efforts to control drug use create serious social problems, and that social conditions would be much improved if drugs were legalized. A strong governmental effort—like the current war on drugs—threatens people's civil liberties and provides criminals with a financial incentive to engage in illegal drug trafficking.

The Drug Enforcement Administration (DEA) opposes Cussen and Block at almost every turn. Moreover, the DEA's position, as outlined here, is not just a simple restatement of the law, but an articulate series of arguments that directly respond to the claims and arguments of legalization supporters such as Cussen and Block. The DEA begins from a point that supporters of legalization must face. If, under legalization, there would be increased availability of drugs, and little or no social sanction against using them, then there would be an increase in use and in drug abuse, and the consequences that follow from that (for example, more drug addicts).

Neither Cussen and Block nor the DEA distinguishes "soft" drugs from "hard" drugs. Perhaps, if such a distinction could be well articulated, it might turn out that one side in this dispute (the YES side) is correct for soft drugs, while the other side (the NO side) is correct for hard drugs. Yet, on the other hand, even if only the hard drugs remained illegal, financial incentives for a black market would still be there—along with violence and crime. Also, neither side considers what limited or regulated legalization might be like. Suppose, for example, that there were an age limit for purchasing drugs, just as there is in the case of tobacco and alcohol. But then again there would still be financial incentives for a black market for underage purchasers. The same social ills that Cussen and Block identify would follow. (But one difference is that the scope of these might be smaller, although drug dealers wouldn't have to worry about their product having to be smuggled into the country, since it would be readily available for adult buyers.)

Cussen and Block and the DEA sometimes seem to occupy extreme positions. It is difficult to find and defend a middle position here. Is there a middle position?

For further reading on this issue, see James A. Inciardi, *The War on Drugs III: The Continuing Saga of the Mysteries and Miseries of Intoxication, Addiction, Crime, and Public Policy* (Allyn & Bacon, 2001); Robert J. MacCoun and Peter Reuter, *Drug War Heresies: Learning from Other Vices, Times, and Places* (Cambridge University Press, 2001); Douglas Husak, *Drugs and Rights* (Cambridge University Press, 2002); Jeffrey A. Miron, *Drug War Crimes: The Consequences of Prohibition* (Independent Institute, 2004); Douglas Valentine, *The Strength of the Wolf: The Secret History of America's War on Drugs* (Verso, 2006); Sergio Ferragut,

A Silent Nightmare: The Bottom Line and the Challenge of Illicit Drugs (http://www.lulu.com, 2007); Doris Marie Provine, *Unequal Under Law: Race in the War on Drugs* (University of Chicago, 2007); Gary "Rusty" Fleming, *Drug Wars: Narco Warfare in the 21st Century* (BookSurge, 2008); and Peggy J. Parks, *Drug Legalization* (Referencepoint Press, 2008).

ISSUE 10

Is Gambling Immoral?

YES: Lisa Newton, from "Gambling: A Preliminary Inquiry," *Business Ethics Quarterly* (vol. 3, no. 4, 1993)

NO: Peter Collins, from "Is Gambling Immoral? A Virtue Ethics Approach," in Mark Timmons, ed., *Disputed Moral Issues* (Oxford University Press, 2007)

ISSUE SUMMARY

YES: Lisa Newton, a philosopher at Fairfield University, argues that gambling is immoral on the grounds that it violates stewardship (and not on the grounds that it violates anyone's rights or that it leads to negative results). Most of the paper examines the concept of stewardship and how it relates to gambling. Stewardship, which is an old concept that is known to us primarily through religious tradition, can also be given a modern secular form.

NO: Peter Collins, a British philosopher, argues that gambling is not immoral. He addresses gambling from both traditional utilitarian (or consequentialist) and Kantian perspectives—and finds the critiques from these perspectives lacking. He then specifically considers the more recent criticism that is based on the idea of stewardship—this too he finds lacking. Collins concludes with the idea of true happiness, and expresses the judgment that although gambling is not necessarily a part of a truly happy life, it is morally trivial.

Gambling has traditionally been considered a vice. It has traditionally been considered immoral. But it may be difficult to specify what exactly is wrong with it. For example, it is not difficult to realize that theft and lying are wrong. But with the case of gambling, determining if it's wrong becomes somewhat more difficult. It is not hard to realize that theft and lying violate people's rights, but while some cases of gambling violate people's rights, some do not. For example, if I take the rent money and gamble it away, then I have trespassed against the rights of those who are depending on me to take care of the rent. You could say that I have wrongfully deprived them of what was theirs—just as in the case of theft. But that would be the case if I just spent the rent money on books—and no one says that reading is immoral. But if there is something wrong with gambling in particular, we still haven't managed to say exactly what that is. Now, it's sometimes the case that gamblers will waste their time and that others have a claim on that time. This point can be granted, but people can waste time on a variety of things without those things having to be thought immoral. What is it, we ask, that is immoral about gambling?

One way of looking at this issue invites us to step away from "rights-talk" and think not in terms of rights but—to use a rather old-fashioned word—virtues. The language of rights encourages us to look for the absolute minimum that one person owes another. But the language of virtues encourages us to look higher than the minimum. Thus, for example, if I do not steal from someone, at least I am not violating that person's rights—but this a minimum. People don't think that they are good people on the grounds that they don't steal. That is, it's hardly a claim to moral goodness that one isn't a thief. Of course, being a thief is a *disqualification* from being a good person. But is that all that people should do in order to be good? Avoid the disqualifications?

One non-rights approach to gambling (and to ethics in general) suggests that we use the language of *virtues*. "Responsible," for example, is a virtue word. (I'm thinking of the sense of the term in which a person you can count on is said to be a *responsible* person, not the sense in which the thief who took the money is said to be *responsible* for its disappearance.) One difference between this sort of word and a rights-word is that different people can have various *degrees* of the virtue. One person may be highly responsible, for example—far more responsible than another responsible individual.

Lisa Newton, in her article below on gambling, speaks of *stewardship*. Here again, we can see that this old-fashioned-sounding term suggests degrees: There is the idea of being a good steward, or an even better steward, or possibly a poor steward, while rights-talk encourages an all-or-nothing approach. (If you violate someone's rights, that action is wrong; there are no "low-level" violations that gradually shade off into non-violations. But if you are a poor steward of some resources, then this could gradually shade off into higher and higher levels of stewardship, including—at some distance—even good stewardship.)

The author of the answering article, Peter Collins, not only examines gambling from a variety of viewpoints, but includes specific criticism of the ideas of stewardship. His conclusion is that gambling is "morally trivial."

YES

Lisa Newton

Gambling: A Preliminary Inquiry

Abstract: In all the criticisms that have shadowed the financial industry in recent years, the burden seems to be, that the reckless (as opposed to malicious) bankers too often took money of which they were the appointed stewards, and used it for speculation, especially in junk bonds. As Shaheen Borna and James Lowry argue in their "Gambling and Speculation" (the only article on gambling that I was able to raise on my computer[1]) business speculation is probably wrong, since it is very like gambling, which everyone knows is wrong. But why is gambling wrong? If we, as the ethicists of business, are to adopt an uncharacteristically judgmental posture toward the most venerable American institutions, occupying the tallest and closest of American buildings, by calling their residents "gamblers," then surely we ought to be able to provide an account of the blameworthiness of gambling itself.[2] That, at any rate, is the challenge I set myself for this paper.

Why Is Gambling Wrong?

Not because it injures others than the gambler. Others are surely injured, and every chronicle of gambling details the miseries of the gamblers' families and friends as they struggle to survive themselves, cover for the gambler and pay the debts. But the injury is not a violation of their rights, and whether or not they "accept" the gambling, they accept the situation overall and voluntarily remain in it [to one who is willing no injury is done]. Nor is the injury one that the law punishes whether or not the victim accepts it: whatever the peculiar mental anguish of the gambler's family, the only material damage they suffer is impoverishment, and they might suffer that from any number of causes (if the family breadwinner is laid off from work, for instance), without anyone thinking an injury has been done.

Not because it injures the gambler. When the gambler voluntarily engages in the activity, he or she accepts the possibility of loss of as much money as is wagered—that is the definition of gambling, is it not?—so the results of the gamble are apparently acceptable. The gambler may claim that they are not, but from the fact that he or she repeatedly engages in the activity we have reason to doubt the sincerity of the claim. In any case, the loss suffered is no different from that imposed on the family—loss of money—which can result from any number of misguided voluntary actions (making a bad investment

From *Business Ethics Quarterly,* vol. 3, issue 4, 1993, pp. 405–413. Copyright © 1993 by Business Ethics Quarterly. Reprinted by permission.

in the stock market, for instance) without any claim of injury arising. The literature that grounds our societal commitment to individual rights is eloquent in its defense of the right to make mistakes without thereby inviting social intervention; after all, what other right makes any sense without that one?

The origin of the moral condemnation of gambling (as opposed to the literature of regret for the social consequences) seems to lie in the duty of *stewardship,* and the egregious violation of that duty constituted by gambling, at an individual and societal level. Since the term has not been common in recent literature, especially in the literature of business ethics, a few words of review might be in order.

Stewardship has essentially to do with property not your own, and is governed more by what we now call "agency theory" than any other set of moral principles. It designates simultaneously the occupancy of a position (the position of "steward," one hired by a property owner to watch out for his property in his absence), and the duties associated with that position. If you are a steward, you have property that has been entrusted to you to take care of by the owner, and it is your duty to make sure that it is well maintained, well used by those who use it, improved as appropriate, self-sustaining and profitable. The duties extend to whatever new property may arise out of the entrusted property; if the cows calve, the calves must be taken care of, and if the property yields a substantial income, the money must be appropriately invested. The investments must be "safe," as opposed to "risky," unless the owner has given specific instructions to take risks (and specified the risks), for the duty to keep the property safe and whole outweighs any duty to make it profitable. At no time is the steward free to use, or use up, the property at will.

Yes, but what has this to do with the gambler's gambling with the gambler's own money? Three lines of reasoning lead from that duty to the gambler's risk. First, stewardship actually derives from ownership: the primary command for the steward, or agent, is to treat the property of the master, or principal, as if it were one's own. But at the time the concept was cemented into the moral tradition, "ownership" was understood to carry an enormous baggage of duties with it, duties less familiar in this century. The property the human race has known for 99% of its settled existence has been the land we farmed and the animals we kept for food, milk and wool. Land and animals are uncompromising: you will take care of them, or you will get no good of them, either for yourself (in immediate use for food or cloth) or for trade, in exchange for other things you might need. Your living depends upon judicious investment in the future of your property, digging wells, buying new rams, or purchasing new seed or machines; above all you must maintain the property in good condition. You could assume new positions only by liquidating (selling or otherwise consuming) part of your property in order to enhance others; that was the element of capitalistic flexibility that made our ancestors good businessmen and businesswomen.

Of course there was always the theoretical possibility of liquidating *all* your property—selling off all your sheep, seed, acreage and buildings, for cash—but then, of course (the story of the Prodigal Son), you would have nothing left after the cash was spent. Life depended on a very careful balance between investment (saving) and liquidation (spending), with the balance always tipped to saving. Let the balance tip the other way, and that particular community was destined for bankruptcy, and extinction. That is the way we lived from neolithic times through the last century, in which the habits cultivated over millennia were transferred without remainder to the factories and industrial empires of the burgeoning industries of iron and steel, rail transportation and petroleum. Communities that did not understand the duties of ownership presumably died out in hard times, vanished without a trace, and are not available for comparison. So the necessities of sheer survival created, not exactly a duty (for we cannot get an ought from an is), but a fact situation in which those who did not adopt certain hypothetical imperatives as duties failed to transmit their culture to descendants—making such duty part, I suppose, of what H. L. A. Hart would call the "minimum natural law."[3]

So the gambler, first, in ignoring the duties of ownership to property, violates a taboo of great antiquity. Second, and perhaps more immediately for our Calvinist ancestors, there is a question whether property can be "owned" by humans at all. For the earth, come to that, is the Lord's, as is the yield thereof—the world, and they that dwell therein; for He founded it upon the seas, and established it upon the floods. To the extent that we "own" property, under the secular laws of our land at this time, we actually hold it in trust for God, we are His stewards, and (to put a finer point on it) we can be called from this life at any moment to render an account to God of our stewardship of that which was never really ours. It would not be pleasant to have that moment arrive as we sat at the green felt gaming tables.

Third, there is a secular version of the argument above, to the effect that there is a strong social interest in the care and conservation of all property in the commonwealth, that gives the public a justified and lively concern with the way people dispose of wealth that by law is their private property. The law and its regulations, after all, are never far from the exercise of property rights: I am compelled to spend my money on things I may not want (casualty insurance); I am prohibited from spending my money on things I may want (controlled substances, including non-approved medications); I must maintain my land, especially if it contains salt marshes, in accordance with zoning and other regulations. Only diehard libertarians seriously oppose such regulation, which amounts to a strong state interest in the management of property as a whole. (In passing, we may note that if the gambler ends in poverty, the taxpayers end up footing the welfare bills.) Our duty of "stewardship" of the nation's property in general, then, can entail that putting that property at risk at the gaming tables is seriously wrong.

The conclusion that gambling is wrong, because it is a violation of our duty of stewardship of property, is consistent with several otherwise anomalous facts in the checkered career of the activity in this country: that gambling is illegal or severely restricted in most jurisdictions, although no basis can be found for opposition to gambling in rights theory, which is elsewhere our first (and usually last) court of appeal; that gambling has been publicly prohibited or carefully controlled through much of our history by most of our legislatures even though (see next section) there is no utilitarian warrant for public prohibition of gambling; and that the Protestant churches that most controlled the country's moral life until this century consistently condemned gambling, in the absence of any Biblical warrant for such condemnation. As a preliminary suggestion for further research, we might want to follow up the notion of "stewardship" for other applications at the border of private behavior and business enterprise.

If Gambling Is Wrong, Should It Be Against the Law?

Probably not. Very powerful arguments have been advanced, that the criminalization of gambling and other consensual transactions creates a whole new class of "crimes without victims," and does much more harm than good.[4] We need not rehearse these familiar arguments in any detail. In brief, it has been observed that where the "crime" consists of a transaction between consenting adults, its commission is extremely difficult to detect; information is very difficult to gather, involving the police in distasteful recruitment of spies and informants; the police find it impossible to resist corruption of their own number in protection rackets for the activity in question; the participants in the activity are driven underground and isolated from the help and community support that might draw them into healthier lines of work and recreation; blackmail, loansharking, and organized crime in general rapidly take over the conduct of the activity and corrupt the community as a whole. As long as there is a willing market for gambling, prostitution, and narcotics purchases (older accounts include abortion and homosexual encounters), and as long as there is money available to pay for them, they will take place, and their criminalization will have no effect but to degrade participants and law enforcement alike.

Then Should the Society Encourage Gambling?

This is the question of the hour. The costs and benefits of two forms of societal encouragement of gambling—the state lotteries, for one, and the legalization of casino gambling, for the other—are debated as we speak in legislatures across the country, including my home state of Connecticut. Benefits and costs are simple enough to discover; the problem is one of weighting. Let us run through the exercise, very briefly.

The benefits of legalized gambling are public revenue and jobs. Any legal income can be taxed, and that includes gambling income; any legal enterprise is subject to business taxes, Federal, state and local. A casino or other gambling establishment is a new source of revenue for the state, politically palatable (unlike new taxes) and endlessly profitable. Because the casino is so sure to make money, entrepreneurs (and the banks that back them) gladly venture the capital to construct them, without government subsidy or tax breaks, and even in locations that have found it difficult to attract other sorts of business (the crumbling downtown districts of the older cities, for instance). The building alone cleans out the slums, cleans up the streets, and provides construction jobs at union wages. Once the casinos begin operating, they provide more jobs immediately suitable for the unskilled inner-city unemployed—work in the restaurants, maintenance, maid service. (We may assume that the executive-level and skilled jobs—croupiers and the like—will come from outside.) And they pay taxes: real estate taxes to cities long unused to successful industry, state taxes for public education, and federal taxes, to fund new programs for the inner cities.

And the beauty of it all is, that the whole profitable deal is entirely voluntary and without limit. No one loses money at the tables who has not asked to do so. The gambler is probably aware that the house skims a percent off the top of every transaction; and is also probably aware that the state does too; but the gambling continues. There is no apparent natural limit on the amount of money the enterprise will yield: the more casinos, and the more hours they are open, the higher the state revenue from casino gambling. What could be the objections to this goose of endless golden eggs?

The state lottery, a different form of state encouragement of gambling, is a lower budget version of the same argument. Here the state takes all the profit, but incurs all the expenses. Its moral status, whatever that turns out to be, is the same as that of the collection of revenue from casino gambling, and the decision to emphasize one or the other is a simple business decision. Again, since all play is voluntary, no effort is required to collect the revenue, and no political consequences follow from advocating an expansion.

The drawbacks of legalized gambling are also reasonably well known. First, there is the sleaze factor. There is little evidence that, legalized, these activities suddenly become clean and harmless ways for the citizenry to spend their time. Another literature surveys the communities that make their living on gambling, notably Las Vegas and Atlantic City, and concludes that most of the evils of illegal gambling followed the law into the legal casino, where they continue to hold sway.[5] Nor is it clear that the proposed benefits to the inner cities actually took place. The picture given of the life of the casinos, and of the pockets of poverty in the cities that harbor them, is of human associations severely unbalanced, engines to produce human misery behind the shield of "voluntary participation." Given the experience of Las Vegas and especially Atlantic City (since the decision to permit casino gambling there was more recent and self-conscious), communities should think long and hard about the decision to cash in on the easy revenues.

The second objection, the objection from Rawlsian justice, is harder to calculate. John Rawls has asked us to evaluate each scheme for the betterment of the society by one simple test: does it improve the lot of the least advantaged?[6] Gambling does not, except maybe it does. First, if we look only to the objective, material, effects, gambling (legal or illegal) takes from the poor, who gamble, and gives to the rich. If the only one to profit is the policy banker, the injustice is clear; but even if the take from gambling is distributed through the state education system, it remains the case that the least well off of society have contributed their money for the benefit of an aggregate on average richer than the contributors. In effect, gambling is worse than a regressive tax, which takes from all equally; gambling takes disproportionately from the poor and almost none from the successful professional class. This is clearly unjust.

The injustice is compounded by deception, or arguable deception, in the advertising of the state lotteries or other legal opportunities to gamble. The odds of winning—*against* winning—are well known, by cognoscenti—but how many of the poor fall into that category? Meanwhile, the percent of the take distributed to *actual* winners may be much less than that, since the state gets to keep an extra percentage of every pot that is not won. Should it not be wrong to add to the temptation to gamble by the slick advertising campaigns now in use?

On the other hand, there is evidence that suggests that not only are the disadvantaged themselves much happier for having the opportunity to gamble, but that it is indeed rational for them to do so. In districts where hope is in short supply, the numbers chit or lottery ticket is hope, and that alone is worth the price of the ticket. Second, the hope is not irrational: if your goal is to achieve the material American Dream, you should know that saving your pennies, including the extra two dollars a week that you spend on the lottery, from a minimum wage job in the inner city, will never get you there; a hit on the numbers, or the lottery, will do that. Never mind that the chances are miniscule; without the ticket, they are nonexistent. Finally, the very fact that the lowest of the rackets, the numbers game, is confined to the ghetto, renders it a special area of activity and expertise, a social event with its own gratifying rituals and non-material rewards.[7]

Do I have the right to enslave an unsuspecting tribe of masochists that plead with me to enslave them? Do I have the right to profit from the hopes of the poor, when the society that has treated me so well has created the conditions that make the gambling, from which I profit, their only hope?

The third objection, from the teaching responsibility of the State, is related to the second, but more amorphous yet. What is our responsibility for creating the conditions for a good life for all citizens—not necessarily a materially good life, but a life in which they can be good? Suppose it should turn out, and I suspect it might, that it is easier to resist temptation and develop justice and kindness as traits of character in settings where the encouragement of virtue and the condemnation (and punishment) of vice is part of public commitment—in short, where virtue is publicly rewarded, and vice is against the law (one remembers Sparta)? What is the responsibility of the political association to form its citizens into virtuous people? We cannot pursue this objection in this paper, but the classical conservative political tradition takes it very seriously.[8]

Can Gambling Be Good Business?

If by "good business" all we mean is "profitable," the question is not worth asking. Las Vegas continues to build casinos, Atlantic City processes enormous amounts of cash on a daily basis, the Pequot Indians of Connecticut know more prosperity than they have had since the White Man first landed on their shores. Of course it can be, and is, profitable. (But then, have you ever known organized crime to get into a line of work that was *not* profitable?)

But if we mean to determine the moral status of the enterprise, the question is more interesting, and again, surprisingly unasked, in any literature with which I am familiar. This is no time for any attempt at detailed evaluation of the ethical dimensions of Las Vegas and its relatives; the following preliminary sketch of the issues may be enough to get us started:

1. Is there any way that gambling can be useful, or at least entertaining and harmless? (Does it have, we may ask, any redeeming social value?) If so, then the ethical casino would make good faith attempts to ensure that gambling happened there only in that way. The analogy that suggests itself is the manufacture and sale of alcoholic beverages. We know that if the product is misused, terrible injury can result (from violence, drunken operation of machinery or automobiles, or alcohol-related disease); we know that there are an indefinitely large number of people who will, by reason of their physical or psychological predispositions, misuse it; and we suspect that non-alcohol-related aspects of our society are being compromised by it (50% of hospital admissions are alcohol related, entailing a large but incalculable effect of alcohol consumption on our national health care bill). But alcohol can be consumed affordably, harmlessly, and enjoyably, so it is possible to run a manufactury, tavern, or wine and liquor emporium, to cater to that trade alone. On the other hand, it would be difficult to conceive of an ethical trade in cocaine, as it is becoming harder to imagine an ethical trade in cigarettes. Along the spectrum from the harmless entertainment (subject to misuse by some) to the obnoxious product with no redeeming features, where does gambling fall?

2. Is it possible to run the industry in such a way as to extract it from organized crime? If not, is there an ethical way to include, and deal with, the Mob? If we can free the industry from organized crime, who would run it? Could we justify keeping gambling as a government monopoly, as a source of revenue for the states, especially if it turns out that private operators cannot stay clear of criminal associations? If it turns out that it is impractical to have the government run it, that private operators are inevitably part of the Mafia or rapidly become captured by it, is that reason enough, in the absence of other reasons, to criminalize gambling?

3. What, if any, responsibility does the industry bear for the compulsive gambler? Is there something wrong with placing the means of one more addiction in front of people already addicted? The liquor industry takes no responsibility for the alcoholic *per se,* but the bartender is responsible for refusing to serve someone obviously drunk. Should the casino take responsibility for ascertaining the financial means of each patron, and barring from play any who go over a preset limit?

These are not easy questions to answer. It is no real help to flesh out the analogy of the ethical tavern with the analogy of Prohibition, to point out that, as above, gambling will take place illegally if not legally, so we might as well try to run ethical casinos as at least a small improvement. Prohibition of the manufacture and sale of alcohol clearly "did not work"—it was a disaster for law enforcement and demoralized (and criminalized) the middle class, never something a lawgiver wants to do. But while it was in effect, alcohol-caused disease dropped significantly, especially among the poor. By reverse projection, we may expect that if casino gambling is legalized, the take from illegal gambling will drop, and the middle class will no longer gamble illegally. And we may also expect that gambling losses over the whole population will increase significantly, especially among the poor. Is it worth it?

To conclude, at very long last, what do we, as a people, expect of ourselves? There is an ironic justice in the fact that our eagerness to legalize casino gambling for the sake of the revenues follows directly from our unwillingness to assess ourselves a fair and adequate amount in taxes. The problems with our public character dovetail with the problems in our private character. There is a good possibility that we will make progress on neither until we are willing to address both.

Notes

1. *Journal of Business Ethics* 6(3):219–224 (April, 1987). That isn't quite true, actually. The computer search showed a fascinating literature, now over ten years old, on John Harris' proposal (in the spirit of Jonathan Swift) for a mandatory "survival lottery"—requiring an unlucky "donor" to be sacrificed if two or more persons with otherwise terminal diseases could be saved by the use of his organs. The proposal can be shown to maximize survival if not happiness, and to accord with certain rules of justice, but the thought of it makes some of us a little queasy. See Harris, John, "The Survival Lottery," *Philosophy* 50(191):81–87 (January 1975); Hanink, J. G. "On the Survival Lottery," *Philosophy* 51:223–225 (April 1976); Morillo, Carolyn R. "As Sure as Shooting," *Philosophy* 51:80–89 (January 1976); Singer, Peter, "Utility and the Survival Lottery," *Philosophy* 52:218–222 (April 1977); Green, Michael B., "Harris's Modest Proposal," *Philosophy* 54:400–406 (July 1979); Trammell, Richard L. and Wren, Thomas E., "Fairness, Utility and Survival," *Philosophy* 52:331–337 (July 1977); Harris, John, "Hanink on the Survival Lottery," *Philosophy* 53:100–101 (January 1978). All of which brings us back to the original question: since the profession seems to have no problem tackling the issues of games of chance when they are far-fetched and imaginary, why the avoidance of games of chance real, actual, and grossing a billion dollars a day all around us?
2. We may note in passing that the industry under consideration here, the industry that provides and draws its profits from the slot machines and card games of Las Vegas and Atlantic City, prefers to call itself the "gaming" industry, not "gambling." "Gaming" certainly sounds better, conjuring up visions of children playing games for amusement. We take the two activities to be conceptually distinct: "Gaming" means playing games, no more or less; "gambling" means placing property at risk, as described below in the paper. We are concerned with the ethical implications of the latter, not the former, so we retain the term "gambling" to describe our subject.
3. H. L. A. Hart, *The Concept of Law,* Oxford: Oxford University Press, 1961.
4. See the report by the American Friends Service Committee, *Struggle for Justice: A Report on Crime and Punishment in America,* New York: Hill and Wang, 1971; also Troy Duster, *The Legislation of Morality,* New York: The Free Press, 1970; Gilbert Geis, *Not the Law's Business? An Examination of Homosexuality, Abortion, Prostitution, Narcotics, and Gambling in the United*

States, National Institute of Mental Health, Crime and Delinquency Monograph Series, Washington, DC: U.S. Government Printing Office, 1972; *The Knapp Commission Report on Police Corruption,* New York: George Braziller, 1972;

Herbert L. Packer, *The Limits of the Criminal Sanction,* Stanford: Stanford University Press, 1968; Edwin M. Schur, *Crimes Without Victims,* Englewood Cliffs, NJ: Prentice-Hall, Inc. 1965; Schur, *Labeling Deviant Behavior,* New York: Harper and Row, 1971; Schur, "The Case for Abolition," in *Victimless Crimes: Two Sides of a Controversy,* by Edwin Schur and Hugo Adam Bedau, Englewood Cliffs, NJ: Prentice-Hall, Inc., 1974. All of these have something to do with gambling; other literature on publicly condemned consensual transactions (for instance, the *Report* of the Wolfenden Committee on Homosexual Offences and Prostitution, Home Office, London, 1972) base their conclusions on similar observation and argument.

5. See Wallace Turner, *Gamblers' Money: The New Force in American Life,* Cambridge, MA: The Riverside Press, 1965; Ed Reid and Ovid Demaris, *The Green Felt Jungle,* New York: Trident Press, 1963; Ovid Demaris, *(How Greed, Corruption and the Mafia Turned Atlantic City into) The Boardwalk Jungle,* New York: Bantam Books, 1986. See also, for a gamblers' eye view of gambling, Stuart Winston and Harriet Harris, M.D. *Nation of Gamblers: America's Billion Dollar a Day Habit,* Englewood Cliffs, NJ: Prentice-Hall, 1984.
6. John Rawls, *A Theory of Justice,* Cambridge, MA: Harvard University Press, 1971.
7. Or so Gilbert Geis argues, citing abundant sources. Geis, *op. cit.,* pp. 225 ff.
8. See George F. Will, *Statecraft as Soulcraft: What Government Does,* New York: Simon and Schuster, 1983.

Peter Collins

Is Gambling Immoral? A Virtue Ethics Approach

1. Introduction

The question of whether gambling should be prohibited or legalised and, if legalised, how it should be regulated has received considerable attention from people who think about public policy. It is no part of my purpose here to try to contribute to answering those questions. Clearly, in as far as these questions raise moral issues, they are issues of public rather than private morality. That is, they are about what governments should or should not use their coercive powers to do rather than about how we individually should conduct our lives in conformity with what morality requires.

Historically, gambling along with other activities deemed to constitute vices has been legally proscribed because two beliefs were widely held: first that gambling is immoral and second, that it is the business of government to try to stamp out activities which are immoral. The second of these beliefs, however, has for better or for worse been largely discredited in pluralist societies committed to the principles of liberal democracy, on the grounds that it is neither morally defensible nor politically practicable. As a consequence, advocates of banning or limiting legal gambling tend to avoid invoking the claim that gambling is intrinsically immoral even though this is a belief which many of them hold. Instead they focus on trying to show that prohibition or legal restriction is justified on the basis of the illegitimate harm that legalised gambling does to gamblers themselves, to third parties and to society as a whole.

But is gambling immoral? Suppose it were agreed, on the purest libertarian grounds, that the State should do absolutely nothing to try to prevent or discourage people from gambling as much as they like; would there still be any good reasons why you and I should nevertheless decide on moral grounds that gambling ought to play little or no part in the way we conduct our daily lives?

I want to anchor this discussion by identifying [two] reasons why this question deserves substantial attention from moral philosophers and certainly more attention than it has recently received.[1] . . .

First, the role which pleasure and pleasures should play in our lives is a fundamental issue in moral philosophy to the extent that it addresses the question of how ordinary people ought to conduct their everyday lives. Gambling furnishes

From *2005 Collection of Papers on Self Study and Institutional Improvement,* April 2005. Published in 2005 by the Higher Learning Commission of the North Central Association of Colleges and Schools. Reprinted by permission of Peter Collins. ncahlc.org.

a particularly good case study for this kind of philosophising since it not only tends to consume considerable time and money which could arguably be better spent but also has a propensity to become addictive. For reasons which may be largely self-serving we tend to avoid reflection on this kind of question when it applies to our own pleasures or those of our friends. But it becomes inescapable when we think about the need to offer rational guidance to children about how they should conduct themselves in relation to different kinds of pleasure. And as soon as we ask: "What should we teach children about gambling?" we confront the question of the morality or otherwise of gambling.

Secondly, it is clear that gambling provides an interesting case against which to test different types of ethical theory. As we shall see, some people argue that gambling violates the principle of utility. Others claim on Kantian grounds that it is inconsistent with conduct of a rational and autonomous person. Gambling has also, of course, been condemned by those who espouse a puritan ethic whether based on religious convictions or on secular considerations.

Finally we need to consider the claim that gambling is incompatible with living the best or most fulfilling kind of life of which human beings are capable. . . .

2. What Is Gambling?

Before we can properly address questions about the morality of gambling we need to make some conceptual points about the nature of the activity we are discussing.

The standard definition of gambling is that it involves three components:

- Something valuable is placed at risk (staked).
- With the prospect of winning something more valuable if one set of events occurs and of losing one's stake if another set of events occurs.
- Where the outcome is wholly or partly unpredictable by the gambler.

This definition, however, seems to leave some important questions unanswered amongst which I wish to single out two because of their relevance to the moral issues.

First there is the question of whether buying stocks and shares is gambling. The thought here is that a pro-gambling argument might be developed along the following lines. If there is no difference between speculating on the stock market and gambling in a casino, the latter activity can only be morally culpable if the former is too. But it would obviously be absurd to condemn investing on the stock exchange as immoral. Therefore it is absurd to condemn gambling in casinos as immoral.

In order to refute this argument it is not necessary to rebut the full (and considerable) force of Marx's arguments to the effect that those who make money out of the mere ownership of capital in the form of shares are robbing workers of the private property which is rightfully theirs because it was created by their labour. All that is necessary is to point out that the stock exchange is not in its essence a provider of gambling services but rather of opportunities for genuine investment. The stock exchange thus differs from a casino or lottery in at least two crucial ways. First, success on the stock exchange depends primarily on the exercise of rational judgment. Second, investing in the stock market is not a zero sum game. That is, making profits on the stock exchange does not necessitate the making of losses by others: in the normal case it depends on the creation of new wealth. It is true that some investing on the stock exchange is, from the point of view of the investor, exactly like gambling—for example, if they pick their investments using a pin. Similarly, some gambling is indeed like investing on the stock exchange: the professional poker player or the bettor on horse races who is an expert on form is trying to make money out of superior knowledge and judgment. But the essence of investing in the stock market does not consist in people literally "trying their luck" in circumstances where one person's gain is always another's loss. The essence of gambling—or at least of the most widespread forms of gambling with whose morality this essay is mainly concerned—consists in just this.

This is why some of the most telling arguments against gambling are that, unlike investing, it is an irrational activity which is unproductive, at best, and destructive of wealth, at worst.

The second distinction which needs to be added to the standard definition of gambling is that between social gambling and commercial gambling. In the heyday of temperance movements, opponents of gambling argued that playing low-stakes social bridge was no less to be condemned on moral grounds than betting on horses, playing roulette or going to a gambling den. For the purposes of the present discussion, however, I shall assume that there could be a great deal of difference from a moral point of view between:

- games of skill engaged in as a social pastime and spiced up with wagers which all participants have a formally equal chance of winning, and
- gambling on games where the outcome is unavoidably and mainly dependent on luck, in commercial contexts where the games are set up so as to make it certain that the players will in the long run lose.

Thus the morality of gambling on slot machines, as opposed to having a bet on a game of golf, may be significantly affected by the fact that anyone who plays gaming machines ought to know that over time they are bound to lose. This may, for example, strengthen the claim that such gambling must be irrational and as such morally wrong. Note also that such an argument would not be affected by whether the amount wagered was large or small.

A very important question for conceptual analysis which underlies the question of what principles we should adopt in shaping both personal conduct and public policy in regard to gambling is: "To what extent is gambling like and unlike other pleasures which have historically been banned on the grounds that they are immoral?" At one extreme some would claim that gambling is like taking hard drugs and should be eschewed on the grounds that it is immoral and banned on the grounds that it is highly dangerous. At the other extreme, people argue that gambling is no more vicious or dangerous than going to the theatre or cinema which was also once much disapproved of by puritans. Rather than discussing these questions fully here, I simply note that to the extent that gambling is both similar to and different from other pleasurable activities to which we devote time and money we will benefit in our thinking about both public and private morality if we accept the demands of consistency in this area, i.e., if we accept that we should take the same position with respect to all pleasures except to the extent that we can demonstrate relevant differences between them. The discussion which follows, therefore, is implicitly though not explicitly concerned that a satisfactory answer can be given to the question: "What are the morally relevant differences, if any, between gambling and, say, dancing, playing golf (on the Sabbath), watching sexually exciting movies or consuming psychotropic drugs for pleasure?"

To summarise these considerations, then, I shall be here predominantly concerned with the morality of individuals' playing games of chance in commercial contexts where the odds are systematically stacked against them. The paradigm will be games like roulette or slot machine gambling. I shall also be concerned with table games played in casinos such as poker or blackjack where the opportunities to exercise skill are rendered systematically nugatory, as well as with lotteries and other number games like keno and bingo. With respect to most sports- and other event-betting I take it that ignorance of the relevant facts for most punters is sufficient to make the outcome the equivalent to one which is predominantly determined by luck. By contrast, I shall not concern myself with the morality of either professional gamblers who rely on superior knowledge and skill in order to make money or of the suppliers of gambling services who earn their money by offering only games in which the odds always favour the House.

I shall proceed by considering what light may be shed on the first question I identify above, namely how does gambling relate to a general moral theory of pleasure, by considering what light may be shed on this question by the four types of ethical theory alluded to above. Not only does applying these theories illuminate the ethics of gambling but we also learn something about the power of the theories by testing them against the case of gambling.

In general, I shall argue that a strong puritan position—it is always good to deny oneself pleasure—is indefensible. I shall also argue against a weaker puritan position which says that it is wrong to engage in any wasteful and addictive activities of which gambling is clearly one. On the other hand, I do not take the view—though I do take it seriously—that gambling is unconditionally good for one's moral health. Perhaps rather tamely, I conclude by adopting what I take to be an Aristotelian view of the morality of gambling and I hope that this position is sustainable with respect to all those pleasures which have been and continue to be deemed by some to be "vices."

3. Mill, Utilitarianism and Vice

A good place to begin considering whether we ought to refrain from or restrict our indulgence in gambling even if the law does not oblige us to do so is with John Stuart Mill's extraordinarily rich, subtle and sensible Chapter 5 of *On Liberty*. Here he treats of each of fornicating, gambling, drunkenness and drugs.

Under the title "Applications," Mill addresses the question of what would happen in terms of actual policy and legislation if his two great principles were adopted by government. The principles are that:

- "That the individual is not accountable to society for his actions, in so far as these concern the interests of no person but himself"
- "That for such actions as are prejudicial to the interests of others, the individual is accountable and may be subjected either to social or to legal punishment if society is of the opinion that the one or the other is requisite for its protection."[2]

Clearly on Mill's view, we cannot outlaw consensual fornication, gambling or self-intoxication. Nor, according to Mill can we subject people who engage in such activities to social sanctions such as ostracism. This is because in an ideal libertarian society, the State makes no attempt to stop people enjoying themselves in whatever way they choose provided only that they do not illegitimately harm others. In such a state anyone may do as they please within the limits of the harm proviso; and in particular, there are no restrictions on indulgence in all manner of pleasures deemed to be vices, no matter how widespread and deeply ingrained the conviction may be that these activities are immoral. But this does not mean, according to Mill, that there are no good moral grounds for refraining from indulgence in vicious pleasures. His felicific ethics as expounded in *Utilitarianism* allow him at least two arguments.

The first is that vicious self-indulgence may be contrary to the principle of utility to the extent that it is self-damaging and conducive for the individual to a preponderance of misery over pleasure in the long run. The second is that fornication, gambling and drunkenness are "lower pleasures" which ought to be abstained from in favour of higher pleasures such as enjoying works of great art.

Neither of these reasons is very convincing as they stand. The first turns on matters of empirical fact: for example, will my indulgence in drugs or gambling ultimately lead to the madness and misery of addiction? The answer in at least many cases is "No" and as Mill himself says, "no-one but the person himself can judge of the motive which may prompt him to incur the risk."[3] Consequently, the most others may legitimately do is to ensure that "he be warned of the danger."[4]

With regard to the argument from higher pleasures, apart from the well-known difficulty which this notion creates for the utilitarian calculus generally, it is also far from clear that the vices would always fail Mill's own test. This test consists in asking moral or hedonic experts who have experience of both higher pleasures such as reading poetry and lower pleasures such as playing pushpin, which of the two activities afford them the greater pleasure. Unfortunately for puritans, however, plenty of people who thoroughly appreciate Picasso's paintings, nevertheless rate the pleasures of fornication even more highly. (Perhaps Picasso himself did.)

On the other hand, I think both kinds of argument have some force in relation to at least the commonest forms of gambling, namely wagering on mechanical devices like roulette wheels or slot machines. Even non-pathological gambling consumes significant amounts of time and money on an activity which arguably affords no significant intellectual or physical stimulation, which, in other words is literally mechanical and mindless. On a purely utilitarian calculus of maximising personal pleasure it is probably easy for most people to get a bigger bang for their leisure buck. I also think that gambling fares poorly in relation to the question of higher pleasures and that it ought to be possible for most people to get a better as well as a bigger bang for their buck.

However, as far as Mill is concerned, the truth is, I believe, that the logic of his position really supports the hedonistic, "whatever-turns-you-on" permissivism. However, Mill didn't embrace such an ethic himself partly because he was concerned to defend utilitarianism against criticism from high-minded Victorian moralists but more because he was himself largely in sympathy with their puritanism, at least in relation to traditional vices. He would almost certainly have regarded modern permissivism as decadent.

However, even if Mill's arguments against vices in general are inadequate to shore up a general defence of puritanism against permissivism, there may be some other and better arguments against unrestrained self-indulgence at least in relation to gambling even though these arguments do not support stronger forms of puritanism or a moral requirement for teetotalism in respect of gambling. Kantian moral reasoning might furnish such arguments.

4. Kantian Arguments and Gambling

The general form of Kantian arguments vetoing particular practices is that one could not rationally desire the world to be a place in which everyone acted in accordance with the principle of conduct which informs the particular practice under discussion. Thus, one could not rationally want the world to be a place where everyone told lies or broke promises whenever it suited them. This seems plausible to the extent that there does seem to be something very like a piece of self-contradiction in asserting: "It would be a good thing if people always told lies when they felt like it" or "Everyone ought to break their promises if they think they will gain thereby." It also seems plausible to claim that there would be something not just bad but mad about someone who asserted without any further explanation that it is just or right for blue-eyed people to be paid much more than brown-eyed people for doing the same job.

The most plausible way in which Kantian reasoning has been used against gambling is by focussing on the fact the whole point of gambling is to distribute property randomly: to make some people richer who have done nothing to deserve it and others poorer simply as a consequence of chance. Allied to this is the thought that gamblers are people who want something for nothing. A Kantian might then argue that one could not rationally desire a world in which what people possess bears no relation to what they deserve in terms of their natural endowments, the talents they cultivate and deploy, their industry and/or their general contribution to the welfare of society.

One objection to this line of reasoning would be a sort of socialist argument which pointed out that, as a matter of fact, property in society mostly has been and mostly still is distributed according to accidents of birth. It might then be further urged that it would be much fairer and perhaps less divisive if, instead of allowing people to inherit wealth (and otherwise benefit materially from fortunate accidents of birth), differences in at least unearned wealth should be entirely determined by a literal lottery rather than the so-called "lottery of life."

This is perhaps fanciful. A more down-to-earth objection to the Kantian anti-gambling argument is to deny that gambling is all about wanting something for nothing. On the contrary, it may plausibly be urged, gambling is merely a pastime in which some people take pleasure and for which they are willing to pay in the form of the losses which they incur as a result of the fact that the odds are set, to a modest degree, against the player and in favour of the House. Surely, there is nothing irrational about the principle that people should be able to spend their own time and money on entertainments of their own choosing. . . .

There may, however, be a more persuasive and subtle argument against at least the forms of gambling whose paradigm is the gambling machine. This argument is usually couched in Kantian terms and suggests that gambling is an anti-rational activity which runs counter to our character as autonomous agents and, in some sense, requires us to surrender our freedom of will, something which it can no more be rationally right to do than to choose to submit to a condition of slavery. It can, however, also be articulated in utilitarian terms, employing Bentham's notion of the importance of the fecundity of pleasures and pains in doing the felicific calculus as well as noting the role of the principle of diminishing returns. On this view, we should judge pleasures and pains in respect of their propensity to spawn other pleasures and pains, as well as in the tendency of pleasures to grow stale on us the more we indulge in them.

Thus, the kinds of reason that one is intuitively most disposed to urge against regularly gambling on slot machines is that it is a vapid, pointless and mindless activity. As such, it may actually undermine or degrade the intelligence, given that there is no skill involved and that perhaps one becomes inveigled into deceiving oneself into believing that one may actually win in the long run. From a Kantian point of view, this may be thought to be inconsistent with living as a fully rational and autonomous human being. From a utilitarian point of view, it is at least a waste of time and money which could be more usefully employed. It may also actually blunt one's capacity for more profound pleasures.

The difficulty with this line of reasoning is partly that so are many of the other activities—playing solitaire, watching soap operas, etc.—which human beings divert themselves in their moments of leisure in the interval between birth and death. It is not obvious that it is more *rational* to spend time listening to Beethoven rather than playing roulette. On the other hand for many people who enjoy gambling, Beethoven's music sadly remains mere noise no matter how sincerely they attempt to appreciate it. What is obviously true as a matter of fact is that lots of people actually do get a lot of pleasure from gambling, that it does them no harm, and that they get as much benefit from it as others (such as Wittgenstein) get from other forms of recreation such as reading thrillers.

Of course, any time or money whatsoever which we spend on enjoying ourselves could in principle be used to improve ourselves or the lot of our fellow human beings, often in a manner that would be required of a fairly narrowly construed felicific calculus. Perhaps this means that we should regard gambling as indeed but one among many available diversions. However, in this case we might say, with Pascal, that any diversion which serves to distract us from the business of contemplating our ultimate destiny and thereby learning the truths which are necessary for the salvation of our immortal souls is *eo ipso* sinful. This brings us directly to a consideration of the religious case against gambling and secular versions of the same case.

5. Puritan Arguments and Gambling

The view that all indulgence in worldly pleasures is immoral is associated with the more fundamentalist and ascetic strands of all religions. It has a secular counterpart in the views of people who ascribe to political commitment the same importance as others ascribe to religious faith: the pursuit of private pleasure distracts from the work of establishing the political kingdom of heaven. An interesting, if eccentric, puritan view about gambling is to be found in Freud's claim that gambling is really a substitute for masturbation and, as such, an impediment to achieving the ideal of full genitality.

It is perhaps also worth mentioning that some people are puritanical about some pleasures on grounds that are more akin to aesthetic than moral ones. Very obviously people have objections of this kind to all sorts of sexual practices probably preferring to describe those who engage in them as disgusting rather than wicked. It is certainly true that many people who disapprove of Las Vegas would now be inclined to describe it as a monument to crassness and vulgarity rather than as a den of iniquity.

It must be conceded that by far the most common objections to gambling come from people who are in principle opposed to it on religious grounds which they take to possess the self-evidence of revealed truth. Typically they feel the same about sexual activity outside marriage as well as about getting drunk or high. Since, in the nature of the case, puritans tend to appeal either to contested authority or to faith or to taste, it is not clear what arguments could effectively be urged against them. Clearly, they would be right if in fact it turns out that those who indulge themselves in certain kinds of pleasure are going to suffer greatly after they are dead while those who abstain receive great blessings. But this seems equally clearly to be in the realm of the publicly unshowable even if it is not strictly unknowable.

Against puritanism one can urge but not demonstrate that pleasure is always a good and, as such, always a good prima facie reason for action. Thus, if there is anything morally wrong about indulging in any alleged vice, this cannot be a function of the character of the pleasure it offers, let alone of the fact that it offers pleasure at all. It is difficult to see how gambling could be rationally adjudged immoral merely on the grounds that people enjoy it. Like any other activity in which people take pleasure, if it is immoral this must be because of its propensity for corrupting character or otherwise doing damage to those who engage in it or to others. This must be to a significant extent an empirical issue and on this the evidence seems to be that in most cases gambling does not do any harm including harm to people's character.

A much more persuasive basis for arguments against dissipation of all sorts derives from the idea of stewardship. Here the religious version claims that our minds and bodies, our time and our talents, are all gifts of God. We are the stewards of our lives and our nature is such that we can only find true fulfillment and happiness by living in a manner befitting the creatures of God. We do this by attending to the workings of divine grace within us and engaging in works which are pleasing in the sight of our Creator. At all events we should not squander our lives in trivialities and we should acknowledge that a life given over to self-indulgence is an ultimately unsatisfying one.

The secular version of the stewardship argument sometimes appeals to the general economic well-being of society which allegedly requires a good deal of self-denial. More generally it appeals to our alleged obligations to future generations. In its simplest and, I think, strongest form it asserts that this life is all we have. Consequently, we should do everything in our power to ensure that we live it as well as we can and do not waste the only chance at living which we shall ever get.

Thinking in either of these ways enables us to make sense of what people have been getting at in their hostility to drugs, gambling and promiscuity. In each case a plausible argument can be made for the view that loveless sex is not a right use of the body, that consigning one's property to chance is improper stewardship of one's possessions, and that altering one's state of mind with chemicals is an abuse of one's mind. Arguments of this kind will never be decisive but that does not mean they are without rational force. And the force of these stewardship arguments is to alert us in what may be a very salutary way to the dangers of squandering our lives. It does not, however, support the view, nor is it usually taken as supporting the view, that any particular pleasures are in themselves wrong, including gambling.

6. Eudaimonic Ethics and the Place of Pleasure in the Good Life

At this point I think the stewardship argument becomes part of what I take to be the most convincing of all ethical theories, namely what I call eudaimonic ethical theory which most explicitly characterises Greek ethical thought but which is also at the basis of all moral systems which derive from religious creeds or secular belief systems such as Marxism or Psychoanalysis. The fundamental tenet of this kind of theory is that the answers to ethical questions are to be found by discovering what is the best kind of life that a human being can lead. Here the best kind of life is understood as the one which is most conducive to true inner well-being or happiness. This may be thought to have a different answer for different people or a general answer which is true for everyone. It is also clear that there are many different views about what constitutes the summum bonum or supreme good for human beings.

The great strength of such theories is that they make all ethical judgments ultimately a matter of enlightened self-interest and thus render the facts about human nature and human experience crucial for determining how we ought to live. In technical terms, it is analytic that one ought to live the best possible life of which one is capable and it is also analytic that the best possible life is the one which most conduces to eudaimonia or true happiness.

If this line of reasoning is to be helpful in answering the question: "Is gambling immoral?" we need to ask the question which is asked by the Greeks in a self-consciously philosophical way and to which all religions and secular ideologies offer (usually dogmatic) answers, namely: "What is the role of pleasure generally and of individual pleasures specifically in the life of a truly happy man?"

At this point I want to claim that, in general, the view of Aristotle is superior to that, not only of later religious puritans, but also to that of other secular philosophers in both the ancient and the modern worlds. For Aristotle, pleasure is indeed an important part of the best kind of life which a human being can lead, as is wealth. A life in which there is no fun can no more be accounted a happy life than a life of grinding poverty.

But pleasure, like money, is not the only ingredient in a truly happy human life nor is it the most important ingredient. And indeed a life which is exclusively devoted to the pursuit of either pleasure or money will not be a happy one. Hence the famous doctrine of the golden mean which in this case would require finding the right median course between the opposing vices of an excessive asceticism, on the one hand, and of hedonistic over-indulgence on the other.

Obviously for many people gambling will not be an important source of pleasure in their lives. But for those who do derive significant pleasure from gambling, what Aristotle defends in respect of pleasure generally seems to be a sensible view to take in respect of gambling. This is the Delphic injunction: "Nothing in excess."

The virtue of temperance which this maxim recommends is one which it is highly plausible to see as an essential ingredient in living the best kind of life of which we are capable, especially in respect of the commonest sources of pleasurable recreation. Not only does temperance obviously avoid the dangers of addiction but it is not unreasonable to suppose that it issues in a life which is better than one of total abstinence. Thus it may in fact be the case that more people who drink in moderation, have temperate sex lives, and even enjoy the occasional game of chance have lives which are not only more enviable but also more admirable than those who eschew all such pleasures. Their obvious advantages over both the hedonist and the ascetic is that their wants are tempered to their ability to satisfy them. Moreover, they do not find themselves in the condition of permanent tantalization which Schopenhauer believed to be our natural lot.

At least this is a way I can imagine we might talk to our children about "adult pleasures" with honesty and helpfulness.

7. Conclusion

I want to conclude by first trying to express as forcefully as I can what I take to be a synthesis of all the anti-gambling views we have considered from all philosophical standpoints and then to say some things which seem to me to be relevant to a defence of gambling against these charges.

The worst that can be said about the sort of gambling which is typified by repetitively inserting money into gambling machines is that as a way of spending time and money it is mindless, anti-social, boring, dehumanizing, vulgar, ugly, degrading, depraving, cretinising, soul-destroying, feckless and stupid.

Against this need to be set a number of considerations which relate to why people actually engage in this activity and what the actual effect on their character may be supposed to be.

In the first place people who spend money on gambling are buying three distinct kinds of product. The first is the pleasure of play. People play slot machines and table games pretty much as they play pinball machines or games of patience. Precisely because it is not intellectually or physically taxing, some people find this an especially relaxing form of amusement. It is hard to make a serious moral case against indulging in the pleasures of playing games for recreation or entertainment. Secondly, people who gamble on machines which offer large jackpots, who buy lottery tickets or do the pools are really buying (through theft losses) fuel for their fantasies of getting suddenly and fabulously rich beyond the dreams of avarice. In itself this puts gambling in the same morally trivial category as other forms of innocuous escapism such as watching soap operas or reading sex-and-shopping novels. From one point of view, indeed, buying a lottery ticket may not only be a harmless form of escapism but also a rational investment. For the poor who have no other prospect of ever becoming really rich no matter how hard they work, it is better to have a very remote chance of attaining great wealth than no chance at all. Thirdly, people pay for the ancillary pleasures they associate with gambling—the conviviality of the bingo hall or the betting shop, the glamour of the casino or the racetrack, and in all cases the defence against loneliness. This seems to be not just harmless but positively benign.

We should perhaps also consider the view that gambling may actually be good for the character. Perhaps gambling accustoms us to sit more loosely than we otherwise would towards money and material possessions and this may be morally desirable. Perhaps, too, gambling inculcates the virtues of courage, equanimity, and graciousness in adversity and good fortune alike. . . .

In some ways it would be nice to conclude with the suggestion that not only is gambling generally good for the moral character but that gambling for very high stakes is particularly likely to develop moral heroism. The truth of the matter, however, is almost certainly much duller. This is that for the vast majority of people who engage in it gambling has no significant impact on their moral character at all. Moreover, when it appears to, it is more likely to be an expression of character traits which for better or worse are already established rather than being the cause of the emergence of new vices or virtues which otherwise would not have developed.

If this is so, then it looks as if the truth about gambling is that, despite all the passion which continues to inform the attacks of opponents of gambling, it is in fact for the most part a morally trivial issue. What is of course not morally trivial is that no one ought to devote too much of their time, their talents, their energies and their resources to activities which are morally trivial, and that includes gambling.

Notes

1. Amongst the articles which have addressed recently this issue, the following deserve mention: Barrett, Will: "Gambling and Public Policy." *Public Affairs Quarterly.* Vol. 14. No 1, January 2000; Lorenz, Valerie C: "Gambling" in *Encyclopaedia of Applied Ethics.* San Diego Academic Press. 1998; Newton, Lisa: "Gambling, A Preliminary Inquiry." *Business Ethics Quarterly.* Vol. 3. Issue 4. 1993. Murphy, Jeffrie. "Indian Casinos and the Morality of Gambling." *Public Affairs Quarterly*, Vol. 12. Jan 1998. Versions of all the anti-gambling arguments discussed here can also be found in a form which repays philosophical analysis in MacKenzie, W. Douglas: *The Ethics of Gambling.* (4th Edition). The Sunday School Union. London 1899.
2. J.S. Mill: *On Liberty.* (1859) Everyman's Library Edition Edited by H.B. Acton. 1910. New Edition 1972. pp. 162–3.
3. Ibid., p. 165.
4. Ibid.

POSTSCRIPT

Is Gambling Immoral?

Gambling is an unusual issue in this respect: Whereas many social issues have both proponents and opponents, gambling seems to have opponents but no real proponents. (Even libertarians and other who support the right to do with one's money as one pleases, as long as it doesn't infringe on anyone else's rights, do not argue that one of the good things about their view is that we will be free to gamble. Freedom to gamble may well be a result, or implication, of that view. But they do not tout it as one of things that makes their viewpoint appealing.) They too might agree with Collins that gambling itself is "morally trivial"—it's just another way of disposing of one's money. Almost no one thinks that gambling is a positively good thing. Thus, for example, we generally do not find gambling clubs alongside sports clubs, coin-collecting clubs, cycling clubs, photography clubs, etc. In fact, the only gambling group one is likely to find is something like Gamblers Anonymous.

In this way, gambling is somewhat like drinking alcohol. Some people say drinking is wrong—in fact, whole religions forbid it, and at one time the U.S. Constitution did so too. But many people regard it as "morally trivial." In both cases, of course, some individuals become "over-involved" and indulge in problematic compulsive behavior (or addiction), as evidenced by the very existence of such groups as Alcoholics Anonymous and Gamblers Anonymous. But these are dismissed as "not the usual case."

We generally apply the language of *rights* to behavior. And we find that individuals are within their rights when they engage in gambling. But the focus of such "rights-talk" is on the individual and the isolated act. What some people find problematic in gambling is not that rights are violated, or even that there is some problem about an isolated act, but that the individual who regularly gambles is irresponsible. So in some ways, Peter Collins is correct that gambling (on a one-time basis) is morally trivial. So is daydreaming (on a one-time basis). But a person who habitually gambles (or habitually daydreams) is not a responsible human being. Yet we can't press the analogy between gambling and daydreaming too far—after, all, there are no compulsive daydreamers.

The views of Peter Collins are further elaborated in his book, *Gambling and the Public Interest* (Praeger, 2003). For a detailed history of gambling, see David G. Schwartz, *Roll the Bones: The History of Gambling* (Gotham, 2006). For an interesting account of gambling, written by a man who is both a gambler himself and a therapist who works with compulsive gamblers, see Neil Isaacs, *You Bet Your Life: The Burdens of Gambling* (University Press of Kentucky, 2001). See also Mike W. Martin, *From Morality to Mental Health: Virtue and Vice in a Therapeutic Culture* (Oxford University Press, 2006).

ISSUE 11

Is Affirmative Action Fair?

YES: Albert G. Mosley, from "Affirmative Action: Pro," in Albert G. Mosley and Nicholas Capaldi, eds., *Affirmative Action: Social Justice or Unfair Preference?* (Rowman & Littlefield, 1996)

NO: Louis P. Pojman, from "The Case Against Affirmative Action," *International Journal of Applied Philosophy* (Spring 1998)

ISSUE SUMMARY

YES: Professor of philosophy Albert G. Mosley argues that affirmative action is a continuation of the history of black progress since the *Brown v. Board of Education* desegregation decision of 1954 and the Civil Rights Act of 1964. He defends affirmative action as a "benign use of race."

NO: Professor of philosophy Louis P. Pojman contends that affirmative action violates the moral principle that maintains that each person is to be treated as an individual, not as representative of a group. He stresses that individual merit needs to be appreciated and that respect should be given to each person on an individual basis.

Throughout history, women and minority groups have been discriminated against in the United States. However, it might be difficult for many of us today to appreciate the extent of past discrimination and the ways in which social, legal, and political institutions were discriminatory.

Slavery is probably the most blatant form of past racism. We know that people were bought and sold, but the words are so familiar that the realities they stand for may never rise to consciousness. Many particular events and experiences lie behind a simple word like *slavery*. For example, the importation of slaves to this country was illegal before slaveholding itself became so. When ships at sea bringing African slaves to America found themselves in danger of being confronted by the law, it was easy to do what smugglers on the high seas always do with their contraband: the blacks, chained together and weighted down, were dropped overboard. Even after the Civil War, blacks were denied the right to vote, to testify in court, to own land, or to make contracts. In many states, laws restricted blacks in every conceivable aspect of their lives, including education, employment, and housing.

With respect to discrimination against women, consider the following, written by U.S. Supreme Court justice Joseph Bradley in concurring with the Court's decision in *Bradwell v. Illinois* (1873) that the state of Illinois was justified in denying Myra Bradwell a license to practice law on the grounds that she was a woman:

> [T]he civil law, as well as nature herself, has always recognized a wide difference in the respective spheres and destinies of man and woman. Man is, or should be, woman's protector and defender. The natural and proper timidity and delicacy which belongs to the female sex evidently unfits it for many of the occupations of civil life. The constitution of the family organization, which is founded in the divine ordinance, as well as in the nature of things, indicates the domestic sphere as that which properly belongs to the domain and functions of womanhood. The harmony . . . of interests and views which belong . . . to the family institution is repugnant to the idea of a woman adopting a distinct and independent career from that of her husband. . . . The paramount destiny and mission of woman are to fulfill the noble and benign offices of wife and mother.

Such thoughts are rarely openly expressed these days, and segregation and discrimination do not have legal support. One wonders, though, how much attitudes have actually changed. The law can change, but old attitudes can persist, and they can even be preserved and passed down from generation to generation. Moreover, the results of past social injustices are with us today.

Some of the consequences of past discrimination are systemic rather than individual-based. However much *individuals* might reject certain attitudes and practices of the past, there will usually be some *systemic* problems that are not so easily eliminated. There are systemic consequences of racist and sexist practices in the professions, in housing, in education, in the distribution of wealth, etc. For example, even if previously "white only" schools take down their "white only" signs, and the individuals involved agree to accept applicants of any race, the school system itself would be left virtually unchanged from its segregationist days. The situation of white-only schools would systematically perpetuate itself. This is where many feel that affirmative action can step in and change the system.

Albert G. Mosley places controversies surrounding affirmative action in a historical context and considers the justification of affirmative action both from the "backward-looking" perspective of corrective justice and from the "forward-looking" perspective of the social distribution of harms and benefits. Louis P. Pojman explains what he means by the term *affirmative action*. He maintains that affirmative action requires us to practice *reverse discrimination*, to fail to treat people as individuals, and to undervalue merit.

YES

Albert G. Mosley

Affirmative Action: Pro

Legislative and Judicial Background

In 1941, Franklin Roosevelt issued Executive Order 8802 banning discrimination in employment by the federal government and defense contractors. Subsequently, many bills were introduced in Congress mandating equal employment opportunity but none were passed until the Civil Rights Act of 1964. The penalty for discrimination in Executive Order 8802 and the bills subsequently proposed was that the specific victim of discrimination be "made whole," that is, put in the position he or she would have held were it not for the discriminatory act, including damages for lost pay and legal expenses.

The contemporary debate concerning affirmative action can be traced to the landmark decision of *Brown v. Board of Education* (1954), whereby local, state, and federal ordinances enforcing segregation by race were ruled unconstitutional. In subsequent opinions, the Court ruled that state-mandated segregation in libraries, swimming pools, and other publicly funded facilities was also unconstitutional. In *Swann v. Charlotte-Mecklenburg* (1971), the Court declared that "in order to prepare students to live in a pluralistic society" school authorities might implement their desegregation order by deciding that "each school should have a prescribed ratio of Negro to White students reflecting the proportion for the district as a whole."[1] The ratio was not to be an inflexible one, but should reflect local variations in the ratio of Whites to Blacks. But any predominantly one-race school in a district with a mixed population and a history of segregation was subject to "close scrutiny." This requirement was attacked by conservatives as imposing a "racial quota," a charge that reverberates in the contemporary debate concerning affirmative action.

With the Montgomery bus boycotts of the mid-1950s, Blacks initiated an era of nonviolent direct action to publicly protest unjust laws and practices that supported racial discrimination. The graphic portrayals of repression and violence produced by the civil rights movement precipitated a national revulsion against the unequal treatment of African Americans. Blacks demanded their constitutional right to participate in the political process and share equal access to public accommodations, government-supported programs, and employment opportunities. But as John F. Kennedy stated in an address to Congress: "There is little value in a Negro's obtaining the right to be admitted to hotels and restaurants if he has no cash in his pocket and no job."[2]

From *Affirmative Action: Social Justice or Unfair Preference?* by Albert G. Mosley and Nicholas Capaldi, eds. (1996, pp. 1–3, 23–28, 44–48, 50). Copyright © 1996 by Rowman & Littlefield. Reprinted by permission.

Kennedy stressed that the issue was not merely eliminating discrimination, but eliminating as well the oppressive economic and social burdens imposed on Blacks by racial discrimination.[3] To this end, he advocated a weak form of affirmative action, involving eliminating discrimination and expanding educational and employment opportunities (including apprenticeships and on-the-job training). The liberal vision was that, given such opportunities, Blacks would move up the economic ladder to a degree relative to their own merit. Thus, a principal aim of the Civil Rights Act of 1964 was to effect a redistribution of social, political, and economic benefits and to provide legal remedies for the denial of individual rights.

The Civil Rights Act of 1964

The first use of the phrase "affirmative action" is found in Executive Order 10952, issued by President John F. Kennedy in 1961. This order established the Equal Employment Opportunity Commission (EEOC) and directed that contractors on projects funded, in whole or in part, with federal funds "take affirmative action to ensure that applicants are employed, and employees are treated during their employment, without regard to the race, creed, color, or national origin."

As a result of continuing public outrage at the level of violence and animosity shown toward Blacks, a stronger version of the Civil Rights Bill was presented to the Congress than Kennedy had originally recommended. Advocates pointed out that Blacks suffered an unemployment rate that was twice that of Whites and that Black employment was concentrated in semiskilled and unskilled jobs. They emphasized that national prosperity would be improved by eliminating discrimination and integrating Black talent into its skilled and professional workforce.[4]

Fewer Blacks were employed in professional positions than had the requisite skills, and those Blacks who did occupy positions commensurate with their skill level had half the lifetime earnings of Whites. Such facts were introduced during legislative hearings to show the need to more fully utilize and reward qualified Blacks throughout the labor force, and not merely in the unskilled and semiskilled sectors. . . .

Conceptual Issues

There are many interests that governments pursue—maximization of social production; equitable distribution of rights, opportunities, and services; social safety and cohesion; restitution—and those interests may conflict in various situations. In particular, governments as well as their constituents have a prima facie obligation to satisfy the liabilities they incur. One such liability derives from past and present unjust exclusionary acts depriving minorities and women of opportunities and amenities made available to other groups.

"Backward looking" arguments defend affirmative action as a matter of *corrective justice,* where paradigmatically the harmdoer is to make restitution to the harmed so as to put the harmed in the position the harmed most likely

would have occupied had the harm not occurred. An important part of making restitution is the acknowledgment it provides that the actions causing injury were unjust and such actions will be curtailed and corrected. In this regard Bernard Boxill writes:

> Without the acknowledgement of error, the injurer implies that the injured has been treated in a manner that befits him. . . . In such a case, even if the unjust party repairs the damage he has caused . . . nothing can be demanded on legal or moral grounds, and the repairs made are gratuitous. . . . justice requires that we acknowledge that this treatment of others can be required of us; thus, where an unjust injury has occurred, the injurer reaffirms his belief in the other's equality by conceding that repair can be demanded of him, and the injured rejects the allegation of his inferiority . . . by demanding reparation.[5]

This view is based on the idea that restitution is a basic moral principle that creates obligations that are just as strong as the obligations to maximize wealth and distribute it fairly.[6] If x has deprived y of opportunities y had a right not to be deprived of in this manner, then x is obligated to return y to the position y would have occupied had x not intervened; x has this obligation irrespective of other obligations x may have. . . .

[An] application of this principle involves the case where x is not a person but an entity, like a government or a business. If y was unjustly deprived of employment when firm F hired z instead of y because z was White and y Black, then y has a right to be made whole, that is, brought to the position he/she would have achieved had that deprivation not occurred. Typically, this involves giving y a position at least as good as the one he/she would have acquired originally and issuing back pay in the amount that y would have received had he/she been hired at the time of the initial attempt.

Most critics of preferential treatment acknowledge the applicability of principles of restitution to individuals in specific instances of discrimination. The strongest case is where y was as or more qualified than z in the initial competition, but the position was given to z because y was Black and z was White.[7] Subsequently, y may not be as qualified for an equivalent position as some new candidate z′, but is given preference because of the past act of discrimination by F that deprived y of the position he or she otherwise would have received.

Some critics have suggested that, in such cases, z′ is being treated unfairly. For z′, as the most qualified applicant, has a right not to be excluded from the position in question purely on the basis of race; and y has a right to restitution for having unjustly been denied the position in the past. But the dilemma is one in appearance only. For having unjustly excluded y in the past, the current position that z has applied for is not one that F is free to offer to the public. It is a position that is already owed to y, and is not available for open competition. Judith Jarvis Thomson makes a similar point:

> suppose two candidates [A and B] for a civil service job have equally good test scores, but there is only one job available. We could decide

> between them by coin-tossing. But in fact we do allow for declaring for A straightway, where A is a veteran, and B is not. It may be that B is a non-veteran through no fault of his own. . . . Yet the fact is that B is not a veteran and A is. On the assumption that the veteran has served his country, the country owes him something. And it is plain that giving him preference is not an unjust way in which part of that debt of gratitude can be paid.[8]

In a similar way, individual Blacks who have suffered from acts of unjust discrimination are owed something by the perpetrator(s) of such acts, and this debt takes precedence over the perpetrator's right to use his or her options to hire the most qualified person for the position in question.

Many White males have developed expectations about the likelihood of their being selected for educational, employment, and entrepreneurial opportunities that are realistic only because of the general exclusion of women and non-Whites as competitors for such positions. Individuals enjoying inflated odds of obtaining such opportunities because of racist and sexist practices are recipients of an "unjust enrichment."

Redistributing opportunities would clearly curtail benefits that many have come to expect. And given the frustration of their traditional expectations, it is understandable that they would feel resentment. But blocking traditional expectations is not unjust if those expectations conflict with the equally important moral duties of restitution and just distribution. It is a question, not of "is," but of "ought": not "Do those with decreased opportunities as a result of affirmative action feel resentment?" but "Should those with decreased opportunities as a result of affirmative action feel resentment?". . .

Since Title VII [of the Civil Rights Act of 1964] protects bona fide seniority plans, it forces the burden of rectification to be borne by Whites who are entering the labor force rather than Whites who are the direct beneficiaries of past discriminatory practices. Given this limitation placed on affirmative action remedies, the burden of social restitution may, in many cases, be borne by those who were not directly involved in past discriminatory practices. But it is generally not true that those burdened have not benefited at all from past discriminatory practices. For the latent effects of acts of invidious racial discrimination have plausibly bolstered and encouraged the efforts of Whites in roughly the same proportion as it inhibited and discouraged the efforts of Blacks. Such considerations are also applicable to cases where F discriminated against y in favor of z, but the make-whole remedy involves providing compensation to y rather than y. This suggests that y is an *undeserving beneficiary* of the preferential treatment meant to compensate for the unjust discrimination against y, just as z above appeared to be the innocent victim forced to bear the burden that z benefited from. Many critics have argued that this misappropriation of benefits and burdens demonstrates the unfairness of compensation to groups rather than individuals. But it is important that the context and rationale for such remedies be appreciated.

In cases of "egregious" racial discrimination, not only is it true that F discriminated against a particular Black person y, but F's discrimination advertised a general disposition to discriminate against any other Black person who might seek such positions. The specific effect of F's unjust discrimination was that y was refused a position he or she would otherwise have received. The latent (or dispositional) effect of F's unjust discrimination was that many Blacks who otherwise would have sought such positions were discouraged from doing so. Thus, even if the specific y actually discriminated against can no longer be compensated, F has an obligation to take affirmative action to communicate to Blacks as a group that such positions are indeed open to them. After being found in violation of laws prohibiting racial discrimination, many agencies have disclaimed further discrimination while in fact continuing to do so.[9] In such cases, the courts have required the discriminating agencies to actually hire and/or promote Blacks who may not be as qualified as some current White applicants until Blacks approach the proportion in F's labor force they in all likelihood would have achieved had F's unjust discriminatory acts not deterred them.

Of course, what this proportion would have been is a matter of speculation. It may have been less than the proportion of Blacks available in the relevant labor pool from which applicants are drawn if factors other than racial discrimination act to depress the merit of such applicants. This point is made again and again by critics. Some, such as Thomas Sowell, argue that cultural factors often mitigate against Blacks meriting representation in a particular labor force in proportion to their presence in the pool of candidates looking for jobs or seeking promotions.[10] Others, such as Michael Levin, argue that cognitive deficits limit Blacks from being hired and promoted at a rate proportionate to their presence in the relevant labor pool.[11] What such critics reject is the assumption that, were it not for pervasive discrimination and overexploitation, Blacks would be equally represented in the positions in question. What is scarcely considered is the possibility that, were it not for racist exclusions, Blacks might be over rather than under represented in competitive positions.

Establishing Blacks' presence at a level commensurate with their proportion in the relevant labor market need not be seen as an attempt to actualize some valid prediction. Rather, given the impossibility of determining what level of representation Blacks would have achieved were it not for racist discrimination, the assumption of proportional representation is the only *fair* assumption to make. This is not to argue that Blacks should be maintained in such positions, but their contrived exclusion merits an equally contrived rectification.[12]

Racist acts excluding Blacks affected particular individuals, but were directed at affecting the behavior of the group of all those similar to the victim. Likewise, the benefits of affirmative action policies should not be conceived as limited in their effects to the specific individuals receiving them. Rather, those benefits should be conceived as extending to all those identified with the recipient, sending the message that opportunities are indeed available to qualified Black candidates who would have been excluded in the past. . . .

Forward-Looking Justifications of Affirmative Action

. . . [Some] have defended preferential treatment but denied that it should be viewed as a form of reparation. This latter group rejects "backward looking" justifications of affirmative action and defends it instead on "forward-looking" grounds that include distributive justice, minimizing subordination, and maximizing social utility.

Thus, Ronald Fiscus argues that backward-looking arguments have distorted the proper justification for affirmative action policies.[13] Backward-looking arguments depend on the paradigm of traditional tort cases, where a specific individual x has deprived another individual y of a specific good t through an identifiable act a, and x is required to restore y to the position y would have had, had a not occurred. But typically, preferential treatment requires that x (rather than x) restore y′ (instead of y) with a good t′ that y′ supposedly would have achieved had y not been deprived of t by x. The displacement of perpetrator (x′ for x) and victim (y′ for y) gives rise to the problem of (1) White males who are innocent of acts having caused harm nonetheless being forced to provide restitution for such acts; and (2) Blacks who were not directly harmed by those acts nonetheless becoming the principal beneficiaries of restitution for those acts. . . .

Fiscus argues that the backward-looking argument reinforces the perception that preferential treatment is unfair to innocent White males, and so long as this is the case, both the courts and the public are likely to oppose strong affirmative action policies such as quotas, set-asides, and other preferential treatment policies.

In contrast, Fiscus recommends that preferential treatment be justified in terms of distributive justice, which as a matter of equal protection, "requires that individuals be awarded the positions, advantages, or benefits they would have been awarded under fair conditions," that is, conditions under which racist exclusion would not have precluded Blacks from attaining "their deserved proportion of the society's important benefits." Conversely, "distributive justice also holds that individuals or groups may not claim positions, advantages, or benefits that they would not have been awarded under fair conditions."[14] These conditions jointly prohibit White males from claiming an unreasonable share of social benefits and protects White males from having to bear an unreasonable share of the redistributive burden.

Fiscus takes the position that any deviation between Blacks and Whites from strict proportionality in the distribution of current goods is evidence of racism. Thus, if Blacks were 20 percent of a particular population but held no positions in the police or fire departments, that is indicative of past and present racial discrimination. . . .

Because the Equal Protection Clause of the Fourteenth Amendment protects citizens from statistical discrimination on the basis of race, the use of race as the principal reason for excluding certain citizens from benefits made available to other citizens is a violation of that person's constitutional rights. This was one basis for [Alan] Bakke's suit against the UC-Davis medical school's

16 percent minority set-aside for medical school admission. There were eighty-four seats out of the one hundred admission slots that he was eligible to fill, and he was excluded from competing for the other sixteen slots because of his race. On the basis of the standard criteria (GPA, MCAT scores, etc.), Bakke argued that he would have been admitted before any of the Black applicants admitted under the minority set-aside. He therefore claimed that he was being excluded from the additional places available because he was White.

Currently, Blacks have approximately 3.25 times fewer physicians than would be expected given their numbers in the population. Native Americans have 7 times fewer physicians than what would have been expected if intelligent, well-trained, and motivated Native Americans had tried to become physicians at the same rate as did European Americans.

For Fiscus, the underrepresentation of African and Native Americans among physicians and the maldistribution of medical resources to minority communities is clearly the effect of generations of racist exclusions. . . . Not only are qualified members of the oppressed group harmed by . . . prejudice, but even more harmed are the many who would have been qualified but for injuries induced by racial prejudice.

For Fiscus, individuals of different races would have been as equally distributed in the social body as the molecules of a gas in a container and he identifies the belief in the inherent equality of races with the Equal Protection Clause of the Fourteenth Amendment.[15] In a world without racism, minorities would be represented among the top one hundred medical school applicants at UC-Davis in the same proportion as they were in the general population. Accordingly, because Bakke did not score among the top eighty-four Whites, he would not have qualified for admission. Thus, he had no right to the position he was contesting, and indeed if he were given such a position in lieu of awarding it to a minority, Bakke would be much like a person who had received stolen goods. "Individuals who have not personally harmed minorities may nevertheless be prevented from reaping the benefits of the harm inflicted by the society at large."[16]

Justice O'Connor has voiced skepticism toward the assumption that members of different races would "gravitate with mathematical exactitude to each employer or union absent unlawful discrimination."[17] She considers it sheer speculation as to "how many minority students would have been admitted to the medical school at Davis absent past discrimination in educational opportunities."[18] I likewise consider it speculative to assume that races would be represented in every area in proportion to their proportion of the general population. But because it is impossible to reasonably predict what that distribution would have been absent racial discrimination, it is not mere speculation but morally fair practice to assume that it would have been the same as the proportion in the general population. Given the fact of legally sanctioned invidious racism against Blacks in U.S. history, the burden of proof should not be on the oppressed group to prove that it would be represented at a level proportionate to its presence in the general population. Rather, the burden of proof should be on the majority to show why its overrepresentation among the most well off is not the result of unfair competition imposed by racism.

We are morally obligated to assume proportional representation until there are more plausible reasons than racism for assuming otherwise. . . .

Thus, it should be the responsibility of the Alabama Department of Public Safety to show why no Blacks were members of its highway patrol as of 1970, even though Blacks were 25 percent of the relevant workforce in Alabama. It should be the responsibility of the company and the union to explain why there were no Blacks with seniority in the union at the Kaiser plant in Louisiana, although Blacks made up 39 percent of the surrounding population. Likewise, it should be the responsibility of the union to explain why no Blacks had been admitted to the Sheet Metal Workers' Union in New York City although minorities were 29 percent of the available workforce. If no alternative explanations are more plausible, then the assumption that the disparity in representation is the result of racism should stand.

The question should not be whether White males are innocent or guilty of racism or sexism, but whether they have a right to inflated odds of obtaining benefits relative to minorities and women. A White male is innocent only up to the point where he takes advantage of "a benefit he would not qualify for without the accumulated effects of racism. At that point he becomes an accomplice in, and a beneficiary of, society's racism. He becomes the recipient of stolen goods."[19]. . .

Cass Sunstein also argues that the traditional compensation model based on the model of a discrete injury caused by one individual (the tort-feasor or defendant) and suffered by another individual (the plaintiff) is inadequate to capture the situation arising from racial and sexual discrimination.[20] With the traditional tortlike model, the situation existing prior to the injury is assumed to be noncontestable, and the purpose of restitution is to restore the injured party to the position that party would have occupied if the injury had not occurred. But in cases where the injury is not well defined, where neither defendant nor plaintiff are individuals connected by a discrete event, and where the position the injured party would have occupied but for the injury is unspecifiable, then in such cases dependence on the traditional model of compensatory justice is questionable.[21]

In contrast to the position taken by Fiscus, Sunstein argues that the claim that affirmative action and preferential treatment is meant to put individuals in the position they would have occupied had their groups not been subject to racial and sexual discrimination is nonsensical: "What would the world look like if it had been unaffected by past discrimination on the basis of race and sex? . . . the question is unanswerable, not because of the absence of good social science, but because of the obscure epistemological status of the question itself."[22]

Affirmative action must be justified in terms of alternative conceptions of the purpose of legal intervention, and Sunstein recommends instead the notion of "risk management" (intended to offset increased risks faced by a group rather than compensate the injuries suffered by a particular individual) and the "principle of nonsubordination" (whereby measures are taken to reverse a situation in which an irrelevant difference has been transformed by legally sanctioned acts of the state into a social disadvantage). The notion of risk management is meant to apply to cases where injuries are "individually small but collectively large" so that pursuing each case individually would be too costly both in terms of time and effort.[23] In such cases, those harmed may be unable to establish a direct causal link between their injuries and the plaintiff's actions. Thus, a person who develops a certain type of cancer associated with a toxin produced by a particular company might have developed that condition even in the absence of the company's negligent behavior. At most, they can argue that the company's actions caused an increased risk of injury, rather than any specific instance of that injury.

Harms suffered in this way systematically affect certain groups with higher frequency than other groups, without it being possible to establish causal links between the injuries of specific plaintiffs and the actions of the defendant. Regulatory agencies should be designed to address harms that are the result of increased risks rather than of a discrete action.[24] One of their principal aims should be not to compensate each injured party (and only injured parties), "but instead to deter and punish the risk-creating behavior" by redistributing social goods.[25] . . .

The principle of nonsubordination is meant to apply to cases where the existing distribution of wealth and opportunities between groups are the result of law rather than natural attributes.[26] The purpose of affirmative action from a forward-looking perspective should be to end social subordination and reverse the situation in which irrelevant differences have been, through social and legal structures, turned into systematic disadvantages operative in multiple spheres that diminish participation in democratic forms of life.[27] . . .

> affirmative action does not appear an impermissible 'taking' of an antecedent entitlement. Because the existing distribution of benefits and burdens between Blacks and Whites and men and women is not natural . . . and because it is in part a product of current laws and practices having discriminatory effects, it is not decisive if some Whites and men are disadvantaged as a result.[28]

A central question in the debate over affirmative action is the extent to which racial classifications are important in accomplishing the goal of relieving the subordinate status of minorities and women. Given the aim of improving safety in transportation, classifying people in terms of their race is rationally irrelevant, while classifying them in terms of their driving competency, visual acuity, and maturity is essential. On the other hand, given the aim of improving health care in Black neighborhoods, classifying applicants for medical school in terms of their race is, in addition to their academic and clinical abilities, a very relevant factor.

To illustrate, African Americans, Hispanics, and Native Americans make up 22 percent of the population but represent only 10 percent of entering medical students and 7 percent of practicing physicians. A number of studies have shown that underrepresented minority physicians are more likely than their majority counterparts to care for poor patients and patients of similar ethnicity. Indeed, "each ethnic group of patients was more likely to be cared for by a physician of their own ethnic background than by a physician of another ethnic background."[29] This suggests that sociocultural factors such as language, physical identity, personal background, and experiences are relevant factors in determining the kinds of communities in which a physician will establish a practice. If this is the case, then the race of a medical school applicant would be an important factor in providing medical services to certain underrepresented communities. Thus, while there might be some purposes for which race is irrelevant, there might be other purposes in which race is important (though perhaps not necessary) for achieving the end in view.[30] The remedy targets Blacks as a group because racially discriminatory practices were directed against Blacks as a group.[31]

. . . Preferential treatment programs are meant to offset the disadvantages imposed by racism so that Blacks are not forced to bear the principal costs of that error.

. . . To condemn polices meant to correct for racial barriers as themselves erecting barriers is to ignore the difference between action and reaction, cause and effect, aggression and self-defense. . . .

Conclusion

Racism was directed against Blacks whether they were talented, average, or mediocre, and attenuating the effects of racism requires distributing remedies similarly. Affirmative action policies compensate for the harms of racism (overt and institutional) through antidiscrimination laws and preferential policies. Prohibiting the benign use of race as a factor in the award of educational, employment and business opportunities would eliminate compensation for past and present racism and reinforce the moral validity of the status quo, with Blacks overrepresented among the least well off and underrepresented among the most well off.

It has become popular to use affirmative action as a scapegoat for the increased vulnerability of the White working class. But it should be recognized that the civil rights revolution (in general) and affirmative action (in particular) has been beneficial, not just to Blacks, but also to Whites (e.g., women, the disabled, the elderly) who otherwise would be substantially more vulnerable than they are now.

Affirmative action is directed toward empowering those groups that have been adversely affected by past and present exclusionary practices. Initiatives to abolish preferential treatment would inflict a grave injustice on African Americans, for they signal a reluctance to acknowledge that the plight of African Americans is the result of institutional practices that require institutional responses.

Notes

1. Kent Greenawalt, *Discrimination and Reverse Discrimination* (New York: Alfred A. Knopf, 1983), 129 ff.
2. Kathanne W. Greene, *Affirmative Action and Principles of Justice* (New York: Greenwood Press, 1989), 22.
3. Kennedy stated: "Even the complete elimination of racial discrimination in employment—a goal toward which this nation must strive—will not

put a single unemployed Negro to work unless he has the skills required." Greene, *Affirmative Action*, 23.

4. Greene, *Affirmative Action*, 31.
5. Bernard Boxill, "The Morality of Reparation" in *Social Theory and Practice*, 2, no. 1, Spring 1972: 118–119. It is for such reasons that welfare programs are not sufficient to satisfy the claims of Blacks for restitution. Welfare programs contain no admission of the unjust violation of rights and seek merely to provide the basic means for all to pursue opportunities in the future.
6. I am presuming that most of us would recognize certain primae facie duties such as truth telling, promise keeping, restitution, benevolence, justice, nonmalficience as generally obligatory. See W. D. Ross, *The Right and the Good* (Oxford: Clarendon Press, 1930).
7. Even in the case where y was only as qualified as z, a fair method of choice between candidates should produce an equitable distribution of such positions between Blacks and Whites in the long run if not in the short.
8. Judith Jarvis Thompson, *Philosophy and Public Affairs,* 2 (Summer 1973): 379–380.
9. *Sheet Metal Workers v. EEOC* (1986); *United States v. Paradise* (1987).
10. Thomas Sowell, *Ethnic America* (New York: Basic Books, 1981); *Preferential Policies: An International Perspective* (New York: William Morrow, 1990); For a recent critique of Sowell's position, see Christopher Jencks, *Rethinking Social Policy: Race, Poverty, and the Underclass* (New York: Harper, 1993), chap. 1.
11. Michael Levin, "Race, Biology, and Justice" in *Public Affairs Quarterly*, 8, no. 3 (July 1994). There are many good reasons for skepticism regarding the validity of using IQ as a measure of cognitive ability. See *The Bell Curve Wars* ed. Steven Fraser (New York: Basic Books, 1995); *The Bell Curve Debate,* ed. by Russell Jacoby and Naomi Glauberman (New York: Times Books, 1995); Allan Chase, *The Legacy of Malthus* (Urbana: University of Illinois Press, 1980); Steven J. Gould, *The Mismeasure of Man* (New York: Norton, 1981); R. C. Lewontin, S. Rose, L. J. Kamin, *Not in Our Genes* (New York: Pantheon Books, 1984).
12. See Robert Fullinwider, *The Reverse Discrimination Controversy: A Moral and Legal Analysis* (Totowa, N.J.: Rowman & Littlefield, 1980), 117. Ronald Fiscus, *The Constitutional Logic of Affirmative Action* (Durham, N.C.: Duke University Press, 1992).
13. Ronald J. Fiscus, *The Constitutional Logic of Affirmative Action* (Durham, N.C.: Duke University Press, 1992).
14. Fiscus, *Constitutional Logic*, 13.
15. Fiscus, *Constitutional Logic*, 20–26.
16. Fiscus, *Constitutional Logic*, 38.
17. *Sheet Metal Workers v. EEOC*, 478 US 421, 494 (1986); Fiscus, *Constitutional Logic*, 42.
18. *City of Richmond v. J. A. Croson Co.*, 109 S.Ct. at 724 (1989); Fiscus, *Constitutional Logic*, 42.
19. Fiscus, *Constitutional Logic*, 47. With regard to the problem of so-called "undeserving beneficiaries" of affirmative action Fiscus writes: "When the rightful owner of stolen goods cannot be found, the law . . . may or may not award possession to the original but wrongful claimant; but if it does

not, if it awards possession to a third party whose claim is arguable, the original claimant cannot justifiably feel morally harmed. And the government's action cannot be said to be arbitrary unless it awards the goods to an individual whose claim is even less plausible than that of the original claimant" (49).

20. Cass Sunstein, "Limits of Compensatory Justice" in *Nomos* 33, *Compensatory Justice*, ed. John Chapman (New York: New York University Press, 1991), 281–310.
21. "It is not controlling and perhaps not even relevant that the harms that affirmative action attempts to redress cannot be understood in the usual compensatory terms. . . . the nature of the problem guarantees that the legal response cannot take the form of discrete remedies for discrete harms" (Sunstein, "Limits," 297).
22. Sunstein, "Limits," 303.
23. The orientation of the EEOC toward investigating individual cases of alleged discrimination is one explanation of its extraordinary backlog of over 80,000 cases. This orientation precludes it from focusing on systemic practices that affect many individuals, and instead forces it to expend resources dealing with particular instances. See "The EEOC: Pattern and Practice Imperfect" by Maurice Munroe in *Yale Law and Policy Review*, 13, no. 2, (1995): 219–80.
24. Sunstein, "Limits," 292.
25. Sunstein, "Limits," 289.
26. "The current distribution of benefits and burdens as between blacks and whites and women and men is not part of the state of nature but a consequence of past and present social practices" (Sunstein, "Limits," 294).
27. See also Thomas H. Simon, *Democracy and Social Justice* (Lanham, Md.: Rowman & Littlefield, 1995), chap. 5.
28. Sunstein, "Limits," 306.
29. Gang Xu, Sylvia Fields, et al., "The Relationship between the Ethnicity of Generalist Physicians and Their Care for Underserved Populations," Ohio University College of Osteopathic Medicine, Athens, Ohio, 10.
30. Of course, we may ask whether the use of race is necessary for the achievement of the end in view or whether it is one among alternative ways of achieving that end. For instance, it might be possible to induce doctors to practice in Black neighborhoods by providing doctors, irrespective of their race, with suitable monetary incentives. But given the importance of nonmonetary factors in physician-patient relationships, it is doubtful that purely monetary rewards would be sufficient to meet the needs of underserved populations.
31. Remedial action based on the imbalance between blacks in the available work force and their presence in skilled jobs categories presumes that imbalance is caused by racial discrimination. This assumption has been challenged by many who cite cultural and cognitive factors that might equally be the cause of such imbalances. See Thomas Sowell, *Markets and Minorities* (New York: Basic Books, 1981); Richard Herrenstein and Charles Murray, *The Bell Curve* (New York: The Free Press, 1994). This literature has itself been subject to critique: for Sowell, see Christopher Jencks, *Rethinking Social Policy* (New York: Harper, 1993); for Herrenstein and Murray, see *The Bell Curve Wars*, ed. Steven Fraser (New York: Basic Books, 1995).

Louis P. Pojman

The Case Against Affirmative Action

Let us agree that despite the evidences of a booming economy, the poor are suffering grievously, with children being born into desperate material and psychological poverty; for them the ideal of "equal opportunity for all" is a cruel joke. Many feel that the federal government has abandoned its guarantee to provide the minimum necessities for each American, so that the pace of this tragedy seems to be worsening daily. In addition to this, African-Americans have a legacy of slavery and unjust discrimination to contend with, and other minorities have also suffered from injustice. Women have their own peculiar history of being treated unequally in relevant ways. What is the answer to this national problem? Is it increased welfare? More job training? More support for education? Required licensing of parents to have children? Negative income tax? More support for families or for mothers with small children? All of these have merit and should be part of the national debate. But, my thesis is, however tragic the situation may be (and we may disagree on just how tragic it is), one policy is *not* a legitimate part of the solution and that is *reverse, unjust discrimination* against young white males. Strong Affirmative Action, which implicitly advocates reverse discrimination, while no doubt well intentioned, is morally heinous, asserting, by implication, that *two wrongs make a right.*

The *Two Wrongs Make a Right* Thesis goes like this: Because *some* Whites once enslaved some Blacks, the descendants of those slaves (some of whom now may enjoy high incomes and social status) have a right to opportunities and offices over better qualified Whites who had nothing to do with either slavery or the oppression of Blacks (and who may even have suffered hardship comparable to that of poor Blacks). In addition, Strong Affirmative Action creates a new Hierarchy of the Oppressed: Blacks get primary preferential treatment, women second, Native Americans third, Hispanics fourth, Handicapped fifth, and Asians sixth and so on until White males, no matter how needy or well qualified, must accept the leftovers. . . .

Before analyzing arguments concerning Affirmative Action, I must define my terms.

By *Weak Affirmative Action* I mean policies that will increase the opportunities of disadvantaged people to attain social goods and offices. It includes such things as dismantling of segregated institutions, widespread advertisement to groups not previously represented in certain privileged positions,

From *International Journal of Applied Philosophy,* vol. 12, Spring 1998, pp. 97–115. Copyright © 1998 by International Journal of Applied Philosophy. Reprinted by permission.

special scholarships for the disadvantaged classes (e.g., the poor, regardless of race or gender), and even using diversity or under-representation of groups with a history of past discrimination as a tie breaker when candidates for these goods and offices are relatively equal. The goal of *Weak Affirmative Action* is equal opportunity to compete, not equal results. We seek to provide each citizen regardless of race or gender a fair chance to the most favored positions in society. . . .

By *Strong Affirmative Action* I mean preferential treatment on the basis of race, ethnicity or gender (or some other morally irrelevant criterion), discriminating in favor of underrepresented groups against overrepresented groups, aiming at roughly equal results. *Strong Affirmative Action* is *reverse discrimination*. It says it is right to do wrong to correct a wrong. This is the policy currently being promoted under the name of *Affirmative Action*, so I will use that term or "AA" for short throughout this essay to stand for this version of affirmative action. I will not argue for or against the principle of *Weak Affirmative Action*. Indeed, I think it has some moral weight. *Strong Affirmative Action* has none, or so I will argue.

This essay concentrates on AA policies with regard to race, but the arguments can be extended to cover ethnicity and gender. I think that if a case for Affirmative Action can be made it will be as a corrective to racial oppression. I will examine eight arguments regarding AA. The first six will be *negative*, attempting to show that the best arguments for Affirmative Action fail. The last [two] will be *positive* arguments for policies opposing Affirmative Action:

A Critique of Arguments for Affirmative Action

The Need for Role Models

This argument is straightforward. We all have need of role models, and it helps to know that others like us can be successful. We learn and are encouraged to strive for excellence by emulating our heroes and "our kind of people" who have succeeded.

In the first place it's not clear that role models of one's own racial or sexual type are necessary (let alone sufficient) for success. One of my heroes was Gandhi, an Indian Hindu, another was my grade school science teacher, Miss DeVoe, and another Martin Luther King, behind whom I marched in Civil Rights demonstrations. More important than having role models of one's "own type" is having genuinely good people, of whatever race or gender, to emulate. Our common humanity should be a sufficient basis for us to see the possibility of success in people of virtue and merit. To yield to the demand, however tempting it may be, for "role-models-just-like-us" is to treat people like means not ends. . . .

The Compensation Argument

The argument goes like this: blacks have been wronged and severely harmed by whites. Therefore white society should compensate blacks for the injury caused them. Reverse discrimination in terms of preferential hiring, contracts, and scholarships is a fitting way to compensate for the past wrongs.[1]

This argument actually involves a distorted notion of compensation. Normally, we think of compensation as owed by a specific person A to another person B whom A has wronged in a specific way C. For example, if I have stolen your car and used it for a period of time to make business profits that would have gone to you, it is not enough that I return your car. I must pay you an amount reflecting your loss and my ability to pay. If I have made $5,000 and only have $10,000 in assets, it would not be possible for you to collect $20,000 in damages—even though that is the amount of loss you have incurred. . . .

On the face of it, demands by blacks for compensation do not fit the usual pattern. Southern States with Jim Crow laws could be accused of unjustly harming blacks, but it is hard to see that the United States government was involved in doing so. Much of the harm done to blacks was the result of private discrimination, not state action. . . . Furthermore, it is not clear that all blacks were harmed in the same way or whether some were *unjustly* harmed or harmed more than poor whites and others (e.g., short people). Finally, even if identifiable blacks were harmed by identifiable social practices, it is not clear that most forms of Affirmative Action are appropriate to restore the situation. The usual practice of a financial payment seems more appropriate than giving a high level job to someone unqualified or only minimally qualified. . . .

Still, there may be something intuitively compelling about compensating members of an oppressed group who are minimally qualified. Suppose that the Hatfields and the McCoys are enemy clans and some youths from the Hatfields go over and steal diamonds and gold from the McCoys, distributing it within the Hatfield economy. Even though we do not know which Hatfield youths did the stealing, we would want to restore the wealth, as far as possible, to the McCoys. One way might be to tax the Hatfields, but another might be to give preferential treatment in terms of scholarships and training programs and hiring to the McCoys.

This is perhaps the strongest argument for Affirmative Action, and it may well justify some weaker versions of AA, but it is doubtful whether it is sufficient to justify strong versions with quotas and goals and time tables in skilled positions. There are at least two reasons for this. First, we have no way of knowing how many people of any given group would have achieved some given level of competence had the world been different. . . . Secondly, the normal criterion of competence is a strong prima facie consideration when the most important positions are at stake. There are three reasons for this: (1) treating people according to their merits respects them as persons, as ends in themselves, rather than as means to social ends (if we believe that individuals possess a dignity which deserves to be respected, then we ought to treat that individual on the basis of his or her merits, not as a mere instrument for social policy); (2) society has given people expectations that if they attain certain levels of excellence they will be awarded appropriately; and (3) filling the most important positions with the best qualified is the best way to ensure efficiency in job-related areas and in society in general. These reasons are not absolutes.

They can be overridden.[2] But there is a strong presumption in their favor, so that a burden of proof rests with those who would overrride them. . . .

The Argument for Compensation From Those Who Innocently Benefitted From Past Injustice

Young White males as innocent beneficiaries of unjust discrimination against blacks and women have no grounds for complaint when society seeks to level the tilted field. They may be innocent of oppressing blacks, other minorities, and women, but they have unjustly benefitted from that oppression or discrimination. So it is perfectly proper that less qualified women and blacks be hired before them.

The operative principle is: He who knowingly and willingly benefits from a wrong must help pay for the wrong. Judith Jarvis Thomson puts it this way. "Many [white males] have been direct beneficiaries of policies which have downgraded blacks and women . . . and even those who did not directly benefit . . . had, at any rate, the advantage in the competition which comes of the confidence in one's full membership [in the community] and of one's right being recognized as a matter of course."[3] That is, white males obtain advantages in self respect and self-confidence deriving from a racist/sexist system which denies these to blacks and women.

Here is my response to this argument: As I noted in the previous section, compensation is normally individual and specific. If A harms B regarding x, B has a right to compensation from A in regards to x. If A steals B's car and wrecks it, A has an obligation to compensate B for the stolen car, but A's son has no obligation to compensate B. Furthermore, if A dies or disappears, B has no moral right to claim that society compensate him for the stolen car—though if he has insurance, he can make such a claim to the insurance company. Sometimes a wrong cannot be compensated, and we just have to make the best of an imperfect world. . . .

The Diversity Argument

It is important that we learn to live in a pluralistic world, learning to get along with those of other races, conditions, and cultures, so we should have schools and employment situations as fully integrated as possible. . . . Diversity is an important symbol and educative device. Thus, proponents of AA argue, preferential treatment is warranted to perform this role in society.

Once again, there is some truth in these concerns. Diversity of ideas challenges us to scrutinize our own values and beliefs. . . . Diversity may expand our moral horizons. But, again, while we can admit the value of diversity, it hardly seems adequate to override the moral requirement to treat each person with equal respect. *Diversity for diversity's sake is moral promiscuity*, since it obfuscates rational distinctions, undermines treating individuals as ends, treating them, instead as mere means (to the goals of social engineering), and, furthermore, unless those hired are highly qualified, the diversity factor threatens to become a fetish. . . .

There may be times when diversity may seem to be "crucial" to the well-being of a diverse community, such as for a police force. Suppose that White policemen tend to overreact to young Black males and the latter group distrusts White policemen. Hiring more less qualified Black policemen, who would relate better to these youth, may have overall utilitarian value. But such a move, while we might make it as a lesser evil, could have serious consequences in allowing the demographic prejudices to dictate social policy. A better strategy would be to hire the best police, that is, those who can perform in [a] disciplined, intelligent manner, regardless of their race. A White policeman must be able to arrest a Black burglar, even as a Black policeman must be able to arrest a White rapist. The quality of the police man or woman, not their race or gender, is what counts.

On the other hand, if a Black policeman, though lacking some of the formal skills of the White policeman, really is able to do a better job in the Black community, this might constitute a case of merit, not Affirmative Action. As Stephen Kershnar points out, this is similar to the legitimacy of hiring Chinese men to act as undercover agents in Chinatown.[4]

The Equal Results Argument

Some philosophers and social scientists hold that human nature is roughly identical, so that on a fair playing field the same proportion from every race and ethnic group and both genders would attain to the highest positions in every area of endeavor. It would follow that any inequality of results itself is evidence for inequality of opportunity.

> History is important when considering governmental rules like Test 21 because low scores by blacks can be traced in large measure to the legacy of slavery and racism: segregation, poor schooling, exclusion from trade unions, malnutrition, and poverty have all played their roles. Unless one assumes that blacks are naturally less able to pass the test, the conclusion must be that the results are themselves socially and legally constructed, not a mere given for which law and society can claim no responsibility.
>
> The conclusion seems to be that genuine equality eventually requires equal results. Obviously blacks have been treated unequally throughout U.S. history, and just as obviously the economic and psychological effects of that inequality linger to this day, showing up in lower income and poorer performance in school and on tests than whites achieve. Since we have no reason to believe that differences in performance can be explained by factors other than history, equal results are a good benchmark by which to measure progress made toward genuine equality (John Arthur, *The Unfinished Constitution* [Belmont, CA: Wadsworth Publishing Co, 1990], p. 238)

. . . Albert G. Mosley develops a similar argument. "Establishing Blacks' presence at a level commensurate with their proportion in the relevant labor market need not be seen as an attempt to actualize some valid prediction.

Rather, given the impossibility of determining what level of representation Blacks would have achieved were it not for racial discrimination, the assumption of proportional representation is the only *fair* assumption to make. This is not to argue that Blacks should be maintained in such positions, but their contrived exclusion merits equally contrived rectification."[5]. . . However, Arthur [and] Mosley . . . fail even to consider studies that suggest that there are innate differences between races, sexes, and groups. If there are genetic differences in intelligence, temperament, and other qualities within families, why should we not expect such differences between racial groups and the two genders? Why should the evidence for this be completely discounted?

Mosley's reasoning is as follows: Since we don't know for certain whether groups proportionately differ in talent, we should presume that they are equal in every respect. So we should presume that if we were living in a just society, there would be roughly proportionate representation in every field (e.g., equal representation of doctors, lawyers, professors, carpenters, airplane pilots, basketball players, and criminals). Hence, it is only fair—productive of justice—to aim at proportionate representation in these fields.

But the logic is flawed. Under a situation of ignorance we should not presume equality or inequality of representation—but conclude that we *don't know* what the results would be in a just society. Ignorance doesn't favor equal group representation any more than it favors unequal group representation. It is neutral between them . . .

The "No One Deserves His Talents" Argument Against Meritocracy

According to this argument, the competent do not deserve their intelligence, their superior character, their industriousness, or their discipline; therefore they have no right to the best positions in society; therefore it is not unjust to give these positions to less (but still minimally) qualified blacks and women. In one form this argument holds that since no one deserves anything, society may use any criteria it pleases to distribute goods. The criterion most often designated is social utility. Versions of this argument are found in the writings of John Arthur, John Rawls, Bernard Boxill, Michael Kinsley, Ronald Dworkin, and Richard Wasserstrom. Rawls writes, "No one deserves his place in the distribution of native endowments, any more than one deserves one's initial starting place in society. The assertion that a man deserves the superior character that enables him to make the effort to cultivate his abilities is equally problematic; for his character depends in large part upon fortunate family and social circumstances for which he can claim no credit. The notion of desert seems not to apply to these cases."[6] Michael Kinsley is even more adamant:

> Opponents of affirmative action are hung up on a distinction that seems more profoundly irrelevant: treating individuals versus treating

groups. What is the moral difference between dispensing favors to people on their "merits" as individuals and passing out society's benefits on the basis of group identification?

Group identifications like race and sex are, of course, immutable. They have nothing to do with a person's moral worth. But the same is true of most of what comes under the label "merit." The tools you need for getting ahead in a meritocratic society—not all of them but most: talent, education, instilled cultural values such as ambition—are distributed just as arbitrarily as skin color. They are fate. The notion that people somehow "deserve" the advantages of these characteristics in a way they don't "deserve" the advantage of their race is powerful, but illogical.[7]

It will help to put the argument in outline form.

1. Society may award jobs and positions as it sees fit as long as individuals have no claim to these positions.
2. To have a claim to something means that one has earned it or deserves it.
3. But no one has earned or deserves his intelligence, talent, education or cultural values which produce superior qualifications.
4. If a person does not deserve what produces something, he does not deserve its products.
5. Therefore better qualified people do not deserve their qualifications.
6. Therefore, society may override their qualifications in awarding jobs and positions as it sees fit (for social utility or to compensate for previous wrongs).

So it is permissible if a minimally qualified black or woman is admitted to law or medical school ahead of a white male with excellent credentials or if a less qualified person from an "underutilized" group gets a professorship ahead of an eminently better qualified white male. Sufficiency and underutilization together outweigh excellence.

My response: Premise 4 is false. To see this, reflect that just because I do not deserve the money that I have been given as a gift (for instance) does not mean that I am not entitled to what I get with that money. If you and I both get a gift of $100 and I bury mine in the sand for 5 years while you invest yours wisely and double its value at the end of five years, I cannot complain that you should split the increase 50/50 since neither of us deserved the original gift. . . .

But there is no good reason to accept the argument against [moral] desert. We do act freely and, as such, we are responsible for our actions. We deserve the fruits of our labor, reward for our noble feats and punishment for our misbehavior.[8]

We have considered six arguments for Affirmative Action and have found no compelling case for Strong AA and only one plausible argument (a version of the compensation argument) for Weak AA. We must now turn to the arguments against Affirmative Action to see whether they fare any better.

Arguments Against Affirmative Action

Affirmative Action Requires Discrimination Against a Different Group

Weak AA weakly discriminates against new minorities, mostly innocent young white males, and Strong Affirmative Action strongly discriminates against these new minorities. . . . [T]his discrimination is unwarranted, since, even if some compensation to blacks were indicated, it would be unfair to make innocent white males bear the whole brunt of the payments. . . . [I]t is poor white youth who become the new pariahs on the job market. The children of the wealthy have little trouble getting into the best private grammar schools and, on the basis of superior early education, into the best universities, graduate schools, managerial and professional positions. Affirmative Action simply shifts injustice, setting Blacks, Hispanics, Native Americans, Asians and women against young white males, especially ethnic and poor white males. It makes no more sense to discriminate in favor of a rich Black or female who had the opportunity of the best family and education available against a poor White, than it does to discriminate in favor of White males against Blacks or women. It does little to rectify the goal of providing equal opportunity to all. . . .

Respect for persons entails that we treat each person as an end in him or herself, not simply as a means to be used for social purposes. What is wrong about discrimination against Blacks is that it fails to treat Black people as individuals, judging them instead by their skin color not their merit. What is wrong about discrimination against women is that it fails to treat them as individuals, judging them by their gender, not their merit. What is equally wrong about *Affirmative Action* is that it fails to treat White males with dignity as individuals, judging them by *both their race and gender*, instead of their merit. *Current Strong Affirmative Action* is both racist and sexist. . . .

An Argument From the Principle of Merit

Traditionally, we have believed that the highest positions in society should be awarded to those who are best qualified. Rewarding excellence both seems just to the individuals in the competition and makes for efficiency. Note that one of the most successful acts of racial integration, the Brooklyn Dodgers's recruitment of Jackie Robinson in the late 40s, was done in just this way, according to merit. If Robinson had been brought into the major league as a mediocre player or had batted .200 he would have been scorned and sent back to the minors where he belonged.

As mentioned earlier, merit is not an absolute value, but there are strong *prima facie* reasons for awarding positions on that basis, and it should enjoy a weighty presumption in our social practices.

. . .We generally want the best to have the best positions. . . . Only when little is at stake do we weaken the standards and content ourselves with sufficiency (rather than excellence)—there are plenty of jobs where "sufficiency" rather than excellence is required. Perhaps we have even come to feel that medicine or law or university professorships are so routine that they can be performed by minimally qualified people—in which case AA has a place.

Note! no one is calling for quotas or proportional representation of *underutilized* groups in the National Basketball Association where blacks make up 80% of the players. But, surely, if merit and merit alone reigns in sports, should it not be valued at least as much in education and industry?

The case for meritocracy has two pillars. One pillar is a deontological argument which holds that we ought to treat people as ends and not merely means. By giving people what they deserve as *individuals*, rather than as members of *groups*, we show respect for their inherent worth. . . .

The second pillar for meritocracy is utilitarian. In the end, we will be better off by honoring excellence. We want the best leaders, teachers, policemen, physicians, generals, lawyers, and airplane pilots that we can possibly produce in society. So our program should be to promote equal opportunity, as much as is feasible in a free market economy, and reward people according to their individual merit.[9]

Conclusion

Let me sum up my discussion. The goal of the Civil Rights movement and of moral people everywhere has been justice for all, including equal opportunity. The question is: how best to get there. Civil Rights legislation removed the unjust legal barriers, opening the way towards equal opportunity, but it did not tackle the deeper causes that produce differential results. Weak Affirmative Action aims at encouraging minorities to strive for excellence in all areas of life, without unduly jeopardizing the rights of majorities. The problem of Weak Affirmative Action is that it easily slides into Strong Affirmative Action where quotas, "goals and timetables," "equal results"—in a word—*reverse discrimination*—prevail and are forced onto groups, thus promoting mediocrity, inefficiency, and resentment. Furthermore, AA aims at the higher levels of society—universities and skilled jobs, but if we want to improve our society, the best way to do it is to concentrate on families, children, early education, and the like, so all are prepared to avail themselves of opportunity. Affirmative Action, on the one hand, is too much, too soon and on the other hand, too little, too late. . . .

Martin Luther said that humanity is like a man mounting a horse who always tends to fall off on the other side of the horse. This seems to be the case with Affirmative Action. Attempting to redress the discriminatory iniquities of our history, our well-intentioned social engineers now engage in new forms of discriminatory iniquity and thereby think that they have successfully mounted the horse of racial harmony. They have only fallen off on the other side of the issue.[10]

Notes

1. For a good discussion of this argument see B. Boxill, "The Morality of Reparation," in *Social Theory and Practice* 2:1 (1972) and Albert G. Mosley in his and Nicholas Capaldi, *Affirmative Action; Social Justice or Unfair Preference?* (Rowman and Littlefield, 1996), pp. 23–27.

2. Merit sometimes may be justifiably overridden by need, as when parents choose to spend extra earnings on special education for their disabled child rather than for their gifted child. Sometimes we may override merit for utilitarian purposes. E.g., suppose you are the best shortstop on a baseball team but are also the best catcher. You'd rather play shortstop, but the manager decides to put you at catcher because, while your friend can do an adequate job at [shortstop], no one else is adequate at catcher. It's permissible for you to be assigned the job of catcher. Probably, some expression of appreciation would be due you.
3. Judith Jarvis Thomson, "Preferential Hiring," in Marshall Cohen, Thomas Nagel and Thomas Scanlon, eds., *Equality and Preferential Treatment* (Princeton: Princeton University Press, 1977).
4. Stephen Kershnar pointed this out in written comments (December 22, 1997).
5. See Mosley, op cit., p. 28, and Bernard Boxill, *Blacks and Social Justice* (Rowman & Littlefield, 1984), whom Mosley quotes in his article, also defends this position.
6. John Rawls, *A Theory of Justice* (Harvard University Press, 1971), p. 104. See Bernard Boxill, "The Morality of Preferential Hiring," *Philosophy and Public Affairs* 7:3 (1983).
7. Michael Kinsley, "Equal Lack of Opportunity," *Harper's* (June 1983).
8. My point does not depend on any particular theory of free will. One is reminded of Nozick's point that Rawls' professed aim of articulating the enormous worth of each individual seems contrary to the reductive determinism in his natural lottery argument.
9. For further discussion of this point see my "Equality and Desert," *Philosophy* 72 (1997).
10. Some of the material in this essay appeared in "The Moral Status of Affirmative Action," *Public Affairs Quarterly* 6:2 (1992). I have not had space to consider all the objections to my position or discuss the issue of freedom of association which, I think, should be given much scope in private but not in public institutions. Barbara Bergmann (*In Defense of Affirmative Action* [New York: Basic Books, 1996], pp. 122–25) and others argue that we already offer preferential treatment for athletes and veterans, especially in university admissions, so being consistent, we should provide it for women and minorities. My answer is that I am against giving athletic scholarships, and I regard scholarships to veterans as a part of a contractual relationship, a reward for service to one's country. But I distinguish entrance programs from actual employment. I don't think that veterans should be afforded special privilege in hiring practice, unless it be as a tiebreaker.

    I should also mention that my arguments from merit and respect apply more specifically to public institutions than private ones, where issues of property rights and freedom of association carry more weight.

POSTSCRIPT

Is Affirmative Action Fair?

That racial discrimination and sexual discrimination have existed in the United States is a matter of historical record and beyond dispute. But the question remains, What follows for us here and now?

Opponents of affirmative action say that nothing at all follows, except perhaps that we might be more careful and vigilant about allowing any form of discrimination, including modern forms of reverse discrimination.

Proponents of strong affirmative action say that although these views might *look* fair and aim to *be* fair, they are not fair. Just preventing discrimination without taking positive action to improve minorities' positions in society would simply freeze an unfairly established status quo. As American society is now, blacks are not represented in professions, in graduate schools, in business boardrooms, or in positions of social and political leadership in a way that is consistent with their numbers in the population. This is not for lack of interest or ability; it is a legacy of social injustice. To insist that we now freeze this status quo and proceed "fairly," on a case-by-case basis, will guarantee that the white-biased social momentum will continue for at least the foreseeable future. Advocates of affirmative action want to eradicate the effects of past discrimination and to put an end to the bias in momentum as soon as possible. They call for active measures to achieve this.

Sources that are relevant to this issue include Gertrude Ezorsky, *Racism and Justice: The Case for Affirmative Action* (Cornell University Press, 1991); Andrew Kull, *The Colorblind Constitution* (Harvard University Press, 1992); Bernard R. Boxhill, *Blacks and Social Justice*, rev. ed. (Rowman & Littlefield, 1992); Andrew Hacker, *Two Nations: Black and White, Separate, Hostile, Unequal* (Scribner, 1992); Stanley Fish, "Reverse Racism, or How the Pot Got to Call the Kettle Black," *The Atlantic Monthly* (November 1993); Steven M. Cahn, ed., *Affirmative Action and the University* (Temple University Press, 1993); Carl Cohen, *Naked Racial Preference: The Case Against Affirmative Action* (Madison Books, 1995); Ralph R. Reiland, "Affirmative Action or Equal Opportunity?" *Regulation* (vol. 18, 1995), pp. 19–23; and Steven M. Cahn, ed., *The Affirmative Action Debates*, 2d ed. (Routledge, 2002).

Other sources on this controversial policy are George E. Curry, ed., *The Affirmative Action Debate* (Addison-Wesley, 1996); Richard F. Thomasson, Faye J. Crosby, and Sharon D. Herzberger, *Affirmative Action: The Pros and Cons of Policy and Practice* (University Press of America, 1996); John David Skrentny, *The Ironies of Affirmative Action: Politics, Culture, and Justice in America* (University of Chicago Press, 1996); Robert Emmett Long, ed. , *Affirmative Action* (H. W. Wilson, 1996); Barbara Bergmann, *In Defense of Affirmative Action* (Basic Books, 1996); Terry Eastland, *Ending Affirmative Action: The Case for Colorblind*

Justice (Basic Books, 1996); Jewelle Taylor Gibbs, *Color of Justice: Rodney King, O. J. Simpson, and Race in America* (Jossey-Bass, 1996); K. Anthony Appiah and Amy Gutmann, *Color Conscious: The Political Morality of Race* (Princeton University Press, 1996); David Theo Goldberg, *Racial Subjects: Writing on Race in America* (Routledge, 1997); Michael Levin, *Why Race Matters: Race Differences and What They Mean* (Greenwood Publishing Group, 1997); Abigail Thernstrom and Stephen Thernstrom, *America in Black and White: One Nation, Indivisible* (Simon & Schuster, 1997); Peter Skerry, "The Strange Politics of Affirmative Action," *Wilson Quarterly* (Winter 1997); Francis J. Beckwith, Todd E. Jones, eds., *Affirmative Action: Social Justice or Reverse Discrimination?* (Prometheus Books, 1997); Glenn C. Loury, "How to Mend Affirmative Action," *The Public Interest* (Spring 1997); Charles R. Lawrence III and Mari Matsuda, *We Won't Go Back: Making the Case for Affirmative Action* (Houghton Mifflin, 1997); David K. Shipler, *A Country of Strangers: Blacks and Whites in America* (Alfred A. Knopf, 1997); Lincoln Caplan, *Up Against the Law: Affirmative Action and the Supreme Court* (Century Foundation, 1997); Jim Sleeper, *Liberal Racism* (Viking Penguin, 1997); "Racism and the Law: The Legacy and Lessons of Plessy," a special issue of *Law and Philosophy* (May 1997); "The Affirmative Action Debate," a special issue of *Report From the Institute for Philosophy and Public Policy* (Winter–Spring 1997); Bryan K. Fair, *Notes of a Racial Caste Baby: Color Blindness and the End of Affirmative Action* (New York University Press, 1997); John Davis Skrentny, "Affirmative Action: Some Advice for the Pundits," *American Behavioral Scientist* (April 1998); *Focus on Law Studies* (Spring 1998) (this entire issue concerns affirmative action); Matt Cavanagh, *Against Equality of Opportunity* (Clarendon Press, 2002); Samuel Leiter and William M. Leiter, *Affirmative Action in Antidiscrimination Law and Policy: An Overview and Synthesis* (State University of New York Press, 2002); Charles V. Dale, *Affirmative Action Revisited* (Nova Science Publishers, 2002); and Fred L. Pincus, *Reverse Discrimination: Dismantling the Myth* (Lynne Rienner Publishers, 2003).

A concise account of civil rights history (including the birth of the phrase "affirmative action") is Hugh Davis Graham, *Civil Rights and the Presidency: Race and Gender in American Politics, 1960–1972* (Oxford University Press, 1992). Another useful historical account is Paul D. Moreno, *From Direct Action to Affirmative Action: Fair Employment Law and Policy in America, 1933–1972* (Louisiana State University Press, 1999). The position that affirmative action policies are necessary for women is defended by Susan D. Clayton and Faye J. Crosby, *Justice, Gender and Affirmative Action* (University of Michigan Press, 1992).

ISSUE 12

Should Licensing for Handguns Be More Restrictive?

YES: Jon S. Vernick, James G. Hodge, Jr., and Daniel W. Webster, from "The Ethics of Restrictive Licensing for Handguns: Comparing the United States and Canadian Approaches to Handgun Regulation," *Journal of Law, Medicine & Ethics* (Winter 2007)

NO: Daniel D. Polsby, from "The False Promise of Gun Control," *The Atlantic Monthly* (March 1994)

ISSUE SUMMARY

YES: Gun control and health policy professionals Vernick, Hodge, and Webster argue that there are trade-offs and competing values at stake in gun control debates. In particular, a comparison between public health policy and gun control in Canada and the United States shows the benefits of placing the value of public health above that of the right to own guns.

NO: Professor of law Daniel D. Polsby asserts that gun control legislation is misguided. He maintains that if there were a ban on handguns, criminals would still arm themselves, but law-abiding citizens would not, resulting in more crime and more innocent victims.

Murder and violence are serious problems in the United States and guns play a significant role. In the wake of recent tragedies such as the Littleton, Colorado, high school killings and the murders at Virginia Tech, we are especially conscious of the role guns play. But beyond these striking events is the more routine, day-to-day violence that involves guns and killing.

The resulting question is: What should be done to prevent further killing?

One suggestion is to regulate the traffic in guns, in particular, handguns. It is thought by some that this would have a favorable impact by eliminating some of the violence and killing associated with the possession of guns. It would lessen the ability of career criminals to obtain weapons and use them to commit crimes and it would prevent situations in which noncriminals might cause damage through the use of guns that they later regret but which cannot be undone. Ideally, the number of guns in circulation would be so limited that it would be difficult (or impossible) for a criminal to obtain a gun even through the black market.

Some would argue that these positive results are seriously overestimated. They counter that regulating the traffic in guns does not reduce the number of guns in circulation. Instead, regulations reduce the number of guns that are sold on open markets, where people follow restrictions, while there is little or no impact on the number of guns sold through black markets, where people do not follow restrictions. As a result, law-abiding citizens would not have guns—but criminals would. In this case, with law-abiding people at the mercy of criminals, the situation would be far worse, not better.

Gun control is one of those topics that generally separate political conservatives from political liberals. Conservatives tend to stand by the right of citizens to possess guns, while liberals tend to stand by the right of society to outlaw guns (or to restrict their sale or use). Conservatives tend to think that gun restrictions will have a larger impact on law-abiding citizens (who will follow restrictions) than on criminals (who will not); liberals tend to think that bringing the overall number of guns down will definitely have a beneficial impact on a society that is prone to use guns for the wrong reasons. Conservatives sometimes point out that guns don't kill people: people kill people. They often believe that what is required is personal responsibility and self-control, not gun control. Some liberals state that ideas of "personal responsibility" apply in an ideal world, but not in the real world, which contains excessive violence in the media and inner-city poverty.

In the selections that follow, Vernick, Hodge, and Webster argue for tighter restrictions on the sale and use of handguns. They compare the stricter restrictions in Canada to the view that prevails in the United States, and argue for the moral superiority of the Canadian approach. Daniel D. Polsby counters that gun control will not deliver the positive effects that its proponents hope for and that the roots of U.S. gun violence actually lie elsewhere.

YES

Jon S. Vernick, James G. Hodge, Jr., and Daniel W. Webster

The Ethics of Restrictive Licensing for Handguns: Comparing the United States and Canadian Approaches to Handgun Regulation

I. Introduction

On April 16, 2007, Cho Seung-Hui used two semiautomatic handguns to kill 32 persons and then himself at Virginia Tech University in the largest campus shooting in U.S. history. Mr. Cho purchased his handguns from a pawnshop and a gun store in Virginia, where under state law a background check was conducted to determine whether he had any disqualifying criminal or mental health history. The paperwork for the background check was completed at the gun store, and the check itself was conducted through an "instant" system facilitated by a toll-free telephone number. The entire transaction took approximately 20 minutes.[1] At no point was Mr. Cho asked why he wished to purchase the guns. And although he had been deemed a potential danger to himself by a state magistrate in 2005—which should have disqualified his purchase of a gun under federal law—this information never reached those conducting the background check.[2]

The process by which Mr. Cho acquired his handguns in Virginia is consistent with the approach adopted by many U.S. states. In general, persons in the U.S. without a very specific disqualifying criminal or mental health history, or some other prohibited status such as a dishonorable discharge from the armed forces, may purchase or possess firearms. It is not necessary, in most states, for prospective purchasers to provide any reason for wanting or needing to own a gun, nor do authorities retain any discretion to deny guns to those who have certain indicia of dangerousness but who do not otherwise fit one of the statutorily defined prohibited categories.[3]

The U.S. approach to the purchase and possession of firearms reflects a public policy choice with important implications for public health. This policy choice generally allows most people who wish to own a handgun to do so. As a result, in the United States, more than 200 million firearms rest in civilian

From *Journal of Law, Medicine and Ethics*, vol. 34, no. 4, Winter 2007, pp. 668–778 (excerpts).
Copyright © 2007 by American Society of Law, Medicine & Ethics. Reprinted by permission.

hands, at least one firearm can be found in 38 percent of all homes, and 16 percent of adults own a handgun.[4] The public health consequences of widespread firearm availability are enormous. In 2004, nearly 30,000 persons were killed by firearms, including homicides, suicides, and unintentional deaths, for an annual rate of ten per 100,000.[5] Almost another 70,000 persons suffered non-fatal gunshot wounds serious enough to warrant at least a visit to an emergency room in 2005.[6] And in the same year, there were also 419,640 gun-related violent crimes in the U.S., many of which involved threats or shots fired with no physical wounds.[7] Despite a decline beginning in the mid-1990s, firearm-related crime has recently begun to increase in many parts of the U.S.,[8] resulting in an estimated social cost of $100 billion annually.[9]

The U.S. approach to the sale and possession of firearms, particularly handguns, is unusual among high-income, developed countries. Although laws vary somewhat, Canada and some Western European countries, for example, require prospective buyers to first obtain a permit to purchase a handgun.[10] In order to get the permit, the buyer must undergo an extensive background check often requiring weeks to complete. Importantly, the buyer must also demonstrate a valid reason for needing the handgun, such as an especially dangerous occupation or participation in a certified shooting club.[11]

These differing policy approaches to handgun possession, we argue, raise ethical issues as well. They reflect a common ethical dilemma about where to place the benefits and burdens of widespread gun availability. The U.S. approach emphasizes the ability of individuals to own guns and even carry concealed weapons in public, whereas the Canadian approach generally places a premium on the health and safety of communities. Proponents of the U.S. approach often cast the debate in terms of individuals' "freedom" to have guns. Proponents of the Canadian approach might respond that individual freedom is actually enhanced by maximizing community safety.

In this article, we explore the ethical dimensions of the U.S. versus Canadian approaches to the regulation of handguns through the three major themes of autonomy, prevention of harms, and social justice. We argue that the Canadian approach is ethically justified. Our aim is to inform future public policy, as the U.S. and other countries wrestle with the appropriate policy responses to tragedies like the Virginia Tech shootings as well as the daily toll of gun violence within the population.

II. Overview of Handgun Regulation in the U.S. and Canada

A. United States

To conduct an appropriate ethical analysis, it is frst necessary to better understand the existing systems of regulation for handguns in the U.S. and Canada. We choose to focus on handguns, rather than on all firearms, because the majority of all gun-related homicides, suicides, and crimes in the United States are committed with handguns. . . . Of the firearms owned by civilians in the U.S., only about 40 percent are handguns.[12]

. . . Under federal law, anyone at least 21 years of age[13] who lives in the state where the handgun is being acquired[14] can legally purchase and possess a handgun unless they are the following: (1) a felon; (2) under a felony indictment; (3) a fugitive from justice; (4) addicted to a controlled substance; (5) "adjudicated as a mental defective" or have been "committed to any mental institution"; (6) an illegal alien; (7) dishonorably discharged from the armed forces; (8) subject to certain domestic violence restraining orders; or (9) convicted of a misdemeanor crime of domestic violence.[15] These exclusionary criteria, however, may miss many potentially dangerous individuals. For example, although the vast majority of homicide offenders have a criminal record, only 43 percent had a prior felony conviction.[16] Handgun purchasers with misdemeanor convictions are five to ten times more likely to commit crimes involving violence or guns as are handgun purchasers without such a criminal history.[17]

In the U.S., systems for determining whether individuals meet the legal criteria for gun ownership are far from perfect. Persons in the business of selling firearms must be licensed by the federal government.[18] When an individual wishes to purchase a handgun from a licensed dealer, a background check must be conducted,[19] but an estimated 40 percent of all firearm transactions do not involve licensed dealers.[20] When a handgun is purchased from someone who is not a licensed dealer, no background check is required under federal law. . . . And once a handgun has been purchased, no national registration system exists to make it easier for law enforcement to track a firearm from owner to owner.[21] Furthermore, the background check system is only as good as the information it contains. Potentially disqualifying information, other than felony conviction status, is often missing or incomplete.[22] . . .

States may impose additional requirements for the purchase and possession of handguns, resulting in a patchwork quilt of varying regulations. For example, three states (California, Maryland, and Virginia) limit handgun purchases to a maximum of one per person per month, and 15 states require background checks for all handgun sales.[23] But only a few U.S. states or localities—including New Jersey, Massachusetts, and New York City—have enacted relatively restrictive licensing systems that limit handgun ownership to those who can pass a comprehensive background check.[24] . . .

One non-ethical objection that is often raised to the enactment of more restrictive gun laws in the U.S. is that such laws would violate the Second Amendment of the U.S. Constitution. The Second Amendment states, "A well regulated Militia, being necessary to the security of a free State, the right of the people to keep and bear Arms, shall not be infringed."[25] Although there remains a robust public and academic debate about the meaning of the Second Amendment,[26] U.S. courts have had remarkably little trouble determining the effect of the amendment on gun laws.[27] With only one exception . . . no federal appellate court has ever struck down any gun law as a violation of the Second Amendment.[28] Until and unless the Supreme Court changes this prevailing judicial interpretation, the Second Amendment is generally not a legal obstacle to Canadian-style handgun licensing. Of course, public opinion and its effect on the political process in the U.S. also affect gun policy.

In public opinion polls, for example, a majority of Americans consistently report that they believe the Second Amendment protects an individual's right to own guns.[29]

B. Canada

By comparison, like some Western European countries, Canada has a form of restrictive licensing system for handguns. Beginning in 1977, handguns were classified at the national level as "restricted weapons," meaning that a permit is required before persons may purchase handguns. In order to obtain the permit, a person must: (1) need the gun for specific occupations; (2) be part of an approved shooting club; (3) be a collector; or (4) demonstrate that the gun is needed for self-protection because of a danger from which the police could not protect him or her.[30] Restricted weapons must also be registered, and authorizations are required to transport them from one location to another. . . .

Beginning in 1991, a mandatory training course, an improved screening process including references and a photograph, and a 28-day waiting period were implemented. Safe-storage provisions were also instituted requiring all guns to be unloaded and locked up when not in use.[31] Finally, in 1995 the law was further amended to include, among other features, mandatory licensing and registration of all guns. . . .

Although estimates vary, there are about seven million firearms in Canada, including an estimated one million handguns[32]—roughly three handguns for every 100 Canadians. Although Canada has ten provinces and three territories, firearm regulation in Canada (unlike the U.S.) is largely national in scope, thus limiting the effects of illegal trafficking from one jurisdiction to another. However, a large proportion of Canada's crime guns originate in the United States.[33] . . .

III. Risks and Benefits of Widespread Gun Availability for Individuals and Communities

A. Potential Benefits and Harms of Gun Availability for Individuals

Handguns are associated with a number of potential benefits for their owners. . . . [W]hen considering the potential benefits of handguns, most [people] primarily contemplate issues of personal protection. In fact, the majority of handgun owners report personal protection as their main reason for owning the gun.[34]

Firearms can indeed be used by law-abiding citizens to protect themselves. No consensus exists on how commonly law-abiding citizens in the U.S. use firearms to interrupt or ward off criminal attacks against persons or property, but . . . [r]egardless of the actual frequency with which handguns are used for protection, clearly some people derive psychological benefit from having a firearm in case they are threatened.

However, research has generally shown gun ownership, at the individual or household level, to be associated with an increased risk of death. A number of studies have demonstrated that homes with guns are more likely to experience the suicide of a household member than those without guns;[35] that risk is especially acute for young persons. Other studies have shown that those who purchase guns are also at elevated risk of suicide.[36]

It may be more difficult to study the effects of gun ownership on the risk of homicide because many factors that can influence homicide, other than gun ownership, are hard to measure. . . . A national . . . study . . . estimated that, after controlling for . . . demographic differences, adults in homes with firearms had a 41 percent higher homicide risk than adults in homes without firearms.[37]

In high-risk settings such as in homes with domestic violence, abusers' ownership of a firearm increases the lethality of domestic violence five fold.[38] In another analysis, intimate partner assaults that involved a firearm were 12 times more likely to result in death than those that did not involve a gun.[39] The presence of a firearm also increases the risk of an unintentional gunshot death in the home.[40] Although the weight of evidence indicates that household members are on average at greater risk when a firearm is kept in the home, for some individuals gun ownership may be, on balance, protective.

Finally, it is also important to recognize that the harms associated with widespread gun availability are not equally distributed throughout the population. For example, among males aged 15 to 24, rates of firearm homicide victimization are 23 times higher for Blacks than for non-Hispanic Whites.[41]

B. Potential Benefits and Harms of Widespread Gun Availability for Communities

"An armed society is a polite society."[42] The underlying message of this pro-gun aphorism is the belief that widespread availability and carrying of firearms in a community forces residents to behave in a more civil, peaceful manner toward one another. This belief has one of its clearest policy expressions in U.S. state laws that make it easy to obtain a permit to carry a concealed weapon—so-called "shall issue" or "right-to-carry" concealed carry laws. Advocates of these laws, notably John Lott in his book *More Guns, Less Crime*, argued that they would actually reduce violent crime by deterring criminals from attacking law-abiding citizens who might be armed.[43] In his evaluations of the effects of "shall issue" laws, Lott found that the laws were indeed associated with fewer homicides.[44] Although some researchers agreed with Lott's conclusions,[45] when other researchers reexamined the data, correcting for (in their view) methodological and others problems with the initial analyses, no convincing evidence showed a beneficial effect for these laws.[46] In a recent review of the research on "shall issue" laws, a National Research Council panel concluded that it was "not possible to determine that there is a causal link between the passage of right-to-carry laws and crime rates."[47]

In addition to protection from crime, proponents of easy access to guns sometimes argue that private ownership of guns acts as a bulwark against government tyranny.[48] They claim that private citizens can use their guns to deter and even resist a government that tries to inappropriately usurp the rights of individuals. Some also see private gun ownership as a protection against potential foreign or terrorist invasion. It is difficult to assess the validity of these perspectives, except to question whether, in this age of high tech weapons and professional armies, it is truly realistic to expect handgun-owning civilians to challenge government forces. . . .

On average, high-income nations with a relatively high prevalence of gun ownership, such as the U.S., have more homicides than do other high income countries with fewer guns after controlling for differences in age structure, racial/ethnic heterogeneity, and levels of government social support.[49] The high homicide rate in the U.S. cannot be explained by higher overall rates of criminality because U.S. non-lethal crime rates are similar to those of most other high-income, developed countries.[50] In one comparison of death rates in the early 1990s, U.S. firearm-related homicides rates were 19 times greater than the pooled rate of 25 other high-income countries. The U.S. overall homicide rate was about 3.5 times higher than the nearest other high-income country (excluding Northern Ireland, whose homicide rate during a time of internal turmoil was still only about 59 percent as great as that of the U.S.).[51] Comparing the U.S. with Canada more specifically, the age-adjusted U.S. homicide rate was almost five times higher than Canada's in 1992, a difference primarily explained by a more than ten-fold greater U.S. firearm homicide rate. More recently, in 2004 the Canadian homicide rate was 1.95 per 100,000 persons,[52] compared with a U.S. rate of 5.9.[53] . . .

Even among U.S. cities and states, however, notable differences exist in the prevalence of firearm ownership likely associated, at least in part, with differences in the restrictiveness of their firearm laws. In a series of analyses conducted by researchers at the Harvard School of Public Health, U.S. states with fewer guns had lower rates of firearm-related suicide, homicide, and unintentional deaths after adjusting for other socio-demographic differences.[54] The states with the lowest prevalence of gun ownership were generally those with the most restrictive handgun licensing laws.

Our own research also reveals another harm associated with the easy availability of firearms in some U.S. states: illegal gun trafficking.[55] Guns used for crime in cities and states with more restrictive laws are more likely to have first been sold by out-of-state retailers in places with weaker laws. In particular, cities located in states with restrictive licensing, often coupled with firearm registration laws, have a much smaller share of their crimes originating from in-state dealers than other cities. Even guns owned by law-abiding citizens contribute to illegal gun trafficking and gun crime in communities. An estimated 500,000 firearms are stolen from U.S. homes every year, and thus directly enter the criminal market.[56] Some evidence suggests that higher rates of gun ownership within communities actually increase the risk for home burglaries, perhaps because firearms are an attractive item for burglars to steal.[57]

Just as the individual-level harms associated with guns are not evenly distributed, so too do some communities bear a disproportionate burden of gun-related violence. On average, more urban, poorer neighborhoods—often with a higher proportion of African Americans—have higher rates of gun violence and all of the associated social harms.[58]

Firearm-related suicides and unintentional shootings also affect communities as well as individuals. These deaths and injuries generate police, medical, and lost productivity costs for communities. They are, of course, also associated with emotional and other less-easily quantifiable costs for survivors. Overall rates of suicide in the U.S. and Canada are similar, though a direct comparison of race-specific rates is not possible with readily available data. One estimate based on U.S. data suggests that "the elimination of unintentional shootings and gun suicides in 1997 would be worth as much as $20 billion."[59] . . .

IV. Assessing the Ethics of Comparative Handgun Policies

Ethical principles, like laws, are interpreted and applied based on facts. What is ethical from a policy perspective is thus contingent on available, accurate data. From our assessment of domestic and international handgun laws, several important conclusions can be drawn: (1) the presence of firearms is associated, on average, with a greater incidence of homicide, suicide, and unintentional firearm-related deaths in households and/or populations, after controlling for other factors associated with these outcomes; (2) the burden of firearm-related death, crime, and injury in the United States is not evenly distributed through the population; and (3) handguns are generally less prevalent in household settings and on the streets in jurisdictions with more restrictive licensing laws. . . .

In the sections below, we explore the scope and limits of individual and communal interests in restricting access to handguns through restrictive licensing by addressing three major ethical themes: respect for persons, preventing harms, and promoting social justice.

A. Understanding the Limits of Autonomy Concerning Communal Interests

The Canadian approach to regulating access to handguns does not allow individuals an unfettered choice to purchase a handgun for recreation, satisfaction, self-defense, or certain other purposes. Under broad conceptions of the moral principle of autonomy, individuals with the capacity for making choices enjoy a realm of personal decision-making that is free from external burdens or controlling factors.[60] Canada's licensing laws may be challenged as infringing an individual's "right"[61] to own a gun, even though ownership of firearms, particularly rifles and shotguns, for many is still possible.[62] Governments that implement restrictive gun laws may be viewed as paternalistic[63] and lacking in deference to the wishes of law-abiding adults who perceive a need to own firearms for self-protection, or who simply enjoy firearms.

Such perspectives grounded in individual autonomy cannot be ignored.[64] In societies that value the rights of individuals to act freely, respect for persons is supported by legal norms (e.g., liberty, privacy, due process)[65] and is characterized as a universal ethical principle.[66] However, deference to individual autonomy does not override all other values.[67] Individuals may be constrained when their personal choices or actions affect the legitimate rights or well-being of others individually or collectively.[68] Recognition of the limits of autonomy gives rise to many governmental efforts to protect the public's health.[69] Government actions to protect community health commonly infringe upon individual choices in some ways, but these actions can often be justified by the need to protect populations from risks to health and safety for which individuals cannot fully or easily protect themselves.[70]

In the context of gun ownership, the prevalence of handguns in the U.S., coupled with other factors, affects the health of populations. Morbidity and mortality related to firearm use in the U.S. are significantly higher, on average, than other high-income, industrialized democracies with generally more restrictive gun laws.[71] Similarly, U.S. jurisdictions with fewer firearms have, on average, lower rates of homicides, suicides, and unintentional shootings after controlling for other socio-demographic differences.[72]

Laws that are designed to reduce gun violence may infringe some individuals' interests in gun possession, but they further the autonomy of a majority of the population that seeks to live in a safer society with a reduced risk of gun-related violence. Lowering a society's risk of gun violence enhances the freedom of individuals to choose where to live, work, go to school, recreate, and interact with others without the fear of violence limiting those choices. Recast in this consequentialist way, restrictive gun laws in Canada actually facilitate the autonomy of many while infringing the choices of a few. Reinforcing this perspective are polling data indicating that even a majority of gun owners in the U.S. would support a variety of enhanced restrictions on the ability to purchase or possess firearms.[73] That U.S. gun policies are often dictated by the gun industry and a small percentage of the population who are gun enthusiasts presents its own set of ethical issues. . . .

Differences in cultural factors that affect support for strong regulation of gun ownership may also affect rates of violence. . . . If Canada's lower homicide rates are more attributable to . . . cultural or other factors and not to its firearms laws, then it becomes more difficult to ethically justify a policy that may place some individuals in danger by denying them access to handguns. In our view, however, existing research on the connection between firearm ownership and increased mortality risks as well as data and theory regarding the effects of handgun licensing are persuasive enough to provide an ethical justification for Canada's restrictive licensing approach.

B. Advancing Individual and Communal Benefits through the Prevention of Harm

Potentially contradicting the argument that the Canadian approach is consistent with individual autonomy is the claim that handguns offer unique benefits for some that cannot be accommodated in a restrictive licensing scheme. For example, while firearm enthusiasts may continue to enjoy the benefits of gun ownership in Canada (provided they have a valid reason for the gun, get past screening, take a training course, wait for 28 days, and register their guns), some may perceive an imminent need for a gun for self-defense. Imagine the victim of an escalating case of domestic violence who cannot be fully protected by law enforcement authorities. In both countries, this individual may be able to purchase a firearm, but in Canada it may be substantially more difficult absent an emergency exception to its licensing policies. Is this ethically problematic given that a handgun may be viewed by some victims as an effective means of self-protection?

While the potential victim in this case may have a perceived need to immediately obtain a handgun, it does not necessarily mean she has an ethical right to one, nor is there good evidence that her access to a gun will enhance her safety. Several possible outcomes could result from the intention to use a firearm to interrupt or deter an assault, only one of which (self-defense) is beneficial. A domestic violence victim's acquisition of a firearm may prompt the abuser to resort to more lethal methods, including using the victim's firearm against her. Victims of domestic violence are also at increased risk of attempting suicide;[74] thus, access to a firearm increases the lethality of suicide attempts. Firearms also increase the risk of suicide and unintentional shootings among adolescents living in the home.[75] None of these outcomes benefits the victim. Moreover, the potential for protection afforded the victim by acquiring a firearm might also be realized by other actions that pose fewer risks to victims and others (e.g., having the abuser arrested, obtaining a protective order, installing security systems, or seeking outside shelter).

Still, the psychological benefit of possessing a handgun to potentially deter lethal force may be powerful for some. The victim's perception of safety arising from her gun possession cannot be discounted. It can, however, be qualified. A victim's need for a handgun in the U.S. is arguably stronger because of the easier availability of guns to dangerous people. Notably, her aggressor may also possess one. A rational person facing a potential lethal threat is not necessarily wrong to want to try to meet this threat with a correspondingly lethal weapon. What is ethically suspect from the public health perspective is a government policy that allows widespread gun access that may benefit a few individuals at the expense of higher population-level risks for lethal violence and accompanying social costs. Furthermore, U.S.-style handgun policies are likely to place more victims of domestic violence at risk of losing their lives by making it easier for their abusive partners to obtain firearms.

C. Promoting Social Justice by Protecting the Public's Health

Principles of justice evoke an array of ethical norms, including fairness, equity, and impartiality.[76] From a public policy perspective, justice addresses known or perceived issues of fairness in the application of governmental policies. Whether intended or inadvertent, public health policies that negatively impact specific individuals or groups in unreasonable, unwarranted, or nefarious ways may be deemed unjust.[77] Emerging theories of social justice suggest that all persons are owed "a sufficient amount of each of the essential elements of well-being, of which health is one."[78] Consistent with this theme, justice as a foundation of public health ethics supports the need to improve human health, particularly by focusing on the "most disadvantaged."[79]

Though the dimensions of justice are subject to ethical debate, its core meaning is not: individuals are entitled to fair and appropriate treatment in the application of governmental policies.[80] Therefore, to be ethically acceptable, any firearm policy must be implemented and enforced fairly. On their faces, the different handgun laws of the U.S. and Canada both seemingly support this fundamental norm. Each is applied uniformly across affected populations (noting that Canada's restrictive licensing law is national in scope, whereas many gun laws in the U.S. are state-specific). Neither approach singles out specific categories of persons to prevent firearm ownership, except those who most agree should not have guns (e.g., felons, fugitives, certain domestic abusers). . . .

Assessing the social justice aspects of restrictive licensing laws also requires considering their effects on racial or ethnic minorities. Gun violence in the U.S. is a national problem, but its impact is felt disproportionately in urban, poorer neighborhoods—often with a higher proportion of African Americans or other minorities.[81] Many reasons account for the higher rates of gun violence in these areas, but most experts agree that easy access to guns is an important component of the problem. This unequal burden of gun violence on persons living in urban, poorer environments is a problem of social justice, no matter how the laws are intended to apply.

However, the issue of social justice can also be viewed from a different perspective. Inequities in the U.S. criminal justice system may cause African Americans in some parts of the country to be more likely to be convicted of a crime that disqualifies them from purchasing a gun. In addition, persons living in dangerous inner-city neighborhoods may arguably have a greater need (whether real or perceived) for a handgun for protection. But efforts to reduce gun prevalence and violence within a community may lessen the perceived need for a gun, helping to provide an ethical justification for restrictive licensing approaches. Of course, any unfairness in the criminal justice system should also be addressed.

V. Conclusion

Restrictive licensing for handguns represents a classic ethical dilemma. Some individuals may be harmed so that communities can be safer. Safer communities, in turn, enhance the well-being of most individuals. In this way, restrictive licensing is analogous to mandatory vaccination laws. Some individuals will suffer harmful side-effects from the vaccine, but most will not. Because the community will benefit from reduced infection rates and so-called herd immunity—with enough persons vaccinated, the virus is unable to gain a foothold—mandatory vaccination laws are routinely justified on ethical and legal grounds.

One difference between mandatory vaccination laws and restrictive licensing laws, however, is the strength and specificity of the evidence that restrictive licensing laws significantly contribute to Canada's (and other jurisdictions') lower rates of homicide and gun violence. In our view, evidence that greater availability of firearms in homes and/or communities is associated with higher homicide, suicide, and gun violence rates, after controlling for other factors, is reasonably strong. Yet international and cross-jurisdictional research is challenging given the other factors that can affect violence.

Governments must often act in the absence of perfect data. Although we are not unsympathetic to the desire of some persons to own firearms, our analysis demonstrates that the Canadian approach to handgun regulation is an ethical one. These same policy choices continue to arise in the United States as well. In a nation with 80 firearm-related deaths every day,[82] U.S. policymakers must be prepared to appropriately balance individual and community interests. However, policymakers should also understand that the greater "autonomy" of the community as a whole may be served by a policy that best promotes freedom from violence.

References

1. A. Buncombe and J. Taylor, "Massacre—The Dealer's Defence: 'I Just Sold Him the Gun,'" *The Independent* (U.K.), April 18, 2007. . . .
2. M. Luo, "U.S. Rules Made Killer Ineligible to Purchase Guns," *New York Times*, April 21, 2006.
3. J. S. Vernick and J. S. Mair, "How the Law Affects Gun Policy in the United States: Law as Intervention or Obstacle to Prevention," *Journal of Law, Medicine & Ethics* 30, no. 4 (2002): 692–704.
4. L. Hepburn, M. Miller, D. Azrael, and D. Hemenway, "The U.S. Gun Stock: Results from the 2004 National Firearms Survey," *Injury Prevention* 13 (2007): 15–19.
5. National Center for Injury Prevention and Control, Centers for Disease Control and Prevention, "Web-Based Injury Statistics Query and Reporting System." . . .
6. *Id.*
7. "Key Facts at a Glance: Nonfatal Firearm-Related Violent Crimes, 1993–2005," Office of Justice Programs, Bureau of Justice Statistics, U.S. Department of Justice, 2007. . . .
8. "2006 Crime in the United States: Preliminary Annual Uniform Crime Report," Federal Bureau of Investigation, U.S. Department of Justice, 2007. . . .
9. P. J. Cook and J. Ludwig, *Gun Violence: The Real Costs* (New York: Oxford University Press, 2000): at 113.
10. *Graduate Institute of International Studies, Small Arms Survey 2002: Counting the Human Cost* (Oxford: Oxford University Press, 2002).
11. W. Cukier and V. W. Sidel, *The Global Gun Epidemic* (Westport, CT: Praeger Security International, 2006).
12. See Hepburn et al., *supra* note 4.
13. 18 U.S.C. § 922(b)(1) (2007).
14. 18 U.S.C. § 922(b)(3) (2007).
15. 18 U.S.C. § 922(d) (2007).
16. P. J. Cook, J. Ludwig, and A. A. Braga, "Criminal Records of Homicide Offenders," *JAMA* 294 (2005): 598–601.
17. G. J. Wintemute, C. M. Drake, J. J. Beaumont, M. A. Wright, and C. A. Parrham, "Prior Misdemeanor Convictions as a Risk Factor for Later Violent and Firearm-Related Criminal Activity among Authorized Purchasers of Handguns," *JAMA* 280 (1998): 2083–7.
18. 18 U.S.C. § 923(a) (2007).

19. 18 U.S.C. § 922(t) (2007).
20. P. J. Cook and J. Ludwig, *Guns in America: Results of a Comprehensive National Survey on Firearms Ownership and Use* (Washington, D.C.: Police Executive Research Forum, 1996).
21. 18 U.S.C. § 926(a) (2007).
22. M. Bowling, G. Lauver, M. J. Hickman, and D. B. Adams, *Background Checks for Firearm Transfers,* Office of Justice Programs, Bureau of Justice Statistics, Washington, D.C., U.S. Department of Justice, 2006.
23. J. S. Vernick and D. W. Webster, "Policies to Prevent Firearm Trafficking," *Injury Prevention* 13 (2007): 78–9.
24. Bureau of Alcohol, Tobacco, Firearms and Explosive, *State Laws and Published Ordinances—Firearms,* U.S. Department of Justice, Washington, D.C., 2005.
25. U.S. Constitution, amend. 2.
26. S. Cornell, *A Well-Regulated Militia: The Founding Fathers and the Origins of Gun Control in America* (New York: Oxford University Press, 2007).
27. J. S. Vernick and S. P. Teret, "Firearms and Health: The Right to Be Armed with Accurate Information about the Second Amendment," *American Journal of Public Health* 83 (1993): 1773–77.
28. J. S. Vernick and J. S. Mair, "How the Law Affects Gun Policy in the United States: Law as Intervention or Obstacle to Prevention," *Journal of Law, Medicine & Ethics* 30, no. 4 (2002): 692–704.
29. J. S. Vernick, S. P. Teret, K. A. Howard, M. D. Teret, and G. J. Wintemute, "Public Opinion Polling on Gun Policy," *Health Affairs* 12 (1993): 198–208.
30. Canada Firearms Centre, "Frequently Asked Questions." . . .
31. S. Jacobs, "Toward a More Reasonable Approach to Gun Control: Canada as a Model," *New York Law School Journal of International and Comparative Law* 15 (1995): 315–43.
32. W. Cukier, "Firearms Regulation: Canada in the International Context," *Chronic Diseases in Canada* 19 (1998): 25–34.
33. Graduate Institute of International Studies, *Small Arms Survey 2002: Counting the Human Cost* (Oxford: Oxford University Press, 2002): at 135.
34. See Cook and Ludwig, *supra* note 20.
35. D. A. Brent, J. A. Perper, C. J. Allman, G. M. Moritz, M. E. Wartella, and J. P. Zelenak, "The Presence and Accessibility of Firearms in the Homes of Adolescent Suicides: A Case-Control Study," *JAMA* 266 (1991): 2989–95; A. L. Kellermann, F. P. Rivara, and G. Somes et al., "Suicide in the Home in Relation to Gun Ownership," *New England Journal of Medicine* 327 (1992): 467–72.
36. P. Cummings, T. D. Keopsell, D. C. Grossman, J. Svarion, and R. S. Thompson, "The Association between the Purchase of a Handgun and Homicide or Suicide," *American Journal of Public Health* 87 (1997): 974–78; G. J. Wintemute, C. A. Parham, J. J. Beaumont, M. Wright, and C. Drake, "Mortality among Recent Purchasers of Handguns," *New England Journal of Medicine* 341 (1999): 1583–89.

37. D. J. Wiebe, "Homicide and Suicide Risks Associated with Firearms in the Home: A National Case-Control Study," *Annals of Emergency Medicine* 41 (2003): 771–82.

38. J. C. Campbell, D. Webster, and J. Koziel-McLain et al., "Risk Factors for Femicide in Abusive Relationships: Results from a Multisite Case Control Study," *American Journal of Public Health* 93 (2003): 1089–97.

39. L. E. Saltzman, J. A. Mercy, P. W. O'Carroll, M. L. Rosenberg, and P. H. Rhodes, "Weapon Involvement and Injury Outcomes in Family and Intimate Assaults," *JAMA* 267 (1992): 3043–7.

40. D. J. Wiebe, "Firearms in U.S. Homes as a Risk Factor for Unintentional Gunshot Fatality," *Accident Analysis and Prevention* 35 (2003): 711–16.

41. See National Center for Injury Prevention and Control, Centers for Disease Control and Prevention, *supra* note 5.

42. The phrase has been attributed to science-fiction writer Robert Heinlein. R. A. Heinlein, *Beyond This Horizon* (Riverdale, NY: Baen Books, 2002). It has since been used by those supporting greater access to firearms.

43. J. R. Lott, *More Guns, Less Crime: Understanding Crime and Gun Control Laws* (Chicago: The University of Chicago Press, 2000).

44. J. R. Lott and D. B. Mustard, "Crime, Deterrence, and Right-to-Carry Concealed Handguns," *Journal of Legal Studies* 26 (1997): 1–68.

45. F. Plassman and J. E. Whitley, "Comments: Confirming More Guns, Less Crime," *Stanford Law Review* 55 (2003): 1313–69.

46. D. A. Black and D. S. Nagin, "Do Right-to-Carry Laws Deter Violent Crime?" *Journal of Legal Studies* 27 (1998): 209–19; I. Ayres and J. Donohue, "Shooting Down the More Guns, Less Crime Hypothesis," *Stanford Law Review* 55 (2003): 1194–1312.

47. Committee to Improve Research Information and Data on Firearms, *National Research Council, Firearms and Violence: A Critical Review* (Washington, D.C.: National Academies Press, 2005): at 150.

48. A. M. Gottlieb, *Gun Rights Fact Book* (Bellevue, WA: Merril Press, 1989).

49. A. W. Hoskin, "Armed Americans: The Impact of Firearm Availability on National Homicide Rates," *Justice Quarterly* 18 (2001): 569–92; L. M. Hepburn and D. Hemenway, "Firearm Availability and Homicide: A Review of the Literature," *Aggression and Violent Behavior* 9 (2004): 417–40; D. Hemenway and M. Miller, "Firearm Availability and Homicide Rates across 26 High-Income Countries," *Journal of Trauma* 49 (2000): 985–88.

50. F. E. Zimring and G. Hawkins, *Crime Is Not the Problem: Lethal Violence in America* (New York: Oxford University Press, 1999); D. Hemenway, "The Public Health Approach to Reducing Firearm Injury and Violence," *Stanford Law & Policy Review* 17 (2006): 635–56.

51. E. G. Krug, K. E. Powell, and L. L. Dahlberg, "Firearm-Related Deaths in the United States and 35 Other High- and Upper-Middle-Income Countries," *International Journal of Epidemiology* 27 (1998): 214–21.

52. "Statistics Canada," Statistics Canada Web site. . . .

53. See National Center for Injury Prevention and Control, Centers for Disease Control and Prevention, *supra* note 5.

54. M. Miller, D. Azrael, and D. Hemenway, "Rates of Household Firearm Ownership and Homicide across U.S. Regions and States, 1988–1997," *American Journal of Public Health* 92 (2002): 1988–1993; M. Miller, D. Azrael, and D. Hemenway, "Household Firearm Ownership and Suicide Rates in the United States," *Epidemiology* 13 (2002): 517–24; M. Miller, S. J. Lippmann, D. Azrael, and D. Hemenway, "Household Firearm Ownership and Rates of Suicide across the 50 United States," *Journal of Trauma* 62 (2007): 1029–35; D. Miller, D. Azrael, and D. Hemenway, "Firearm Availability and Unintentional Firearm Deaths, Suicide, and Homicide among 5–14 Year Olds," *Journal of Trauma* 52 (2002): 267–75.
55. D. W. Webster, J. S. Vernick, and M. T. Bulzacchelli, *Association Between Regulations and Oversight of Firearm Dealers and Gun Trafficking*, paper to be presented at the Annual Meeting of the American Society of Criminology, Atlanta, Georgia, November 2007; D. W. Webster, J. S. Vernick, and L. M. Hepburn, "The Relationship between Licensing, Registration and Other State Gun Sales Laws and the Source State of Crime Guns," *Injury Prevention* 7 (2001): 184–89.
56. See Cook and Ludwig, *supra* note 20.
57. P. J. Cook and J. Ludwig, "Guns and Burglary," in P. J. Cook and J. Ludwig, eds., *Evaluating Gun Policy: Effects on Crime and Violence* (Washington, D.C.: Brookings Institution Press, 2003): 74–118.
58. A. J. Reiss and J. A. Roth, eds., *Understanding and Preventing Violence* (Washington, D.C.: National Academy Press, 1993).
59. P. J. Cook and J. Ludwig, *Gun Violence: The Real Costs* (New York: Oxford University Press, 2000): at 115.
60. T. L. Beauchamp and J. F. Childress, *Principles of Biomedical Ethics*, 4th ed. (New York: Oxford University Press, 1994): at 327.
61. We use the term "right" in this context to refer to ethical, not legal or constitutional, conceptions of "rights."
62. H. La Follette, "Gun Control," *Ethics* 110 (2000): 263–81.
63. M. Boylan, "Gun Control in the United States: Ethical Perspective for the Twenty-First Century," *Clinical Orthopaedics and Related Research* 408 (2003): 17–27.
64. See Beauchamp and Childress, *supra* note 68, at 288–91.
65. L. O. Gostin, *Public Health Law: Power, Duty, Restraint* (Berkeley: University of California Press, 2000): at 88.
66. R. M. Veatch, *The Basics of Bioethics: Second Edition* (New Jersey: Prentice Hall, 2003): at 12.
67. L. Turner, "Bioethics, Public Health, and Firearm-Related Violence: Missing Links between Bioethics and Public Health," *Journal of Law, Medicine & Ethics* 25, no. 1 (1997): 42–8.
68. See Beauchamp and Childress, *supra* note 74, at 126.
69. See Gostin, *supra* note 65, at 88.
70. J. G. Hodge and L. O. Gostin, "Legal Methods," in J. Sugarman and D. P. Sulmasy, eds., *Methods in Medical Ethics* (Washington, D.C.: Georgetown University Press, 2001): 88–103.

71. See *supra* notes 49 to 53 and accompanying text.
72. See *supra* note 54 and accompanying text.
73. S. P. Teret, D. W. Webster, and J. S. Vernick et al., "Public Support for Innovative Gun Policies: The Results of Two National Surveys," *New England Journal of Medicine* 339 (1998): 813–8.
74. A. C. Gielen, K. A. McDonnell, P. J. O'Campo, and J. G. Burke, "Suicide Risk and Mental Health Indicators: Do They Differ by Abuse and HIV Status?" *Women's Health Issues* 15 (2005): 89–95.
75. See *supra* notes 35 and 40 and accompanying text.
76. See Beauchamp and Childress, *supra* note 60, at 288–91.
77. N. E. Kass, "An Ethics Framework for Public Health," *American Journal of Public Health* 91 (2001): 1776–82.
78. M. Powers and R. Faden, *Social Justice* (New York: Oxford University Press, 2006): at 9.
79. *Id.*, at 10.
80. See Beauchamp and Childress, *supra* note 60, at 288–91.
81. A. J. Reiss and J. A. Roth, eds., *Understanding and Preventing Violence* (Washington, D.C.: National Academy Press, 1993).
82. See National Center for Injury Prevention and Control, Centers for Disease Control and Prevention, *supra* note 5.

Daniel D. Polsby

The False Promise of Gun Control

During the 1960s and 1970s the robbery rate in the United States increased sixfold, and the murder rate doubled; the rate of handgun ownership nearly doubled in that period as well. Handguns and criminal violence grew together apace, and national opinion leaders did not fail to remark on the coincidence.

It has become a bipartisan article of faith that more handguns cause more violence. Such was the unequivocal conclusion of the National Commission on the Causes and Prevention of Violence in 1969, and such is now the editorial opinion of virtually every influential newspaper and magazine, from *The Washington Post* to *The Economist* to the *Chicago Tribune*. Members of the House and Senate who have not dared to confront the gun lobby concede the connection privately. Even if the National Rifle Association can produce blizzards of angry calls and letters to the Capitol virtually overnight, House members one by one have been going public, often after some new firearms atrocity at a fast-food restaurant or the like. And [in] November [1993] they passed the Brady bill.

Alas, however well accepted, the conventional wisdom about guns and violence is mistaken. Guns don't increase national rates of crime and violence—but the continued proliferation of gun-control laws almost certainly does. Current rates of crime and violence are a bit below the peaks of the late 1970s. . . . The rising generation of criminals will have no more difficulty than their elders did in obtaining the tools of their trade. Growing violence will lead to calls for laws still more severe. Each fresh round of legislation will be followed by renewed frustration.

Gun-control laws don't work. What is worse, they act perversely. While legitimate users of firearms encounter intense regulation, scrutiny, and bureaucratic control, illicit markets easily adapt to whatever difficulties a free society throws in their way. Also, efforts to curtail the supply of firearms inflict collateral damage on freedom and privacy interests that have long been considered central to American public life. Thanks to the seemingly never-ending war on drugs and long experience attempting to suppress prostitution and pornography, we know a great deal about how illicit markets function and how costly to the public attempts to control them can be. It is essential that we make use of this experience in coming to grips with gun control.

From *The Atlantic Monthly,* March 1994, pp. 57–60, 62–64, 68–70. Copyright © 1994 by Daniel D. Polsby. Reprinted by permission of Daniel D. Polsby.

The thousands of gun-control laws in the United States are of two general types. The older kind sought to regulate how, where, and by whom firearms could be carried. More recent laws have sought to make it more costly to buy, sell, or use firearms (or certain classes of firearms, such as assault rifles, Saturday-night specials, and so on) by imposing fees, special taxes, or surtaxes on them. The Brady bill is of both types: it has a background-check provision, and its five-day waiting period amounts to a "time tax" on acquiring handguns. All such laws can be called scarcity-inducing, because they seek to raise the cost of buying firearms, as figured in terms of money, time, nuisance, or stigmatization.

Despite the mounting number of scarcity-inducing laws, no one is very satisfied with them. Hobbyists want to get rid of them, and gun-control proponents don't think they go nearly far enough. Everyone seems to agree that gun-control laws have some effect on the distribution of firearms. But it has not been the dramatic and measurable effect their proponents desired.

Opponents of gun control have traditionally wrapped their arguments in the Second Amendment to the Constitution. Indeed, most modern scholarship affirms that so far as the drafters of the Bill of Rights were concerned, the right to bear arms was to be enjoyed by everyone, not just a militia, and that one of the principal justifications for an armed populace was to secure the tranquillity and good order of the community. But most people are not dedicated antiquitarians, and would not be impressed by the argument "I admit that my behavior is very dangerous to public safety, but the Second Amendment says I have a right to do it anyway." That would be a case for repealing the Second Amendment, not respecting it.

Fighting the Demand Curve

Everyone knows that possessing a handgun makes it easier to intimidate, wound, or kill someone. But the implication of this point for social policy has not been so well understood. It is easy to count the bodies of those who have been killed or wounded with guns, but not easy to count the people who have avoided harm because they had access to weapons. Think about uniformed police officers, who carry handguns in plain view not in order to kill people but simply to daunt potential attackers. And it works. Criminals generally do not single out police officers for opportunistic attack. Though officers can expect to draw their guns from time to time, few even in big-city departments will actually fire a shot (except in target practice) in the course of a year. This observation points to an important truth: people who are armed make comparatively unattractive victims. A criminal might not know if any one civilian is armed, but if it becomes known that a large number of civilians do carry weapons, criminals will become warier.

Which weapons laws are the right kinds can be decided only after considering two related questions. First, what is the connection between civilian possession of firearms and social violence? Second, how can we expect gun-control laws to alter people's behavior? Most recent scholarship raises serious questions about the "weapons increase violence" hypothesis. The second question is emphasized here, because it is routinely overlooked and often mocked when noticed; yet it is crucial. Rational gun control requires understanding not only the relationship between weapons and violence but also the relationship between laws and people's behavior. Some things are very hard to accomplish with laws. The purpose of a law and its likely effects are not always the same thing. Many statutes are notorious for the way in which their unintended effects have swamped their intended ones.

In order to predict who will comply with gun-control laws, we should remember that guns are economic goods that are traded in markets. Consumers' interest in them varies. For religious, moral, aesthetic, or practical reasons, some people would refuse to buy firearms at any price. Other people willingly pay very high prices for them.

Handguns, so often the subject of gun-control laws, are desirable for one purpose—to allow a person tactically to dominate a hostile transaction with another person. The value of a weapon to a given person is a function of two factors: how much he or she wants to dominate a confrontation if one occurs, and how likely it is that he or she will actually be in a situation calling for a gun.

Dominating a transaction simply means getting what one wants without being hurt. Where people differ is in how likely it is that they will be involved in a situation in which a gun will be valuable. Someone who *intends* to engage in a transaction involving a gun—a criminal, for example—is obviously in the best possible position to predict that likelihood. Criminals should therefore be willing to pay more for a weapon than most other people would. Professors, politicians, and newspaper editors are, as a group, at very low risk of being involved in such transactions, and they thus systematically underrate the value of defensive handguns. (Correlative, perhaps, is their uncritical readiness to accept studies that debunk the utility of firearms for self-defense.) The class of people we wish to deprive of guns, then, is the very class with the most inelastic demand for them—criminals—whereas the people most likely to comply with gun-control laws don't value guns in the first place.

Do Guns Drive Up Crime Rates?

Which premise is true—that guns increase crime or that the fear of crime causes people to obtain guns? . . .

If firearms increased violence and crime, then rates of spousal homicide would have skyrocketed, because the stock of privately owned handguns has increased rapidly since the mid-1960s. But according to an authoritative study of spousal homicide in the *American Journal of Public Health,* by James Mercy and Linda Saltzman, rates of spousal homicide in the years 1976 to 1985 fell. If firearms increased violence and crime, the crime rate should have increased throughout the 1980s, while the national stock of privately owned handguns increased by more than a million units in every year of the decade. It did not. Nor should the rates of violence and crime in Switzerland, New Zealand, and Israel be as low as they are, since the number of firearms per civilian household is comparable to that in the United States. Conversely, gun-controlled Mexico and South Africa should be islands of peace instead of having murder rates more than twice as high as those here. The determinants of crime and law-abidingness are, of course, complex matters, which are not fully understood and certainly not explicable in terms of a country's laws. But gun-control enthusiasts, who have made capital out of the low murder rate in England, which is largely disarmed, simply ignore the counterexamples that don't fit their theory.

If firearms increased violence and crime, Florida's murder rate should not have been falling since the introduction . . . of a law that makes it easier for ordinary citizens to get permits to carry concealed handguns. Yet the murder rate has remained the same or fallen every year since the law was enacted, and it is now lower than the national murder rate (which has been rising). As of November [1993] 183,561 permits had been issued, and only seventeen of the permits had been revoked because the holder was involved in a firearms offense. It would be precipitate to claim that the new law has "caused" the murder rate to subside. Yet here is a situation that doesn't fit the hypothesis that weapons increase violence.

If firearms increased violence and crime, programs of induced scarcity would suppress violence and crime. But—another anomaly—they don't. Why not? A theorem, which we could call the futility theorem, explains why gun-control laws must either be ineffectual or in the long term actually provoke more violence and crime. Any theorem depends on both observable fact and assumption. An assumption that can be made with confidence is that the higher the number of victims a criminal assumes to be armed, the higher will be the risk—the price—of assaulting them. By definition, gun-control laws should make weapons scarcer and thus more expensive. By our prior reasoning about demand among various types of consumers, after the laws are enacted criminals should be better armed, compared with noncriminals, than they were before. Of course, plenty of noncriminals will remain armed. But even if many noncriminals will pay as high a price as criminals will to obtain firearms, a larger number will not.

Criminals will thus still take the same gamble they already take in assaulting a victim who might or might not be armed. But they may appreciate that the laws have given them a freer field, and that crime still pays—pays even better, in fact, than before. What will happen to the rate of violence? Only a relatively few gun-mediated transactions—currently, five percent of armed robberies committed with firearms—result in someone's actually being shot (the statistics are not broken down into encounters between armed assailants and unarmed victims, and encounters in which both parties are armed). It seems reasonable to fear that if the number of such transactions were to increase because criminals thought they faced fewer deterrents, there would be a corresponding increase in shootings. Conversely, if gun-mediated transactions declined—if criminals initiated fewer of them because they feared encountering an armed victim or an armed good Samaritan—the number of shootings would go down. The magnitude of these effects is, admittedly, uncertain. Yet it is hard to doubt the general tendency of a change in the law that imposes legal burdens on buying guns. The futility theorem suggests that gun-control laws, if effective at all, would unfavorably affect the rate of violent crime. . . .

Are there empirical studies that can serve to help us choose between the futility theorem and the hypothesis that guns increase violence? Unfortunately, no: the best studies of the effects of gun-control laws are quite inconclusive. Our statistical tools are too weak to allow us to identify an effect clearly enough to persuade an open-minded skeptic. But it is precisely when we are dealing with undetectable statistical effects that we have to be certain we are using the best models available of human behavior.

Sealing the Border

Handguns are not legally for sale in the city of Chicago, and have not been since April of 1982. Rifles, shotguns, and ammunition are available, but only to people who possess an Illinois Firearm Owner's Identification [FOID] card. It takes up to a month to get this card, which involves a background check. Even if one has a FOID card there is a waiting period for the delivery of a gun. In few places in America is it as difficult to get a firearm legally as in the city of Chicago.

Yet there are hundreds of thousands of unregistered guns in the city, and new ones arriving all the time. It is not difficult to get handguns—even legally. Chicago residents with FOID cards merely go to gun shops in the suburbs. Trying to establish a city as an island of prohibition in a sea of legal firearms seems an impossible project.

Is a state large enough to be an effective island, then? Suppose Illinois adopted Chicago's handgun ban. Same problem again. Some people could just get guns elsewhere: Indiana actually borders the city, and Wisconsin is only forty miles away. Though federal law prohibits the sale of handguns in one state to residents of another, thousands of Chicagoans with summer homes in other states could buy handguns there. And, of course, a black market would serve the needs of other customers.

When would the island be large enough to sustain a weapons-free environment? In the United States people and cargoes move across state lines without supervision or hindrance. Local shortages of goods are always transient, no matter whether the shortage is induced by natural disasters, prohibitory laws, or something else.

Even if many states outlawed sales of handguns, then, they would continue to be available, albeit at a somewhat higher price, reflecting the increased legal risk of selling them. Mindful of the way markets work to undermine their efforts, gun-control proponents press for federal regulation of firearms, because they believe that only Congress wields the authority to frustrate the interstate movement of firearms.

Why, though, would one think that federal policing of illegal firearms would be better than local policing? The logic of that argument is far from clear. Cities, after all, are comparatively small places. Washington, D.C., for example, has an area of less than 45,000 acres. Yet local officers have had little luck repressing the illegal firearms trade there. Why should federal officers do any better watching the United States' 12,000 miles of coastline and millions of square miles of interior? Criminals should be able to frustrate federal police forces just as well as they can local ones. Ten years of increasingly stringent federal efforts to abate cocaine trafficking, for example, have not succeeded in raising the street price of the drug. . . .

In firearms regulation, translating theory into practice will continue to be difficult, at least if the objective is to lessen the practical availability of firearms to people who might abuse them. On the demand side, for defending oneself against predation there is no substitute for a firearm. Criminals, at least, can switch to varieties of law-breaking in which a gun confers little or no advantage (burglary, smash-and-grab), but people who are afraid of confrontations with criminals, whether rationally or (as an accountant might reckon it) irrationally, will be very highly motivated to acquire firearms. . . . [P]eople's demand for personal security and for the tools they believe provide it will remain strong.

On the supply side, firearms transactions can be consummated behind closed doors. Firearms buyers, unlike those who use drugs, pornography, or prostitution, need not recurrently expose themselves to legal jeopardy. One trip to the marketplace is enough to arm oneself for life. This could justify a consumer's taking even greater precautions to avoid apprehension, which would translate into even steeper enforcement costs for the police. . . .

Administering Prohibition

. . . Unless people are prepared to surrender their guns voluntarily, how can the U.S. government confiscate an appreciable fraction of our country's nearly 200 million privately owned firearms? We know that it is possible to set up weapons-free zones in certain locations—commercial airports and many courthouses and, lately, some troubled big city high schools and housing projects. The sacrifices of privacy and convenience, and the costs of paying guards, have been thought worth the (perceived) gain in security. No doubt it would be possible, though it would probably not be easy, to make weapons-free zones of shopping centers, department stores, movie theaters, ball parks. But it is not obvious how one would cordon off the whole of an open society.

Voluntary programs have been ineffectual. From time to time community-action groups or police departments have sponsored "turn in your gun" days, which are nearly always disappointing. Sometimes the government offers to buy guns at some price. . . . If the price offered exceeds that at which a gun can be bought on the street, one can expect to see plans of this kind yield some sort of harvest—as indeed they have. But it is implausible that these schemes will actually result in a less-dangerous population. Government programs to buy up surplus cheese cause more cheese to be produced without affecting the availability of cheese to people who want to buy it. So it is with guns.

One could extend the concept of intermittent roadblocks of the sort approved by the Supreme Court for discouraging drunk driving. Metal detectors could be positioned on every street corner, or ambulatory metal-detector squads could check people randomly, or hidden magnetometers could be installed around towns, to detect concealed weapons. As for firearms kept in homes (about half of American households), warrantless searches might be rationalized on the well-established theory that probable cause is not required when authorities are trying to correct dangers to public safety rather than searching for evidence of a crime. . . .

Ignoring the Ultimate Sources of Crime and Violence

The American experience with prohibition has been that black marketeers—often professional criminals—move in to profit when legal markets are closed down or disturbed. In order to combat them, new laws and law-enforcement techniques are developed, which are circumvented almost as soon as they are put in place. New and yet more stringent laws are enacted, and greater sacrifices of civil liberties and privacy demanded and submitted to. But in this case the problem, crime and violence, will not go away, because guns and ammunition (which, of course, won't go away either) do not cause it. One cannot expect people to quit seeking new weapons as long as the tactical advantages of weapons are seen to outweigh the costs imposed by prohibition. Nor can one expect large numbers of people to surrender firearms they already own. The only way to make people give up their guns is to create a world in which guns are perceived as having little value. This world will come into being when criminals choose not to use guns because the penalties for being caught with them are too great, and when ordinary citizens don't think they need firearms because they aren't afraid of criminals anymore.

Neither of these eventualities seems very likely without substantial departures in law-enforcement policy. Politicians' nostrums—increasing the punishment for crime, slapping a few more death-penalty provisions into the code—are taken seriously by few students of the crime problem. The existing penalties for predatory crimes are quite severe enough. The problem is that they are rarely meted out in the real world. The penalties formally published by the code are in practice steeply discounted, and criminals recognize that the judicial and penal systems cannot function without bargaining in the vast majority of cases.

This problem is not obviously one that legislation could solve. . . .

The problem is not simply that criminals pay little attention to the punishments in the books. Nor is it even that they also know that for the majority of crimes, their chances of being arrested are small. The most important reason for criminal behavior is this: the income that offenders can earn in the world of crime, as compared with the world of work, all too often makes crime appear to be the better choice.

. . . More prisons means that fewer violent offenders will have to be released early in order to make space for new arrivals; perhaps fewer plea bargains will have to be struck—all to the good. Yet a moment's reflection should make clear that one more criminal locked up does not necessarily mean one less criminal on the street. The situation is very like one that conservationists and hunters have always understood. Populations of game animals readily recover from hunting seasons but not from loss of habitat. Mean streets, when there are few legitimate entry level opportunities for young men, are a criminal habitat, so to speak, in the social ecology of modern American cities. Cull however much one will, the habitat will be reoccupied promptly after its previous occupant is sent away. So social science has found.

Similarly, whereas increasing the number of police officers cannot hurt, and may well increase people's subjective feelings of security, there is little evidence to suggest that doing so will diminish the rate of crime. Police forces are basically reactive institutions. . . .

There is a challenge here that is quite beyond being met with tough talk. Most public officials can see the mismatch between their tax base and the social entropies they are being asked to repair. There simply isn't enough money; existing public resources, as they are now employed, cannot possibly solve the crime problem. But mayors and senators and police chiefs must not say so out loud: too-disquieting implications would follow. For if the authorities are incapable of restoring public safety and personal security under the existing ground rules, then obviously the ground rules must change. . . .

Communities must, in short, organize more effectively to protect themselves against predators. No doubt this means encouraging properly qualified private citizens to possess and carry firearms legally. It is not morally tenable—nor, for that matter, is it even practical—to insist that police officers, few of whom are at a risk remotely as great as are the residents of many city neighborhoods, retain a monopoly on legal firearms. It is needless to fear giving honest men and women the training and equipment to make it possible for them to take back their own streets.

Over the long run, however, there is no substitute for addressing the root causes of crime—bad education and lack of job opportunities and the disintegration of families. Root causes are much out of fashion nowadays as explanations of criminal behavior, but fashionable or not, they are fundamental. *The root cause of crime is that for certain people, predation is a rational occupational choice.* Conventional crime-control measures, which by stiffening punishments or raising the probability of arrest aim to make crime pay less, cannot consistently affect the behavior of people who believe that their alternatives to crime will pay virtually nothing. Young men who did not learn basic literacy and numeracy skills before dropping out of their wretched public schools may not [be] worth hiring at the minimum wage. . . . Their legitimate opportunities, always precarious in a society where race and class still matter, often diminish to the point of being for all intents and purposes absent. . . .

The solution to the problem of crime lies in improving the chances of young men. Easier said than done, to be sure. No one has yet proposed a convincing program for checking all the dislocating forces that government assistance can set in motion. One relatively straightforward change would be reform of the educational system. Nothing guarantees prudent behavior like a sense of the future, and with average skills in reading, writing, and math, young people can realistically look forward to constructive employment and the straight life that steady work makes possible.

But firearms are nowhere near the root of the problem of violence. As long as people come in unlike sizes, shapes, ages, and temperaments, as long as they diverge in their taste for risk and their willingness and capacity to prey on other people or to defend themselves from predation, and above all as long as some people have little or nothing to lose by spending their lives in crime, dispositions to violence will persist.

This is what makes the case for the right to bear arms, not the Second Amendment. It is foolish to let anything ride on hopes for effective gun control. As long as crime pays as well as it does, we will have plenty of it, and honest folk must choose between being victims and defending themselves.

POSTSCRIPT

Should Licensing for Handguns Be More Restrictive?

Vernick, Hodge, and Webster argue that there are good public health reasons to make licenses for handguns more restrictive. But we must also consider whether there are equally good reasons *not* to do so. Polsby considers, for example, the idea that handguns are a useful part of self-defense. But Vernick, Hodge, and Webster maintain that it is often only the psychological *feeling* of safety that gun owners may possess, not the reality. Certainly there are cases in which one's assailant takes away one's gun, cases in which one causes damage (or even death) accidentally—so one isn't so safe after all—but there must also be cases in which handguns serve the self-defense purpose that many people say is their original reason for purchasing a handgun in the first place. Moreover, it is very hard, if not impossible, to get a good count of these self-defense cases. For one thing, the very fact that one is armed may provide the self-defense that is needed; it may not be necessary to actually use the gun. The gun's effectiveness in achieving self-defense may not rise to the attention of others, but if you accidentally shoot a family member and he goes to the emergency room, there will be reports to be filed, and doctors and police and maybe journalists who also know of this accident. Successful self-defense, on the other hand, although it *can* be dramatic, *need not* involve drama, the emergency room, or the police.

This same argument can also be used with regard to the effectiveness of gun control laws. Those laws didn't stop Cho Seung-Hui from buying the weapons he used at Virginia Tech, and they certainly don't keep burglars and other criminals from illegally getting hold of a gun either by stealing it from a licensed gun-owner or by buying it from another criminal. But such laws and regulations must *sometimes* work. We just can't get a reliable count of the cases in which they *do* work; sometimes at least, those who have been deemed a danger to themselves or others are actually caught and successfully screened out. Some individuals won't even attempt to go through the screening process because they know that their felony conviction will be sure to come to light. And—Vernick, Lodge, and Webster suggest—if restrictions are tighter, there will be fewer handguns in circulation for criminals to steal.

It seems that some amount of speculation is necessary to both the "pro" and the "con" side here. *Will* tighter restrictions on the purchase of handguns bring about greater positive result? Will it only make matters worse? Since we can't run experiments on this, it is useful to have the comparison with Canada.

Polsby takes a position that is rather unusual for opponents of gun control. He emphasizes that the root cause of crime lies in social conditions such as the breakdown of families, poor schooling, and lack of occupational opportunities—especially in the case of young men. According to his view, these are social conditions that have to be addressed, possibly in the form of social programs. It is here, he suggests—and not in laws and regulations about guns—that we can come to grips with the real problems. Polsby goes so far as to say that, for certain people, the decision to prey on others (and, presumably, use a handgun in order to facilitate their preying) is a *rational* one. That is, given the facts of their situation, using a handgun and committing crimes may be a more rational thing for them to do than to seek a minimum-wage job—which, realistically, they may never even be able to find.

The problem of guns and violent crime is immense, and many-sided. Recent publications that deal with the matter of gun control, gun rights, and gun ownership are John R. Lott, Jr., *More Guns, Less Crime: Understanding Crime and Gun-Control Laws* (University of Chicago Press, 1998); Philip J. Cook and Jens Ludwig, *Gun Violence: The Real Costs* (Oxford University Press, 2002); Richard Poe, *The Seven Myths of Gun Control: Reclaiming the Truth About Guns, Crime, and the Second Amendment* (Three Rivers Press, 2003); Wayne LaPierre, *Guns, Freedom, and Terrorism* (WND Books, 2003); Kristen A. Goss, *Disarmed: The Missing Movement for Gun Control in America* (Princeton University Press, 2006); and Mark V. Tushnet, *Out of Range: Why the Constitution Can't End the Battle over Guns* (Oxford University Press, 2007). A book that gives a Canadian view is Gregory W. McClinchey, *Stickin' to His Guns: A Through-the-Keyhole Look at Mr. Paul Daniel Steckle* (iUniverse-Indigo, 2007).

ISSUE 13

Should the Death Penalty Be Abolished?

YES: Michael Welch, from *Punishment in America: Social Control and the Ironies of Imprisonment* (Sage, 1999)

NO: Ernest van den Haag, from "The Death Penalty Once More," *U.C. Davis Law Review* (Summer 1985)

ISSUE SUMMARY

YES: Criminologist Michael Welch argues that the death penalty encourages murder and is applied in a biased and mistake-laden way to growing groups of people. Much of the recent popular support of capital punishment is due to ignorance of the facts.

NO: Professor of law Ernest van den Haag argues that the death penalty is entirely in line with the U.S. Constitution and that although studies of its deterrent effect are inconclusive, the death penalty is morally justified and should not be abolished.

Since punishment involves the intentional infliction of harm upon another person, and since the intentional infliction of harm is generally wrong, the idea of punishment itself is somewhat problematic. Punishment requires some strong rationale if it is not to be just another form of wrongdoing; capital punishment requires an especially strong rationale.

Consider some actual cases of capital punishment: Socrates was tried in ancient Athens and condemned to die (by drinking poison) for not believing in the gods of the state and for corrupting young people. In 1977 a princess and her lover were executed (by firing squad and beheading, respectively) in Saudi Arabia for adultery. Also in 1977 Gary Gilmore insisted that he receive the death penalty and was executed by a firing squad in Utah for murder.

Justification for capital punishment usually comes down to one of two different lines of reasoning. One is based on the idea of justice, the other on the idea of deterrence.

Justice, it is said, demands that certain criminal acts be paid for by death. The idea is that some people deserve death and have to pay for their criminal acts with their lives.

There are several objections to this view. One of the most important of these focuses on the idea of a person "paying" for a crime by death (or even in some other way). What concept of "paying" is being used here? It does not seem like an ordinary case of paying a debt. It seems to be a kind of vengeance, as when one person says to another "I'll make you pay for that," meaning "I'll make you suffer for that." Yet one of the ideas behind state-inflicted punishment is that it is supposed to be very official, even bureaucratic, and it is designed to eliminate private vendettas and personal vindictiveness. The state, in a civilized society, is not supposed to be motivated by revenge or vindictiveness. The state's only intent is to support law and order and to protect its citizens from coming to harm at the hands of wrongdoers.

The other major line of reasoning in support of capital punishment is based on the idea of deterrence. According to this view, capital punishment must be retained in order to deter criminals and potential criminals from committing capital crimes. An old joke reflects this view: A Texan tells a visitor that in the old days the local punishment for horse-stealing was hanging. The visitor is shocked. "You used to hang people just for taking horses?" "Nope," says the Texan, "horses never got stolen."

Unlike the argument about "paying," the logic behind deterrence is supposed to be intuitively easy to understand. However, assertions concerning deterrence do not seem to be clearly borne out by actual statistics and empirical evidence.

Your intuition may support the judgment that the death penalty deters crime, but the empirical evidence is not similarly uniform and clear, and in some cases the evidence even points to the opposite conclusion. (For example, some people may be more likely to murder an innocent victim if they are reasonably certain of achieving their own death and perhaps some notoriety.) Or consider the example of the failure of deterrence that occurred in England when public hanging was the punishment for the crime of pickpocketing. Professional pickpockets, undeterred by the activity on the gallows, circulated among the crowd of spectators, aware that a good time to pick pockets was when everyone's attention was focused on something else—in this case, when the rope tightened around the neck of the convicted pickpocket.

Further thought about this matter of deterrence raises more questions. Consider this scenario: Two men get into an argument while drinking, and one pulls a gun and shoots the other, who dies. Do we suppose that this killer is even aware of the punishment for murder when he acts? Would he be deterred by the prospect of capital punishment but be willing to shoot if the punishment were only 20 years or life in prison?

In the following selection, Michael Welch argues for the abolition of the death penalty. He refers to its brutalizing effects and to a host of difficulties involving who actually receives the punishment. Then Ernest van den Haag argues against its abolition, discussing the constitutionality, possible deterrent effect, and moral justification of the death penalty.

YES

Michael Welch

The Machinery of Death: Capital Punishment and the Ironies of Social Control

Mechanical terms abound in criminal justice, connoting efficiency, stability, and equilibrium. Consider, for instance, the depiction of criminal justice as a *system* with law *enforcement*. Even critics rely on mechanical metaphors while describing criminal justice as a social control *apparatus* whose *mechanisms* function as *tools* of the ruling class (Lynch & Groves, 1989; Welch, 1996a, 1996b). Contributing to this lexicon, Justice Harry A. Blackmun referred to capital punishment as a *machinery* of death (also see Harlow, Matas, & Rocamora, 1995). The momentum behind executions has increased dramatically since the late 1970s due to several social forces, including political pandering to—and manipulation of—public opinion, the expansion of capital crimes, and the reduction of appeals, which hastens executions. . . .

The efficiency of the machinery of death has been streamlined recently in accordance with the principles of Frederick Taylor's "scientific management."[1] For example, in Arkansas, a triple execution was carried out in 1997 (the second of its kind since capital punishment was resumed). It has been said by prison officials that "such multiple executions minimize overtime costs and reduce stress on prison employees" (Kuntz, 1997, p. E-7). . . .

Although the death penalty is portrayed by its supporters as a precise, reliable, and necessary armament of criminal justice, in reality this machinery of death has proven to be imprecise, unreliable, and reckless. Opponents criticize capital punishment for perpetuating injustice because it is fraught with errors, contradictions, and various ironies. . . . [Here,] we apply Marx's (1981) notions of escalation, nonenforcement, and covert facilitation to capital punishment to illuminate its contradictions. In addition to exploring how the machinery of death produces counterdeterrent effects, creates new categories of violators and victims, and falsely convicts the innocent, we shall remain mindful of the significance of racism and classism in shaping the patterns of executions.

Escalation

. . . [Escalation] implies that "by taking enforcement action, authorities unintentionally encourage rule breaking" (Marx, 1981, p. 222). In this analysis of capital punishment, murder is one type of rule breaking we shall examine;

From *Punishment in America: Social Control and the Ironies of Imprisonment* by Michael F. Welch, 1999, pp. 159–186 (excerpts). Copyright © 1999 by Sage Publications. Reprinted by permission via Copyright Clearance Center.

thus, it is argued that executions not only fail to deter homicide but, ironically, promote violence. To support this claim, there is an emerging body of research documenting that capital punishment may indeed have counterdeterrent effects.

Brutalization Versus Deterrence

Despite the volume of empirical studies demonstrating that there is *no* conclusive evidence linking deterrence with capital punishment, the myth persists. Walker (1994) characterized the myth of deterrence as a crime control theology, a belief that resembles a religious conviction more than an intellectual position because it rests on faith rather than on facts. But the issue is not whether the death penalty offers greater deterrence than no penalty at all—of course it does. Rather, the issue is whether the death penalty deters more than other severe penalties, such as life imprisonment without parole. . . .

Proponents of deterrence theory argue that publicizing executions is a necessary component of capital punishment because it is through such publicity that the tough "law and order" message of death sentences is widely communicated. Conversely, a competing theory about publicized executions has challenged the notion of deterrence. Brutalization theory suggests that publicized executions not only fail to deter violence but, paradoxically, increase it. To appreciate fully brutalization theory, we must deconstruct the central element of deterrence theory, namely the assumption that potential killers are restrained from committing murder because they *identify* with those who have been executed. Brutalization theory suggests that *some* persons, rather than identifying with the condemned, identify with the executioner (Bowers & Pierce, 1980). It is crucial here to return to the principal message inherent in capital punishment: Those who commit heinous crimes *deserve* to die. Supporting this perspective, advocates of the death penalty view executions as a "public service" performed by the state, ridding society of its despicable members.

According to brutalization theory, however, publicized executions create an *alternative identification process* that promotes imitation, not deterrence. Bowers and Pierce (1980) found an increase in homicides soon after well-publicized executions, suggesting that some murderers liken their victims to the condemned. This finding was presented as evidence of a counterdeterrent effect (also see Bailey, 1983, 1998; Bowers, 1988; Cochran, Chamlin, & Seth, 1994; Decker & Kohfeld, 1990; Forst, 1983; King, 1978). It is important to emphasize that Bowers and Pierce specified that the brutalization effect has an impact on individuals who are prone to violence, not persons who are generally nonviolent; in such cases, the publicized execution reinforces the belief that lethal vengeance is justified. Executions devalue human life and "demonstrate that it is appropriate to kill those who have gravely offended us" (Bowers & Pierce, 1980, p. 456). In the context of social control, evidence engendered by brutalization studies supports the claim that capital punishment produces an ironic and escalating effect by promoting, rather than deterring, murder.

The Creation of New Categories and Net Widening

. . .

Juvenile Offenders

Increasingly, the application of the death penalty has expanded to include juveniles. Although eight states do not specify a minimum age at which the death penalty may be imposed, 14 states and the federal system require a minimum age of 18, and 16 states indicate an age of eligibility between 14 and 17 (Snell, 1996; see Table 1). In 1997, California Governor Pete Wilson reported

Table 1

Minimum Age Authorized for Capital Punishment, 1996

Age 16 or Less	Age 17	Age 18	None Specified
Alabama (16)	Georgia	California	Arizona
Arkansas (14)[a]	New Hampshire	Colorado	Idaho
Delaware (16)	North Carolina[b]	Connecticut[c]	Montana
Florida (16)	Texas	Federal system	Louisiana
Indiana (16)		Illinois	Pennsylvania
Kentucky (16)		Kansas	South Carolina
Mississippi (16)[d]		Maryland	South Dakota[e]
Missouri (16)		Nebraska	Utah
Nevada (16)		New Jersey	
Oklahoma (16)		New Mexico	
Virginia (14)[f]		New York	
Wyoming (16)		Ohio	
		Oregon	
		Tennessee	
		Washington	

Source: Snell (1997, p. 5).

Note: Reporting by states reflects interpretations by state attorney general offices and may differ from previously reported ages.

a. See Arkansas Code Ann. 9-27-318(b)(1)(Repl. 1991).

b. The age required is 17 unless the murderer was incarcerated for murder when a subsequent murder occurred; then the age may be 14.

c. See Conn. Gen. Stat. 53a-46a(g)(1).

d. The minimum age defined by statute is 13, but the effective age is 16, based on a Mississippi Supreme Court decision.

e. Juveniles may be transferred to adult court. Age can be a mitigating factor.

f. The minimum age for transfer to adult court is 14 by statute, but the effective age for a capital sentence is 16, based on interpretation of a U.S. Supreme Court decision by the state attorney general's office.

that he would consider a state law allowing executions of 14-year olds, and Cruz M. Bustamante said he might support executions for "hardened criminals" as young as 13 (Verhovek, 1998, p. A-7). Texas State Representative Jim Pitts in 1998 proposed the death penalty for 11-year-old killers. Pitts reasoned: "This is a drastic step. . . . But some of the kids are growing up today, they just aren't the 'Leave it to Beaver' kids that I grew up with" (Verhovek, 1998, p. A-7). Reacting to the 1998 Arkansas schoolyard killings, Pitts argued that the state needs to "send a message to our kids that they can't do these kinds of crimes"(Verhovek, 1998, p. A-7).

Mentally Handicapped Offenders

The new categories of offenders eligible for the death penalty also include the emotionally and mentally handicapped. Although in recent memory the U.S. Supreme Court has prohibited the execution of emotionally disturbed capital defendants (*Ford v. Wainwright,* 1986; Miller & Radelet, 1993; Paternoster, 1991), such restrictions have been not been uniformly enforced. In 1995, Varnall Weeks, a convicted murderer diagnosed by psychiatric experts as a paranoid schizophrenic, was executed in Alabama. Weeks was clearly disturbed: Living in a maze of delusions, he believed that "he would come back to life as a giant flying tortoise that would rule the world" (Bragg, 1995, p. 7). At one of his hearings, Weeks described himself as God, wore a domino on a band around his shaved head, and responded to the court's question with a "rambling discourse on serpents, cybernetics, albinos, Egyptians, the Bible, and reproduction. . . . [He also] sat in his cell naked in his own feces, mouthing senseless sounds" (Shapiro, 1995, p. A-29). Although prosecution and defense acknowledged that he suffered from paranoid schizophrenia, the courts contended that he was sane enough to be executed. The U.S. Supreme Court unanimously rejected his appeal. To date, legislators and the courts have not established a consistent or humane definition of how sane or competent a capital defendant needs to be in order to be executed.

Whereas the death penalty for mentally ill murderers is characterized by inconsistent court rulings, there are no such obstacles interfering with the execution of mentally retarded capital defendants (those scoring below 70 on a standardized intelligence test). It has been speculated that throughout history, mildly retarded offenders have been commonly executed but that their level of intelligence was never known to the courts because such tests were not conducted. Today, defendants are routinely administered intelligence tests; thus, the courts are fully aware of the defendant's level of intelligence. In 1989, the High Court ruled in *Penry v. Lynaugh* that states have the right to execute mentally retarded persons convicted of capital murder.

Critics point out that executing mentally retarded (even mildly retarded) offenders raises serious moral and ethical issues, especially because mental retardation constitutes a serious liability affecting every dimension of that person's life. "Many individuals who are sentenced to death and executed in this country have mental retardation" (Harlow et al., 1995, p. 1; Reed, 1993). Persons with mental retardation are quite susceptible to suggestion and have serious difficulty in logic, planning, and understanding consequences. With this in mind, Professor of Special Education Ruth Luckasson asked, "Can you imagine anyone easier to execute?" (quoted in Harlow et al., 1995, p. 1). Luckasson added, "I have seen people with mental retardation sitting in their own capital trials, with their lives at stake, who had absolutely no understanding of what was going on" (quoted in Harlow et al., 1995, p. 1). In 1992, Bill Clinton, then governor of Arkansas, refused to halt the execution of Ricky Ray Rector, who had blown away part of his brain in a suicide attempt just after he had killed a police officer. At the time of his trial, Rector was so mentally retarded that "he did not understand that death was permanent" (Ridgeway, 1994, p. 23). On the day of his death, he told his lawyer that "he planned to vote for Mr. Clinton that November" (Shapiro, 1995, p. A-29) and asked the guards to "save his dessert for a snack before bedtime" (Terry, 1998, p. 22).

In 1995, Mario Marquez was executed by the state of Texas after being convicted of double murder and rape. Marquez, a grade-school dropout with an IQ of 65, was the 10th of 16 children born to a migrant farmworker. As a child, he was beaten with a horsewhip by his father and abandoned to the streets and a life of drug abuse at the age of 12. During the trial, Marquez asked his lawyer "if he [Marquez] was going to have a good job when he goes to heaven" and wanted his lawyer to tell him "if he could get a job being a gardener, or taking care of animals" (Hentoff, 1995, p. 30). . . .

In sum, capital punishment generates an escalating, counterdeterrent effect because, by taking enforcement action (i.e., performing executions), authorities unintentionally encourage a type of rule breaking, namely homicide. The irony of this form of social control is supported by brutalization research. To reiterate, a particularly important analytic element of escalation is the creation of new categories of violators and victims. Such categories are the products of legislation, driven by relentless political pandering to the public on crime. Not only do these self-serving political activities widen the net of capital punishment, but they tend to snare violators—juveniles, the mentally handicapped, the emotionally disturbed—who paradoxically become vulnerable victims of an overzealous criminal justice apparatus.

Nonenforcement

. . . [Nonenforcement] constitutes another irony of social control in that authorities, by taking no enforcement action, intentionally permit rule breaking (Marx, 1981). Arguably one of the more tragic examples of nonenforcement can be found in America's history of vigilante "justice," particularly lynching. Authorities deliberately encouraged these travesties of justice by refusing to impose sanctions on persons who carried them out. In addition, many of these incidents of nonenforcement were motivated by racism, in that blacks served as convenient scapegoats.

Contemporary examinations of racism and the death penalty should not neglect the history of formal (executions) and informal (lynchings) penalties imposed on black defendants and suspects. Following the Civil War, black codes were *formally* established to perpetuate the economic subordination of former slaves. Such codes employed harsher penalties for crimes committed by blacks and led to a disproportionate number of black executions. *Informally*, black men also were subject to lynching (illegal execution) by vigilante mobs. Bowers (1984) reported that in the 1890s there were more lynchings (1,540) than legal executions (1,098). Though lynchings gradually declined, nearly 2,000 illegal executions occurred in the early part of the 20th century: Between 1900 and 1909 there were 885 reported lynchings, between 1910 and 1919, 621 lynchings, and in the 1920s, 315 (Bowers, 1984; also see Brundage, 1993; Jackson, 1996; Tolnay & Beck, 1992, 1994).[2]

Nowadays, a long-standing criticism of the death penalty is that despite efforts to guard against arbitrariness (as enumerated in *Gregg v. Georgia*, 1976), it continues to be administered in ways that are racially biased. Casual observers of the death penalty controversy might assume that the death penalty is racially discriminatory because black murderers, compared to white murderers, are disproportionately sentenced to death. This assumption, however, would be too simplistic. To clarify the extent of racism evident in the death penalty, one must look at the race of the victim as well as the race of the offender. In the United States, approximately half of those murdered each year are black. However, since 1977, about 85% of capital defendants who have been executed had killed a white person, whereas only 11% had murdered a black person (Baldus, Woodworth, & Pulaski, 1990). Research continues to demonstrate that killers of whites are more likely than killers of blacks to be sentenced to death: Paternoster (1983) revealed that blacks who kill whites have a 4.5 times greater chance of facing the death penalty than blacks who kill blacks. When the race of the victim is ignored, the chances of blacks' and whites' receiving a death sentence are almost equal. Furthermore, Keil and Vito (1989) found that when controlling for seriousness of the murder (in Kentucky), "Prosecutors were more likely to seek the death penalty in cases in which blacks killed whites and . . . juries were more likely to sentence to death blacks who killed whites" (p. 511). Baldus et al. (1990) concluded that when the murder victim was white, the chance of a death penalty was roughly doubled in certain kinds of cases: in particular, those cases catalogued as "middle-ground" incidents in which the victim was killed during the commission of a felony (e.g., homicide during a robbery).[3] In a recent study on racial disparities in capital punishment, Baldus (in press) reported that in Philadelphia, black defendants in murder cases are four times more likely than other defendants to be sentenced to death, even when the circumstances of the killings are the same (see Butterfield, 1998). . . .

The racial bias in capital punishment should be viewed as another irony of social control, especially in the realm of nonenforcement. Given that only 11% of all executions involve capital defendants convicted of killing a black person, there is the appearance that the lives of white victims are more valuable than black victims. From 1977 to 1995, 88 black men were executed for murdering whites, whereas only 2 white men have been executed for killing blacks (Eckholm, 1995). To date, Texas—the all-time leader of executions with 404 at year end 1996—has never executed *anyone* for killing a black person. . . .

Incidentally, in Virginia in 1998, Louis Ceparano pleaded guilty to burning alive a black man, Garnett P. Johnson, and chopping off his head with an ax. Ceparano was one of two white men accused of soaking Johnson with gasoline and subjecting him to racial slurs, then setting fire to him. Ceparano was spared the death penalty and received two consecutive life terms without possibility of parole ("White Man Pleads Guilty," 1998).

Advocates who believe that the death penalty can be modified to eliminate its racial bias (van den Haag & Conrad, 1983) are likely to encounter an even greater irony. Because in most murders, the assailant and the victim are of the same race, eliminating the disparity linked to the race of the victim would be likely to result in a higher proportion of blacks sentenced to death.

> If killers of black people were executed at the rate of killers of whites, many more blacks would receive death sentences. If, on the other hand, killers of whites were executed at the same rate as killers of blacks, many whites would be spared. (Eckholm, 1995, p. B-4)

The history of black lynchings in America serves as a reminder of egregious acts of nonenforcement that authorized and perpetuated the racist practice of unlawful executions. Nowadays, incidents of nonenforcement are not as clear-cut and obvious. Admittedly, it is unlikely that authorities *intentionally* encourage lethal violence against blacks. Still, executions remain significantly patterned by the race of the victim, thereby suggesting that in the eyes of the state, white murder victims are inherently more valuable than their black counterparts. Thus, racial disparities in capital punishment contradict fundamental principles of justice in a democratic society.

Covert Facilitation

Although sentencing disparities according to the race of murder victims violate basic ideals of fairness, such contradictions are compounded when innocent people are falsely convicted, and worse, executed. False convictions in capital crimes may be the result of error, wrongdoing, or a combination of the two. Whereas the former serves as evidence of an imperfect criminal justice system, the latter reveals an insidious side of the machinery of death. The deliberate prosecution of innocent people typically emerges in the form of covert facilitation: hidden or deceptive enforcement action in which authorities intentionally encourage rule breaking (Marx, 1981). In this context, *rule breaking* refers to wrongdoing by the prosecutors and police that is encouraged by the state for the purpose of securing capital convictions, even if the suspect is innocent (e.g., framing a suspect, prosecutorial misconduct, allowing perjured testimony). Cases of false conviction shed additional light on racism and classism because people of color and the impoverished are more vulnerable to these miscarriages of justice.

Capital punishment experts have long speculated that numerous innocent persons have been convicted, and in some instances, executed; still, a general understanding of such injustices was previously based on anecdotal and unsystematic research. Then, in 1987, Hugo Bedau and Michael Radelet published a systematic study of 350 defendants believed to have been wrongly convicted in capital (or potential capital) cases between the years 1900 and 1985. It is important to note that Bedau and Radelet did not simply include any case that appeared suspect. Rather, they applied strict standards of miscarriages of justice and accepted cases only on the basis of *overwhelming* evidence that an innocent person had been falsely convicted. In an expanded volume of their work, Radelet, Bedau and Putnam released *In Spite of Innocence: Erroneous Convictions in Capital Cases* (1992), cataloguing 416 cases of falsely convicted capital defendants between 1900 and 1991. Approximately one-third of these defendants were sentenced to death, and the authors persuasively documented 23 cases in which innocent people were executed. Most of the remaining defendants, though initially trapped in the machinery of justice, fortunately escaped execution. Radelet et al. referred to them as the lucky ones. Nevertheless, they still experienced years of incarceration along with the agony of uncertainty; consequently, their lives were virtually ruined (also see Dieter, 1997; Huff, Rattner, & Sagarin, 1996).

Covert facilitation is commonly found in the most egregious cases of false convictions, and as we shall see, racism and classism also permeate many such travesties of justice. Consider Walter McMillian, who, after spending 6 years on Alabama's death row, was released in 1993. Upon further scrutiny, different prosecutors conceded that the state had withheld evidence from his lawyers and had relied on perjured testimony to falsely convict McMillian. In a case that fits the "middle-ground" category of homicide, Ronda Morrison, an 18-year-old white female clerk, was murdered by a black male during a robbery in Monroeville, Alabama—coincidentally, the home town of Harper Lee, author of *To Kill a Mockingbird* (1960), a story of race and justice in the Jim Crow South. While being interrogated in connection to another killing, Ralph Myers, an ex-con with a lengthy criminal record, accused McMillian of murdering Morrison. In an unusual move, McMillian was assigned to death row before his trial. After a one-and-a-half day trial, McMillian was convicted on the testimony of three witnesses, including that of Myers and another criminal suspect. The defense lawyer called a dozen witnesses who each testified that McMillian was at home the day of the murder, socializing with friends at a fish fry. The prosecution offered no physical evidence linking McMillian to the murder; thus, critics insist that the trial was driven by racism. It was well known that McMillian was dating a white woman and that one of his sons had married a white woman; both McMillian and his attorney believed that these interracial relationships motivated the prosecution (Dieter, 1997).

The Alabama Bureau of Investigation eventually discredited the prosecution's case against McMillian. All three witnesses recanted their testimony, and Myers also reported that he was pressured by law officers to accuse McMillian. The case emerged at a time when federal appeals for capital defendants were becoming increasingly restricted, a reminder of how flawed—and corrupt—the machinery of death can be. Bryan Stevenson, McMillian's attorney, said, "It's clear that he had nothing to do with this crime. There are other folks in prison who don't have the money or the resources or the good fortune to have folks come in and help them" (Applebome, 1993, p. B-11).

In another recent case, all charges were dropped against three black men who were incarcerated in an Illinois prison from 1978 to 1996 for a double murder they did not commit. Dennis Williams spent much of that sentence waiting on death row, as did Verneal Jimerson, a fourth black inmate whose charges were dismissed a month earlier. Their case not only underscores the flaws of the criminal justice system but sheds additional light on the controversy over the restriction of federal death penalty appeals recently affirmed by the U.S. Supreme Court. The reduction of federal appeals for capital defendants is expected to cut in half the time between conviction and execution (from approximately 8 to 4 years). Richard C. Dieter, director of the Death Penalty Information Center, warns that these restrictions mean that the length of appeals would "fall well below the average time it takes to discover new evidence of innocence. . . . This rush to get on with the death penalty by shortening the appeals process will raise the danger of executing innocent people" (Terry, 1996, p. A-14).

The case against Williams, Jimerson, and their codefendants, Willie Rainge and Kenneth Williams, stems from the murder of a white couple in suburban Chicago in 1978, but new DNA evidence, witness recantations, and a jailhouse confession led to their release. Cook County State's Attorney Jack O'Malley said his office was trying to determine how the original investigation "got derailed and why it is the wrong people were charged" (Terry, 1996, p. A-14). To this, Dennis Williams quickly responded *racism*: "The police just picked up the first young black men they could and that was it. . . . They didn't care if we were guilty or innocent. . . . We are victims of this crime too" (Terry, 1996, p. A-14). In a strange turn of events, Jimerson had been previously released when the only witness connecting him to the crime recanted; later, in a deal to get released from prison, the witness changed her testimony again. Jimerson was then rearrested, convicted, and sentenced to die. Jimerson and his codefendants believe they were indeed *framed* by the prosecution.

Contrary to popular belief, capital cases often are not meticulously litigated. Indigent defendants assigned court-appointed attorneys stand a good chance of being consumed by the machinery of death. . . .

Although the term *presumed innocence* rings of democratic notions of justice, many prosecutors smugly overlook its importance. Even Edwin R. Meese, while serving as U.S. Attorney General, stated that "suspects who are innocent of a crime should [have the right to have lawyer present during police questioning]. But the thing is, you don't have many suspects who are innocent of a crime. That's contradictory. If a person is innocent of a crime, he is not a uspect" ("Attorney General Speaks," 1985, p. 67). . . .

[The] concept covert facilitation is useful in analyzing the complex ironies of capital punishment. From this perspective, we can look beyond *honest* mistakes occurring in capital cases and examine activities that are truly pernicious. In these cases, capital defendants not only face a flawed criminal justice process but also risk being falsely convicted by unethical prosecutors willing to frame suspects to advance their political aspirations. Again, minorities, the impoverished, and the mentally handicapped remain easy targets of covert facilitation.

Conclusion

Despite clear and compelling evidence that the system of capital punishment has glaring biases and errors, its popularity continues to rise. Approximately 80% of the U.S. population favors the death penalty for offenders convicted of first-degree murder (Moore, 1994), and this level of support is the highest since 1936 (Bohm, 1991).[4] Researchers have found, however, that Americans are greatly misinformed about capital punishment (Bohm, 1991, 1996; Bowers, 1993). Ironically, then, the enormous public support for the death penalty is based, not on a sophisticated understanding of the facts, but on beliefs rooted in popular myths of criminal justice.

[Here] we explored the machinery of death as it pertains to the ironies of social control, namely escalation, nonenforcement, and covert facilitation. To summarize, [we] confronted significant contradictions apparent in American capital punishment. The United States is the only Western industrialized democracy to execute offenders, and this practice continues to violate contemporary standards of decency, especially the execution of juveniles and the mentally retarded. Contradictions also are found in the death penalty's failure to offer a deterrent effect, protect the community (including police; Bailey & Peterson, 1987), eliminate racial and socioeconomic biases, and ensure that innocent people are not falsely convicted or executed. In addition, the death penalty is confounded by several other problems that reveal deep structural contradictions in the social control apparatus, including financial costs, the alliance between the state and certain physicians and psychiatrists who facilitate the execution protocol, and the recent restriction of appeals, all of which paradoxically make errors more likely. . . .

The nation's enthusiasm for the death penalty has become a "fatal attraction" insofar as its contradictions and ironies lead to a self-defeating form of social control. In addition to producing a counterdeterrent effect (i.e., brutalization), a greater commitment to capital punishment creates more categories of violators (and victims), resulting in a higher volume of death sentences. A greater commitment to expediting capital cases by eliminating appeals also means more mistakes are likely to occur.[5] In the end, capital punishment policy is reckless and unjust—especially for people of color, the impoverished, and the mentally handicapped.

Notes

1. Frederick Taylor (1856–1915) promoted the "efficiency movement" in managing the industrial workforce, emphasizing the optimum use of time and motion.
2. A discussion of racism and the death penalty ought to include references to *racial hoaxes* in which black men are easily targeted as criminal suspects. Consider the cases of Charles Stuart, Susan V. Smith, and Jesse Anderson, all of whom committed premeditated murder and falsely reported to police that their crimes were the acts of a black man (Russell, 1998; Welch, 1996a).

3. Baldus et al. (1990) showed that disparities in the death penalty are more clearly understood by classifying murders into three types. The first category includes crimes of passion and killings in barroom brawls; these rarely draw the death penalty. The second category includes grisly murders such as mass and serial killings; these are typically sanctioned by capital punishment, regardless of race. However, racial disparities most commonly arise in the third category, known as "middle-ground" incidents in which homicide occurs during the commission of a felony (e.g., armed robbery); in this type of murder, the race of the victim is a crucial factor in determining the penalty. The killing of a white victim under these circumstances, especially when the perpetrator is black, has the highest chance of drawing capital punishment.
4. Researchers also conclude that the support for the death penalty may not be as deep as the polls suggest. When given the choice between favoring the death penalty and life imprisonment with absolutely no possibility of parole, support for the death penalty drops to less than half (Bohm, 1991, 1996; Bowers, 1993; Gallup & Newport, 1991; McGarrell & Sandys, 1996).
5. Opponents of the death penalty are alarmed and enraged over Congress's passing of the Anti-Terrorism and Effective Death Penalty Act of 1996, which sharply limits the prisoner's ability to file more than one habeas corpus petition. In 1996, Congress also voted to stop funding ($20 million) the Post-Conviction Defender Organizations that have played a vital role in representing death row inmates. In reaction to this move and to Congress's curtailing of federal habeas corpus protections, the American Bar Association in 1997 called for the suspension of the death penalty until the system is changed to afford adequate due process ("A Lawyerly Cry of Conscience," 1997). Regarding the defender's program, the *New York Times* editorialized, "It deserves to live. A Congress committed to the death penalty cannot in good conscience deny competent legal counsel. Abolishing the Defender Organizations harms the causes of economy, speed, and justice" ("Shortchanging Inmates," 1995, p. A-32).

References

Applebome, P. (1993, March 3). Alabama releases man held on death row for six years. *New York Times,* pp. A-1, B-11.

Attorney General speaks. (1985, October 14). *U.S. News and World Report,* p. 67.

Bailey, W. C. (1983). Disaggregation in deterrence and death penalty research: The case of murder in Chicago. *Journal of Criminal Law and Criminology, 74,* 827–859.

Bailey, W. C. (1998). Deterrence and brutalization, and the death penalty. *Criminology, 36,* 711–734.

Bailey, W. C., & Peterson, R. D. (1987). Police killings and capital punishment: The post-Furman period. *Criminology, 25,* 1–26.

Baldus, D. (in press). The death penalty in black and white: Who lives, who dies, who decides. *Cornell Law Review.*

Baldus, D., Woodworth, G., & Pulaski, C. (1990). *Equal justice and the death penalty: A legal and empirical analysis.* Boston: Northeastern University Press.

Bohm, R. (1991). American death penalty opinion, 1936–1986: A critical examination of the Gallup polls. In R. Bohm (Ed.), *The death penalty in America: Current research* (pp. 113–145). Cincinnati, OH: Anderson.

Bohm, R. (1996). Understanding and changing public support for capital punishment. *Corrections Now, 1*(1), 1–4.

Bowers, W. J. (1984). *Legal homicide: Death as punishment in America, 1864–1982.* Boston: Northeastern University Press.

Bowers, W. J. (1988). The effect of execution is brutalization, not deterrence. In K. Hass & J. Inciardi (Eds.), *Challenging capital punishment: Legal and social science approaches* (pp. 49–90). Newbury Park, CA: Sage.

Bowers, W. J. (1993). Capital punishment and contemporary values: People's misgivings and the court's misperceptions. *Law and Society Review, 27,* 157–175.

Bowers, W. J., & Pierce, G. (1980). Deterrence or brutalization: What is the effect of executions. *Crime and Delinquency, 26,* 453–484.

Bragg, R. (1995, May 13). A killer racked by delusions dies in Alabama's electric chair. *New York Times,* p. 7.

Brundage, W. (1993). *Lynching in the New South: Georgia and Virginia, 1880–1930.* Champaign: University of Illinois Press.

Butterfield, F. (1998, June 7). New study adds to evidence of bias in death sentences. *New York Times,* p. 20.

Cochran, J. K., Chamlin, M., & Seth, M. (1994). Deterrence or brutalization? An impact assessment of Oklahoma's return to capital punishment. *Criminology, 32,* 107–134.

Decker, S., & Kohfeld, C. (1990). The deterrent effect of capital punishment in the five most active execution states: A time series analysis. *Criminal Justice Review, 15,* 173–191.

Dieter, R. (1997). *Innocence and the death penalty: The increasing danger of executing the innocent.* Washington, DC: Death Penalty Information Center.

Eckholm, E. (1995, February 25). Studies find death penalty tied to race of the victims. *New York Times,* pp. B-1, B-2.

Ford v. Wainwright, 477 U.S. 699 (1986).

Forst, B. (1983). Capital punishment and deterrence: Conflicting evidence? *Journal of Criminal Law and Criminology, 74,* 927–942.

Gallup, A., & Newport, F. (1991, June). Death penalty support remains strong. *Gallup Monthly Report,* No. 321, pp. 3–5.

Gregg v. Georgia, 428 U.S. 153 (1976).

Harlow, E., Matas, D., & Rocamora, J. (1995). *The machinery of death: A shocking indictment of capital punishment in the United States.* New York: Amnesty International.

Hentoff, N. (1995, February 21). Executing the retarded in our name. *Village Voice,* pp. 30–31.

Huff, C. R., Rattner, A., & Sagarin, E. (1996). *Convicted but innocent: Wrongful conviction and public policy.* Thousand Oaks, CA: Sage.

Jackson, J. (1996). *Legal lynching: Racism, injustice, and the death penalty.* New York: Marlowe.

Keil, T., & Vito, G. (1989). Race, homicide severity, and application of the death penalty: A consideration of the Barnett Scale. *Criminology, 27,* 511–536.

King, D. (1978). The brutalization effect: Execution publicity and the incidence of homicide in South Carolina. *Social Forces, 57,* 683–687.

Kuntz, T. (1997, January 12). Banality, nausea, triple execution: Guards on inmates' final hours. *New York Times,* p. E-7.

A lawyerly cry of conscience. (1997, February 22). *New York Times,* p. 20.

Lee, H. (1960). *To kill a mockingbird.* New York: HarperCollins.

Lynch, M., & Groves, W. B. (1989). *A primer in radical criminology.* New York: Harrow & Heston.

Marx, G. (1981). Ironies of social control: Authorities as contributors to deviance through escalation, nonenforcement, and covert facilitation. *Social Problems, 28,* 221–233.

McGarrell, E. F., & Sandys, M. (1996). Misperception of public opinion toward capital punishment: Examining the spuriousness explanation of death penalty support. *American Behavioral Scientist, 39,* 500–513.

Miller, K., & Radelet, M. (1993). *Executing the mentally ill: The criminal justice system and the case of Alvin Ford.* Newbury Park, CA: Sage.

Moore, D. W. (1994, September). Majority advocate death penalty for teenage killers. *Gallup Poll Monthly,* No. 321, pp. 2–5.

Paternoster, R. (1983). Race of the victim and location of crime: The decision to seek the death penalty in South Carolina. *Journal of Criminal Law and Criminology, 74,* 754–785.

Paternoster, R. (1991). *Capital punishment in America.* New York: Lexington.

Penry v. Lynaugh, 57 U.S.L.W. 4958 (1989).

Radelet, M., Bedau, H., & Putnam, C. (1992). *In spite of innocence: Erroneous convictions in capital cases.* Boston: Northeastern University Press.

Reed, E. (1993). *The Penry penalty: Capital punishment and offenders with mental retardation.* Landam, MD: University Press of America.

Ridgeway, J. (1994, October 11). Slaughterhouse justice: Race, poverty, and politics: The essential ingredients for a death penalty conviction. *Village Voice,* pp. 23–24.

Russell, K. (1998). *The color of crime: Racial hoaxes, white fear, black protectionism, police aggression and other macroaggressions.* New York: New York University Press.

Shapiro, A. (1995, May 11). An insane execution. *New York Times,* p. A-29.

Shortchanging inmates on death row. (1995, October 13). *New York Times,* p. A-32.

Snell, T. (1997). *Capital punishment 1996.* Washington, DC: Bureau of Justice Statistics.

Terry, D. (1996, July 3). After 18 years in prison, 3 are cleared of murders. *New York Times,* p. A-14.

Terry, D. (1998, April 12). Jury to decide if condemned man comprehends his fate. *New York Times,* p. 22.

Tolnay, S., & Beck, E. (1994). Lethal social control in the South: Lynchings and executions between 1880 and 1930. In G. Bridges & M. Myers (Eds.), *Inequality, crime, and social control* (pp. 176–194). Boulder, CO: Westview.

van den Haag, E., & Conrad, J. (1983). *The death penalty: A debate.* New York: Plenum.

Verhovek, S. (1998, April 18). Texas legislator proposes the death penalty for murderers as young as 11. *New York Times,* p. A-7.

Walker, S. (1994). *Sense and nonsense about crime and drugs: A policy guide* (3rd ed.). Belmont, CA: Wadsworth.

Welch, M. (1996a). *Corrections: A critical approach.* New York: McGraw-Hill.

Welch, M. (1996b). Critical criminology, social justice, and an alternative view of incarceration. *Critical Criminology: An International Journal, 7*(2), 43–58.

White man pleads guilty to killing a black man. (1998, May 31). *New York Times,* p. 22.

Ernest van den Haag

The Death Penalty Once More

People concerned with capital punishment disagree on essentially three questions: (1) Is it constitutional? (2) Does the death penalty deter crime more than life imprisonment? (3) Is the death penalty morally justifiable?

Is the Death Penalty Constitutional?

The fifth amendment, passed in 1791, states that "no person shall be deprived of life, liberty, or property, without due process of law." Thus, with "due process of law," the Constitution authorizes depriving persons "of life, liberty or property." The fourteenth amendment, passed in 1868, applies an identical provision to the states. The Constitution, then, authorizes the death penalty. It is left to elected bodies to decide whether or not to retain it.

The eighth amendment, reproducing almost verbatim a passage from the English Bill of Rights of 1689, prohibits "cruel and unusual punishments." This prohibition was not meant to repeal the fifth amendment since the amendments were passed simultaneously. "Cruel" punishment is not prohibited unless "unusual" as well, that is, new, rare, not legislated, or disproportionate to the crime punished. Neither the English Bill of Rights, nor the eighth amendment, hitherto has been found inconsistent with capital punishment.

Evolving Standards

Some commentators argue that, in *Trop v. Dulles,* the Supreme Court indicated that "evolving standards of decency that mark the progress of a maturing society" allow courts to declare "cruel and unusual," punishments authorized by the Constitution. However, *Trop* was concerned with expatriation, a punishment that is not specifically authorized by the Constitution. The death penalty is. *Trop* did not suggest that "evolving standards" could de-authorize what the Constitution repeatedly authorizes. Indeed, Chief Justice Warren, writing for the majority in *Trop,* declared that "the death penalty . . . cannot be said to violate the constitutional concept of cruelty."[1] Furthermore, the argument based on "evolving standards" is paradoxical: the Constitution would be redundant if current views, enacted by judicial fiat, could supersede what it plainly says. If "standards of decency" currently invented or evolved could, without formal

The Death Penalty Once More, copyright © 1985 by Ernest van den Haag, originally published in 18 *U. C. Davis L. Rev.* 957 (1985), copyright 1985 by the Regents of the University of California. Reprinted with permission.

amendment, replace or repeal the standards authorized by the Constitution, the Constitution would be superfluous.

It must be remembered that the Constitution does not force capital punishment on the population but merely authorizes it. Elected bodies are left to decide whether to use the authorization. As for "evolving standards," how could courts detect them without popular consensus as a guide? Moral revelations accepted by judges, religious leaders, sociologists, or academic elites, but not by the majority of voters, cannot suffice. The opinions of the most organized, most articulate, or most vocal might receive unjustified deference. Surely the eighth amendment was meant to limit, but was not meant to replace, decisions by the legislative branch, or to enable the judiciary [to] do what the voters won't do.[2] The general consensus on which the courts would have to rely could be registered only by elected bodies. They favor capital punishment. Indeed, at present, more than seventy percent of the voters approve of the death penalty. The state legislatures reflect as much. Wherefore, the Supreme Court, albeit reluctantly, rejected abolition of the death penalty by judicial *fiat.* This decision was subsequently qualified by a finding that the death penalty for rape is disproportionate to the crime,[3] and by rejecting all mandatory capital punishment.

Caprice

Laws that allowed courts too much latitude to decide, perhaps capriciously, whether to actually impose the death penalty in capital cases also were found unconstitutional. In response, more than two-thirds of the states have modified their death penalty statutes, listing aggravating and mitigating factors, and imposing capital punishment only when the former outweigh the latter. The Supreme Court is satisfied that this procedure meets the constitutional requirements of non-capriciousness. However, abolitionists are not.

In *Capital Punishment: The Inevitability of Caprice and Mistake,*[4] Professor Charles Black contends that the death penalty is necessarily imposed capriciously, for irremediable reasons. If he is right, he has proved too much, unless capital punishment is imposed more capriciously now than it was in 1791 or 1868, when the fifth and fourteenth amendments were enacted. He does not contend that it is. Professor Black also stresses that the elements of chance, unavoidable in all penalizations, are least tolerable when capital punishment is involved. But the irreducible chanciness inherent in human efforts does not constitutionally require the abolition of capital punishment, unless the framers were less aware of chance and human frailty than Professor Black is. (I shall turn to the moral as distinguished from the legal bearing of chanciness anon.)

Discrimination

Sociologists have demonstrated that the death penalty has been distributed in a discriminatory pattern in the past: black or poor defendants were more likely to be executed than equally guilty others. This argues for correction of the distributive process, but not for abolition of the penalty it distributes, unless constitutionally excessive maldistribution ineluctably inheres in the penalty.

There is no evidence to that effect. Actually, although we cannot be sure that it has disappeared altogether, discrimination has greatly decreased compared to the past.[5]

However, recently the debate on discrimination has taken a new turn. Statistical studies have found that, *ceteris paribus,* a black man who murders a white has a much greater chance to be executed than he would have had, had his victim been black.[6] This discriminates against black *victims* of murder: they are not as fully, or as often, vindicated as are white victims. However, although unjustified per se, discrimination against a class of victims need not, and here does not, amount to discrimination against their victimizers. The pattern discriminates *against* black murderers of whites and *for* black murderers of blacks. One may describe it as discrimination for, or discrimination against, just as one may describe a glass of water as half full or half empty. Discrimination against one group (here, blacks who kill whites) is necessarily discrimination in favor of another (here, blacks who kill blacks).

Most black victims are killed by black murderers, and a disproportionate number of murder victims is black. Wherefore the discrimination in favor of murderers of black victims more than offsets, numerically, any remaining discrimination against other black murderers.[7]

Comparative Excessiveness

Recently lawyers have argued that the death penalty is unconstitutionally disproportionate if defendants, elsewhere in the state, received lesser sentences for comparable crimes. But the Constitution only requires that penalties be appropriate to the gravity of the crime, not that they cannot exceed penalties imposed elsewhere. Although some states have adopted "comparative excessiveness" reviews, there is no constitutional requirement to do so.

Unavoidably, different courts, prosecutors, defense lawyers, judges and juries produce different penalties even when crimes seem comparable. Chance plays a great role in human affairs. Some offenders are never caught or convicted, while others are executed; some are punished more than others guilty of worse crimes. Thus, a guilty person, or group of persons, may get away with no punishment, or with a light punishment, while others receive the punishment they deserve. Should we let these others go too, or punish them less severely? Should we abolish the penalty applied unequally or discriminatorily?[8]

The late Justice Douglas suggested an answer to these questions:

> A law that . . . said that blacks, those who never went beyond the fifth grade in school, those who made less than $3,000 a year, or those who were unpopular or unstable should be the only people executed [would be wrong]. A law which in the overall view reaches that result in practice has no more sanctity than a law which in terms provides the same.[9]

Justice Douglas' answer here conflates an imagined discriminatory law with the discriminatory application of a non-discriminatory law. His imagined law would be inconsistent with the "equal protection of the laws" demanded by the fourteenth amendment, and the Court would have to invalidate it *ipso facto*. But discrimination caused by uneven application of non-discriminatory death penalty laws may be remedied by means other than abolition, as long as the discrimination is not intrinsic to the laws.

Consider now, albeit fleetingly, the moral as distinguished from the constitutional bearing of discrimination. Suppose guilty defendants are justly executed, but only if poor, or black and not otherwise. This unequal justice would be morally offensive for what may be called tautological reasons:[10] if any punishment for a given crime is just, then a greater or lesser punishment is not. Only one punishment can be just for all persons equally guilty of the same crime.[11] Therefore, different punishments for equally guilty persons or group members are unjust: some offenders are punished more than they deserve, or others less.

Still, equality and justice are not the same. "Equal justice" is not a redundant phrase. Rather, we strive for two distinct ideals, justice and equality. Neither can replace the other. We want to have justice and, having it, we want to extend it equally to all. We would not want equal injustice. Yet, sometimes, we must choose between equal injustice and unequal justice. What should we prefer? Unequal justice is justice still, even if only for some, whereas equal injustice is injustice for all. If not every equally guilty person is punished equally, we have unequal justice. It seems preferable to equal injustice—having no guilty person punished as deserved.[12] Since it is never possible to punish equally all equally guilty murderers, we should punish, as they deserve, as many of those we apprehend and convict as possible. Thus, even if the death penalty were inherently discriminatory—which is not the case—but deserved by those who receive it, it would be morally just to impose it on them. If, as I contend, capital punishment is just and not inherently discriminatory, it remains desirable to eliminate inequality in distribution, to apply the penalty to all who deserve it, sparing no racial or economic class. But if a guilty person or group escaped the penalty through our porous system, wherein is this an argument for sparing others?

If one does not believe capital punishment can be just, discrimination becomes a subordinate argument, since one would object to capital punishment even if it were distributed equally to all the guilty. If one does believe that capital punishment for murderers is deserved, discrimination against guilty black murderers and in favor of equally guilty white murderers is wrong, not because blacks receive the deserved punishment, but because whites escape it.

Consider a less emotionally charged analogy. Suppose traffic police ticketed all drivers who violated the rules, except drivers of luxury cars. Should we abolish tickets? Should we decide that the ticketed drivers of nonluxury cars were unjustly punished and ought not to pay their fines? Would they become innocent of the violation they are guilty of because others have not been ticketed? Surely the drivers of luxury cars should not be exempted. But the fact that they were is no reason to exempt drivers of nonluxury cars as well. Laws could never be applied if the escape of one person, or group, were accepted as ground for not punishing another. To do justice is primarily to punish as deserved, and only secondarily to punish equally.

Guilt is personal. No one becomes less guilty or less deserving of punishment because another was punished leniently or not at all. That justice does not catch up with all guilty persons understandably is resented by those caught. But it does not affect their guilt. If some, or all, white and rich murderers escape the death penalty, how does that reduce the guilt of black or poor murderers, or make them less deserving of punishment, or deserving of a lesser punishment?

Some lawyers have insisted that the death penalty is distributed among those guilty of murder as though by a lottery and that the worst may escape it.[13] They exaggerate, but suppose one grants the point. How do those among the guilty selected for execution by lottery become less deserving of punishment because others escaped it? What is wrong is that these others escaped, not that those among the guilty who were selected by the lottery did not.

Those among the guilty actually punished by a criminal justice system unavoidably are selected by chance, not because we want to so select them, but because the outcome of our efforts largely depends on chance. No murderer is punished unless he is unlucky enough both to be caught and to have convinced a court of his guilt. And courts consider evidence not truth. They find truth only when the evidence establishes it. Thus they may have reasonable doubts about the guilt of an actually guilty person. Although we may strive to make justice as equal as possible, unequal justice will remain our lot in this world. We should not give up justice, or the death penalty, because we cannot extend it as equally to all the guilty as we wish. If we were not to punish one offender because another got away because of caprice or discrimination, we would give up justice for the sake of equality. We would reverse the proper order of priorities.

Is the Death Penalty More Deterrent Than Other Punishments?

Whether or not the death penalty deters the crimes it punishes more than alternative penalties—in this case life imprisonment with or without parole—has been widely debated since Isaac Ehrlich broke the abolitionist ranks by finding that from 1933–65 "an additional execution per year . . . may have resulted on the average in seven or eight fewer murders."[14] Since his article appeared, a whole cottage industry devoted to refuting his findings has arisen.[15] Ehrlich, no slouch, has been refuting those who refuted him.[16] The result seems inconclusive.[17] Statistics have not proved conclusively that the death penalty does or does not deter murder more than other penalties.[18] Still, Ehrlich has the merit of being the first to use a sophisticated statistical analysis to tackle the problem, and of defending his analysis, although it showed deterrence. (Ehrlich started as an abolitionist.) His predecessors cannot be accused of mathematical sophistication. Yet the academic community uncritically accepted their abolitionist results. I myself have no contribution to make to the mathematical analyses of deterrent effects. Perhaps this is why I have come to believe that they may becloud the issue, leading us to rely on demonstrable deterrence as though decisive.

Most abolitionists believe that the death penalty does not deter more than other penalties. But most abolitionists would abolish it, even if it did.[19] I have discussed this matter with prominent abolitionists such as Charles Black, Henry Schwarzchild, Hugo Adam Bedau, Ramsey Clark, and many others. Each told me that, even if every execution were to deter a hundred murders, he would oppose it. I infer that, to these abolitionist leaders, the life of every murderer is more valuable than the lives of a hundred prospective victims, for these abolitionists would spare the murderer, even if doing so would cost a hundred future victims their lives.

Obviously, deterrence cannot be the decisive issue for these abolitionists. It is not necessarily for me either, since I would be for capital punishment on grounds of justice alone. On the other hand, I should favor the death penalty for murderers, if probably deterrent, or even just possibly deterrent. To me, the life of any innocent victim who might be spared has great value; the life of a convicted murderer does not. This is why I would not take the risk of sacrificing innocents by not executing murderers.

Even though statistical demonstrations are not conclusive, and perhaps cannot be, I believe that capital punishment is likely to deter more than anything else. They fear most death deliberately inflicted by law and scheduled by the courts. Whatever people fear most is likely to deter most. Hence, I believe that the threat of the death penalty may deter some murderers who otherwise might not have been deterred. And surely the death penalty is the only penalty that could deter prisoners already serving a life sentence and tempted to kill a guard, or offenders about to be arrested and facing a life sentence. Perhaps they will not be deterred. But they would certainly not be deterred by anything else. We owe all the protection we can give to law enforcers exposed to special risks.

Many murders are "crimes of passion" that, perhaps, cannot be deterred by any threat. Whether or not they can be would depend on the degree of passion; it is unlikely to be always so extreme as to make the person seized by it totally undeterrable. At any rate, offenders sentenced to death ordinarily are guilty of premediated murder, felony murder, or multiple murders. Some are rape murderers, or hit men, but, to my knowledge, no one convicted of a "crime of passion" is on death row. Whatever the motive, some prospective offenders are not deterrable at all, others are easily deterred, and most are in between. Even if only some murders were, or could be, deterred by capital punishment, it would be worthwhile. . . .

Almost all convicted murderers try to avoid the death penalty by appeals for commutation to life imprisonment. However, a minuscule proportion of convicted murderers prefer execution. It is sometimes argued that they murdered for the sake of being executed, of committing suicide via execution. More likely, they prefer execution to life imprisonment. Although shared by few, this preference is not irrational per se. It is also possible that these convicts accept the verdict of the court, and feel that they deserve the death penalty for the crimes they committed, although the modern mind finds it hard to imagine such feelings. But not all murderers are ACLU humanists. . . .

Is the Death Penalty Moral?

Miscarriages

Miscarriages of justice are rare, but do occur. Over a long enough time they lead to the execution of some innocents.[20] Does this make irrevocable punishments morally wrong? Hardly. Our government employs trucks. They run over innocent bystanders more frequently than courts sentence innocents to death. We do not give up trucks because the benefits they produce outweigh the harm, including the death of innocents. Many human activities, even quite trivial ones, forseeably cause wrongful deaths. Courts may cause fewer wrongful deaths than golf. Whether one sees the benefit of doing justice by imposing capital punishment as moral, or as material, or both, it outweighs the loss of innocent lives through miscarriages, which are as unintended as traffic accidents.

Vengeance

Some abolitionists feel that the motive for the death penalty is an un-Christian and unacceptable desire for vengeance. But though vengeance be the motive, it is not the purpose of the death penalty. Doing justice and deterring crime are the purposes, whatever the motive. Purpose (let alone effect) and motive are not the same.

The Lord is often quoted as saying "Vengeance is mine." He did not condemn vengeance. He merely reserved it to Himself—and to the government. For, in the same epistle He is also quoted as saying that the ruler is "the minister of God, a revenger, to execute wrath upon him that doeth evil." The religious notion of hell indicates that the biblical God favored harsh and everlasting punishment for some. However, particularly in a secular society, we cannot wait for the day of judgment to see murderers consigned to hell. Our courts must "execute wrath upon him that doeth evil" here and now.

Charity and Justice

Today many religious leaders oppose capital punishment. This is surprising, because there is no biblical warrant for their opposition. The Roman Catholic Church and most Protestant denominations traditionally have supported capital punishment. Why have their moral views changed? When sharing secular power, the churches clearly distinguished between justice, including penalization as deserved, a function of the secular power, and charity, which, according to religious doctrine, we should feel for all those who suffer for whatever reasons. Currently, religious leaders seem to conflate justice and charity, to conclude that the death penalty and, perhaps, all punishment, is wrong because uncharitable. Churches no longer share secular power. Perhaps bystanders are more ready to replace justice with charity than are those responsible for governing.

Human Dignity

Let me return to the morality of execution. Many abolitionists believe that capital punishment is "degrading to human dignity" and inconsistent with the "sanctity of life." Justice Brennan, concurring in *Furnam,* stressed these phrases repeatedly.[21] He did not explain what he meant.

Why would execution degrade human dignity more than life imprisonment? One may prefer the latter; but it seems at least as degrading as execution. Philosophers, such as Immanuel Kant and G. F. W. Hegel, thought capital punishment indispensable to redeem, or restore, the human dignity of the executed. Perhaps they were wrong. But they argued their case, whereas no one has explained why capital punishment degrades. Apparently those who argue that it does degrade dignity simply define the death penalty as degrading. If so, degradation (or dehumanization) merely is a disguised synonym for their disapproval. Assertion, reassertion, or definition, do not constitute evidence or argument, nor do they otherwise justify, or even explain, disapproval of capital punishment.

Writers, such as Albert Camus, have suggested that murderers have a miserable time waiting for execution and anticipating it.[22] I do not doubt that. But punishments are not meant to be pleasant. Other people suffer greatly waiting for the end, in hospitals, under circumstances that, I am afraid, are at least as degrading to their dignity as execution. These sufferers have not deserved their suffering by committing crimes, whereas murderers have. Yet, murderers suffer less on death row, unless their consciences bother them.

Lex Talionis

Some writers insist that the suffering the death penalty imposes on murderers exceeds the suffering of their victims. This is hard to determine, but probably true in some cases and not in other cases. However, the comparison is irrelevant. Murderers are punished, as are all offenders, not just for the suffering they caused their victims, but for the harm they do to society by making life insecure, by threatening everyone, and by requiring protective measures. Punishment, ultimately, is a vindication of the moral and legal order of society and not limited by the *Lex Talionis,* meant to limit private retaliation for harms originally regarded as private.

Sanctity of Life

We are enjoined by the Declaration of Independence to secure life. How can this best be achieved? The Constitution authorizes us to secure innocent life by taking the life of murderers, so that any one who deliberately wants to take an innocent life will know that he risks forfeiting his own. The framers did not think that taking the life of a murderer is inconsistent with the "sanctity of life" which Justice Brennan champions. He has not indicated why they were wrong.[23]

Legalized Murder?

Ever since Cesare Bonesana, Marchese di Beccaria, wrote *Dei Delitti e Delle Pene,* abolitionists have contended that executing murderers legitimizes murder by doing to the murderer what he did to his victim. Indeed, capital punishment retributes, or pays back the offender. Occasionally we do punish offenders by doing to them what they did to their victims. We may lock away a kidnapper who wrongfully locked away his victim, and we may kill the murderer who wrongfully killed his victim. To lawfully do to the offender what he unlawfully did to his victim in no way legitimizes his crime. It legitimizes (some) killing, and not murder. An act does not become a crime because of its physical character, which, indeed, it may share with the legal punishment, but because of its social, or, better, antisocial, character—because it is an unlawful act.

Severity

Is the death penalty too severe? It stands in a class by itself. But so does murder. Execution is irreparable. So is murder. In contrast, all other crimes and punishments are, at least partly or potentially, reparable. The death penalty thus is congruous with the moral and material gravity of the crime it punishes.[24]

Still, is it repulsive? Torture, however well deserved, now is repulsive to us. But torture is an artifact. Death is not, since nature has placed us all under sentence of death. Capital punishment, in John Stuart Mills' phrase, only "hastens death"—which is what the murderer did to his victim. I find nothing repulsive in hastening the murderer's death, provided it be done in a nontorturous manner. Had he wished to be secure in his life, he could have avoided murder.

To believe that capital punishment is too severe for any act, one must believe that there can be no act horrible enough to deserve death.[25] I find this belief difficult to understand. I should readily impose the death penalty on a Hitler or a Stalin, or on anyone who does what they did, albeit on a smaller scale.

Conclusion

The death penalty has become a major issue in public debate. This is somewhat puzzling, because quantitatively it is insignificant. Still, capital punishment has separated the voters as a whole from a small, but influential, abolitionist elite. There are, I believe, two reasons that explain the prominence of the issue.

First, I think, there is a genuine ethical issue. Some philosophers believe that the right to life is equally imprescriptible for all, that the murderer has as much right to live as his victim. Others do not push egalitarianism that far. They believe that there is a vital difference, that one's right to live is lost when one intentionally takes an innocent life, that everyone has just the right to one life, his own. If he unlawfully takes that of another he, *eo ipso,* loses his own right to life.

Second, and perhaps as important, the death penalty has symbolic significance. Those who favor it believe that the major remedy for crime is punishment. Those who do not, in the main, believe that the remedy is anything but punishment. They look at the causes of crime and conflate them with compulsions, or with excuses, and refuse to blame. The majority of the people are less sophisticated, but perhaps they have better judgment. They believe that everyone who can understand the nature and effects of his acts is responsible for them, and should be blamed and punished, if he could know that what he did was wrong. Human beings are human because they can be held responsible, as animals cannot be. In that Kantian sense the death penalty is a symbolic affirmation of the humanity of both victim and murderer.

Notes

1. 356 U.S. 99 (1958).
2. The courts have sometimes confirmed the obsolescence of non-repealed laws or punishments. But here they are asked to invent it.
3. In *Coker v. Georgia,* 433 U.S. 584, 592 (1977), the Court concluded that the eighth amendment prohibits punishments that are "'excessive' in relation to the crime committed." I am not sure about this disproportion. However, threatening execution would tempt rapists to murder their victims who, after all, are potential witnesses. By murdering their victims, rapists would increase their chances of escaping execution without adding to their risk. Therefore, I agree with the court's conclusion, though not with its argument.
4. C. BLACK, CAPITAL PUNISHMENT: THE INEVITABILITY OF CAPRICE AND MISTAKE (2d ed. 1981).
5. Most discrimination occurred in rape cases and was eliminated when the death penalty for rape was declared unconstitutional.
6. For a survey of the statistical literature, see, e.g., Bowers, *The Pervasiveness of Arbitrariness and Discrimination under Post-*Furman *Capital Statutes,* 74 J. CRIM. L. & CRIMINOLOGY 1067 (1983). His article is part of a "Symposium on Current Death Penalty Issues" compiled by death penalty opponents.
7. Those who demonstrated the pattern seem to have been under the impression that they had shown discrimination against black murderers. They were wrong. However, the discrimination against black victims is invidious and should be corrected.
8. The capriciousness argument is undermined when capriciousness is conceded to be unavoidable. But even when capriciousness is thought reducible, one wonders whether releasing or retrying one guilty defendant, because another equally guilty defendant was not punished as much, would help reduce capriciousness. It does not seem a logical remedy.
9. *Furman v. Georgia,* 408 U.S. 238, 256 (1971) (Douglas, J., concurring).
10. I shall not consider here the actual psychological motives that power our unending thirst for equality.
11. If courts impose different punishments on different persons, we may not be able to establish in all cases whether the punishment is just, or (it amounts to the same) whether the different persons were equally guilty of the same crime, or whether their crimes were identical in all relevant respects. Thus, we may not be able to tell which of two unequal punishments is just. Both may be, or neither may be. Inequality may not entail more injustice than equality, and equality would entail justice only if we were sure that the punishment meted out was the just punishment.
12. Similarly, it is better that only some innocents suffer undeserved punishment than that all suffer it equally.

13. It would be desirable that all of the worst murderers be sentenced to death. However, since murderers are tried in different courts, this is unlikely. Further, sometimes the testimony of one murderer is needed to convict another, and cannot be obtained except by leniency. Morally, and legally it is enough that those sentenced to death deserve the penalty for their crimes, even if others, who may deserve it as much, or more, were not sentenced to death.
14. Ehrlich, *The Deterrent Effect of Capital Punishment: A Question of Life or Death,* 65 AM. ECON. REV. 397, 414 (1975).
15. *See, e.g.,* Baldus & Cole, *A Comparison of the Work of Thorsten Sellin and Isaac Ehrlich on the Deterrent Effect of Capital Punishment,* 85 YALE L. J. 170 (1975); Bowers & Pierce, *Deterrence or Brutalization: What Is the Effect of Executions?,* 26 CRIME & DELINQ. 453 (1980); Bowers & Pierce, *The Illusion of Deterrence in Isaac Ehrlich's Research on Capital Punishment,* 85 YALE L. J. 187 (1975).
16. Ehrlich, *Fear of Deterrence,* 6 J. LEGAL STUD. 293 (1977); Ehrlich & Gibbons, *On the Measurement of the Deterrent Effect of Capital Punishment and the Theory of Deterrence,* 6 J. LEGAL STUD. 35 (1977).
17. At present there is no agreement even on whether the short run effects of executions delay or accelerate homicides. *See* Phillips, *The Deterrent Effect of Capital Punishment: New Evidence on an Old Controversy,* 86, AM. J. Soc. 139 (1980).
18. As stated in *Gregg v. Georgia,* 428 U.S. 153, 185 (1976), "Although some of the studies suggest that the death penalty may not function as a significantly greater deterrent than lesser penalties, there is no convincing empirical evidence either supporting or refuting this view."
19. Jeffrey Reiman is an honorable exception. *See* Reiman, *Justice, Civilization, and the Death Penalty: Answering van den Haag,* 14 PHIL. & PUB. AFF. 115 (1985).
20. Life imprisonment avoids the problem of executing innocent persons to some extent. It can be revoked. But the convict also may die in prison before his innocence is discovered.
21. "[T]he Cruel and Unusual Punishments Clause prohibits the infliction of uncivilized and inhuman punishments. The State, even as it punishes, must treat its members with respect for their intrinsic worth as human beings." *Furman v. Georgia,* 408 U.S. 238, 270 (1972) (Brennan, J., concurring). "When we consider why [certain punishments] have been condemned, . . . we realize that the pain involved is not the only reason. The true significance of these punishments [that have been condemned] is that they treat members of the human race as nonhumans, as objects to be toyed with and discarded." *Id.* at 272–73.

    > In determining whether a punishment comports with human dignity, we are aided also by a second principle inherent in the Clause—that the State must not arbitrarily inflict a severe punishment. This principle derives from the notion that the State does not respect human dignity when, without reason, it inflicts upon some people a severe punishment that it does not inflict upon others.

    Id. at 274. "Death is truly an awesome punishment. The calculated killing of a human being by the State involves, by its very nature, a denial of the executed person's humanity." *Id.* at 290. "In comparison to all other punishments today, then, the deliberate extinguishment of human life by the State is uniquely degrading to human dignity." *Id.* at 291.

22. In *Reflections on the Guillotine,* Camus stated that "[t]he parcel [the condemned person] is no longer subject to the laws of chance that hang over the living creature but to mechanical laws that allow him to foresee accurately the day of his beheading. . . . The Greeks, after all, were more humane with their hemlock." A. CAMUS, RESISTANCE, REBELLION AND DEATH 175, 202 (1960).
23. "Sanctity of life" may mean that we should not take, and should punish taking innocent life: "*homo homini res sacra.*" In the past this meant that we should take the life of a murderer to secure innocent life, and stress its sacredness. Justice Brennan seems to mean that the life of the murderer should be sacred too—but no argument is given for this premise.
24. Capital punishment is not inconsistent with *Weems v. United States,* 217 U.S. 349 (1910), which merely held that punishment cannot be excessive, that is, out of proportion to the gravity of the crime. Indeed, if life imprisonment suffices for anything else, it cannot be appropriate for murder.
25. The notion of deserving is strictly moral, depending exclusively on our sense of justice, unlike the notion of deterrence, which depends on the expected factual consequences of punishment. Whilst deterrence alone would justify most of the punishments we should impose, it may not suffice to justify all those punishments that our sense of justice demands. Wherefore criminal justice must rest on desert as well as deterrence, to be seen as morally justified.

POSTSCRIPT

Should the Death Penalty Be Abolished?

The argument is sometimes made that even if capital punishment is not a deterrent (or, more radically, even if capital punishment actually encourages crime), justice demands that certain criminals be executed. For example, former Nazis who killed many innocent people are today tracked down and brought to trial. Usually, these are elderly men who have lived many years without killing anyone. If the death penalty is demanded for these people, would this demand receive support from the deterrence line of reasoning? Probably not. First, these people have already stopped killing and so do not need to be deterred. Second, should we suppose that executing them will deter potential future Nazis, Aryan supremacists, and other racists from murder? More likely, in these cases, the argument is that these former Nazis should die for what they have done as a matter of justice.

A special issue for Americans is whether or not the death penalty is constitutional—in particular, whether or not it is cruel and unusual punishment. In a series of important legal cases (including *Furman v. Georgia,* 1972, and *Gregg v. Georgia,* 1976), the U.S. Supreme Court found that capital punishment *as then applied* was indeed unconstitutional. The main problem was that a lack of explicit standards in applying the death penalty gave much room for discretion, which in turn allowed prejudice and racism to hide behind legality. But the Court allowed the development of procedures of administering capital punishment that did not violate the Constitution.

One of the major points on which Welch and van den Haag seem to differ is over the extent to which we can separate and correct the bias, error, and other negative features to which Welch draws our attention from the death penalty itself. Van den Haag would argue that all the negative features that Welch has identified can be addressed without the moral acceptability of the death penalty being brought into question. Welch would probably respond that the moral acceptability of the death penalty is not its moral acceptability in an ideal world but in the real world that we live in.

Much has been written about the death penalty. Useful recent sources are Mark Grossman, *Encyclopedia of Capital Punishment* (ABC-CLIO, 1998); Hugo Bedau and Paul Cassell, eds., *Debating the Death Penalty: Should America Have Capital Punishment?* (Oxford University Press, 2004); and Bill Kurtis, *The Death Penalty on Trial: Crisis in American Justice* (Public Affairs, 2004).

ISSUE 14

Is Torture Ever Justified?

YES: Mirko Bagaric and Julie Clarke, from "Not Enough Official Torture in the World?" *University of San Francisco Law Review* (Spring 2005)

NO: Christopher W. Tindale, from "Tragic Choices: Reaffirming Absolutes in the Torture Debate," *International Journal of Applied Philosophy* (vol. 19, no. 2, 2005)

ISSUE SUMMARY

YES: Bagaric and Clarke remind us, first of all, that torture, although prohibited by international law, is nevertheless widely practiced. A rational examination of torture, and a consideration of hypothetical (but realistic) cases shows that torture is justifiable in order to prevent great harm. Torture should be regulated and carefully practiced as an information-gathering technique in extreme cases.

NO: Christopher Tindale argues that torture is absolutely wrong; it is not just wrong under ordinary circumstances, but even when the stakes are high. Hypothetical cases of imminent danger unless we torture a terrorist are always unrealistic to some extent, since, in the real world, we can never be sure of the facts. And once we become torturers, there is no going back. We have undergone a moral loss, and there is no assurance of gain.

This is a question that might not even have arisen in a serious way if it were not for current events and the War on Terrorism. Actually, philosophers had been talking about questions like this before 9/11, but only in a purely hypothetical way. No one anticipated that seemingly crazy ideas about buildings being blown up in New York and thousands of people being killed would actually become a reality.

But times have changed. And the question is now asked as a reflection of the times. Yet, to ask the question does not mean that one is considering torture as a possibility. For some of those who address this very question—Christopher Tindale, for example—would insist that the answer is no and would further insist that in this day of terrorism one of the important values that distinguishes us from the terrorists is that our answer should be that torture is absolutely out of the question. We should not try to imagine situations or conditions under which we torture people. So, on this view, we should not try to "draw a line," for one side of the line will be the side where torture is justified. Part of what we would be doing is determining an area in which we believed that torture is justified. But, in order to stay faithful to a negative answer to the issue question, there should not be any such area.

Opponents of the view that torture is never justified might construct various scenarios. Suppose, for example, that there was a ticking bomb that was hidden in a secret location and was set to go off at a certain time and would be sure to kill hundreds or thousands of innocent people. And suppose that the authorities had in their custody an individual who had detailed information about the bomb, including its location and the time it was set to go off. If this person were unwilling to disclose the information voluntarily, would torture be justified? After all, so much is at stake. If that one person were tortured, the very lives of a great many innocent people lie in the balance. How, it might be asked, could his well-being outweigh theirs?

The opponents of torture would probably respond that the question of torturing the person does not really have to do with his well-being at all, but rather with our own actions. The imagined scenario seems to suggest that so much is (potentially) at stake that we must be prepared to torture people. If so, we can't lay claim to ideas about human rights, the sacredness of life, etc. For example, if we really are going to be prepared to torture people, we have to have trained torturers who know how to do their job well. Even in the imagined "ticking bomb" scenario, the innocent people wouldn't be saved if we used an incompetent torturer who bungled the job and did something that resulted in the person's death—in which case we'd never find out any information about the ticking bomb. But the torturer has to cause some serious pain nevertheless. Proponents of torture seem to need someone who is a trained torturer, someone who is not doing this for the first time. So one question is whether we should initiate action now to produce such people in case they might be used.

In the first reading, Bagaric and Clarke argue that torture is already being practiced widely—although unmonitored and "underground." Their idea is to acknowledge it, endorse it to some extent, but draw lines. In the second reading, Christopher Tindale acknowledges that torture takes place, but does not wish to condone it. On Tindale's view, the current situation in which we abhor torture is a civilized achievement that we should not lose.

YES

Mirko Bagaric and Julie Clarke

Not Enough Official Torture in the World? The Circumstances in Which Torture Is Morally Justifiable

Recent events stemming from the "war on terrorism" have highlighted the prevalence of torture, both as an interrogation technique and as a punitive measure. Torture is almost universally deplored. It is prohibited by international law and is not officially sanctioned by the domestic laws of any state. The formal prohibition against torture is absolute—there are no exceptions to it. This is not only pragmatically unrealistic, but unsound at a normative level. Despite the absolute ban on torture, it is widely used. Contrary to common belief, torture is not the preserve of despot military regimes in third world nations. For example, there are serious concerns regarding the treatment by the United States of senior Al Qaeda leader Khalid Shaikh Mohammad. There is also irrefutable evidence that the United States tortured large numbers of Iraqi prisoners, as well as strong evidence that it tortured prisoners at Guantanamo Bay prison in Cuba, where suspected Al Qaeda terrorists are held. More generally Professor Alan Dershowitz has noted, "[C]ountries all over the world violate the Geneva Accords [prohibiting torture]. They do it secretly and hypothetically, the way the French did it in Algeria."

Dershowitz has also recently argued that torture should be made lawful. His argument is based on a harm minimization rationale from the perspective of victims of torture. He said, "Of course it would be best if we didn't use torture at all, but if the United States is going to continue to torture people, we need to make the process legal and accountable." Our argument goes one step beyond this. We argue that torture is indeed morally defensible, not just pragmatically desirable. The harm minimization rationale is used to supplement our argument.

While a "civilized" community does not typically condone such conduct, this Article contends that torture is morally defensible in certain circumstances, mainly when more grave harm can be avoided by using torture as an interrogation device. The pejorative connotation associated with torture should be abolished. A dispassionate analysis of the propriety of torture indicates that it is morally justifiable. At the outset of this analytical discussion, this Article

From *University of San Francisco Law Review,* vol. 39, Spring 2005, pp. 581–616. Copyright © 2005 by University of San Francisco Law Review. Reprinted by permission.

requires readers to move from the question of whether torture is *ever* defensible to the issue of the circumstances in which it is morally permissible.

Consider the following example: A terrorist network has activated a large bomb on one of hundreds of commercial planes carrying over three hundred passengers that is flying somewhere in the world at any point in time. The bomb is set to explode in thirty minutes. The leader of the terrorist organization announces this intent via a statement on the Internet. He states that the bomb was planted by one of his colleagues at one of the major airports in the world in the past few hours. No details are provided regarding the location of the plane where the bomb is located. Unbeknown to him, he was under police surveillance and is immediately apprehended by police. The terrorist leader refuses to answer any questions of the police, declaring that the passengers must die and will do so shortly.

Who in the world would deny that all possible means should be used to extract the details of the plane and the location of the bomb? The answer is not many. The passengers, their relatives and friends, and many in society would expect that all means should be used to extract the information, even if the pain and suffering imposed on the terrorist resulted in his death.

Although the above example is hypothetical and is not one that has occurred in the real world, the force of the argument cannot be dismissed on that basis. As C.L. Ten notes, "fantastic examples" that raise fundamental issues for consideration, such as whether it is proper to torture wrongdoers, play an important role in the evaluation of moral principles and theories. These examples sharpen contrasts and illuminate the logical conclusions of the respective principles to test the true strength of our commitment to the principles. Thus, fantastic examples cannot be dismissed summarily merely because they are "simply" hypothetical.

Real life is, of course, rarely this clear cut, but there are certainly scenarios approaching this degree of desperation, which raise for discussion whether it is justifiable to inflict harm on one person to reduce a greater level of harm occurring to a large number of blameless people. Ultimately, torture is simply the sharp end of conduct whereby the interests of one agent are sacrificed for the greater good. As a community, we are willing to accept this principle. Thus, although differing in degree, torture is no different in nature from conduct that we sanction in other circumstances. It should be viewed in this light.

Given this, it is illogical to insist on a blanket prohibition against torture. Therefore, the debate must turn to the circumstances when torture is morally appropriate. This is the topic of this Article.

International law defines torture as severe pain and suffering, generally used as an interrogation device or as a punitive measure. This Article focuses on the use of torture as an interrogation device and poses that the device is only permissible to prevent significant harm to others. In these circumstances, there are five variables relevant in determining whether torture is permissible and the degree of torture that is appropriate. The variables are (1) the number of lives at risk; (2) the immediacy of the harm; (3) the availability of other means to acquire the information; (4) the level of wrongdoing of the agent; and (5) the likelihood that the agent actually does possess the relevant information.

This Article analyzes the meaning of torture and the nature and scope of the legal prohibition against torture [and] examines whether torture is morally defensible. It is argued that torture is no different than other forms of morally permissible behavior and is justifiable on a utilitarian ethic. It is also argued that, on close reflection, torture is also justifiable against a backdrop of a non-consequentialist rights-based ethic, which is widely regarded as prohibiting torture in all circumstances. Thus, the Article concludes that torture is morally justifiable in rare circumstances, irrespective of which normative theory one adopts. [We] examine the circumstances in which torture is justifiable. Finally, [we] debunk the argument that torture should not be legalized because it will open the floodgates to more torture.

Torture: Reality and Legal Position

The Law on Torture

Pursuant to international law, "torture" is defined as:

> Any act by which severe pain or suffering, whether physical or mental, is intentionally inflicted on a person for such purposes as obtaining from him or a third person information or a confession, punishing him for an act he or a third person has committed or is suspected of having committed, or intimidating or coercing him or a third person, or for any reason based on discrimination of any kind, when such pain or suffering is inflicted by or at the instigation of or with the consent or acquiescence of a public official or other person acting in an official capacity. It does not include pain or suffering arising only from, inherent in or incidental to lawful sanctions.

Torture is prohibited by a number of international documents. It is also considered to carry a special status in customary international law, that of *jus cogens,* which is a "peremptory norm" of customary international law. The significance of this is that customary international law is binding on all states, even if they have not ratified a particular treaty. At the treaty level, there are both general treaties that proscribe torture and specific treaties banning the practice.

In terms of general treaties, torture is prohibited by a number of international and regional treaties. . . .

The rigidity of the rule against torture is exemplified by the fact that it has a non-derogable status in human rights law. That is, there are no circumstances in which torture is permissible. This prohibition is made clear in Article 2(2) of the U.N. Convention Against Torture, which states, "No exceptional circumstances whatsoever, whether a state of war or a threat of war, internal political instability or any other public emergency, may be invoked as a justification of torture." Thus, the right not to be tortured is absolute. . . .

This absolute prohibition is frequently highlighted by Amnesty International and other human rights organizations. For example, Amnesty International states, "The law is unequivocal—torture is absolutely prohibited in all circumstances. . . . The right to be free from torture is absolute. It cannot be denied to anyone in any circumstances."

Torture is also prohibited as a war crime, pursuant to humanitarian law. In addition, torture is considered to be a crime against humanity when the acts are perpetrated as part of a widespread or systematic attack against a civilian population, whether or not they are committed in the course of an armed conflict.

The Reality of Torture

As with many legal precepts, the black letter law must be considered against the context of reality. As this part shows, various forms of torture are used despite the legal prohibition of it.

1. Forms of Torture

As is noted by Dershowitz, torture comes in many different forms and intensities:

> Torture is a continuum and the two extremes are on the one hand torturing someone to death—that is torturing an enemy to death so that others will know that if you are caught, you will be caused excruciating pain—that's torture as a deterrent. . . . At the other extreme, there's non-lethal torture which leaves only psychological scars. The perfect example of this is a sterilised needle inserted under the fingernail, causing unbearable pain but no possible long-term damage. These are very different phenomena. What they have in common of course is that they allow the government physically to come into contact with you in order to produce pain.

Various methods of torture have and continue to be applied in a multitude of countries. The most common methods are beating, electric shock, rape and sexual abuse, mock execution or threat of death, and prolonged solitary confinement. Other common methods include sleep and sensory deprivation, suspension of the body, "shackling interrogees in contorted painful positions" or in "painful stretching positions," and applying pressure to sensitive areas, such as the "neck, throat, genitals, chest and head."

2. The Benefits of Torture: An Effective Information Gathering Device

The main benefit of torture is that it is an excellent means of gathering information. Humans have an intense desire to avoid pain, no matter how short term, and most will comply with the demands of a torturer to avoid the pain. Often even the threat of torture alone will evoke cooperation. To this end, Dershowitz cites a recent kidnapping case in Germany in which the son of a distinguished banker was kidnapped. The eleven-year-old boy had been missing for three days. The police had in their custody a man they were convinced had perpetrated the kidnapping. The man was taken into custody after being seen collecting a ransom that was paid by the boy's family. During seven hours of interrogation the man "toyed" with police, leading them to one false location after another. After exhausting all lawful means of interrogation, the deputy commissioner of the Frankfurt police instructed his officers, in writing, that they could try to extract information "by means of the infliction of pain, under medical supervision and subject to prior warning." Ten minutes after the warning was given the suspect told the police where the boy was; unfortunately the boy was already dead, having been killed shortly after the kidnapping.

3. The Widespread Use of Torture

a. Torture Around the World Despite the contemporary abhorrence against it, dozens of countries continue to use torture. A study of 195 countries and territories by Amnesty International between 1997 and mid-2000 found reports of torture or ill-treatment by state officials in more than 150 countries and in more than seventy countries that torture or ill-treatment was reported as "widespread or persistent." It is also clear that torture is not limited to military regimes in third world nations. Amnesty International recently reported that in 2003 it had received reports of torture and ill-treatment from 132 countries, including the United States, Canada, Japan, France, Italy, Spain, and Germany. . . .

The Circumstances in Which Torture Is Acceptable

The only situation where torture is justifiable is where it is used as an information gathering technique to avert a grave risk. In such circumstances, there are five variables relevant in determining whether torture is permissible and the degree of torture that is appropriate. The variables are (1) the number of lives at risk; (2) the immediacy of the harm; (3) the availability of other means to acquire the information; (4) the level of wrongdoing of the agent; and (5) the likelihood that the agent actually does possess the relevant information. Where (1), (2), (4) and (5) rate highly and (3) is low, all forms of harm may be inflicted on the agent—even if this results in death.

The Harm to Be Prevented

The key consideration regarding the permissibility of torture is the magnitude of harm that is sought to be prevented. To this end, the appropriate measure is the number of lives that are likely to be lost if the threatened harm is not alleviated. Obviously, the more lives that are at stake, the more weight that is attributed to this variable.

Lesser forms of threatened harm will not justify torture. Logically, the right to life is the most basic and fundamental of all human rights—non-observance of it would render all other human rights devoid of meaning. Every society has some prohibition against taking life, and "the intentional taking of human life is . . . the offence which society condemns most strongly." The right to life is also enshrined in several international covenants. For example, Article 2 of the

European Convention on Human Rights (which in essence mirrors Article 6 of the International Covenant on Civil and Political Rights) provides that "everyone's right to life shall be protected by law. No one shall be deprived of his life intentionally save in the execution of a sentence of a court following his conviction of a crime for which this penalty is provided by law."

Torture violates the right to physical integrity, which is so important that it is only a threat to the right to life that can justify interference with it. Thus, torture should be confined to situations where the right to life is imperiled.

Immediacy of Harm and Other Options to Obtain Information

Torture should only be used as a last resort and hence should not be utilized where there is time to pursue other avenues of forestalling the harm. It is for this reason that torture should only be used where there is no other means to obtain the relevant information. Thus, where a terrorist has planted a bomb on a plane, torture will not be permissible where, for example, video tapes of international airports are likely to reveal the identity of the plane that has been targeted.

The Likelihood of Knowledge or Guilt

As a general rule torture should normally be confined to people that are responsible in some way for the threatened harm. This is not, however, invariably the case. People who are simply aware of the threatened harm, that is "innocent people," may in some circumstances also be subjected to torture.

Regardless of the guilt of the agent, it is most important that torture is only used against individuals who actually possess the relevant information. It will be rare that conclusive proof is available that an individual does, in fact, possess the required knowledge; for example, potential torturees will not have been through a trial process in which their guilt has been established. This is not a decisive objection, however, to the use of torture. The investigation and trial process is simply one means of distinguishing wrongdoers from the innocent. To that end, it does not seem to be a particularly effective process. There are other ways of forming such conclusions. One is by way of lie-detector tests. The latest information suggests that polygraphs are accurate about eighty to ninety per cent of the time. There has been little empirical research done to ascertain the number of innocent people who are ultimately convicted of criminal offenses. As one example, however, research carried out in the United Kingdom for the Royal Commission on Criminal Justice suggests that up to eleven percent of people who plead guilty claim innocence. The wrongful acquittal rate would no doubt be even higher than this.

Moreover, it is important to note that even without resort to polygraphs there will be many circumstances where guilt or relevant knowledge is patently obvious. A clear example is where a person makes a relevant admission that discloses information that would only be within the knowledge of the wrongdoer. Another example occurred in the recent German kidnapping case, referred to earlier, where the man in custody had been witnessed collecting a ransom and had indicated to the police that the kidnapped boy was still alive. Where lesser forms of evidence proving guilt are available, the argument in favor of torture is lower.

The Formula

Incorporating all these considerations, the strength of the case in favor of torture can be mapped as follows:

$$\frac{W + L + P}{T \times O}$$

Where:

W = whether the agent is the wrongdoer
L = the number of lives that will be lost if the information is not provided
P = the probability that the agent has the relevant knowledge
T = the time available before the disaster will occur ("immediacy of the harm")
O = he likelihood that other inquiries will forestall the risk

W is a weighting that is attributable to whether the agent has had any direct connection with the potential catastrophe. Where the person is responsible for the incident—for example, planted or organized the bomb—more emphasis should be attached. Where the agent is innocent and has simply stumbled on the relevant information—for example, she saw the bomb being planted or overheard the plan to plant the bomb—this should be reduced by a certain amount. The prohibition against inflicting harm on the innocent is certainly strong, but it is not inviolable.

Torture should be permitted where the application of the variables exceeds a threshold level. Once beyond this level, the higher the figure the more severe the forms of torture that are permissible. There is no bright line that can be drawn concerning the point at which the "torture threshold" should be set. More precision can, however, be obtained by first ascribing unit ranges to each of the above variables (depending on their relative importance), then applying the formula to a range of hypothetical situations, and then making a judgment about the numerical point at which torture is acceptable.

There is obviously a degree of imprecision attached to this process and considerable scope for discussion and disagreement regarding the *exact* weight that should be attached to each variable. It is important to emphasize, however, that this is not an argument against our proposal. Rather it is a signal for further discussion and refinement. This is a call that we are confident other commentators will take up. The purpose of this Article is not to set in stone the full range of circumstances where torture is justifiable. Our aim is more modest—to convince readers that torture is justifiable in some circumstances and to set out the variables that are relevant to such an inquiry.

Regulation Better Than Prohibition

In addition to the moral argument for torture as an interrogation device, Dershowitz has argued that torture should be legalized for harm minimization reasons. Dershowitz has pushed for the introduction of "a torture warrant," which would place a "heavy burden on the government to demonstrate by factual evidence the necessity to administer this horrible, horrible technique of torture." He further adds:

> I think that we're much, much better off admitting what we're doing or not doing it at all. I agree with you, it will much better if we never did it. But if we're going to do it and subcontract and find ways of circumventing, it's much better to do what Israel did. They were the only country in the world ever directly to confront the issue, and it led to a supreme court decision, as you say, outlawing torture, and yet Israel has been criticized all over the world for confronting the issue directly. Candor and accountability in a democracy is very important. Hypocrisy has no place.

The obvious counter to this is the slippery slope argument. "If you start opening the door, making a little exception here, a little exception there, you've basically sent the signal that the ends justify the means," resulting in even more torture. The slippery slope argument is often invoked in relation to acts that in themselves are justified, but which have similarities with objectionable practices, and urges that in morally appraising an action we must not only consider its intrinsic features but also the likelihood of it being used as a basis for condoning similar, but in fact relevantly different undesirable practices. The slippery slope argument in the context of torture holds that while torture might be justified in the extreme cases, legalizing it in these circumstances will invariably lead to torture in other less desperate situations.

This argument is not sound in the context of torture. First, the floodgates are already open—torture is widely used, despite the absolute legal prohibition against it. It is, in fact, arguable that it is the existence of an unrealistic absolute ban on torture that has driven torture "beneath the radar screen of accountability" and that the legalization of torture in very rare circumstances would, in fact, reduce the instances of torture because of the increased level of accountability.

Second, there is no evidence to suggest that the *lawful* violation of fundamental human interests will necessarily lead to a violation of fundamental rights where the pre-conditions for the activity are clearly delineated and controlled. Thus, in the United States the use of the death penalty has not resulted in a gradual extension of the offenses for which people may be executed or an erosion in the respect for human life. Third, promulgating the message that the "means justifies the ends [sometimes]" is not inherently undesirable. Debate can then focus on the precise means and ends that are justifiable.

Conclusion

The absolute prohibition against torture is morally unsound and pragmatically unworkable. There is a need for measured discussion regarding the merits of torture as an information gathering device. This would result in the legal use of torture in circumstances where there are a large number of lives at risk in the immediate future and there is no other means of alleviating the threat. While none of the recent high profile cases of torture appear to satisfy these criteria, it is likely that circumstances will arise in the future where torture is legitimate and desirable. A legal framework should be established to properly accommodate these situations.

Christopher W. Tindale

Tragic Choices: Reaffirming Absolutes in the Torture Debate

1. Introduction: Abu Ghraib and the 'Festival of Cruelty'

In the opening years of a new millennium, one buoyed on the accomplishments of the past and filled with promises for the future, torture is in the news. And it is an issue with an immediacy and urgency about it, as politicians and theorists confront attacks on the very structure of life in Western nations and perhaps as some believe on 'civilization' itself. News exposés report on "the darker reaches of intelligence gathering" at Guantánamo Bay[1] and documentation details the abuses at Abu Ghraib and the policies that led to them.[2] At the same time, concerns to uphold the United Nations' Convention against Torture are seen in cases like that of Faryadi Zardad, the former Afghan warlord found guilty in Britain of conspiracy to torture. It is thought to be the first time torture offences committed in one country have been prosecuted in another.[3]

Yet the real urgency of the issue of torture is seen in the way something as significant as the Zardad case has been lost amidst discussions over the terrorist bombings in London. The capture of the principals involved in a failed attack on July 21, 2005 gives rise to questions of what information the accused possess and what means might be used to obtain that information. Are other attacks on innocent people imminent? The hypothetical 'ticking bomb' case that has proved so attractive to philosophers is starting to lose its abstractness.[4] And we suddenly find ourselves riding on buses and in subways in threatened cities conscious that someone's decision to torture or not could have a direct impact on our own welfare. And we further find ourselves scrutinizing our fellow passengers, as they in turn watch us, looking at them as we have never looked at others before. Seeing them as potentially threatening, wondering of what they might be capable. In such a climate of suspicion and fear how solid are the arguments and intuitions that have brought us so far? How firm is our conviction that no circumstances can warrant the torture of another human being? As Michael Davis points out,[5] a subject that had little interest to philosophers suddenly has immediacy, and we must test our arguments again.

From *International Journal of Applied Philosophy,* vol. 19, no. 2, 2005, pp. 209–222 (excerpts).
Copyright © 2005 by International Journal of Applied Philosophy. Reprinted by permission.

Alan M. Dershowitz questions whether an absolute opposition to torture rests not on moral or logical considerations but on ones that are historical and aesthetic,[6] and considers that only the most doctrinaire civil libertarians deny that torture is permissible when the stakes are high.[7] And Oren Gross echoes this sentiment in stating that the untenability of an absolutist position with respect to the ban on torture can be seen by the fact that all but unabashed Kantians recognize the difficulties for an absolutist position presented by extreme cases.[8] While never considering myself a Kantian, unabashed or otherwise, I remain committed to the absolutist position on this issue, even in the face of extreme cases, even while riding the subway registering the gazes of my fellow riders, and I will argue for this in what follows. In any such extreme choice like the ones that torture presents, we must weigh what we might gain against what we might lose, and we always lose too much. . . .

Before we proceed to review the arguments . . . we need to consider how we should understand the key concept at stake: 'interrogational torture.' Interrogational torture can be distinguished from other types in terms of the ends to be achieved. The goal of the process is information of some description. It may be specific information, or it may be more of a 'fact-gathering' mission, but information is what is required. This sets interrogational torture aside from acts intended to punish, deter, or dehumanize, although nothing precludes one act from aiming at more than one such goal.

More difficult is how we are to understand torture itself. Institutional definitions, like that endorsed by the United Nations,[9] tend to a certain vagueness that allows states to abuse the idea with disregard for the intent behind it. The central stress is placed on "severe pain or suffering, whether physical or mental, [being] intentionally inflicted on a person." But consider in this regard the Bush Administration's request for legal advice with respect to Section 2340A of title 18 of the United States Code (which implements the Convention against Torture).[10] The requested advice reports that, on review, the Convention against Torture and Section 2340A reach "only the most heinous acts" that are on "the extreme end of the spectrum of acts" causing pain and suffering.[11] The stress here is on what should count as "severe," and the judgment allows a wide range of pain and suffering that would fall short of being "severe." The judgment further proceeds to offer that even though interrogation methods may cross the line drawn in Section 2340A, under the circumstances then current, certain justification defenses could eliminate criminal liability. Chief among these are the Necessity defense, where the actor believes certain acts to be necessary to avoid harm or evil to himself or another, and the Self-Defense defense, which permits the use of force to prevent harm to another. We will look at both of these defenses below. The author of the report, Assistant Attorney General Jay S. Bybee, concludes:

> [T]orture as defined in and proscribed by Sections 2340–2340A, covers only extreme acts. Severe pain is generally of the kind difficult for the victim to endure. Where pain is physical, it must be of an intensity akin to that which accompanies serious physical injury such as death or organ failure. Severe mental pain requires suffering not just at the moment of

> infliction but it also requires lasting psychological harm. . . . Because the acts inflicting torture are extreme, there is significant range of acts that though they might constitute cruel, inhuman, or degrading treatment or punishment, fail to rise to the level of torture. Further. . . . under the circumstances of the current war against al Qaeda and its allies, application of Section 2340A to interrogations undertaken pursuant to the President's Commander-in-Chief powers may be unconstitutional. Finally, even if an interrogation method might violate Section 2340A, necessity or self-defense could provide justifications that would eliminate any criminal liability.[12]

Such legal advice as this indicates just how difficult it is to determine that torture has taken place, and even where it has, to successfully prosecute it. Still, in what follows, I will stand by the core of the UN definition, noting only that even acts that fall short of torture may still be cruel, inhuman, or degrading, and so have a natural prohibition against them.

2. A Lesser Evil: Supporting the Use of Torture

The legal advice noted above that proposes the use of defenses based on Necessity and Self-Defense is couched in hypotheticals and vagueness. We will look at both of these, taking that of Self-Defense first.

Self-defense

The doctrine of self-defense permits the use of force to prevent harm to others, and it is thought that this doctrine could be extended to justify torture in certain circumstances. The US Department of Justice memo suggests such circumstances *could* include the threat of an impending terrorist attack that would jeopardize the lives of hundreds, even thousands, of Americans. Crucial to the justification, though, would be the degree of certainty attached to the threat.[13] Some commentators see here an analogy with self-defense under a just war scenario where the defense of a collective is at stake.[14] But others have expressed a notable reluctance to see the two situations as sufficiently analogous.[15] Unlike the threatening enemy combatant in the unpredictable circumstances of just war, the torture victim is unarmed and has lost the autonomy which made the situation unpredictable. . . . The Justice Department ruling is alert to such dissimilarity, but argues that if the detained individual has aided in creating the threat, then this culpability allows them to be harmed. Again, though, these requirements are characterized by a high degree of vagueness insofar as they assume knowledge and confidence on the part of the interrogators. The requirements will likely be known only in retrospect, and the interrogators will be under pressure to act quickly. The suggested justifying circumstances are characteristically hypothetical.

The justification of self-defense also involves other specific criteria as detailed by Stephen Kershnar. These include the requirement that the harm used to extract information is proportional to the harm risked and that the agent involved believes the harm to the detainee to be "necessary" to prevent other harm. The first idea, proportionality, involves the difficulty of identifying and then weighing the competing harms involved. If we believe, as many do, that permitting interrogational torture would cause deep and lasting harm to the society that does so, then a much different calculus is involved than that recognized by the proponents of justified torture. The first idea, necessity, acknowledges how the self-defense defense effectively reduces to the necessity defense in most imagined circumstances.

Necessity

Like self-defense, but more overtly, the necessity defense focuses on the beliefs of the agent who would act. In this case, the agent must believe that certain actions, in this case the torture of a detainee, are necessary in order to prevent harm to that agent or another person. Again, the legal judgment requested by the Bush Administration advises that "certain circumstances could support such a defense."[16] Such circumstances are conceived in this instance in the form of a narrative wherein sleeper cells planted in the United States by al Qaeda are planning other attacks similar to or worse than September 11 and a detainee may possess information that could prevent those attacks. The more likely an attack and the greater the expected damage, then the greater the necessity.

What is clear about this defense is that it can only be used after the fact, after the torturer has been criminally indicted. This is evident in the judgment of the Supreme Court of Israel, asked to pronounce on the General Security Service's interrogation methods. They found that while the necessity defense might be available to an investigator in certain 'ticking bomb' scenarios, neither the government nor the security service could authorize "liberty infringing physical means" *during* the interrogation of suspects.[17]

The key problem with this defense, as others have noted, is that it rests with what a person believed rather than what was actually the case. In climates of heightened fear and suspicion we might imagine a rather elastic range of incidents that could fall under this defense. The very fact, though, that such extreme and exceptional justifications must be imagined emphasizes how great our natural prohibition against torture is.

Dershowitz is one of the commentators who have raised concerns about the subjectivity of the necessity defense and decisions like that of the Supreme Court of Israel.[18] In response, Dershowitz has proposed the very controversial and widely misunderstood idea of torture warrants. Dershowitz's position is that since torture is going on, or might be expected to occur, in an unregulated fashion (and we see this variously in the abuses of Abu Ghraib and the promptings of the Bush Administration), then it would be normatively better to have such practices regulated in a way that required accountability, justifications, and records. While his preference is for no torture,[19] he believes, under the circumstances, that this is unrealistic and that arguments resisting proposals like his are irresponsible. Only if a detainee refused to provide the information required would he be "subjected to judicially monitored physical measures designed to cause excruciating pain without leaving any lasting damage."[20]

Dershowitz marshals pragmatic, utilitarian, and historical evidence to support his proposal.

Pragmatically, he refers to the difficulties involved in getting warrants for wiretaps. Early frivolous cases that would never have received judicial approval and more recent cases where lawyers felt the evidence was too weak to seek a warrant indicate that there may well be "less torture with a warrant requirement than without one."[21] Moreover, he appeals to Bentham's "compelling" hypothetical argument (which we will review below) for torturing one guilty person to prevent the torture of a hundred innocent people.[22] And he further cites the sixteenth- and seventeenth-century English legal system, under which torture warrants existed to protect the state. Because it was legal and hence centralized, it was easier to abolish and left no lasting effects.[23] Again, we will return to this question of lasting effects.

In spite of the furor it seems to have created, Dershowitz's position is balanced and clear. Confronted with a choice of evils, he chooses what he takes to be the lesser of those involved. It is a tragic choice, but the dilemmas involved recommend it:

> If we do not torture, we compromise the security and safety of our citizens. If we tolerate torture, but keep it off the books and below the radar screen, we compromise principles of democratic accountability. If we create a legal structure for limiting and controlling torture, we compromise our principled opposition to torture in all circumstances and create a potentially dangerous and expandable situation.[24]

Dershowitz's proposal is not the only pro-torture argument currently fashionable, but it has dominated the literature and subsumes both self-defense and necessity defense arguments. Any argument against the use of torture should consider whether torture warrants are viable. What reasons, for example, do we have to believe things will change if, as Dershowitz insists, torture is being conducted under the radar screen *and* his proposed warrants will be hard to get? Richard Posner goes so far as to recommend against Dershowitz's warrants because officials are bound to want to push the rules beyond the boundaries and so the practice would simply become regular.[25] In their stead, he prefers something more akin to Walzer's "dirty hands" proposal,[26] where officials break the rules when the stakes are high and face the consequences afterwards, hoping in the circumstances to receive absolution.

The forgoing review gives something of the current state of strong argumentation favoring torture in extraordinary circumstances, and provides some of the key points to be challenged below. . . .

3. Kant's Lie and Winston's Dilemma: Defending the Absolutist's Position

Justifications for torture like those for the necessity defense gain their currency from a certain way of looking at consequences. Expected outcomes with values attached to them may be weighed against each other. In cases like those of 'ticking bomb' scenarios the expected significant and imminent loss of life persuades many commentators that unusual means are justified. We might worry both about the value of weighing outcomes in such cases and, if we are moved to do so, whether we are weighing the right outcomes.

Oren Gross argues that "Moral absolutists must maintain their support for the absolute ban on torture even when the outcome of abstaining from the use of torture in any given case is truly catastrophic . . . one must support a ban on torture no matter what."[27] Part of the problem, to his mind, lies with the Kantian perspective, and he does not think we should be brazen Kantians.

> Recall Kant's celebrated example of an unconditional duty, that is, the duty to tell the truth. According to Kant, the duty to tell the truth is not suspended even when an assassin (A) asks a person (B) whether a friend of B whom A wishes to murder is hiding in B's house. . . . Very few people would want to have as a friend someone who tells the assassin the truth rather than lie and save her friend. Similarly, few would want a leader who follows Kant's absolutist view to its extreme rather than act to save the lives of innocent civilians.[28]

The example itself is widely ridiculed and seen as a symptom of Kant's declining powers. Presented in "On the Supposed Right to Lie because of Philanthropic Concerns" (1797),[29] the full example has something of the burlesque about it. Not only does Kant insist that the friend tell the assassin the truth, but he presents the scenario that if the person lies and says her friend is elsewhere, the assassin may leave the house only to run into the friend who has escaped through a window. But what exactly is Kant's point in using this example? It does not seem to be that we should act *regardless of the consequences*. His point seems rather that we have no control over the consequences and we should not act in the moral realm with the false confidence that we do. Kant suggests through this example that moral acts have value in and of themselves and not in relation to other acts. The refusal to lie bears no *predictable* relation to the subsequent fate of the friend, either in the cellar or on the street, because we cannot predict what causal consequences will follow. Thus it is a mistake to tie the morality of the act to any consequences. We cannot control what will happen. But we *can* control our intentions and therein rests the morality of our act, not in any unpredictable outcomes.[30]

This false confidence is seen particularly in the way people approach the 'ticking bomb' examples, treating them with the retrospective benefit of knowing how many people have been saved as a consequence of torturing a detainee. But the examples themselves are so hypothetical and vague that it is only in light of such successful outcomes that they can be justified. Often overlooked is whether we have any grounds for expecting such success. Kant effectively challenges the causal link between the torture and its successful outcome, forcing us to focus on the act of torture itself and its justification *irrespective* of any imagined consequences which are completely unpredictable.

We do not know that the detainee really has the information we need; we do not know whether what he says under torture can be trusted; we do not know whether torture would be successful on fanatics; we do not know what thresholds of pain a particular individual can tolerate and still provide coherent information. And so our outcomes are unpredictable, even if we ignore what Kant may mean by this. All we know is that we are subjecting another human being to excruciating pain.[31]

Nor can we assume that information derived would be used to save lives. That is, the 'guarantees' are weaker than is imagined. Consider the hypothetical example of a political leader who I will call Winston. Through torturing a detainee authorities have discovered significant information relating to the war with al Qaeda including the presence of a ticking bomb which is an imminent threat to a large population of innocent people. But the information also includes extensive details on the al Qaeda network, including the possible whereabouts of its leaders. There is no time to act on both sets of information, that is, *both* locate the bomb and move on the whereabouts of the al Qaeda network. In fact, doing the first will seriously undermine the prospects of success with the second because removing the bomb will alert the enemy to the leak in information. Breaking the al Qaeda network would significantly reduce if not end the war against that enemy and save an unknown number of innocent lives who might be hurt in future attacks. Presented with this scenario, Winston faces a dilemma: should he act to save the innocent lives facing imminent danger; or should he conceal his knowledge of this attack and act for the long-term success of the war against al Qaeda? This is a difficult dilemma, exacerbated by the lack of guarantees. But we cannot be sure that he will decide to save the first group. That is, we cannot be sure in ticking bomb scenarios that even the desired information would be acted upon, as is so obviously assumed in treatments of this case. Like all hypothetical cases,[32] this example is open to a range of objections. But it serves its point: even the best consequences attached to the ticking bomb scenarios are not certain.

Beyond this, as I have suggested several times above, any serious review of the consequences of permitting torture should consider its impact on society as a whole. Whether torture is a lesser evil is relative to what it is measured against. One party seriously implicated in the practice of torture is those who are required to perpetrate the acts. There may be those, as the events at Abu Ghraib indicate, who possess the worst human qualities and engage in the worst human behaviors,[33] but do we seriously want such people acting on our behalf? And if we do, can we believe that we are not in some ways implicated in such actions? As Michael Ignatieff suggests, "Any liberal democratic citizen who supports the physical torture of terrorist suspects in ticking bomb cases is required to accept responsibility for the psychological damage done, not only to a foreign victim, but to a fellow citizen, the interrogator."[34] Mark Osiel details the mental struggles of torturers during Argentina's 'Dirty War,'[35] noting how aware they were of the enormity of their actions. In contrast to the reports from Abu Ghraib, many of the Argentine torturers struggled with a belief that they were still good Christians, and sought absolution from bishops who used arguments drawn from medieval thought to console them.[36] These men, Osiel insists, did not inhabit a separate moral universe. They were being asked to do things that put them in real moral anguish.

From the torturers themselves, we can move to the institutions that legitimize them, political or otherwise. It is the case, as noted earlier, that Bentham offered a utilitarian justification for torture. He imagines applying equal or superior torture to an individual in order to rescue a hundred innocents from torture. And he sets down provisional guidelines that anticipate modern proposals for regulation: that the prisoner be able to comply with what is requested; that the case involve imminent danger; that the harm to be averted be great; that the torture be regulated and limited by law; and that there should be minimal long-term effects of the torture.[37] Being so similar to contemporary suggestions, the proposals fall subject to the problems we have with those modern proposals. In particular, Bentham assumes the certainty governing the knowledge and intentions of the accused that characterizes other accounts. While Bentham's account is flawed and historically limited in what it addresses, Rod Morgan notes a larger utilitarian objection to torture: it deligitimizes the state.[38] The very practices of law on which the authority of the state is established are undermined by permitted actions that stray outside the law or for which the law is stretched to accommodate. We see the latter in some of the responses to Dershowitz's proposed torture warrants, responses that indicate such warrants would undermine the law that authorizes them.

Beyond the state, and perhaps most poignantly, there is the structure of society itself and the civilization it professes. Torture relaxes the constraints that reinforce civilized behavior. The deliberate infliction of pain upon a helpless human being challenges the moral authority of the society which allows it and the principles which justify that society. This is what is put most at risk by anything other than an absolute ban on torture. Moreover, "Torture is also 'world-destroying' in its ability to invert and degrade the ideas of agency, consent, and responsibility that help shape our ideas of self and self-government."[39] As abstract as this sounds, it has real manifestation. The victim who complies under torture complies against his or her will. The victim who refuses to comply becomes "responsible" for the further treatment that is inflicted. This behavior perverts our ideas of agency and responsibility, ideas central to moral understanding.[40] Again, the argument for this is seen most clearly in the Kantian position that stresses an obligation to treat others as moral agents, with the full autonomy we assign to them. To not do so, to judge that some are candidates for treatment that strips them of their agency as well as their integrity as human beings, that reduces them to physical bearers of pain and suffering, is a Kantian contradiction of the greatest magnitude. Hence, torture is more than an attack on our intuitions; it also undermines our moral groundings. . . .

4. Conclusion

It is by no means clear that torture is an effective way of obtaining information. On this question we have "only anecdotes and counter anecdotes."[41] Skilled interrogators do not need to resort to such means and the fanatic will be immune to them anyway.[42] Reports from Guantánamo Bay suggest disclosures come when pressure is removed.[43] We see cases of interrogators using a detainee's own belief set to address him, exploring his situation from his premises, asking the detainee what Allah's plan may be for him and why he has been spared,[44] and, perhaps more problematic, we learn of instances where the Koran has been destroyed. Destroying the Koran is not shocking (in Michael Davis's terms) for us, but it is for the adherent. It causes mental anguish, and if this is not torture, then like torture it causes hatred in the victim. On the other hand, as Posner notes, if it is ineffectual, then the issue is moot since it will always fail a cost-benefit calculation.[45] And Dershowitz, among others, cites several cases where torture has been successful in scenarios like that of the ticking bomb.[46]

Of course, that torture is being practiced as Dershowitz says "under the radar" has never really been in dispute. The issue is more how we could measure success of something that is so clearly contrary to our intuitions and arguments, and how we respond to the practices, like those coming to light from Abu Ghraib. The almost universal condemnation of what has been revealed there confirms our intuitions and refreshes our faith in basic human responses. But there will still be those like Dershowitz who earnestly believe that the more responsible response is to bring such practices into the open through something like his torture warrants. One of Dershowitz's critics offers a counter-hypothetical case, where the suspect in a ticking bomb scenario sees his four-year-old son tortured, and charges that a nation which permits such torture has lost its moral moorings.[47] Dershowitz replies that, on the contrary, a nation loses its moral moorings when decisions of this kind are left to those whose jobs are to protect terrorism at any cost.[48] But surely the two nations are not analogous? The one which allows warrants is not like the one which opposes them even though torture happens. Because the nation that resists this measure has not crossed the line between expediency and morality, and has not made the more tragic of the choices confronting it, one which once made, cannot be unmade.

Endnotes

1. Adam Zagorin and Michael Duffy, "Inside the Interrogation of Detainee 063," *Time*, June 20, 2005.
2. See, Karen J. Greenberg and Joshua L. Dratel, eds. *The Torture Papers: The Road to Abu Ghraib* (New York: Cambridge University Press, 2005).
3. Zardad, who had sought asylum in the UK, was found guilty in July 2005 and sentenced to two twenty-year jail terms to run concurrently. . . .
4. For discussion of this case, see Henry Shue, "Torture," *Philosophy and Public Affairs* 7 (Spring 1978): 124–43; Christopher W. Tindale, "The Logic of Torture," *Social Theory and Practice* 22 (Fall 1996): 349–74; and Oren Gross, "The Prohibition on Torture and the Limits of the Law," *Torture: A Collection*, ed. Sanford Levinson (New York: Oxford University Press, 2004), 229–53, 237–9.
5. Michael Davis, "The Moral Justifiability of Torture and Other Cruel, Inhuman or Degrading Treatment," *International Journal of Applied Philosophy*, this issue, 161–78.

6. Alan M. Dershowitz, *Why Terrorism Works: Understanding the Threat, Responding to the Challenge* (New Haven & London: Yale University Press, 2002), 148.
7. Dershowitz cited in Richard A. Posner, "Torture, Terrorism, and Interrogation," *Torture: A Collection*, Sanford Levinson ed.: 291–8, 295. Posner goes on to offer: "No one who doubts that should be in a position of responsibility."
8. Gross, "The Prohibition on Torture," 231.
9. For the UN definition and more detailed discussions see Michael Davis's paper in this volume and my discussion in 1996.
10. See "Memo 14" from the U.S. Department of Justice, Office of Legal Counsel in *The Torture Papers*, ed. Greenberg and Dratel, 172ff.
11. Ibid, 191.
12. Ibid., 213–4.
13. Ibid., 211.
14. See Stephen Kershnar's use of self-defense, "For Interrogational Torture" *International Journal of Applied Philosophy*, this issue, 223–41.
15. See Shue, "Torture," and Tindale, "The Logic of Torture."
16. "Memo 14," *The Torture Papers*, ed. Greenberg and Dratel, 209.
17. Supreme Court of Israel, "Judgment Concerning the Legality of the General Security Service's Interrogation Methods (September 6, 1999)" *Torture: A Collection*: 165–81, 180.
18. Alan Dershowitz (2002); "The Torture Warrant: A Response to Professor Strauss," *New York Law School Law Review*, vol. 48 (2004a): 275–94; "Tortured Reasoning," (2004b) *Torture: A Collection*: 257–80.
19. Dershowitz, "The Torture Warrant," 277.
20. Dershowitz, *Why Terrorism Works*, 159.
21. Ibid., 159.
22. Ibid., 142–3.
23. Ibid., 157–8.
24. Ibid., 153.
25. Posner, "Torture, Terrorism, and Interrogation," 296.
26. Michael Walzer, "Political Action: The Problem of Dirty Hands," *Philosophy and Public Affairs*, 1973: 160–80. Miller (*International Journal of Applied Philosophy*, this issue, 179–92) seems to share Posner's preference for seeing public officials accept the consequences of committing illegal acts.
27. Gross, "The Prohibition on Torture," 233.
28. Ibid., 238.
29. I. Kant, *Grounding for the Metaphysics of Moral, with On a Supposed Right to Lie because of Philanthropic Concerns* (Indianapolis: Hackett Publishing Company Inc., 1993).
30. My thinking about Kant's example has benefited from Susan Neiman's discussion of it in *Evil in Modern Thought: An Alternative History of Philosophy* (Princeton, NJ: Princeton University Press, 2002), 73–4.

31. For a typical case of ignoring these problems see Seumas Miller, "Is Torture Morally Justifiable?" (this volume), particularly the paragraph which follows his version of the 'ticking bomb' scenario ("Case Study 2"). Note that in spite of the confidence that Miller extends to what is *known* in such cases, one of his later objections to Dershowitz's torture warrants is that the information gained by torture is not reliable: "torture victims typically tell the torturer whatever they think he wants to hear."
32. Readers should recognize in this case an intentional allusion to Winston Churchill's apparent dilemma prior to the German bombing of Coventry, an attack that he may well have been aware of but the consequences of which he could have avoided only by alerting the enemy to the fact that the Allies had broken the German code. Given the debate among historians as to exactly what the historical Winston did know prior to the bombing, I have chosen to simply stress the hypothetical nature of the case. Depending where readers stand with regard to the historical case, they may be more persuaded by the point I am making.
33. *The Torture Papers*, ed. Greenberg and Dratel, 448.
34. Michael Ignatieff, *The Lesser Evil: Political Ethics in an Age of Terror* (Edinburgh: Edinburgh University Press, 2004), 142.
35. Mark Osiel, "The Mental State of Torturers: Argentina's Dirty War," in *Torture: A Collection*, 129–41.
36. Ibid., 132.
37. Jeremy Bentham, "Of Torture," (previously unpublished manuscript) in "Bentham on Torture" ed. Twining & Twining, *Northern Ireland Legal Quarterly* (1973) 24(3): 307–56; 313–5.
38. Rod Morgan, "The Utilitarian Justification of Torture: Denial, Desert and Disinformation," *Punishment & Society* (2000) 2(2): 181–96. See Morgan for a full discussion of the problems in Bentham's paper.
39. John T. Parry, "Escalation and Necessity: Defining Torture at Home and Abroad," in *Torture: A Collection,* 145–64, 153.
40. Nor should the victim lose his right to autonomy as Stephen Kershnar suggests (this volume). At issue is whether a person can choose the degree to which they can continue to be autonomous. It is contentious as to whether someone can choose to give up such autonomy (I incline to the Millian argument that they cannot); but more significantly, what is being denied to victims in the kinds of torture we are discussing is any real control, narrative or otherwise, over their lives. The control the torturer permits is merely artificial. On the way torture targets autonomy itself see also Miller (this volume).
41. Sanford Levinson, "The Debate on Torture: War against Virtual States," *Dissent* (Summer 2003): 79–90, 84.
42. Ignatieff, *The Lesser Evil,* 140; Tindale, "The Logic of Torture," 368.
43. Zagorin and Duffy, "Inside the Interrogation of Detainee 063," 19.
44. Ibid., 16.
45. Posner, "Torture, Terrorism, and Interrogation," 294.
46. May refers to an Israeli case where a ticking time bomb was thwarted (this volume); and Dershowitz (2002):137 refers particularly to a 1995 case in

the Philippines. There, it is believed, authorities tortured a terrorist into disclosing information that may have prevented the assassination of the Pope and attacks on eleven commercial airlines.

47. Mary Strauss, "Torture," *New York Law School Law Review* 48 (2004): 201–74, 273–4.
48. Dershowitz, "The Torture Warrant," 291.

POSTSCRIPT

Is Torture Ever Justified?

Bagaric and Clarke first remind us that torture is a widespread reality. Just because treaties are signed and international agreements are made, we should not assume that there is no torture (or that what little torture there may be is practiced only by rogue states, dictators, international pariahs, etc.). To this, however, there may be two sorts of responses. One is to seek to get a handle on torture, to regulate it in some way, so that the harm is reduced. (Think of a somewhat similar response to the situation in which hard drugs are a social problem: Here a harm reduction strategy may involve the distribution of clean needles. The problem isn't solved in such a way that it no longer exists. Rather, the harm that may result—e.g., the transmission of HIV—is minimized.) Another sort of response is wanting to reinforce the prohibition of torture and not to regulate it. On this view, the occurrence of torture is not something that we have to take into account and come to grips with—it is considered to be in a category like crime: We know that it goes on, but we don't want to *regulate* it. We want to *stamp it out.* We try as hard as we can to prevent others from torturing, but we have ultimate control only over our own actions, not theirs. So the first move in stamping it out is that we ourselves do not practice it.

One problem is that this second approach leaves an opening for "the bad guys" to act in ways that we say and show by our actions that we will not act. So, if we follow this path, some will say that we are really being negligent of our duty, for we have to protect and take care of those near and dear to us. We have to protect innocent people from "the bad guys." Here we face one of the major problems in politics: How to act right in a world in which other people do not act right. For, in the end, this is the kind of world that we live in—the real world, rather than an ideal world.

Further resources on torture are Sanford Levinson, *Torture: A Collection* (Oxford University Press, new edition, 2006); Karen J. Greenberg, *The Torture Debate in America* (Cambridge University Press, 2005); Alfred W. McCoy, *A Question of Torture: CIA Interrogation, from the Cold War to the War on Terror* (American Empire Project) (Owl Books, reprint edition, 2007); Jennifer K. Harbury, *Truth, Torture, and the American Way: The History and Consequences of U.S. Involvement in Torture* (Beacon Press, 2005); Karen J. Greenberg and Joshua L. Dratel, eds., *The Torture Papers: The Road to Abu Ghraib* (Cambridge University Press, 2005); Darius Rejali, *Torture and Democracy* (Princeton University Press, 2007); and James E. White, *Contemporary Moral Problems: War, Terrorism, and Torture,* 3rd ed. (Wadsworth Publishing, 2008).

ISSUE 15

Is Physician-Assisted Suicide Wrong?

YES: Richard Doerflinger, from "Assisted Suicide: Pro-Choice or Anti-Life?" *Hastings Center Report* (January/February 1989)

NO: David T. Watts and Timothy Howell, from "Assisted Suicide Is Not Voluntary Active Euthanasia," *Journal of the American Geriatrics Society* (October 1992)

ISSUE SUMMARY

YES: Admitting that religiously based grounds for the wrongness of killing an innocent person are not convincing to many people, Doerflinger argues on mainly secular grounds having to do with inconsistencies in the arguments of supporters of physician-assisted suicide. He examines the idea of autonomy, and the tendency for something like physician-assisted suicide to spread once it becomes initially accepted in a limited way.

NO: Watts and Howell first claim that it is very important to distinguish between *assisted suicide* and *voluntary active euthanasia.* Basically, the first of these is suicide or killing oneself; the second involves being killed by someone else (e.g., a physician). Watts and Howell argue that most of the opposition to physician-assisted suicide turns out to be really opposition to voluntary active euthanasia; furthermore, they argue that physician-assisted suicide would not have the dire consequence that its opponents predict.

The initial situation here is that someone—usually a terminally ill patient—wishes to die and requests physician assistance. (After all, the doctor knows what drugs will do the job, and there have been cases of laypeople botching a suicide attempt and ending up alive but paralyzed.) But a physician who agrees to this request seems to be going against all his or her training and experience (including the Hippocratic Oath and a career devoted to the preservation of life and health). Not only that but, according to the ordinary understanding of murder (as well according to the legal definition and most religious views), to participate in purposely bringing about the death of an innocent person would be murder. (It is no defense to a charge of murder that the victim asked you to do it—contrast the case of killing in self-defense where such killing is indeed a defense against the charge of murder, and is generally considered not to be wrong anyway.)

Consider one particular case that was reported a few years ago. A physicist who had long been exposed to X-rays in his scientific practice had cancer. The disease was at an advanced stage. During the course of the cancer, the physicist had lost his left hand and two of the fingers on the right hand; he had lost other body parts as well; and he had lost his sight. Hospitalized, and in great pain, he was given about a year to live. He was not able to kill himself and begged his brothers to kill him. The first two brothers refused. But the third brother agreed, brought a gun to the hospital, and shot his dying brother.

Many people would be quite sympathetic in a case like this, but nevertheless warn us of a slippery slope. If we allow physician-assisted suicide, it might be said, the policy would expand. Even if we grant that in fact a case like the physicist is the most appropriate case for physician-assisted suicide, most cases won't be like that. What about a physicist who lapses into a coma and can't express his wishes? Or a person who is still at the early stages of some fatal disease and is not in great pain at the moment, but has nothing to look forward to but death? What about a great athlete who wants to die because he now finds himself confined to a wheelchair? What about elderly people who request that they be killed through physician-assisted suicide because they are not well and do not wish to be "a burden" on their offspring? Perhaps family members who wish to inherit something (rather than see it go for fruitless medical expenses) and will subtly get the message across to their aged relatives that "it's time to go"? The list goes on. The problem, opponents to physician-assisted suicide might say, is that once you begin to allow this in some cases, it's easy to begin sliding down a slippery slope and ending up with results that are not at all what was desired in the first place.

In the following essays, Richard Doerflinger first argues that physician-assisted suicide is wrong and that the whole idea of there being such a thing as "rational suicide" is flawed. Then David Watts and Timothy Howell distinguish between various categories of euthanasia and suicide, and conclude that there really are cases of rational suicide and that physician-assisted suicide is not necessarily wrong.

YES

Richard Doerflinger

Assisted Suicide: Pro-Choice or Anti-Life?

The intrinsic wrongness of directly killing the innocent, even with the victim's consent, is all but axiomatic in the Jewish and Christian worldviews that have shaped the laws and mores of Western civilization and the self-concept of its medical practitioners. This norm grew out of the conviction that human life is sacred because it is created in the image and likeness of God, and called to fulfillment in love of God and neighbor.

With the pervasive secularization of Western culture, norms against euthanasia and suicide have to a great extent been cut loose from their religious roots to fend for themselves. Because these norms seem abstract and unconvincing to many, debate tends to dwell not on the wrongness of the act as such but on what may follow from its acceptance. Such arguments are often described as claims about a "slippery slope," and debate shifts to the validity of slippery slope arguments in general.

Since it is sometimes argued that acceptance of assisted suicide is an outgrowth of respect for personal autonomy, and not lack of respect for the inherent worth of human life. I will outline how autonomy-based arguments in favor of assisting suicide do entail a statement about the value of life. I will also distinguish two kinds of slippery slope argument often confused with each other, and argue that those who favor social and legal acceptance of assisted suicide have not adequately responded to the slippery slope claims of their opponents.

Assisted Suicide versus Respect for Life

Some advocates of socially sanctioned assisted suicide admit (and a few boast) that their proposal is incompatible with the conviction that human life is of intrinsic worth. Attorney Robert Risley has said that he and his allies in the Hemlock Society are "so bold" as to seek to "overturn the sanctity of life principle" in American society. A life of suffering, "racked with pain," is "not the kind of life we cherish."[1]

Others eschew Risley's approach, perhaps recognizing that it creates a slippery slope toward practices almost universally condemned. If society is to help terminally ill patients to commit suicide because it agrees that death is

From *Hastings Center Report,* Special Supplement, vol. 19, no. 1, January/February 1989, pp. 16–19. Copyright © 1989 by The Hastings Center. Reprinted by permission of the publisher and author.

objectively preferable to a life of hardship, it will be difficult to draw the line at the seriously ill or even at circumstances where the victim requests death.

Some advocates of assisted suicide therefore take a different course, arguing that it is precisely respect for the dignity of the human person that demands respect for individual freedom as the noblest feature of that person. On this rationale a decision as to when and how to die deserves the respect and even the assistance of others because it is the ultimate exercise of self-determination—"ultimate" both in the sense that it is the last decision one will ever make and in the sense that through it one takes control of one's entire self. What makes such decisions worthy of respect is not the fact that death is chosen over life but that it is the individual's own free decision about his or her future.

Thus Derek Humphry, director of the Hemlock Society, describes his organization as "pro-choice" on this issue. Such groups favor establishment of a constitutional "right to die" modeled on the right to abortion delineated by the U.S. Supreme Court in 1973. This would be a right to choose *whether or not* to end one's own life, free of outside government interference. In theory, recognition of such a right would betray no bias toward choosing death.

Life versus Freedom

This autonomy-based approach is more appealing than the straight-forward claim that some lives are not worth living, especially to Americans accustomed to valuing individual liberty above virtually all else. But the argument departs from American traditions on liberty in one fundamental respect.

When the Declaration of Independence proclaimed the inalienable human rights to be "life, liberty, and the pursuit of happiness," this ordering reflected a long-standing judgment about their relative priorities. Life, a human being's very earthly existence, is the most fundamental right because it is the necessary condition for all other worldly goods including freedom; freedom in turn makes it possible to pursue (without guaranteeing that one will attain) happiness. Safeguards against the deliberate destruction of life are thus seen as necessary to protect freedom and all other human goods. This line of thought is not explicitly religious but is endorsed by some modern religious groups:

> The first right of the human person is his life. He has other goods and some are more precious, but this one is fundamental—the condition of all the others. Hence it must be protected above all others.[2]

On this view suicide is not the ultimate exercise of freedom but its ultimate self-contradiction: A free act that by destroying life, destroys all the individual's future earthly freedom. If life is more basic than freedom, society best serves freedom by discouraging rather than assisting self-destruction. Sometimes one must limit particular choices to safeguard freedom itself, as when American society chose over a century ago to prevent people from selling themselves into slavery even of their own volition.

It may be argued in objection that the person who ends his life has not truly suffered loss of freedom, because unlike the slave he need not continue to exist under the constraints of a loss of freedom. But the slave does have some freedom, including the freedom to seek various means of liberation or at least the freedom to choose what attitude to take regarding his plight. To claim that a slave is worse off than a corpse is to value a situation of limited freedom less than one of no freedom whatsoever, which seems inconsistent with the premise of the "pro-choice" position. Such a claim also seems tantamount to saying that some lives (such as those with less than absolute freedom) are objectively not worth living, a position that "pro-choice" advocates claim not to hold.

It may further be argued in objection that assistance in suicide is only being offered to those who can no longer meaningfully exercise other freedoms due to increased suffering and reduced capabilities and lifespan. To be sure, the suffering of terminally ill patients who can no longer pursue the simplest everyday tasks should call for sympathy and support from everyone in contact with them. But even these hardships do not constitute total loss of freedom of choice. If they did, one could hardly claim that the patient is in a position to make the ultimate free choice about suicide. A dying person capable of making a choice of that kind is also capable of making less monumental free choices about coping with his or her condition. This person generally faces a bewildering array of choices regarding the assessment of his or her past life and the resolution of relationships with family and friends. He or she must finally choose at this time what stance to take regarding the eternal questions about God, personal responsibility, and the prospects of a destiny after death.

In short, those who seek to maximize free choice may with consistency reject the idea of assisted suicide, instead facilitating all choices *except* that one which cuts short all choices.

In fact proponents of assisted suicide do *not* consistently place freedom of choice as their highest priority. They often defend the moderate nature of their project by stating, with Derek Humphry, that "we do not encourage suicide for any reason except to relieve unremitting suffering." It seems their highest priority is the "pursuit of happiness" (or avoidance of suffering) and not "liberty" as such. Liberty or freedom of choice loses its value if one's choices cannot relieve suffering and lead to happiness; life is of instrumental value, insofar as it makes possible choices that can bring happiness.

In this value system, choice as such does not warrant unqualified respect. In difficult circumstances, as when care of a suffering and dying patient is a great burden on family and society, the individual who chooses life despite suffering will not easily be seen as rational, thus will not easily receive understanding and assistance for this choice.

In short, an unqualified "pro-choice" defense of assisted suicide lacks coherence because corpses have no choices. A particular choice, that of death, is given priority over all the other choices it makes impossible, so the value of choice as such is not central to the argument.

A restriction of this rationale to cases of terminal illness also lacks logical force. For if ending a brief life of suffering can be good, it would seem that ending a long life of suffering may be better. Surely the approach of the California "Humane and Dignified Death Act"—where consensual killing of a patient expected to die in six months is presumably good medical practice, but killing the same patient a month or two earlier is still punishable as homicide—is completely arbitrary.

Slippery Slopes, Loose Cannons

Many arguments against sanctioning assisted suicide concern a different kind of "slippery slope": Contingent factors in the contemporary situation may make it virtually inevitable in practice, if not compelling at the level of abstract theory, that removal of the taboo against assisted suicide will lead to destructive expansions of the right to kill the innocent. Such factors may not be part of euthanasia advocates' own agenda; but if they exist and are beyond the control of these advocates, they must be taken into account in judging the moral and social wisdom of opening what may be a Pandora's box of social evils.

To distinguish this sociological argument from our dissection of the conceptual *logic* of the rationale for assisted suicide, we might call it a "loose cannon" argument. The basic claim is that socially accepted killing of innocent persons will interact with other social factors to threaten lives that advocates of assisted suicide would agree should be protected. These factors at present include the following:

The psychological vulnerability of elderly and dying patients. Theorists may present voluntary and involuntary euthanasia as polar opposites; in practice there are many steps on the road from dispassionate, autonomous choice to subtle coercion. Elderly and disabled patients are often invited by our achievement-oriented society to see themselves as useless burdens on younger, more vital generations. In this climate, simply offering the *option* of "self-deliverance" shifts a burden of proof, so that helpless patients must ask themselves why they are *not* availing themselves of it. Society's offer of death communicates the message to certain patients that they *may* continue to live if they wish but the rest of us have no strong interest in their survival. Indeed, once the choice of a quick and painless death is officially accepted as rational, resistance to this choice may be seen as eccentric or even selfish.[3]

The crisis in health care costs. The growing incentives for physicians, hospitals, families, and insurance companies to control the cost of health care will bring additional pressures to bear on patients. Curt Garbesi, the Hemlock Society's legal consultant, argues that autonomy-based groups like Hemlock must "control the public debate" so assisted suicide will not be seized upon by public officials as a cost-cutting device. But simply basing one's own defense of assisted suicide on individual autonomy does not solve the problem. For in the economic sphere also, offering the option of suicide would subtly shift burdens of proof.

Adequate health care is now seen by at least some policymakers as a human right, as something a society owes to all its members. Acceptance of assisted suicide as an option for those requiring expensive care would not only offer health care providers an incentive to make that option seem attractive—it would also demote all other options to the status of strictly private choices by the individual. As such they may lose their moral and legal claim to public support—in much the same way that the U.S. Supreme Court, having protected abortion under a constitutional "right of privacy," has quite logically denied any government obligation to provide public funds for this strictly private choice. As life-extending care of the terminally ill is increasingly seen as strictly elective, society may become less willing to appropriate funds for such care, and economic pressures to choose death will grow accordingly.

Legal doctrines on "substituted judgment." American courts recognizing a fundamental right to refuse life-sustaining treatment have concluded that it is unjust to deny this right to the mentally incompetent. In such cases the right is exercised on the patient's behalf by others, who seek either to interpret what the patient's own wishes might have been or to serve his or her best interests. Once assisted suicide is established as a fundamental right, courts will almost certainly find that it is unjust not to extend this right to those unable to express their wishes. Hemlock's political arm, Americans Against Human Suffering, has underscored continuity between "passive" and "active" euthanasia by offering the Humane and Dignified Death Act as an amendment to California's "living will" law, and by including a provision for appointment of a proxy to choose the time and manner of the patient's death. By such extensions our legal system would accommodate nonvoluntary, if not involuntary, active euthanasia.

Expanded definitions of terminal illness. The Hemlock Society wishes to offer assisted suicide only to those suffering from terminal illnesses. But some Hemlock officials have in mind a rather broad definition of "terminal illness." Derek Humphry says "two and a half million people alone are dying of Alzheimer's disease."[4] At Hemlock's 1986 convention, Dutch physician Pieter Admiraal boasted that he had recently broadened the meaning of terminal illness in his country by giving a lethal injection to a young quadriplegic woman—a Dutch court found that he acted within judicial guidelines allowing euthanasia for the terminally ill, because paralyzed patients have difficulty swallowing and could die from aspirating their food at any time.

The medical and legal meaning of terminal illness has already been expanded in the United States by professional societies, legislatures, and courts in the context of so-called passive euthanasia. A Uniform Rights of the Terminally Ill Act proposed by the National Conference of Commissioners on Uniform State Laws in 1986 defines a terminal illness as one that would cause the patient's death in a relatively short time if life-preserving treatment is *not* provided—prompting critics to ask if all diabetics, for example, are "terminal" by definition. Some courts already see comatose and vegetative states as "terminal" because they involve an inability to swallow that will lead to death unless artificial feeding is instituted. In the *Hilda Peter* case, the New Jersey Supreme Court declared that the traditional state interest in "preserving life" referred only to "cognitive and sapient life" and not to mere "biological" existence, implying that unconscious patients are terminal, or perhaps as good as dead, so far as state interests are concerned. Is there any reason to think that American law would suddenly resurrect the older, narrower meaning of "terminal illness" in the context of *active* euthanasia?

Prejudice against citizens with disabilities. If definitions of terminal illness expand to encompass states of severe physical or mental disability, another social reality will increase the pressure on patients to choose death: long-standing prejudice, sometimes bordering on revulsion, against people with disabilities. While it is seldom baldly claimed that disabled people have "lives not worth living," able-bodied people often say they could not live in a severely disabled state or would prefer death. In granting Elizabeth Bouvia a right to refuse a feeding tube that preserved her life, the California Appeals Court bluntly stated that her physical handicaps led her to "consider her existence meaningless" and that "she cannot be faulted for so concluding." According to disability rights expert Paul Longmore, in a society with such attitudes toward the disabled, "talk of their 'rational' or 'voluntary' suicide is simply Orwellian newspeak."[5]

Character of the medical profession. Advocates of assisted suicide realize that most physicians will resist giving lethal injections because they are trained, in Garbesi's words, to be "enemies of death." The California Medical Association firmly opposed the Humane and Dignified Death Act, seeing it as an attack on the ethical foundation of the medical profession.

Yet California appeals judge Lynn Compton was surely correct in his concurring opinion in the *Bouvia* case, when he said that a sufficient number of willing physicians can be found once legal sanctions against assisted suicide are dropped. Judge Compton said this had clearly been the case with abortion, despite the fact that the Hippocratic Oath condemns abortion as strongly as it condemns euthanasia. Opinion polls of physicians bear out the judgment that a significant number would perform lethal injections if they were legal.

Some might think this division or ambivalence about assisted suicide in the medical profession will restrain broad expansions of the practice. But if anything, Judge Compton's analogy to our experience with abortion suggests the opposite. Most physicians still have qualms about abortion, and those who perform abortions on a full-time basis are not readily accepted by their colleagues as paragons of the healing art. Consequently they tend to form their own professional societies, bolstering each other's positive self-image and developing euphemisms to blunt the moral edge of their work.

Once physicians abandon the traditional medical self-image, which rejects direct killing of patients in all circumstances, their new substitute self-image may require ever more aggressive efforts to make this killing more widely practiced and favorably received. To allow killing by physicians in certain circumstances may create a new lobby of physicians in favor of expanding medical killing.

The human will to power. The most deeply buried yet most powerful driving force toward widespread medical killing is a fact of human nature: Human beings are tempted to enjoy exercising power over others; ending another person's life is the ultimate exercise of that power. Once the taboo against killing has been set aside, it becomes progressively easier to channel one's aggressive instincts into the destruction of life in other contexts. Or as James Burtchaell has said: "There is a sort of virginity about murder; once one has violated it, it is awkward to refuse other invitations by saying, 'But that would be murder!'"[6]

Some will say assisted suicide for the terminally ill is morally distinguishable from murder and does not logically require termination of life in other circumstances. But my point is that the skill and the instinct to kill are more easily turned to other lethal tasks once they have an opportunity to exercise themselves. Thus Robert Jay Lifton has perceived differences between the German "mercy killings" of the 1930s and the later campaign to annihilate the Jews of Europe, yet still says that "at the heart of the Nazi enterprise . . . is the destruction of the boundary between healing and killing."[7] No other boundary separating these two situations was as fundamental as this one, and thus none was effective once it was crossed. As a matter of historical fact, personnel who had conducted the "mercy killing" program were quickly and readily recruited to operate the killing chambers of the death camps.[8] While the contemporary United States fortunately lacks the anti-Semitic and totalitarian attitudes that made the Holocaust possible, it has its own trends and pressures that may combine with acceptance of medical killing to produce a distinctively American catastrophe in the name of individual freedom.

These "loose cannon" arguments are not conclusive. All such arguments by their nature rest upon a reading and extrapolation of certain contingent factors in society. But their combined force provides a serious case against taking the irreversible step of sanctioning assisted suicide for any class of persons, so long as those who advocate this step fail to demonstrate why these predictions are wrong. If the strict philosophical case on behalf of "rational suicide" lacks coherence, the pragmatic claim that its acceptance would be a social benefit lacks grounding in history or common sense.

References

1. Presentation at the Hemlock Society's Third National Voluntary Euthanasia Conference, "A Humane and Dignified Death," September 25–27, 1986, Washington, DC. All quotations from Hemlock Society officials are from the proceedings of this conference unless otherwise noted.
2. Vatican Congregation for the Doctrine of the Faith, *Declaration on Procured Abortion* (1974), para. 11.
3. I am indebted for this line of argument to Dr. Eric Chevlen.
4. Denis Herbstein, "Campaigning for the Right to Die," *International Herald Tribune,* 11 September 1986.
5. Paul K. Longmore, "Elizabeth Bouvia, Assisted Suicide and Social Prejudice," *Issues in Law & Medicine* 3:2 (1987), 168.
6. James T. Burtchaell, *Rachel Weeping and Other Essays on Abortion* (Kansas City: Andrews & McMeel, 1982), 188.
7. Robert Jay Lifton, *The Nazi Doctors: Medical Killing and the Psychology of Genocide* (New York: Basic Books, 1986), 14.
8. Yitzhak Rad, *Belzec, Sobibor, Treblinka* (Bloomington, IN: Indiana University Press, 1987), 11, 16–17.

David T. Watts
and Timothy Howell

Assisted Suicide Is Not Voluntary Active Euthanasia

Ongoing developments continue to spotlight the controversial issues of voluntary active euthanasia and assisted suicide. In November 1991, Washington State's Initiative 119, which would have allowed physicians, in certain circumstances, to aid terminally ill patients' dying, was defeated by 56% to 44%.[1] Dr. Jack Kevorkian assisted in the suicides of two non-terminally ill women in October 1991, leading to the suspension of his Michigan medical license.[2] Murder charges were later brought against Kevorkian by a grand jury. In New Hampshire, a bill has been introduced which would allow physicians to assist patients' suicides but not perform active euthanasia.[3, 4]

Such developments highlight some of the confusion emerging from discussions of voluntary active euthanasia (V.A.E.) and assisted suicide. A significant source of confusion has been the tendency to join these concepts or even to consider them synonymous. For example, the AGS Position Statement on V.A.E. and a recent article by Teno and Lynn in the *Journal of the American Geriatrics Society* both reject easing restrictions on V.A.E. and assisted suicide while making arguments *only* against euthanasia.[5, 6] The National Hospice Organization also opposes euthanasia and assisted suicide, but it, too, appears to blur the distinction between them in stating that "euthanasia encompasses . . . in some settings, physician-assisted suicide."[7] Others appear to use the terms euthanasia and assisted suicide synonymously in arguing against both.[8]

In contrast, the AMA Ethics and Health Policy Counsel argues against physician-assisted suicide and distinguishes this from euthanasia.[9] The AMA Council on Ethical and Judicial Affairs also acknowledges there is "an ethically relevant distinction between euthanasia and assisted suicide that makes assisted suicide a more attractive option." Yet it then goes on to assert that "the ethical concerns about physician-assisted suicide are similar to those of euthanasia since both are essentially interventions intended to cause death."[10]

In order to weigh and appreciate the merits of the different arguments for and against V.A.E. and physician-assisted suicide, it is critical that appropriate distinctions be made. For example, we believe the arguments made in the references cited above and by others[11, 12] against euthanasia are telling. However, we find that these same arguments are substantially weaker when used against assisted suicide. And while we agree with the AMA Council on Ethical and Judicial Affairs that an ethically relevant distinction exists between euthanasia and

From *Journal of the American Geriatrics Society,* vol. 40, no. 10, October 1992, pp. 1043–1046.
Copyright © 1992 by American Geriatrics Society. Reprinted by permission of Wiley-Blackwell.

assisted suicide, we think it is important to distinguish further between different forms of assisted suicide. Only by doing so can we begin to sort out some of the apparent confusion in attitudes toward these issues. We caution our readers that the literature on this topic, while growing, remains preliminary, with little empirical research yet completed.[13] Our arguments, however, are philosophical in nature and do not ultimately stand or fall on empirical data.

Definitions

Voluntary active euthanasia: Administration of medications or other interventions intended to cause death at a patient's request.

Assisted suicide: Provision of information, means, or direct assistance by which a patient may take his or her own life. Assisted suicide involves several possible levels of assistance: *providing information,* for example, may mean providing toxicological information or describing techniques by which someone may commit suicide; *providing the means* can involve written prescriptions for lethal amounts of medication; supervising or *directly aiding* includes inserting an intravenous line and instructing on starting a lethal infusion.

These levels of assistance have very different implications. Providing only information or means allows individuals to retain the greatest degree of control in choosing the time and mode of their deaths. Physician participation is only indirect. This type of limited assistance is exemplified by the widely reported case of Dr. Timothy Quill, who prescribed a lethal quantity of barbiturates at the request of one of his patients who had leukemia.[14] By contrast, supervising or directly aiding is the type of physician involvement characterizing the case of Dr. Jack Kevorkian and Janet Adkins. Adkins was a 54-year-old woman with a diagnosis of Alzheimer-type dementia who sought Kevorkian's assistance in ending her life. Dr. Kevorkian inserted an intravenous catheter and instructed Mrs. Adkins on activating a lethal infusion of potassium following barbiturate sedation, a process personally monitored by Kevorkian.[15] This form of assisted suicide carries significant potential for physician influence or control of the process, and from it there is only a relatively short step to physician initiation (i.e., active euthanasia). We therefore reject physician-supervised suicide for the arguments commonly made against V.A.E., namely, that legalization would have serious adverse consequences, including potential abuse of vulnerable persons, mistrust of physicians, and diminished availability of supportive services for the dying.[6, 7, 10–12] We find each of these arguments, however, insufficient when applied to more limited forms of physican-assisted suicide (i.e., providing information or means).

Will Assisted Suicide Lead to Abuse of Vulnerable Persons?

A major concern is that some patients will request euthanasia or assisted suicide out of convenience to others.[6, 9] It is certainly possible that a patient's desire to avoid being a burden could lead to such a request. With euthanasia, there is danger that a patient's request might find too ready acceptance. With assisted suicide, however, the ultimate decision, and the ultimate action, are the patient's, not the physician's. This places an important check and balance on physician initiation or patient acquiescence in euthanasia. As the AMA Council on Ethical and Judicial Affairs acknowledges, a greater level of patient autonomy is afforded by physician-assisted suicide than by euthanasia.[10]

Culturally or socially mediated requests for assisted suicide would remain a significant concern. Patients might also request aid in suicide out of fear, pain, ambivalence, or depression.[16] The requirement that patients commit the ultimate act themselves cannot alone provide a sufficient safeguard. It would be incumbent on physicians to determine, insofar as possible, that requests for assisted suicide were not unduly influenced and that reversible conditions were optimally treated. As to how physicians might respond to such requests, data from the Netherlands indicate that about 75% of euthanasia requests in that country are refused.[17] It is our impression that most requests for assisted suicide, therefore, appear to represent opportunities for improved symptom control. We believe most serious requests would likely come from patients experiencing distressing symptoms of terminal illness.[18] By opening the door for counseling or treatment of reversible conditions, requests for assisted suicide might actually lead to averting some suicides which would have otherwise occurred.

Another concern regarding euthanasia is that it could come to be accepted without valid consent and that such a practice would more likely affect the frail and impoverished. The Remmelink Commission's investigation of euthanasia in the Netherlands appeared to justify such concerns in estimating that Dutch physicians may have performed 1,000 acts of involuntary euthanasia involving incompetent individuals.[19] But while euthanasia opens up the possibility of invalid consent, with assisted suicide consent is integral to the process. Because the choice of action clearly rests with the individual, there is substantially less likelihood for the abuse of assisted suicide as a societal vehicle for cost containment. And there is little basis for assuming that requests for assisted suicide would come primarily from frail and impoverished persons. Prolonged debilitation inherent in many illnesses is familiar to an increasing number of patients, family members, and health professionals. Such illnesses represent a greater financial threat to the middle- and upper-middle class, since the poor and disenfranchised have less to spend down to indigency. Thus, we suspect requests to assisted suicide might actually be more common from the educated, affluent, and outspoken.

Patients diagnosed with terminal or debilitating conditions are often vulnerable. We agree that such patients might request assisted suicide out of fear of pain, suffering, or isolation, and that too ready acceptance of such requests could be disastrous. Yet, we believe that patients' interests can be safeguarded by requirements for persistent, competent requests as well as thorough assessments for conditions, such as clinical depression, which could be reversed, treated, or ameliorated. Foley recently outlined an approach to the suicidal cancer patient.[20] We share her view that many such patients' requests to terminate life are altered by the availability of expert, continuing hospice services. We concur with Foley and others in calling for the wider availability of such services,[5, 6] so that requests for assisted suicide arising from pain, depression, or other distressing symptoms can be reduced to a minimum.

Would Assisted Suicide Undermine Trust Between Patients and Physicians?

The cardinal distinction between V.A.E. and assisted suicide is that V.A.E. is killing by physicians, while suicide is self-killing. Prohibiting both euthanasia and physician-supervised suicide (i.e., with direct physician involvement) should diminish worries that patients might have about physicians wrongly administering lethal medicine. At present, physician-patient trust is compromised by widespread concern that physicians try too hard to keep dying patients alive. The very strength of the physician-patient relationship has been cited as a justification for physician involvement in assisted suicide.[21]

A number of ethicists have expressed concern that both euthanasia and assisted suicide, if legalized, would have a negative impact on the way society perceives the role of physicians.[6, 9, 11, 12] Limited forms of assisted suicide, however, have been viewed more positively.[22] Public and professional attitudes appear to be evolving on this issue. A 1990 Gallup poll found that 66% of respondents believed someone in great pain, with "no hope of improvement," had the moral right to commit suicide; in 1975 the figure was 41%.[23] A panel of distinguished physicians has stated that it is not immoral for a physician to assist in the rational suicide of a terminally ill person.[24] The recent publication of a book on techniques of committing or assisting suicide evoked wide interest and significant support for the right of people to take control of their dying.[25] For a significant segment of society, physician involvement in assisted suicide may be welcomed, not feared. Furthermore, while relatively few might be likely to seek assistance with suicide if stricken with a debilitating illness, a substantial number might take solace knowing they could request such assistance.

There is another argument raised against V.A.E. that we believe also falters when used to object to assisted suicide. It has been maintained that prohibiting euthanasia forces physicians to focus on the humane care of dying patients, including meticulous attention to their symptoms.[6, 18] This argument implies that physicians find it easier to relieve the suffering of dying patients by ending their lives rather than attempting the difficult task of palliating their symptoms. But for some patients, the suffering may not be amenable to even the most expert palliation. Even in such instances, some argue that limited forms of assisted suicide should be prohibited on the grounds that not to forbid them would open the door for more generalized, less stringent applications of assisted suicide.

To us, this "slippery slope" argument seems to imply that the moral integrity of the medical profession must be maintained, even if at the cost of prolonged, unnecessary suffering by at least some dying patients. We believe such a posture is itself inhumane and not acceptable. It contradicts a fundamental principle that is an essential ingredient of physician-patient trust: that patient comfort should be a primary goal of the physician in the face of incurable illness. Furthermore, by allowing limited physician involvement in assisted suicide, physicians can respect both the principle of caring that guides them and the patients for whom caring alone is insufficient. We concede that there is another alternative: terminally ill patients who cannot avoid pain while awake may be given continuous anesthetic levels of medication.[6] But this is exactly the sort of dying process we believe many in our society want to avoid.

Will Assisted Suicide and Euthanasia Weaken Societal Resolve to Increase Resources Allocated to Care of the Dying?

This argument assumes that V.A.E. and assisted suicide would both be widely practiced, and that their very availability would decrease tangible concern for those not choosing euthanasia or suicide. However, euthanasia is rarely requested even by terminal cancer patients.[6] In the Netherlands, euthanasia accounts for less than 2% of all deaths.[17] These data suggest that even if assisted suicide were available to those with intractable pain or distressing terminal conditions, it would likely be an option chosen by relatively few. With assisted suicide limited to relatively few cases, this argument collapses. For with only a few requesting assisted suicide, the vast number of patients with debilitating illnesses would be undiminished, and their numbers should remain sufficient to motivate societal concern for their needs. Furthermore, to withhold assisted suicide from the few making serious, valid requests would be to subordinate needlessly the interests of these few to those of the many. Compounding their tragedy would be the fact that these individuals could not even benefit from any increase in therapeutic resources prompted by their suffering, insofar as their conditions are, by definition, not able to be ameliorated.

Conclusion

We have argued that assisted suicide and voluntary active euthanasia are different and that each has differing implications for medical practice and society. Further discussion should consider the merits and disadvantages of each, a process enhanced by contrasting them. We have further argued that different forms of assisted suicide can be distinguished both clinically and philosophically. Although some may argue that all forms of assisted suicide are fundamentally the same, we believe the differences can be contrasted as starkly as a written prescription and a suicide machine.

We do not advocate ready acceptance of requests for suicide, nor do we wish to romanticize the concept of rational suicide.[26] In some situations, however, where severe debilitating illness cannot be reversed, suicide may represent a rational choice. If this is the case, then physician assistance could make the process more humane. Along with other geriatricians, we often face dilemmas involving the management of chronic illnesses in late life. We believe we can best serve our patients, and preserve their trust, by respecting their desire for autonomy, dignity, and quality, not only of life, but of dying.

References

1. Caplan A. Patient rights measure needs push from Bush. Wis State J November 13, 1991, p 11A.
2. Holyfield J. Doctor who helped suicides has his license suspended. Wis State J November 21, 1991, p 5A.
3. Beresford L., ed. Euthanasia movement may be helping spur new additional attention to pain relief. Hospice News Serv 1992;3:1–3.
4. Anonymous. New Hampshire: Lawmakers file suicide bill. Wis State J November 13, 1991, p 3A.
5. AGS Public Policy Committee. Voluntary active euthanasia. J Am Geriatr Soc 1991;39:826.
6. Teno J. Lynn J. Voluntary active euthanasia: The individual case and public policy. J Am Geriatr Soc 1991;39:827–830.
7. National Hospice Organization. Statement of the National Hospice Organization Opposing the Legalization of Euthanasia and Assisted Suicide. Arlington, VA: National Hospice Organization, 1991.
8. Travis R. Two arguments against euthanasia (letter). Gerontologist 1991; 31:561–562.
9. Orentlicher D. Physician participation in assisted suicide. JAMA 1989; 262; 1844–1845.
10. AMA. Report of the Council on Ethical and Judicial Affairs: Decisions Near the End of Life. Chicago, IL: American Medical Association. 1991.
11. Singer PA. Should doctors kill patients? Can Med Assoc J 1988; 138:1001–1001.
12. Singer PA, Siegler M. Euthanasia—a critique. N Engl J Med 1990; 322: 1881–1883.
13. Watts DT, Howell T, Priefer BA. Geriatricians' attitudes toward assisting suicide of dementia patients. J Am Geriatr Soc 1992, September 40:878–885.
14. Quill TE. Death and dignity: A case of individualized decision making. N Engl J Med 1991;324:691–694.
15. Cassel CK, Meier DE. Morals and moralism in the debate over euthanasia and assisted suicide. N Engl J Med 1990;323:750–752.
16. Jackson DL, Youngner S. Patient autonomy and "death with dignity": Some clinical caveats. N Engl J Med 1979;301:404–408.
17. Van der Maas PJ, Van Delden JJM, Pijnenborg L. Looman CWN. Euthanasia and other medical decisions concerning the end of life. Lancet 1991; 338:669–74.
18. Palmore EB. Arguments for assisted suicide (letter). Gerontologist 1991; 31:854.
19. Karel R. Undertreatment of pain, depression needs to be addressed before euthanasia made legal in U.S. Psychiatric News. December 20, 1991, pp 5, 13, 23.
20. Foley KM. The relationship of pain and symptom management to patient requests for physician-assisted suicide. J Pain Symptom Manag 1991; 6:289–297.

21. Jecker NS. Giving death a hand. When the dying and the doctor stand in a special relationship. J Am Geriatr Soc 1991;39:831–835.
22. American College of Physicians ACP to DA, Grand Jury: Dr. Quill acted "humanely." ACP Observer, September, 1991, p 5.
23. Ames K. Wilson L. Sawhill R et al. Last rights. Newsweek August 26, 1991, pp 40–41.
24. Wanzer SH, Federman DD, Adelstein SJ et al. The physician's responsibility toward hopelessly ill patients: A second look. N Engl J Med 1989;320:844–849.
25. Humphry D. Final Exit: The Practicalities of Self-Deliverance and Assisted Suicide for the Dying. Eugene, OR: The Hemlock Society (distributed by Carol Publishing, Secaucus, NJ). 1991.
26. Conwell Y, Caine ED. Rational suicide and the right to die: Reality and myth. N Engl J Med 1991;325:1100–1103.

POSTSCRIPT

Is Physician-Assisted Suicide Wrong?

We normally understand that physician-assisted suicide, if adopted as a matter of policy, will bring with it certain regulations and safeguards. Clearly, just asking a physician for assistance is not going to be sufficient. Even ordinary people are sometimes depressed, and it is understandable that people with a serious illness are even more likely to be depressed. So, at a minimum, people who request physician-assisted suicide would have to be screened for depression.

Moreover, as Watts and Howell, explain, levels of physician-assistance can vary from merely providing information, writing prescriptions, and so on, all the way up to the methods practiced by Dr. Kevorkian, including the use of his "suicide machines." In fact, while much of the public gets its ideas about what physician-assisted suicide is from Dr. Kevorkian, most proponents of physician-assisted suicide regard what he does as an example of what can happen if we *don't* have regulations and safeguards in place.

It is sometimes difficult for young and healthy people to imagine themselves at the end of life. But some people will have lived through their own relatives' deaths. And the very fact that we are all going to die—although no one knows the exact circumstances and whether we will go peacefully or in pain—makes this a real issue for all of us. The uncertainty that exists might make some people lean toward the side of the issue that provides the greater scope for leeway, allowing some provision for physician-assisted suicide, perhaps as a sort of "insurance" that may not even be needed.

Some of the opposition to the idea of physician-assisted suicide might come from a general repulsion against taking life. This is a good reaction to have. But it doesn't mean that the reaction is a substitute for judgment. Likewise, some of the opposition might come from a negative association of this with the Nazis. Again, the negative reaction is good one. What is required here though is an ability to get past purely emotional responses and mental associations. What we need are reasons and careful thinking.

Further resources on this issue can be found in James H. Ondrey, *Physician-Assisted Suicide* (Greenhaven Press, 2006); Gerald Dworkin, R.G. Frey, and Sissela Bok, *Euthanasia and Physician-Assisted Suicide (For and Against)* (Cambridge University Press, 2005); and Ian Dowbiggin, *A Merciful End: The Euthanasia Movement in Modern America* (Oxford University Press, 2007).

Perhaps of unique interest is Derek Humphry's *Final Exit: The Practicalities of Self-Deliverance and Assisted Suicide for the Dying,* 3rd ed. (Delta, 2003). This book was written by a founder of the Hemlock Society (now merged into the Compassion & Choices organization); the book contains useful information and is also a practical "how-to" guide so that "self-deliverance" (suicide) can be successfully achieved.

Internet References . . .

Animal Rights and Vegetarianism

http://www.peta.org/
http://ar.vegnews.org/Animal_Rights.html

UNIT 4

Human Beings and Other Species

Nowadays we recognize that human beings are part of nature and that we share the planet with other species. In former times, human beings and nature were thought to be two entirely different things. Even then, it was realized of course that we shared the planet with other species, but there was little or no question that eating their meat was morally acceptable. Now that we have become accustomed to seeing animals as fellow inhabitants of the natural world, the question arises about our proper relation to them.

- Does Morality Require Vegetarianism?

ISSUE 16

Does Morality Require Vegetarianism?

YES: Michael Allen Fox, from "Why We Should Be Vegetarians," *International Journal of Applied Philosophy* (vol. 20, no. 2, 2006)

NO: Holmes Rolston III, from *Environmental Ethics: Duties to and Values in the Natural World* (Temple University Press, 1988)

ISSUE SUMMARY

YES: Michael Allen Fox believes that the common practice of eating meat is something that we need to apply critical thinking to. He argues that if we care about pain, suffering, and death, and if we are to live up to the demands of justice, then we should take responsibility for our diets and become vegetarians.

NO: Environmental thinker Holmes Rolston III maintains that meat eating by humans is a natural part of the ecosystem. He states that it is important that animals do not suffer needlessly, but it would be a mistake to think that animals, like humans, are members of a culture. Rolston concludes that people too readily project human nature on animal nature.

This issue comes about because humans are rational beings and, at least to some extent, we are able to control our actions. Many other living things eat meat but are not rational beings. Lions, for example, eat meat—but a male lion will often kill all the lion cubs of his new mate, which would certainly seem by human standards to be unreasonable. The idea that we are just following nature when we eat meat may not exactly be true, say many who recognize that some animal behaviors are not to be used as models by people. Instead we must pick and choose the behaviors that we follow.

Moreover, unlike lions, most people do not *have* to eat meat in order to survive. Indeed, some entire cultures are vegetarian. Individual vegetarians can be found in other cultures as well, for example, in American culture. On the other hand, in American culture the practice of meat eating is the norm and is quite widespread—just look at all the McDonald's and Burger Kings!

As a justification for eating meat, some conclude that it is not quite right to say that we are just doing what the other living things do—for we do not follow animal behavior if we think it would be wrong to do so. But if meat eating is a cultural practice, then, like any other cultural practice, it should be subject to rational judgment and moral critique. We know that in the past, many socially accepted practices have been condoned at the time they were practiced but later found to be morally wanting. We can look back now in amazement at the practice of slavery in the South in the early part of the 1800s or the way great poverty was ignored in Victorian England while some people lived lives of luxury. One wonders, "How could people *do* that?" Could it be that future generations will look back at the Americans who thought nothing of consuming Big Macs and likewise wonder, "How could people *do* that?"

Many find the basic problem with meat eating to be the conditions under which animals that are raised for food live. The people who eat meat bring about these deplorable conditions, some argue, because high consumer demand dictates that the supermarkets are well stocked with meat, that fast food outlets sell meat, and therefore make it easier to obtain a meal with meat than one without. Animal husbandry is big business, and it is big business because the customers demand the product. Because of this huge demand, it can be said that many people look the other way when farmers raise animals under conditions that many vegetarians find appalling.

In the following selections, Michael Allen Fox argues that morality does in fact require vegetarianism. He emphasizes the ideas of caring, justice, and living responsibly. Rather than simply accepting cultural norms blindly, we need to subject them—in this case, the widespread practice of meat eating—to critical analysis. Holmes Rolston III then maintains that the human consumption of meat is part of our human interaction with the natural (as opposed to the cultural) environment. He asserts that it is important that animals do not suffer needlessly, of course, but it would be a mistake to think that animals are members of a culture in the same way that human beings belong to a culture. People too readily project human nature on animal nature, he contends.

YES

Michael Allen Fox

Why We Should Be Vegetarians

Introduction

Presenting the ethics of vegetarianism often arouses heated responses because it challenges the norm of meat eating most people subscribe to. This norm is associated with many symbols and rituals and has a lengthy history (Douglas 1975; Twigg 1983; Adams 1991; Fiddes 1991; Fox 1999b). These associations make the norm difficult to dislodge, and imbue it with considerable inertia. But vegetarianism also taps into the uneasiness and guilt-feelings many meat eaters harbor today, as is evident in hostile and defensive responses to vegetarian practices and arguments, ridicule, and frequent demands that vegetarians justify their "deviant" outlook. Vegetarianism is therefore commonly placed in a defensive position: on it rests the onus of showing that meat eating is unnecessary, environmentally unsustainable, wrong, and so on. This essay presents an ethical rationale for vegetarianism that is straightforward in its appeal, and has the additional aim of destabilizing the default position in favor of meat eating. The argument developed here does not rely upon either a specifically utilitarian view (like that of Peter Singer) or a rights-centred theory (like that of Tom Regan), but originates instead in observations that are fundamental to ethical thinking in a more general sense. Against this background, I offer a vigorous ethical argument for vegetarianism that is grounded in considerations of caring and justice. In addition, the relatively new issue of "responsible meat eating" will be examined, and the inadequacies of this concept exposed. I conclude that only by being vegetarians can we consistently honor what ethics is based upon, and by doing so, minimize the harm we cause by our lifestyle choices. What follows represents just a small part of the overall case for vegetarianism, which is presented in detail elsewhere (Wynne-Tyson 1979; Stephens 1994; Hill 1996; Fox 1999b).

Facing and Avoiding the Food Issue

Everyone who is concerned about making the world a better place in which to live must consider, among other things, the food he or she eats. Why? Because food does not come from nowhere, and how people obtain it has always been an indicator of the way they have chosen to live, of what they value, of their

From *International Journal of Applied Philosophy,* vol. 20, no. 2, 2006, pp. 295–310 (excerpts).
Copyright © 2006 by International Journal of Applied Philosophy. Reprinted by permission.

attitudes toward life, each other, and nature in general. I believe most of us today are concerned about the state of the world; and not only this: most of us are concerned about our health. Therefore, we should be doubly concerned about what we eat.

But somehow these concerns often fall by the wayside, failing to translate into an examination of dietary choices. For some—perhaps most in the Western world, and an increasing number in the non-Western world—it seems to be enough to declare simply: "I love my meat and wouldn't think of giving it up," or: "I've heard the arguments against meat eating, but I'm still a carnivore." These responses exemplify an unreflective approach to life, however, and one that a philosopher must therefore question. I do not plan to go into the health-centred reasons for affirming that a diet that does not rely on meat is healthier than one that does. The largest study ever undertaken on this subject was conducted by Cornell University scientists in the People's Republic of China and Taiwan (Campbell and Campbell 2004). According to their findings, plant-based diets are significantly healthier in numerous respects than meat-based ones. Many other studies have confirmed this result in various sample groups. Thus, there would appear to be reason enough to choose being a vegetarian for health (that is, prudential) reasons alone. But there are additional and compelling reasons that can help us make this decision.

The most important among these has to do with the consequences of eating meat for nonhuman animals (see Singer and Mason 2006). First, note the expression just used: "nonhuman animals." We customarily forget or don't even consider that humans are animals too; we just refer to "animals" as all those other things that from time to time we may think resemble us in certain respects or behaviors but that, we comfort ourselves into believing, are not *really* all that much like us. Animals are those lesser beings that don't matter, or don't matter very much at any rate. They are those beings that work for us, serve our needs, and give up their lives for us. And generally we download an abundance of our problems onto them. For example, we experiment on them in order (we suppose) to improve our lives, as if *their* lives had no independent value—to the animals themselves (and perhaps in objective terms as well). We violate their habitats in order to achieve important but also entirely trivial objectives. We make them into slaves of our obsession with commodities and profits. If, on the other hand, we practice thinking of ourselves as animals too, a quite different perspective emerges. Now we enable ourselves to perceive continuity between humans and nonhumans rather than a false and untenable dichotomy. Now we can release the capacity to understand that other beings of value exist besides ourselves; that they have their own purposes independent of ours; experience pain and suffering; and have a will to live. Historically, there have always been voices to express these ideas, but they have been in the minority and have been ignored or marginalized. This is no longer the case. Anyone who is at all aware of new ideas about nonhuman animals—about their intelligence, communication skills, social life, sophisticated behaviors, and evolutionary proximity to us (Pepperberg 1999; Savage-Rumbaugh et al. 2000; Griffin 2001; Rendell and Whitehead 2001; de Waal and Tyack 2003; Linden 2003)—has to face the task of thinking through the complexities of our troubled relationship with them.

I referred above to the consequences for nonhuman animals of turning them into meat for human consumption. The obvious ones are: (1) pain and suffering, and (2) death. The level at which the meat industry inflicts these harms on sentient beings defies belief. Steven M. Wise reports that: "the sheer number of nonhuman animals whom we kill . . . is beyond understanding. More than 300 mammals and birds are killed [in the U.S. alone] each time your heart beats. The number triples for the rest of the world. In the United States, more than 10 billion are slaughtered annually just for food" (Wise 2002: 9). It is easy to see why we call the economic sector that generates these statistics "the meat industry"; but we could just as well label it "the torture and indiscriminate killing industry," because that is a more accurate description. It is difficult to explain why any normal person would not recoil in horror before this unending and insatiable carnage. Today, domesticated nonhuman animals, as they always have been, are purposely bred for eventual slaughter. They are genetically fashioned, selected, carefully confined, nourished, and often chemically enhanced for the ultimate goal of turning them into the products that satisfy people's taste preferences. Nowhere in this process is it ever considered whether our taste preferences can only, or best, be met in this manner, let alone whether our nutritional requirements must be so addressed.

People tend to compartmentalize their relationships with, and responses to, animals (Fox 1999b, chap. 3), so that pets receive lavish affection while domesticated livestock are merely expendable things, regarded for the most part in a purely instrumental manner, and often allowed to languish in miserable conditions. Furthermore, the process by which farmed animals become or yield food for human consumption is removed from view and also from thought by the meat-production system and its Image-makers.[1] Meat, as a prized commodity having considerable cultural and symbolic meaning and value, exercises a strong hold on our imagination, emotions, and desire. Inasmuch as this valuation rests on associations that go beyond our conscious control, it resists being analyzed and deconstructed, and this resistance helps prevent us from seeing connections between our professed belief in humaneness and kindness toward animals, on the one hand, and the brutality that brings meat to our tables, on the other. Failing to make connections likewise subverts the motivation to bring about changes in our dietary attitudes and practices. While philosophical examination can dislodge ethical prejudices against taking animals' moral status seriously, it requires a reorientation of both thought and feeling to allow natural sentiments of compassion and caring to embrace nonhuman creatures.

Animals' Pain and Suffering, and Why It Matters

. . . Why should anyone care about the suffering of nonhuman animals? First of all, why should anyone care about pain and suffering, period? The reason is that pain and suffering hurt; they are "aversive stimuli," or experiences that have a negative impact, are disvalued by us, and we seek to avoid if at all possible. No other reason can be offered: we care about our own pain and suffering because we don't like it and it adversely affects our well-being. I am not denying the obvious here—that pain and suffering are part of life, and that they are sometimes offset by a greater good. What I am talking about is *gratuitous* pain and suffering, which are caused by malice, cruelty, or carelessness, and *unjustified* pain and suffering, which are not outweighed by a greater good. As I shall argue below, the benefits of meat eating do not amount to a greater good that can mitigate or neutralize the harm done to the animals we rear and slaughter for food.

Now, why should we care about other people's pain and suffering, especially if we don't even know them? Again, the answer is: "Because it hurts, they don't like it, and it harms their well-being." To this, the response may be: "So what?" But if someone says, "So what?" then there's nothing else we can offer by way of persuasion. Harming others is bad because it's harmful, and what's harmful is bad. This is a circular statement, to be sure; but the reason is precisely that it is meant to convey a self-evident truth, not an argument. Anyone who refuses to accept that we should not harm others (who are demonstrably like oneself in relevant respects) simply because they don't want to be harmed, is unlikely to be persuaded by a different sort of appeal, or indeed by any appeal at all. We call people like this "amoral" or "sociopaths" or "psychopaths."

Are we, then, like sociopaths in a certain arena of our lives, if we don't care about hurting nonhuman animals? Well, maybe so, in an important sense. But the point here is not to engage in name-calling or laying on guilt-trips. Rather, it's to realize that nonhuman animals can be hurt, that it matters to them, and therefore, should matter to us.[2] I won't try to prove that nonhuman animals can experience pain and suffering. As I noted earlier, this has been confirmed many times over by the evidence. The biggest breakthrough we can make in our thinking about this matter, it seems to me, is to acknowledge that *it makes no difference what kind of creature we're talking about; if it can feel pain and suffer, such pain and suffering matter.* Jeremy Bentham put this view forward more than two centuries ago. Here, I refer to his famous and frequently quoted remark about sentient nonhuman animals. Bentham says, "The question is not, Can they *reason*? nor Can they *talk*? but, Can they *suffer*?" (Bentham 1789: chap. 19, sec. 1). It is relatively easy today to get utilitarians to accept this outlook. But Bentham's insight has a wider appeal, and those who hold different ethical views from his can nonetheless relate to what he is saying with equal facility.[3] Whether pain and suffering are bad in and of themselves or because of their consequences for our well-being (or both) is not really crucial. What *does* count is that they are sometimes harmful, and that beings who have these experiences seek relief from them. In this ethically important respect, humans and nonhuman animals are alike, and justice, as Aristotle observed long ago, means treating like beings alike.[4] Just treatment is to be understood as fair or deserving treatment. If nonhuman animals are like humans in respect to their experiences of pain and suffering, then so far as it is possible to do so, they should be treated alike. What this means in actual practice is not always easy to determine, since it is difficult to compare different beings' mental states with any degree of precision; but an accurate estimate is not always all that hard to arrive at either. In the case of animal pain and suffering, we have ample evidence to go on, as already stated. This evidence entails simply that we should try to avoid gratuitously or unjustifiably causing such hurtful, harmful feelings when (a) it is within our power to do so, and (b) the sacrifice this requires of us is minimal. And the most obvious way in which to apply this principle of conduct to nonhuman animals is to avoid committing direct or indirect acts—such as buying meat to eat—that violate their well-being in the way I have described.

The production of meat is not the only cause of gratuitous and/or unjustified pain and suffering in nonhumans, to be sure; but it is overwhelmingly the main source of the negative impacts we visit on other conscious, sentient creatures. And we can choose to be on the side of either causing or preventing this kind of pain and suffering. Again, whether we are utilitarians or not, we should care about the amount of pain and suffering in the world, and do what we can to make the world less, rather than more, full of these aversive experiences. Surely, this is what we try to do when we give to charities, help those in need, look after people in distress, and so on. We help nonhuman animals when they are the victims of wanton cruelty; why would we not choose to help them escape from the effects of cruel practices that form a more deliberately planned, systemic part of their lives as well? To many people, the answer is obvious: we *would* and *do* choose to help, and we *should* do so. Others evidently need persuasion on this point. While it is the philosopher's job to try to frame a rational appeal, it is often a more complex type of approach that enables us to change our minds. This is why I have invoked the notion of caring in this essay in order to broaden the case I am making in such a way that it links up with the sorts of feelings that are an essential part of our moral orientation. We need to pause for a moment, however, to consider more carefully what "caring" means.

Caring

To say that *a* cares about *b* may entail one (or both) of two things: *a* feels liking or affection toward *b; a* wants to look after or seriously respond to the needs or condition of *b*, in order to contribute to *b*'s welfare. I wish to focus here on *b* (some people do not like animals particularly well, and in any case, liking should not be a precondition for taking up a proper ethical attitude toward a being). It has been argued that: "What establishes a moral obligation to care for someone else is the existence of, or potential for, a relation between oneself and the other, or else the potential for growth in one's relation with the other."[5] I think that this claim is incorrect, because it states at best a sufficient condition for caring, and may just single out a possible (and obviously desirable) side effect of it. Certainly, there can be and is unrequited caring; and someone may feel a caring form of connectedness with other beings that are totally unaware of the carer's existence. Nor are we necessarily aware of the positive outcome of our caring (if there is any) in every case. Caring about another living thing springs from the fundamental sensibilities of sympathy, empathy, and compassion, and it is these that underpin a moral obligation to care. As for the benefits of caring, just as virtue is its own reward, so too does caring lead to inner contentment and personal growth that are not dependent upon reciprocity from the object of care. Furthermore, although unrelated to our present subject, there are other kinds of caring that don't involve reciprocity in principle, or else only do so in an indirect sense: one may care, for example, about the fate of inanimate entities such as natural formations or artworks.

I have said above that caring derives from basic moral sensibilities. "Compassion," etymologically, means "suffering with." The fact that compassion is a pretty nearly universal attribute of humans is indisputable. It exists and manifests itself even in the most jaded, cruel, and evil persons (think of the "Birdman of Alcatraz," who could only relate to stray birds, and whose nuturing of them transformed his life for the better, one might even say, "redeemed" it). The full meaning of "compassion" involves an acute awareness of another's suffering plus the wish to relieve it. We may speculate that, while the origin of compassion is innate, this sensibility (or moral emotion) is cognitively reinforced by an awareness of shared needs; an appreciation of and respect for (valorizing of) the other's independent life and welfare; and, in relation to nonhuman animals, a sense of our evolutionary continuity with them, and our shared interest in survival and flourishing. When I stated earlier that sentient nonhumans, like us, experience pain and suffering, have their own purposes, and display a will to live, I had in mind the kind of enhancement of compassion through knowledge just explained, which might be expected to positively regulate our behavior toward them.

"Sympathy" (etymologically: "feeling with") signifies resonant feeling occasioned in oneself by another's feelings, which one experiences at the same time as the other is having them. "Empathy" (etymologically: "feeling inside") conveys the sense of being able to understand and share another's feelings. Thus, empathy has a more cognitive element than sympathy; it suggests a deeper appreciation of others' affective states. The relationship between compassion, sympathy, and empathy, then, seems to be as follows: sympathy, modified by cognition, leads (or may lead) to empathy, which in turn yields compassion as a form of active involvement wherein one feels the imperative "I must do something" in order to remedy or ameliorate the situation of the other. This does not necessarily imply that only sympathy is an inborn response, for I think humans are too complex for us to make such a bald assertion. Perhaps it's best to say that we have the innate capacity for developing compassion as I have described it, and leave the matter there. . . .

Justice Considerations

One objection that may arise at this point comes from a utilitarian perspective. This is that the amount of pleasure or satisfaction humans derive from eating meat outweighs the amount of animal pain and suffering we cause in the process. Now aside from the fact that balancing benefits and harms in this way is notoriously difficult—even within the human sphere—I want to suggest that such a line of argument is a non-starter. The reason is that the beneficiaries of meat eating are humans and the recipients of harm are nonhumans. I am not talking here merely about the issue of comparing and balancing the experiences of members of different species. Rather, I have in mind an ethically more critical issue, namely, that of weighing benefits to one class of beings against costs to another class of beings. And this seems to me to involve considerations of justice. We can look at this issue in two ways. First, if we consider the experiences of nonhuman animals to be of a comparable character to those of humans, then it has to be manifestly true that the gustatory pleasures of humans cannot outweigh the amount of pain and suffering caused to animals by the process of obtaining these pleasures. At a very basic level, it seems reasonable to assume that the pain and suffering of meat production matter more to the creatures we choose to eat, for only our most rare gustatory experiences are either intensely or sublimely pleasurable (and these are, in any case, of very short duration), whereas the harms experienced by food animals are often agonizing and protracted. Furthermore, the average meat eater is (usually indirectly) responsible for the pain and suffering of scores of nonhuman animals during his or her lifetime. The aggregated pain and suffering of these creatures undoubtedly outweighs the pleasure of one human by a high degree. Finally, if nonhuman animals have an interest in their own well-being in the manner I have suggested, then this surely very basic interest must outweigh the nonbasic interest of humans in eating meat. (Meat eating is a nonbasic interest because for the vast majority of human beings there are alternative food sources capable of providing all of our nutritional needs.[6] And the alternatives can easily generate pleasurable experiences that are at least equal in value to those that meat eaters forfeit by giving up meat.[7])

The second way of looking at the justice issue is to note simply that in weighing human interests against those of nonhumans, we are comparing apples and oranges. That is, we are trying to rationalize something we prefer by shifting the effects of it onto a different class of beings that have no say in the matter and are powerless to resist our actions. This is the same model that fits acts of enslavement, exploitation of children, experimenting on other humans without their consent, and so on. . . .

The Killing of Animals as a Harm

Thus far, I have limited my remarks to pain and suffering. But there is also the matter of causing animals' deaths. Eating meat is essentially tied to killing, unlike many other forms of harm. . . .

Perhaps we should pause to consider here whether death *is* a harm for sentient nonhuman animals, and *why*. I think it is, and that the reasons for saying so are easy to grasp. These are that: (1) such animals show every sign of preferring to live when their lives are threatened, as when we bring them to slaughter; (2) they clearly have pleasurable experiences (or, in human terms, experiences that are of value to them); and (3) each has an identifiable welfare or state of well-being it strives to preserve. For any being that meets these criteria, death is a harm. Hence, death is a harm to livestock animals. An observation from the Jain tradition of India sums this up quite well: "A wise man should be neither glad nor angry, for he should know and consider the happiness of all things. . . . For nothing is inaccessible to death, and all beings are fond of themselves; they love pleasure and hate pain; they shun destruction and cling to life. They long to live. To all things life is dear" (Basham 1954:293). . . .

Many billions of nonhuman animals are consumed worldwide every year. This translates into many billions of deaths that are unnecessary from a nutritional point of view and that violate the justice principle stated earlier. It would seem that only a deformed, desensitized mind could declare that gratuitous, unjustified, human-caused pain and suffering on a very large scale, as in the food industry, do not matter, or are mitigated by aggregated, minor benefits to ourselves. And it is difficult to understand how widely practiced, institutionalized cruelty *of any kind* can contribute to creating decent and just societies and a nonviolent world order. These are the sorts of overarching issues that reflection on our eating habits makes us confront, and they are as important as any in ethics. What seems at first to be a minor affair, and one that concerns taste preferences alone—what we eat—thus turns into a much more significant matter. We are all responsible for the level of harm and violence that we have the ability to reduce or eliminate, and not to do so when we can, without risk to ourselves, and with only minor inconvenience, is negligent behavior we should correct.

Another objection often heard is that we could acquire our meat from smaller-scale producers, such as organic and free range farms, and operations that practice more "humane" methods of transportation and slaughter. Those who run this kind of facility often slaughter their own livestock, which is at least better than placing this burden upon someone else and distancing oneself from the act, as most meat eaters do. (We'll revisit this point later on.) But this improvement does not cancel out the fact that unnecessary killing is the final step in the process, no matter what the scale; nor can pain and suffering be completely eliminated along the way. In any event, many nonhuman animals reared on smaller farms will also end up at large commercial slaughterhouses. And the fact remains that they live equally artificially abbreviated lives in these circumstances. Finally, it is impossible to imagine how the growing demand for meat, by an increasing world population of humans conditioned to eating it and regarding it as high-status food, can be sustained at all, let alone being supplied by small, independent producers (Durning and Brough 1995; Tilston 2004).

At the outset, I posed three questions about the conditions under which meat is produced for human consumption: Why should I care? What can I do? and Will my choices make a difference? The first and second have been answered. Each of us should care because pain and suffering are inherently bad kinds of conscious experiences, no matter to whom or to what they occur. Causing gratuitous or unjustified pain and suffering is wrong. We should all be concerned to avoid being the agents of wrongdoing when circumstances permit. This leads to the second question. What each of us can do in order to avoid causing pain and suffering to nonhuman animals is first and foremost to stop eating meat. . . .

Taking Responsibility for Our Diets

[Y]ou may [say], "*I* don't cause gratuitous, unjustified pain and suffering to nonhuman animals or kill them for trivial or any other reasons. I may eat them, but *other people* are the ones who do these cruel things." True; but as we all know, demand creates supply, and for that reason, each of us must take responsibility for the food production system that depends upon his or her eating preferences. We are habituated to not confronting the consequences of our actions in large areas of life. We prefer to leave the decisions and actions to others, who act on our behalf, and often we avoid both awareness and accountability thereby—as in their own ways so do these others who do the dirty work for us. We are too used to seeing meat arrive magically, as it were, on our grocery shelves and in butcher shops as just "cuts," already wrapped in plastic or waiting to be wrapped in paper—as disembodied parts of living beings from which we remove ourselves in thought and action (Adams 1991). Taking responsibility for our food means understanding fully where it comes from and how it is obtained; that we have a crucial, if indirect, role in these things; and that we need to act morally in light of this knowledge. . . .

Choosing Vegetarianism as a Way of Life

What the foregoing discussion reveals are two central facts about vegetarianism: (1) that it is a committed, caring response to injustice; and therefore (2) that it represents more than a peculiar taste preference or a matter of lifestyle or fashion, but is, instead, part of a comprehensive outlook on how we ought to live. In short, vegetarianism is an ethical way of life. It follows that choosing to be a vegetarian involves developing a sense of responsibility that reaches beyond the human sphere. It entails an appreciation of the kinship between living beings, as well as a decision to make a serious effort at minimizing the amount of harm that flows from our eating preferences and practices. None of us is or ever could be morally perfect, but we all have different alternatives before us among which to choose; and those acts that contribute to lessening the levels of violence and agony in the world are surely to be preferred to those that do not. Again, this is not an endorsement of utilitarianism, but merely an ethical truism. The difficult part is not getting ourselves to agree to this idea; it is getting ourselves to accept that vegetarianism is part of the strategy needed to translate the idea into reality.

I think enough has been said to make it clear that a commitment to vegetarianism is ethically compelling. However, no one should conclude that I am making grandiose claims on behalf of vegetarianism. It isn't an answer to all the world's problems, only one essential aspect of that answer. We might think of it this way: by being vegetarians, we become part of the solution to global injustice rather than part of the problem of it. Again, this seems a manifestly preferable position to be in. This brings me back to a point I made earlier: that the rewards of doing what is right should come from within us. Being committed to making the world a more just and caring place, and to an outlook that helps promote non-violence, contributes to a more satisfying sense of purpose and of self, I would argue, and therefore, has a lot to do with positive personal development. So a change in diet, which to begin with looked like a big, unpleasant sacrifice, really turns out not to be so at all; and vegetarianism, which may appear, on first encounter, like some kind of self-punishing asceticism that assumes a condescending moral vantage-point, is really something quite different in character and very worthwhile in terms of its consequences. Does anything more need to be offered by way of incentives? You be the judge.[8]

Endnotes

1. This is true in general, especially in relation to slaughterhouses, which, in the past century, have been moved away from large urban centres like Chicago to more remote rural areas. But some things aren't so easily hidden from view. My sister recently drove across the U.S. and reported that in Kansas, cattle by the thousands can be seen, mile after mile, standing ankle-deep in their own excrement. The foul smell is completely penetrating and cannot be escaped even in a motel room.
2. For extended discussion on what it means to care about animals' well-being, see Donovan and Adams, eds. (1996).
3. Indeed, the point can be expressed in the form of a valid (and I think sound) logical argument.

   P1 Any sentient living being naturally seeks to avoid or escape from pain and suffering.
   P2 Any sentient living being that engages in such behavior shows that pain and suffering matter to it.
   P3 Humans and many nonhumans are sentient living beings.
   C1 Humans and many nonhumans are beings that naturally seek to avoid or escape from pain and suffering and to which pain and suffering matter.
   P4 If pain and suffering matter to a sentient living being, then they matter morally.
   C2 For both humans and many nonhumans, pain and suffering matter morally.
   P5 If something matters morally, it must be taken into account in our decisions leading to action.
   C3 The pain and suffering of nonhuman animals, like that of humans, must be taken into account in our decisions leading to action.
4. Aristotle (1995), bk. III, chap. 9: 103: "justice is considered to mean equality. It does mean equality—but for those who are equal, and not for all." Of course, for Aristotle, nonhuman animals were inferior beings that had no moral status; but so were various classes of human beings (women, slaves, non-Athenians). And justice for him was a function of one's contribution to society. Nevertheless, we may borrow his notion of justice for our purposes and apply it more broadly and consistently than he was prepared to do.
5. This criterion is attributed to Nel Noddings by Taylor (2003:79).
6. Exceptions include indigenous peoples who live in environments where meat (including fish) is the only food source. Kathryn Paxton George

argues for a much wider range of exceptions (George, 2000), but her case rests on nutritional data that are controversial.

7. The additional pleasure derived from the knowledge that one has got off the food animal exploitation treadmill is also significant.
8. I would like to thank Lesley McLean and Elliot Cohen for helpful comments on earlier drafts of this essay. Previous versions have also been presented at philosophy seminars in Australia (University of New England) and Taiwan (National Central University and National Chung Cheng University). I wish to express my appreciation to these audiences for their feedback.

Bibliography

Adams, Carol J. 1991. *The Sexual Politics of Meat: A Feminist-Vegetarian Critical Theory*. New York: Continuum.

Basham, A. L. 1954. *The Wonder That Was India: A Survey of the Culture of the Indian Subcontinent before the Coming of the Muslims*. New York: Grove Press.

Bentham, Jeremy. 1789. *An Introduction to the Principles of Morals and Legislation*. London: T. Payne.

Campbell, T. Colin, and Thomas M. Campbell. 2004. *The China Study*. Dallas: BenBella Books.

De Waal, F. B. M., and P. L. Tyack. 2003. *Animal Social Complexity: Intelligence, Culture, and Individualized Societies*. Cambridge, MA: Harvard University Press.

Douglas, Mary. 1975. "Deciphering a Meal." In Mary Douglas. *Implicit Meanings: Essays in Anthropology*. London and Boston: Routledge & Kegan Paul. Pp. 249–75.

Durning, Alan T., and Holly B. Brough. 1995. "Animal Farming and the Environment." In *Just Environments: Intergenerational, International and Interspecies Issues*, ed. David E. Cooper and Joy A. Palmer. London and New York: Routledge. 149–64.

Fiddes, Nick. 1991. *Meat: A Natural Symbol*. New York: Routledge.

Fox, Michael Allen. 1999b. *Deep Vegetarianism*. Philadelphia: Temple University Press.

Griffin, Donald R. 2001. *Animal Minds: Beyond Cognition to Consciousness*. Chicago: University of Chicago Press.

Hill, John Lawrence. 1996. *The Case for Vegetarianism: Philosophy for a Small Planet*. Lanham, MD: Rowman Littlefield.

Linden, Eugene. 2003. *The Octopus and the Orangutan: New Tales of Animal Intrigue, Intelligence, and Ingenuity*. New York: Plume.

Pepperberg, Irene. 1999. *The Alex Studies: Cognitive and Communicative Abilities of Grey Parrots*. Cambridge, MA: Harvard University Press.

Rendell, Luke, and Hal Whitehead. 2001. "Culture in Whales and Dolphins." *Behavioral and Brain Sciences*, 24: 309–24, 373–82.

Savage-Rumbaugh, Sue, W. M. Fields, and J. Taglialatela. 2000. "Ape Consciousness—Human Consciousness: A Perspective Informed by Language and Culture." *American Zoologist*, 40: 910–21.

Singer, Peter, and Jim Mason. 2006. *The Way We Eat: Why Our Food Choices Matter.* Emmaus, PA: Rodale Books. (Simultaneously published by Text Publishing in Australia under the title *The Ethics of What We Eat.*)

Stephens, William O. 1994. "Five Arguments for Vegetarianism." *Philosophy in the Contemporary World,* 1: 25–39.

Tilston, John. 2004. *How to Explain Why You're Vegetarian to Your Dinner Guests.* Victoria, BC: Trafford.

Twigg, J. 1983. "Vegetarianism and the Meanings of Meat." In *The Sociology of Food and Eating: Essays on the Sociological Significance of Food,* ed. A. Murcott. Aldershot, Hampshire: Gower. 18–30.

Wise, Steven M. 2002. *Unlocking the Cage: Science and the Case for Animal Rights.* Oxford: Perseus. (Simultaneously published by Perseus in the United States under the title *Drawing the Line.*)

Wynne-Tyson, John. 1979. *Food for a Future: The Complete Case for Vegetarianism.* London: Centaur Press; New York: Universe Books.

Holmes Rolston III

Higher Animals: Duties to Sentient Life

Domestic and Hunted Animals

Domestic Food Animals

Animal agriculture is tangential to an environmental ethic, yet there is a carry-over connecting the one to the other. Domestic animals are breeds, no longer natural kinds. They are "living artifacts,"[1] kept in culture for so long that it is often not known precisely what their natural progenitors were. They fit no environmental niche; the breeding of them for traits that humans desire has removed them from the forces of natural selection. Without human interest in these animals they would soon cease to exist. Most domestic breeds would go extinct; a few might revert to feral conditions; fewer still might resettle homeostatically into environmental niches. Most feral forms, unchecked by predators, competitors, and diseases, are misfits that cause heavy environmental degradation.

But domestic animals cannot enter the culture that maintains them. By all behavioral evidence, sheep, cows, and pigs are oblivious to the economy for which they are reared, much less to the cultural context of the persons who care for them. They cannot live in the world ethically, cognitively, and critically in those superior human ways. Pet dogs may join the life of the family, enthusiastically eating hot dogs at a picnic; nevertheless, pets are not in culture. Although food animals are taken out of nature and transformed by culture, they remain uncultured in their sentient life, cultural objects that cannot become cultural subjects. They live neither in nature nor in culture but in the peripheral rural world. Meanwhile, they can suffer.

This *is* the case, descriptive of their condition. What *ought* to be? . . . [W]e recognize the wild condition from which such animals were once taken and recognize also that they can neither return to the wild nor enter cultural subjectivity. Although tamed, they can have horizons, interests, goods no higher than those of wild subjectivity, natural sentience. They ought to be treated, by the homologous, baseline principle, with no more suffering than might have been their lot in the wild, on average, adjusting for their modified capacities to care

From *Environmental Ethics: Duties to and Values in the Natural World* by Holmes Rolston III, 1988, pp. 78–84, 358, 373 (excerpts). Copyright © 1988 by Temple University Press. Reprinted by permission of Temple University Press. All Rights Reserved.

for themselves. In taking an interest in them, humans have assumed a responsibility for them. (Whether modern industrial farming introduces suffering in excess of ecological norms will have to be investigated elsewhere.)

By a weaker (but significant) hedonist principle, domestic animals ought to be spared pointless suffering, but they have no claim to be spared innocent suffering. The killing and the eating of animals, when they occur in culture, are still events in nature; they are ecological events, no matter how superimposed by culture. Humans are claiming no superiority or privilege exotic to nature. Analogous to predation, human consumption of animals is to be judged by the principles of environmental ethics, not those of interhuman ethics. We step back from culture into agriculture, toward the wild, and fit the ecological pattern. What *is* in nature may not always imply *ought* (and it may seldom do so in interhuman ethics), but *ought* in environmental ethics seldom negates what *is* in wild nature. Humans eat meat, and meat-eating is a natural component of ecosystems, one to which we do not object in nature nor try to eliminate from our cultural interactions with nature.

A troop of half a dozen chimpanzees, our nearest relatives, will kill and eat about a hundred medium-sized animals a year. Hunter-gatherer cultures are the earliest known, and when agricultural cultures replace them, humans have no duty to cease to be omnivores and become herbivores. They might elect to become vegetarians, perhaps on grounds of more efficient food production or better nutrition, but they have no duty to sentient life to do so.

A characteristic argument for vegetarianism runs as follows:

1. Pain is a bad thing, whether in humans or in animals.
2. Humans (at least most of them) can live nutritiously without causing animal pain.
3. It is immoral for humans to kill and eat humans, causing them pain.
4. Food animals suffer pain, similarly to the way humans do, if killed and eaten.
5. There are no morally relevant differences between humans and food animals.
6. It is immoral for humans to kill and eat animals, causing them pain.

Appealing to sentiment and logically attractive in its charitable egalitarianism, such argument fails to distinguish between nature and culture, between environmental ethics and interhuman ethics. We simply see ourselves in fur. But there are morally relevant differences that distinguish persons in culture from food animals in agriculture, where quasi-ecosystemic processes remain. Whether or not there are differences in pain thresholds between sheep and humans, the value destruction when a sheep is eaten is far less, especially since the sheep have been bred for this purpose and would not otherwise exist. Because animals cannot enter culture, they do not suffer the *affliction* (a heightened, cognitively based pain, distinct from physical pain) that humans would if bred to be eaten.

Chickens can live in ignorant bliss of their forthcoming slaughter (until the moment of execution); persons in such a position could not, because they are in the world culturally and critically. Even if such a fate could be kept secret from persons, the value destruction in their killing would still be greater. The fact that there are twilight zones (humans who are pre-persons or failed persons) does not challenge the existence of morally relevant class differences. In recognizing the human superiority, nothing should be subtracted from the natural condition of animals. But we have no strong duty to deny their original ecology, and only a weaker duty to make their lot better by avoiding pointless pain.

It is not "unfair" or "unjust" to eat a pig. Even an alligator that eats humans is not being unfair or unjust (although humans will be reprehensible if they do not try to prevent it). Humans in their eating habits follow nature; they can and ought to do so. But humans do not eat other humans because such events interrupt culture; they destroy those superior ways in which humans live in the world. The eating of other humans, even if this were shown to be an event in nature, would be overridden by its cultural destructiveness. Cannibalism destroys interpersonal relations. But in nature no such relations obtain, or can obtain. (Human cannibalism has been rare and virtually always a cultural event with religious overtones, not a natural event.)

It may be objected that the differences in rules for those with superior gifts means here that the only moral animals should refuse to participate in the meat-eating phase of their ecology, just as they refuse to play the game merely by the rules of natural selection. Humans do not look to the behavior of wild animals as an ethical guide in other matters (marriage, truth-telling, promise-keeping, justice, charity). Why should they justify their dietary habits by watching what animals do? But these other matters are affairs of culture. Marriage, truth-telling, promise-keeping, justice, charity—these are not events at all in spontaneous nature. They are person-to-person events. By contrast, eating is omnipresent in spontaneous nature; humans eat because they are in nature, not because they are in culture. Eating animals is not an event between persons but a human-to-animal event, and the rules for it come from the ecosystems in which humans evolved and which they have no duty to remake. Humans, then, can model their dietary habits on their ecosystems, but they cannot and should not model their interpersonal justice or charity on ecosystems.

It may seem that while animals are not to be treated like persons in all respects, both they and persons have about equally the capacity to feel pain, and so both ought to be treated equally in this relevant respect involving the pain-pleasure scale. But this is not the only relevant scale, because it does not catch the full scale of value destructions at stake. The eating of persons would destroy cultural values, which the eating of animals does not. The eating of animals, though it does destroy values, reallocates such values when humans gain nutrition and pleasure at the sacrifice of animal lives in a manner wholly consistent with the operation of the natural ecosystem in which such animals were once emplaced and are still quasi-placed in their agricultural stations. Different rules do apply to persons, to persons in exchange with persons, and even to persons in exchange with nature. These rules do require that animals lives count morally, but they do not require humans to deny their ecology and replace it with a charity or justice appropriate to culture.

Sentience in nature and sentience in culture are not really the same thing, despite their common physiology and origin. Sentience in nature belongs with food chains and natural selection; sentience in culture has been transformed into another gestalt, that of self-reflective personality and moral agency. Eating an animal implies no disrespect for animal life . . . ; to the contrary, it respects that ecology. Eating a person would disrupt personal life as set in a cultural pattern; it would reduce personal life to the level of animal life in an ecology. It insults persons to treat them as food objects by the criteria of animal ecology; persons may and must treat nonhuman lives as food objects, but it respects animals to treat them so.

Pain is a bad thing in humans or in animals. But this fools us until we distinguish between intrinsic and instrumental pain. Instrumental pain has contributory reference to further goods; intrinsic pain has no such reference. Intrinsic pain is a bad thing, absolutely; but only instrumental pain is characteristic of nature, where intrinsic pain is a nonfunctional anomaly. Pain is routinely instrumental in ecological defenses, captures, and transfers of goods, and the pains imposed in agriculture are homologous. They are not intrinsic pains; they must be judged in their instrumentality and with no presumption against innocent suffering.

Enjoying pleasure and escaping pain are of value, and evolutionary ecosystems are full of devices for accomplishing both. But much pain remains, and much thwarted pleasure. In nature, the pain-pleasure axis is not the only spectrum of value; indeed, it is not the highest value in either human or nonhuman life. It might be said, for instance, that knowing the meaning of life is more important for humans than leading a painless life, that a life with courage and sacrificial charity in it, which requires the presence of some pain, is a richer life than one without it. Similarly, the evolution of a world with carnivorous mammals, primates, humans, and culture is a richer world than one without them, and the presence of pain seems to have been necessary for such evolution. In that sense, advanced values are frequently built on suffering.

Perhaps it is not merely the pain but the indignity of domestication that is deplorable. A gazelle is pure wild grace, but a cow is a meat factory, pure and simple; a cow might even suffer less than a gazelle but be greatly disgraced. Cows cannot know they are disgraced, of course, and the capture of values in nature is not undignified. A lioness destroys a gazelle, and there is nothing unworthy here. Likewise, in domestication, humans parallel ecosystems and capture agriculturally the values in a cow. There is nothing undignified in this event, even though the once-natural values in the cow, like those in the gazelle, have to be destroyed by the predator.

Although we have defended eating animals as a primary, natural event, we have also said, secondarily, that there is an obligation to avoid pointless pain. Consider, for instance, the following case. There are more than 2,000,000 Muslims in Britain; the Jewish community numbers nearly 400,000. Muslims still practice animal sacrifice; a sheep or goat is sacrificed during a feast concluding a month of fasting, and often at the birth of a child. The animal is sacrificed to Allah, and the meat is eaten and enjoyed. Though Jews no longer practice animal sacrifice as they did in former times, they require their meat to be kosher, slaughtered according to religious ritual. Modern secular abattoirs stun animals with a massive blow or an electric shock before butchering them, and this is thought to be more humane. But it makes the animal unacceptable to Jews and Muslims, who must sever the major blood vessels of an unblemished animal. About 1,500,000 sheep and goats and 100,000 cattle are slaughtered by Jews and Muslims each year.

Animal rights activists have pressed to require stunning, and a government report finds that religious methods of slaughter result in a degree of suffering and distress that does not occur in a properly stunned animal. Muslims and Jews have joined forces to defend their practices.[2] But the additional pain that their methods impose, no longer necessary, cannot be interpreted in the context of ecology; it is pain inflicted for culture-based reasons. Unblemished animals make better sacrifices to God; they enhance religious cleanliness. This pain is ecologically pointless; it has point only culturally and, by the account given here, is not justified. This pain is not homologous; it is superfluous. Perhaps both Jews and Muslims can reach reformed religious convictions, in which respect for animal life overrides their previous concepts of cleanliness, or where the mercy of God prohibits pointless suffering.

Notes

1. J. Baird Callicott, "Animal Liberation: A Triangular Affair," *Environmental Ethics 2,* 1980, p. 330.
2. Karen DeYoung, "Ritual Slaughter Sparks Debate," *Washington Post,* 27 December 1985, pp. A19–20.

POSTSCRIPT

Does Morality Require Vegetarianism?

Traditionally, there has been no question with regard to the morality of eating meat. There is no law against it; it is widely practiced; and it is supported by the biblical idea that God gave people animals to eat, and specifically placed people in dominion over animals. So it is to some extent a great change in the moral climate that this question is even being raised at all.

It is partly due to the views of pioneering environmental thinkers such as Rolston that people have begun to think seriously about the place of human beings within the larger biological environment. This naturally leads to questions about animals and human beings and their relationship.

Of course, there is another biblical injunction to the effect that people should exercise stewardship over God's creation. It is, however, not clear how this is to fit in with the other biblical idea (above). Michael Allen Fox's ideas about caring seem to fit closer to the idea of stewardship than they do to the idea of dominion.

From a religious perspective, we might remember that there are millions of people who base vegetarianism on religion. And from a purely cultural perspective, we know that, as widely accepted as meat eating is in our own culture, some cultures practice vegetarianism.

Part of the difficulty for us in coming to grips with moral questions in this area stems from our dual role in nature. On the one hand, we use reason to stand apart from nature; on the other hand, reason tells us that we are part of nature. But even if we think of ourselves as part of nature, this does not solve our problem. For now, we have to think again (as we did in the introduction to this issue) and use reason to decide whether we should be like the lions, who hunt and kill animals to eat, or whether such killing and eating—even if culturally traditional for us—should be left behind.

A classic work in this field is Peter Singer, *Animal Liberation* (New York Review of Books, 1990). Bernard E. Rollin, in *Farm Animal Welfare: Social, Bioethical, and Research Issues* (Iowa State University Press, 1995), and Howard F. Lyman, in *Mad Cowboy: Plain Truth from the Cattle Rancher Who Won't Eat Meat* (Scribner, 1998), address the conditions under which animals are raised for food, and Lyman in particular is critical of the negative impact that this has on human beings. Carol J. Adams, in *The Sexual Politics of Meat: A Feminist-Vegetarian Critical Theory,* 10th anniversary ed. (Continuum Pub Group, 1999), argues that meat eating is connected with male dominance. Also relevant are Craig B. Stanford et al., eds., *Meat-Eating and Human Evolution* (Oxford University Press, 2001); Eric Schlosser, *Fast Food Nation: The Dark Side of the*

All-American Meal (Harper-Collins, 2002); Matthew Scully, *Dominion: The Power of Man, the Suffering of Animals, and the Call to Mercy* (St. Martin's Press, 2002); Charles Patterson, *Eternal Treblinka: Our Treatment of Animals and the Holocaust* (Lantern Books, 2002); Steve F. Sapontzis, *Food for Thought: The Debate over Eating Meat* (Prometheus Books, 2004); Lyle Munro, *Confronting Cruelty: Moral Orthodoxy and the Challenge of the Animal Rights Movement* (Brill Academic, 2005); and Josephine Donovan and Carol Adams, eds., *The Feminist Care Tradition in Animal Ethics* (Columbia University Press, 2007).

Contributors to This Volume

EDITOR

STEPHEN SATRIS was born in New York City. He received a B.A. in philosophy from the University of California, Los Angeles, an M.A. in philosophy from the University of Hawaii at Manoa, and a Ph.D. in philosophy from Cambridge University, England. He has written on moral and philosophical issues for professional journals, and he is the author of *Ethical Emotivism* (Martinus Nijhoff, 1987). He has taught at several American universities, and he currently teaches philosophy at Clemson University in Clemson, South Carolina. Professor Satris is a former president of the South Carolina Society for Philosophy and is currently C. Calhoun Lemon Fellow in Clemson University's Rutland Center for Ethics.

AUTHORS

GEORGE J. ANNAS is the Edward R. Utley Professor of Law and Medicine at Boston University's Schools of Medicine and Public Health in Boston, Massachusetts. He is also director of Boston University's Law, Medicine, and Ethics Program and chair of the department of health law. His publications include *Some Choice: Law, Medicine, and the Market* (Oxford University Press, 1998). He is the author of the third edition of *The Rights of Patients* (Southern Illinois University Press, 2004).

JOHN ARTHUR is a philosopher at the State University of New York at Binghamton. He has published works on social, political, and legal philosophy.

MIRKO BAGARIC is a professor of law at Deakin University's School of Law in Australia. He has published on a wide variety of social issues. His latest book is *How to Live: Being Happy and Dealing with Moral Dilemmas* (University Press of America, 2006).

WALTER BLOCK earned his Ph.D. in economics at Columbia University. He is an author, editor, and co-editor of many books, including *Defending the Undefendable; Lexicon of Economic Thought, Economic Freedom of the World 1975–1995; Rent Control: Myths and Realities; Discrimination, Affirmative Action, and Equal Opportunity; Theology, Third World Development and Economic Justice; Man, Economy, and Liberty: Essays in Honor of Murray N. Rothbard; Religion, Economics, and Social Thought;* and *Economic Freedom: Toward a Theory of Measurement.* Dr. Block has written more than 500 articles for various non-refereed journals, magazines, and newspapers, and is a contributor to such journals as *The Review of Austrian Economics, Journal of Libertarian Studies, The Journal of Labor Economics, Cultural Dynamics,* and the *Quarterly Journal of Austrian Economics.* He is currently a professor and chair of economics, college of business administration, at Loyola University.

HILARY BOK teaches philosophy at the Johns Hopkins University in Baltimore, where she is Luce Professor in Bioethics and Moral and Political Theory. Her publications and research interests are in ethics, bioethics, free will, and the philosophy of Kant.

DAVID BOONIN is an associate professor and Chair of the Department of Philosophy at the University of Colorado. He is the co-editor of the book *What's Wrong?: Applied Ethicists and Their Critics.*

LEWIS BURROWS, M.D., is Professor Emeritus, Surgery, at Mount Sinai School of Medicine, City University of New York.

JAMES F. CHILDRESS is the John Allen Hollingsworth Professor of Ethics and Professor of Medical Education at the University of Virginia. Professor Childress is the recipient of several prestigious academic awards, is the author (or coauthor) of scores of books and articles, and has served on numerous advisory bodies, including the presidentially appointed National

Bioethics Advisory Commission. With Tom L. Beachamp, he is coauthor of *Principles of Biomedical Ethics,* 5th ed. (University of Oxford Press, 2001), a classic work in its field.

JULIE CLARKE teaches law at Deakin University's School of Law in Australia.

PETER COLLINS is director of the Centre for the Study of Gambling, Salford University, England. A specialist on the subject of gambling, Collins has advised numerous government bodies in the United Kingdom and other countries.

MEAGHAN CUSSEN is a graduate of the College of the Holy Cross in Worcester, Massachusetts. She is currently the Director of Business Development at Navigate Health International.

RICHARD DOERFLINGER is deputy director of the secretariat for Pro-Life Activities at the U.S. Conference of Catholic Bishops in Washington, D.C. He is also Adjunct Fellow in Bioethics and Public Policy at the National Catholic Bioethics Center in Boston. Speaking on behalf of the Catholic Bishops, he has prepared policy statements and given congressional testimony on abortion, euthanasia, human embryo research, and other bioethical issues.

THE DRUG ENFORCEMENT ADMINISTRATION's mission is to enforce the controlled substance laws and regulations of the United States and bring to the criminal and civil justice system of the United States, or any other competent jurisdiction, those organizations and principal members of organizations, involved in the growing, manufacture, or distribution of controlled substances appearing in or destined for illicit traffic in the United States; and to recommend and support non-enforcement programs aimed at reducing the availability of illicit controlled substances on the domestic and international markets.

JANE ENGLISH (1947–1978) was a philosopher whose published work was primarily on feminism and social philosophy.

AUTUMN FIESTER is a senior fellow at the Center for Bioethics at the University of Pennsylvania. She teaches and conducts research in moral philosophy, animals and bioethical issues, and clinical professionalism.

MICHAEL ALLEN FOX is professor of philosophy at Queen's University in Canada and Adjunct Professor of Social Science, University of New England in Australia. He is the author of *Deep Vegetarianism* and *The Accessible Hegel.*

ALAN H. GOLDMAN is now Kenan Professor of Philosophy at the College of William and Mary. (Previously, he taught for 25 years at the University of Miami in Florida.) He is the author of numerous books and articles on aesthetics, moral knowledge, and the philosophy of law. His most recent book is *Practical Rules: When We Need Them and When We Don't* (Cambridge, 2002).

GILBERT HARMAN is Stuart Professor of Philosophy at Princeton University. He has published extensively in ethics, epistemology, metaphysics, cognitive science, and the philosophy of language. His most recent book is *Explaining Value and Other Essays in Moral Philosophy* (Clarendon Press, 2000).

JAMES G. HODGE, JR., is an associate professor at the Johns Hopkins Bloomberg School of Public Health, where he teaches Public Health and the Law and Global Health Law. In addition to his primary faculty appointment at JHSPH, Mr. Hodge is an Adjunct Professor of Law at Georgetown University Law Center, where he lectures in public health law, bioethics, international human rights, and health law and policy. He is the Executive Director of the Centers for Law and the Public's Health: A Collaborative at Johns Hopkins and Georgetown Universities; and a Core Faculty member of the Johns Hopkins Berman Institute of Bioethics.

TIMOTHY HOWELL is associate professor of psychiatry and director of the geropsychiatry program at UW Health—a health and medical network affiliated with the University of Wisconsin. He is active in both teaching and clinical care.

JEEF JORDAN is a professor of philosophy at the University of Delaware. He works in metaphysics and the philosophy of religion.

C. STEPHEN LAYMAN is professor of philosophy at Seattle Pacific University. He has published in logic, metaphysics, and the philosophy of religion. His books include: *The Shape of the Good* (University of Notre Dame Press, 1991), *The Power of Logic*, 2d ed. (McGraw-Hill, 2002), and *Letters to a Doubting Thomas: A Case for the Existence of God* (Oxford University Press, 2007).

DON MARQUIS is a professor of philosophy at the University of Kansas in Lawrence, Kansas. He has written on issues in medical ethics.

ALBERT G. MOSLEY, philosopher and musician, is currently at Smith College in Massachusetts. He is the editor of *African Philosophy: Selected Readings* (Pearson Education, 1995) and coauthor, with Nicholas Capaldi, of *Affirmative Action* (Rowman & Littlefied, 1996).

LISA NEWTON teaches philosophy at Fairfield University in Connecticut, where she is director of the Applied Ethics program. She has written on a wide variety of ethical, social, and political topics, including business ethics and the environment.

LOUIS P. POJMAN (1935–2005) was a prolific American philosopher who published (as editor or author) over 30 books and wrote more than 100 articles. His writing extends widely and embraces many areas of philosophy, but Pojman is best remembered as a writer on ethical, social, and political issues. He was particularly concerned to make ideas clear to non-philosophers.

DANIEL D. POLSBY is dean for academic affairs and professor of law at George Mason University's School of Law. Polsby was on the faculty of Northwestern Law School for over 20 years, and for over 10 of those years he was the Kirkland & Ellis Professor of Law. In addition, he has held visiting appointments at the University of Southern California, the University of Michigan, and Cornell University. He has published widely in many areas of law, including voting rights, family law, employment rights, and gun control.

VINCENT C. PUNZO is Professor Emeritus at Saint Louis University in St. Louis, Missouri. His specialties are ethics and political philosophy.

JOHN A. ROBERTSON holds the Vinson and Elkins Chair at the University of Texas School of Law at Austin. He has written and lectured widely on law and bioethical issues. He is the author of *The Rights of the Critically Ill* (Ballinger, 1983) and *Children of Choice: Freedom and the New Reproductive Technologies* (Princeton University Press, 1994). He is also the author of numerous articles on reproductive rights, genetics, organ transplantation, and human experimentation. Robertson has served on or has been a consultant to many national bioethics advisory bodies and is currently chair of the Ethics Committee of the American Society for Reproductive Medicine.

HOLMES ROLSTON III is an internationally known philosopher of the environment. He is University Distinguished Professor at Colorado State University in Fort Collins, Colorado. He has written extensively and lectured widely on the environment, science, and religion. His works have been translated into many languages.

MICHAEL J. SANDEL is the Anne T. and Robert M. Bass Professor of Government at Harvard University, where he has taught political philosophy since 1980. He is the author of *Liberalism and the Limits of Justice* (Cambridge University Press, 1982, 2nd edition, 1997; translated into eight foreign languages), *Democracy's Discontent: America in Search of a Public Philosophy* (Harvard University Press, 1996), *Public Philosophy: Essays on Morality in Politics* (Harvard University Press, 2005), and *The Case Against Perfection: Ethics in the Age of Genetic Engineering* (Harvard University Press, 2007). He has also written for publications such as *The Atlantic Monthly, The New Republic,* and *The New York Times.*

CHRISTOPHER W. TINDALE is a professor of philosophy at the University of Windsor. His primary research interests are in Argumentation Theory and Informal Logic, Greek Philosophy, and Moral Issues. He is the author of several books, including his most recent, *Fallacies and Argument Appraisal* (Cambridge, 2007).

ERNEST VAN DEN HAAG (1914–2002) was a distinguished lecturer at Columbia University, Yale University, and Harvard University. For many years, he was John M. Olin Professor of Jurisprudence at Fordham University and also a scholar at the Heritage Foundation. van den Haag was both a psychoanalyst and a criminologist. He is coauthor, with John P. Conrad, of *The Death Penalty: A Debate* (Plenum, 1983).

JON S. VERNICK is an associate professor of Health Policy and Management at the Johns Hopkins School of Public Health. He is also the co-director of

BJ
1021
.T24
2010

the Johns Hopkins Center for Gun Policy and Research and the deputy director of the Johns Hopkins Center for Injury Research and Policy.

DAVID T. WATTS is a practicing physician, a poet, a radio commentator, and an author. His most recent book is *Bedside Manners: One Doctor's Reflections on the Oddly Intimate Encounters Between Patient and Healer* (Three Rivers Press, 2006).

DANIEL W. WEBSTER is an associate professor of Health Policy and Management at the Johns Hopkins Bloomberg School of Public Health. He is also co-director of the Johns Hopkins Center for Gun Policy and Research.

MICHAEL WELCH is a sociologist and professor of criminal justice at Rutgers University. His work focuses on the ideas of punishment and social control. He is the author of *Detained: Immigration Laws and the Expanding I.N.S. Jail Complex* (Temple University Press, 2002). Welch is the author of several books, including, most recently, *Scapegoats of September 11th: Hate Crimes and State Crimes in the War on Terror* (Rutgers University Press, 2006).